Chronicles of the Age of Chivalry

Chronicles of the Age of Chivalry

General Editor
Elizabeth Hallam

Preface by
Hugh Trevor-Roper

GE

This edition published in 2002 by
Greenwich Editions
10 Blenheim Court
London N7 9NY

A member of the Chrysalis Group plc

ISBN 0-86288-425-X

Printed and bound in Spain

Above *Lead badge of the Black Prince.*

Frontispiece *Edmund Crouchback, earl of Lancaster, and St George wearing their arms on shield, surcoat and banner. The earl's arms are those of England.*

Editorial Director: Tessa Clark

Editorial:
Editor: Cecilia Walters
Sheila Mortimer
Michèle Staple
Fred Gill
Timothy Probart
Paul Mackintosh
Richard Bird
Picture Research:
Sarah Jones
Agnès Viterbi
Nancy Lustgarten

Design and Production:
Eddie Poulton
Rachael Foster
Anthony Short
Joanne Epstein
David Westcott

Specially commissioned photographs:
Marianne Majerus

Maps:
Jeff Edwards

General Editor:
Dr Elizabeth Hallam, *Assistant Keeper of Public Records, Public Record Office, London*

Preface:
Hugh Trevor-Roper

Translators:
Editor: Dr Meryl Foster, *Public Record Office*
Anne Dawtry
Catharine Edwards
Avril Powell
Janet Shirley
Emily Thomas
Brigette Vale
Geoffrey West
Amanda Whitmore

Contributors to illustrated spreads:
Dr Zygmund Baranski, *Head of Italian Studies Department, Reading University*
John Barnes, *Professor of Italian, University College, Dublin*
Dr David Bates, *Senior History Lecturer, University College, Cardiff*
Maurice Beresford, *Emeritus Professor of Economic History Leeds University*
J. Beverley Smith, *Professor of Welsh History, The University College of Wales*
Dr David Carpenter, *Lecturer, Queen Mary College, University of London*
Dr Trevor Chalmers, *Assistant Keeper, Public Record Office*
Margaret M. Condon, *Assistant Keeper, Public Record Office*
Anne Crawford, *Assistant Keeper, Public Record Office*
Dr David Crook, *Assistant Keeper, Public Record Office*
Dr David Crouch, *Director, Medieval Aristocracy Project, Institute of Historical Research*
Dr Lindy Grant, *Conway Library, Courtauld Institute of Art*
Dr Christopher Harper-Bill, *Principal Lecturer in History, St. Mary's College, Strawberry Hill*
Dr Jennifer Harris, *Honorary Lecturer, Whitworth Art Gallery, University of Manchester*
Nicholas Hooper, *Master, Westminster School*
Dr Charles Kightly, *Writer*
Dr Simone C. Macdougall, *Lecturer in Medieval History, University of St. Andrews*
Anthony R. E. North, *Research Assistant, Victoria and Albert Museum*
Dr William Mark Ormrod, *Lecturer in Medieval History, The Queen's University of Belfast*
Dr John B. Post, *Principal Assistant Keeper, Public Record Office*
Dr Edward Powell, *Fellow of Downing College, Cambridge*
Anthony Pryer, *Senior Lecturer in Music, Goldsmith College*
Dr Shirley Winall, *Lecturer, Italian Studies Department, Reading University*

Special help from: J. Allan, *Royal Albert Memorial Museum, Exeter* Janet Burnett, *Lacock Abbey* J. Conway, *British Library* B. J. Cook, *British Museum* Group Captain D. L. Edmonds, *Berkeley Castle* Grace Holmes, *Honorary Archivist, Windsor Castle* J. Hurst, *English Heritage* Carol Morris, *British Museum* Margaret Phillips, *York Minster* F. H. Thompson, *Society of Antiquaries of London* Sir Walter Verco, *Secretary of the Most Noble Order of the Garter* The London Library The National Trust

Editor's Note

WHETHER monks, clerks or laymen, moralists or dramatic fabricators, the chroniclers of the Middle Ages are the authentic voices of their times. Like journalists of today, they either described events as they happened or investigated and interpreted the past, some in a racy, emotive style, others in a detached, judicious fashion. On the whole their intention was not merely to instruct and inform, but to entertain.

Unlike modern newspapers, however, the chronicles were not written for mass circulation. They were, rather, aimed at the literate élite – churchmen and politicians who could understand and appreciate a meaty Latin history or biography, and the knightly classes which had a growing appetite for works of chivalry and romance in French. Nor did the chroniclers see their work as ephemeral: it was carefully constructed with an eye to posterity, and of those who wrote during the reigns of Henry III and the three Edwards some, like Matthew Paris, Joinville and Froissart, have earned the admiration and approbation of later generations. Most of the other chroniclers have, sadly, remained obscure, their wider value and interest as contemporary writers unappreciated outside the academic world.

In our continuing search to bring their vivid, and sometimes controversial, words to new life within the story of the Plantagenets kings, we have drawn on both celebrated and hitherto relatively unknown writers.

The majority are here translated into modern English for the first time. The passages chosen reflect a variety of styles and viewpoints, giving insights into many different milieux and men – from the cloistered monastic annalists of Waverley and Worcester to the sophisticated and well-born canon of Liège, Jean le Bel.

European writers, with different perspectives on events and personalities, have also been chosen to counterpoint the main narrative: Joinville's adulation of his saint-king, Louis IX, has been juxtaposed with Matthew Paris's waspish criticisms of Henry III to exemplify the different ways in which the two monarchs, and royal power itself, were perceived by their 13th-century contemporaries.

The chronicles provide the main historical narrative. They have been translated and linked with explanatory text. Names, titles, dates and places have been added where necessary, as have a few elucidatory phrases in square brackets.

These editorial interventions have been kept to a minimum, for the aim is to bring readers into direct contact with the past, with the primary sources from which history is made, and to let them make historical interpretations for themselves.

As an aid to this, our team of scholars has written a series of notes commenting on events and people in the main narrative, and exploring the artistic and literary as well as the social and economic contexts.

The notes and the chronicles are complemented with photographs which show places mentioned in the text or illustrate objects and buildings of the period, thus bringing the Middle Ages to life in all their varying aspects.

This book belongs to the chroniclers in all their vivid diversity.

Left *The Plantagenet banner; a modern version by Polly Hope from a 16th-century engraving. Three gold lions were on Geoffrey of Anjou's shield.*

Contents

MAPS

Preface

THE year when this volume begins was a black year for the English monarchy. At his death in 1216 King John had been defeated in foreign war and by internal revolt. Stripped of his Norman and Angevin inheritance, save Gascony, he had been forced to surrender to an insolent baronage. The country had been under a papal interdict and was now half occupied by an invading foreign army. The new king was a child. Three centuries later, when England first became Protestant, John's reputation would enjoy a sudden revival as an English nationalist who stood up to an aggressive papacy.

But the revival would be brief. Elizabethan antiquaries would then print the chronicles, and the chroniclers, being monks, were unanimous against him. For their own reasons they backed the barons, who, in retrospect, seemed the champions of modern English liberty, of Magna Carta.

Nor would the chroniclers be much more sympathetic to the new king. In his long reign of 56 years, Henry III did not quarrel with the Church. Far from it. He cultivated the memory of his pious Saxon predecessor Edward the Confessor and rebuilt his most famous monument, Westminster Abbey. But he could not control his barons and, once again, almost all of the chroniclers supported the barons. So this reign too ended with a royal retreat. The rebel Simon de Montfort might be defeated and killed, but his supporters had established a new curb on royal power: parliament.

It was not until the accession of Edward I – the greatest of England's medieval kings – that the monarchy was seen to recover its old power. Edward I was the great legislator, 'the English Justinian'. He was the hammer of the Welsh and the Scots. He is visible to us still in the Stone of Scone carried triumphantly to Westminster Abbey, in his huge castles in Wales, and in Charing Cross, the last of the crosses that marked the funeral journey of his queen. But then comes the melancholy reign of his son when all the old troubles and old grievances recur: baronial revolt against foreign favourites, defeat abroad, family division, invasion and conquest; and finally, deposition and the grim secret murder in Berkeley Castle. After that, we witness the spectacular recovery under Edward III, the great victories of Crécy and Poitiers, the exploits of the Black Prince, the new institutions of chivalry. But soon these glories too are dimmed as the Hundred Years War drags on and the seeds are sown of those later civil wars which are the last convulsions of the feudal monarchy of England.

Such is the general picture of English history from 1216 to 1377, the scope of this volume. However, we must not see England in isolation. Then, as always, it was an inseparable part of Europe, of Christendom. Its kings, its ruling class, its high clergy, were all European. Those barons who, as English patriots, resented the foreign favourites of Henry III and Edward II were themselves of recent immigrant stock. So were the rival kings of Scotland, Balliol and Bruce. So was Simon de Montfort. What later generations saw as national or constitutional struggles were really the internal politics of a European military caste: a caste which was only united by a common chivalric code, a common religious loyalty, and the external expression of both in those brutal wars of conquest which were also a clash of cultures, the crusades.

In 1216 the crusades are still in full swing in all directions. The Christian Empire of Constantinople has recently been conquered: Latin princes now rule in the East and the Greek

Left *Astronomer with his astrolabe and two assistants, one with an abacus. From the Psalter of St Louis and Blanche of Castile (13th century).*

Church is subjected to Rome. The Albigensian heretics of southern France will soon be crushed. The pagans of the Baltic shore, the Muslim settlers of central Spain, the 'Arabs' of Sicily, are all in retreat; and in the heartlands of expanding Christendom great Gothic cathedrals are rising, symbols of conquest and power. New orders of missionary friars are being founded, new universities created. There are great rulers who seek to grasp and wield these new opportunities: St Louis of France, the arbiter of Europe; the Emperor Frederick II, *Stupor Mundi*, the bugbear of successive popes; Boniface VIII, the most outrageous assertor of papal power. There are great thinkers and poets too: St Thomas Aquinas, the universal doctor of the Church; Dante, its universal poet.

The Plantagenet kings of England, facing west and north, struggling to subdue Wales and Scotland, might seem marginal to this Europe that is pushing south and east, but they cannot be separate from it. It is their essential cultural base, to which they are tied by their marriages, their religion, their lands, their necessary economy. To Flanders goes their profitable wool; from Gascony comes their table wine. So they are continually drawn back from their distracting frontier wars and internal struggles, seeking to preserve their continental base and status. They must keep up with the French kings, in prestigious building, in elaborate chivalry, in crusading zeal. Oxford University must contend with its mother in Paris. Henry III's Westminster Abbey must rival St Louis' Sainte-Chapelle. Henry may not be able to control his barons or subdue the Welsh princes, but he must not be left behind in the European competition. He will see his brother made king of the Romans, his younger son must be king of Sicily, and his heir must do his national service in Palestine.

Admittedly, the impetus cannot be maintained. As the 13th century closes, the tide turns. The Franks are driven out of Constantinople. The crusades in the East fail. The Spanish reconquest is halted. The worldly Church absorbs its reformers and discredits itself by schism.

Europe then turns inward. Social strains increase and find expression in familiar ways. 'Enemies of the people' are identified and persecuted. The Jews are expelled from England in 1290, from France in 1306. Monstrous accusations are brought to justify the destruction and expropriation of the Templars. Two years after the battle of Crécy, plague is added to the horrors of an unending war. The Black Death has reached Europe. Flagellants scourge themselves through the cities; peasant *Jacqueries* and 'companies' of disbanded soldiers terrorise the countryside. A world of misery is masked by the exaggerated chivalry of the feudal courts. In the last years of the once glorious reign of Edward III, heresy and peasant revolt are not far away.

The Chroniclers

Such is the background to the political events recorded by the chroniclers of these four reigns. As before, almost all of them are clergy: mainly monks, although there are some secular priests and, by now, an occasional friar. The monks have the advantage of a continuous tradition and a continuing institution: theirs is a collegiate life with a *scriptorium* and a designated chronicler who generally begins by re-hashing or abridging his predecessor or some other earlier writer. Hence, often, a certain 'house style' and much repetition, until the chronicler finds himself on his own and can at last take off and show his personality, if he has any.

The most famous monastic school of history in these years was that of St Albans. A great Benedictine house, conveniently placed a day's journey on the main north road from London, rich, worldly, aristocratic, with 300 horses on call, the monastery was equipped to entertain visiting grandees and hear the gossip of the great world. Henry III stayed there at least nine times, sometimes for a week at a time; other royal persons, papal nuncios, foreign archbishops, dropped in; and barons and bishops were constant visitors.

For nearly two centuries the abbey maintained a continuous historical tradition. First there is Roger of Wendover, a didactive and inventive scribe, who is on his own from 1215 to 1235; then his flamboyant pupil Matthew Paris takes over until 1259. Later there are William Rishanger and Thomas Walsingham.

The monks of St Albans, and indeed of other great abbeys, have a strong collegiate attitude. They are somewhat complacent, proud of their order, their abbey, their tradition, contemptuous of outsiders and of new-fangled institutions, universities, friars, innovations of any kind. Aristocrats of the clerical world, they support the lay aristocracy against the royal court, and are not too deferential to the court of Rome. In a word, they are English Whigs; and the most vocal and prolific of them, Matthew Paris, has been described as a medieval Macaulay: robust, prejudiced, somewhat slipshod, but also, because of his very limitations, irresistibly readable.

If St Albans was in a class of its own among monasteries, so was Matthew Paris among chroniclers. He was not only a vivid narrator but also a skilful illustrator and illuminator of his own work, which had a wide circulation in manuscript. Other monasteries were less well placed to pick up the gossip of the *beau monde* but had particular local opportunities. They had patrons or neighbours who were involved in the wars of Scotland or Wales, or had returned from France or the East, and they were repositories of interesting documents.

The monastery at Guisborough in North Yorkshire, for instance, is described as rich but dull. It had been founded by the local lord, Robert Bruce, in Norman times, and his family remained its patrons. But by 1300 the Bruce family were claiming the crown of Scotland, and Guisborough was well placed to record news from the North. So were the clergy of Cumberland, where the chronicle of Lanercost was compiled, whether at that Augustinian priory on the Roman Wall or, as seems more probable, in a Franciscan friary at Carlisle. Bartholomew Cotton, monk of Norwich, was a great collector of second-hand news and first-hand local trivia, but he had access to real documents, and he showed his discreet 'Whig' sympathies by inserting the single word 'alas' when recording the death of Simon de Montfort.

However, not all abbeys were 'Whig' in their sympathies. Thomas Wykes, a canon regular of Osney at Oxford, who wrote the official chronicle of his abbey in the 13th century, was an

Overleaf ***The Plantagenet kings on the choir screen in York Minster. From left to right: Henry III, Edward I, Edward II, Edward III.***

Henr : - Tertius reg:56
Edward - Primus : reg:35

Edward' Scdus reg
dward' Tertius

exception. He admired Henry III's brother, Richard earl of Cornwall, and the heir to the throne, afterwards Edward I; he was of the 'court' rather than, like the St Albans chroniclers, the 'country' party. He has been seen as 'a progressive royalist'. A later chronicler who also wrote at Osney (though not, it seems, as a canon) was even more royalist. He was Geoffrey le Baker, who came from Swinbrook, not far from Oxford, and belonged to a small circle there: his patron Sir Thomas de la More of Northfield and his fellow chronicler Adam Murimuth of Fifield, who was employed as its agent by Oxford university, and whose chronicle Geoffrey continued. Perhaps Oxford, even then, was a Tory institution.

Geoffrey le Baker certainly was wholehearted about being not only a Tory, but a High Tory. To him Edward II was a saint, whose sufferings could be compared with those of Christ, while his queen, 'that harridan', 'that virago' Isabella of France, was a 'Jezebel' and her clerical allies 'priests of Baal'. Geoffrey was also a sound English patriot who regarded Edward III as rightful king of France and 'that coward', 'that tyrant' Philip VI as a usurper. For a more balanced picture of Edward II we must turn to the anonymous Latin biography which was written by a judicious and perceptive clerk, evidently a moderate supporter of the opposition earls.

For foreign affairs, of course, we must look abroad. Matthew Paris, indeed, knows no frontiers for the world comes to him at St Albans. He has been abroad himself, sent with papal authority to 'reform' an abbey in Norway. Geoffrey le Baker too may have been on a plundering raid in France: he shows an expert's interest in ransom and booty. But for some foreign matters we must turn to foreign chroniclers: the gadding gossiping Franciscan friar Salimbene, who is Matthew Paris's opposite number in Italy; the idealistic and garrulous John, lord of Joinville, loyal friend and disciple of St Louis. Then, in the reign of Edward III, we have the two Hainaulters, Jean le Bel, canon of St Lambert, Liège, and the continuator who eclipsed him, the most colourful of all chroniclers, Jean Froissart, canon of Chimay.

As countrymen of Edward's queen, Philippa, both these men came to England – Jean le Bel took part in the king's Scottish expedition of 1327 and Froissart joined the queen's household in 1361 and accompanied his hero, the Black Prince, to Aquitaine in 1366. These are the chroniclers of glorious action, of the feats of 'le proeu et gentil roy Edwart' and his famous son, of the splendours and miseries of chivalry and war. They write in French, and are more concerned with vivid first-hand narratives of heroism and pageantry than with high politics or dry documents.

So Froissart would become the great favourite of the laity. He has been described as the Herodotus of the Middle Ages. His work would be splendidly illustrated and widely circulated in manuscript; later, in the days of print, it would be endlessly translated and published; and in the 19th century his statue would be set up in his native city. This was more than any other chroniclers could hope for, but who will say that he does not deserve it?

We are told that, in the days of Matthew Paris, 'public men . . . realised that their share in events could be best preserved for posterity by judicious conversations at St Albans'. Similarly, in the 14th century, such men would have eagerly buttonholed Froissart and Jean le Bel. All would have felt rewarded by this volume, dedicated to them.

Hugh Trevor-Roper

Hugh Trevor-Roper

Atlantic Ocean
North Sea
SCOTLAND
IRELAND
Carlisle
Durham
ENGLAND
York
Chester
Lincoln
WALES
Worcester
Lichfield
Hereford
Ely
Gloucester
Wells
London
Exeter
Salisbury
DENMARK
Utrecht
Minden
Soest
Damme
LITHUANIA
POLAND
Erfurt
Naumburg
Cambrai
Tournai
Cologne
Marburg
Freiburg
Bayeux
Rouen
Amiens
Limburg
Coutances
Beauvais
Mainz
Sées
Reims
Trier
Prague
Paris
Evreux
Le Mans
Oppenheim
Nuremburg
Regensburg
Chartres
Troyes
Auxerre
Strasbourg
Vienna
Bourges
HOLY ROMAN EMPIRE
FRANCE
HUNGARY
Clermont
Bordeaux
Lyon
AQUITAINE
Vercelli
Venice
Padua
Bayonne
Burgos
Albi
Genoa
REPUBLIC OF VENICE
WALLACHIA
Black Sea
NAVARRE
Narbonne
Marseille
PAPAL STATES
Sienna
CASTILE
Lerida
Gerona
Assisi
SERBIA
BULGARIA
ARAGON
Barcelona
CORSICA
Orvieto
Toledo
Rome
KINGDOM OF NAPLES
BYZANTINE EMPIRE
Constantinople
Valencia
Palma de Majorca
Naples
Brindisi
SARDINIA
BALEARIC ISLANDS
Cagliari
CORFU
CEPHALONIA
Antioch
KINGDOM OF SICILY
Tunis
CYPRUS
RHODES
MOSLEM STATES
Damascus
CRETE
Mediterranean Sea
Acre
Damietta
Cairo
Paris Main cities
Main Gothic cathedrals, begun or completed 1216–1377
Crusade routes of Louis IX of France:
1248–1254
2 July–12 August 1270
Crusade route of Frederick II 1228–1229
0 200 400 Miles
0 300 600 Km

The Gothic world in the 13th and 14th centuries

England – with the rival kingdom of Scotland and the satellites of Wales and Ireland – was geographically and politically on the fringes of Christendom. Its 13th- and 14th-century kings looked south and east, towards France, Germany, Italy, and were involved in warfare and alliances with many of their rulers.

Edward I won respect for his role as a crusader in the 1270s, but was overshadowed by the earlier achievements of Emperor Frederick II and King Louis IX of France.

The 13th and 14th centuries saw the blossoming of great Gothic cathedrals all over Europe; England, very much a part of the European scene, produced some which were among the finest of their age.

Although Acre, the last crusader outpost in Palestine, fell to the Muslims in 1290, western forces continued their advance against the caliphs in Spain and the Slavonic tribes in the Baltic. Progress was, however, slow, and the Byzantine Empire, formerly a valuable bastion, was now under ever increasing pressure from the Turks.

Christendom, on the defensive, was on the lookout for allies. Beyond the Turks lay the Mongols, who at the height of their power dominated Asia from China to the Black Sea. Few westerners had direct experience of these people – with the exception of Marco Polo and his family, who were unusually intrepid travellers – but the unrealistic hope that the Mongols might prove useful allies against Islam was nourished by many.

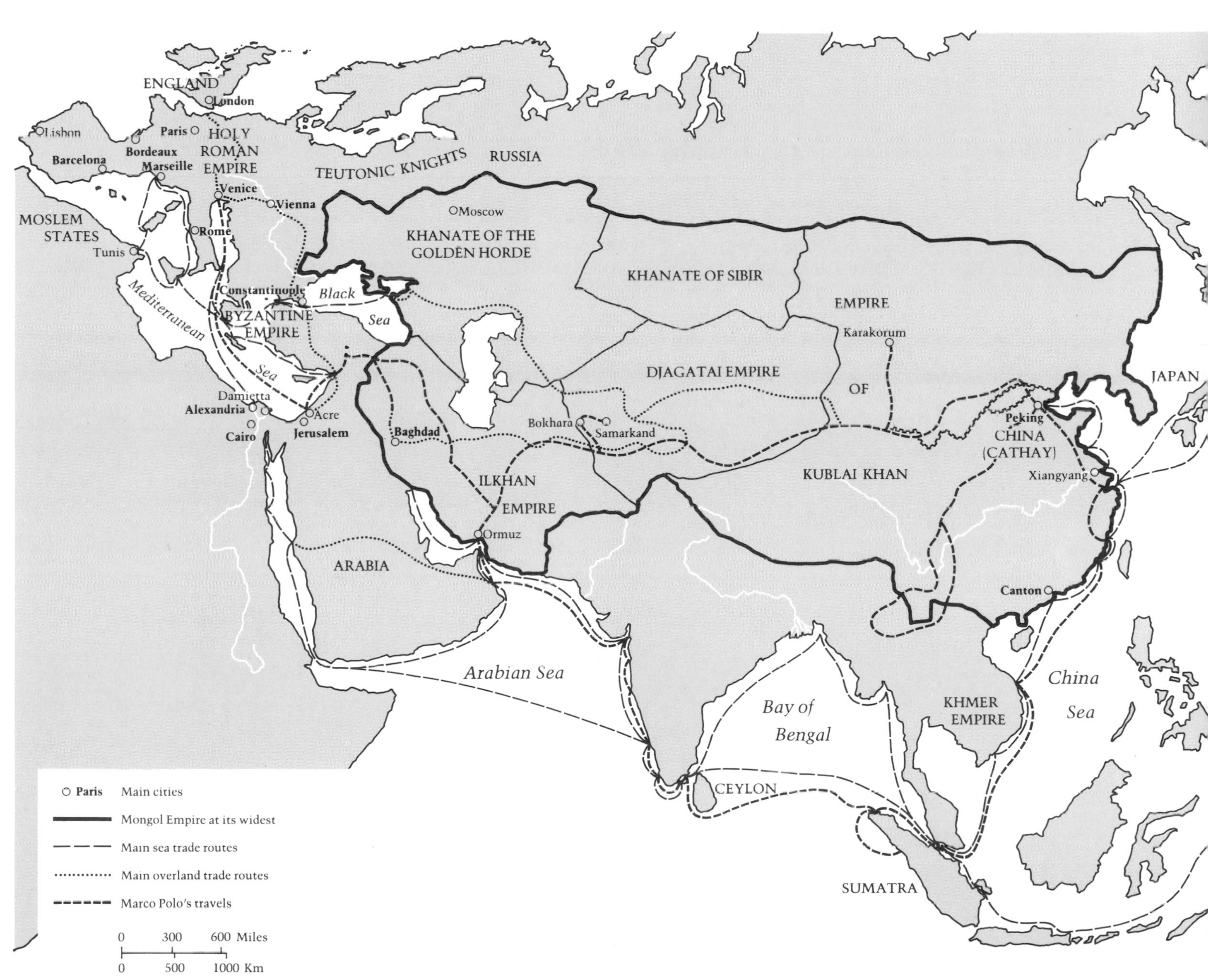

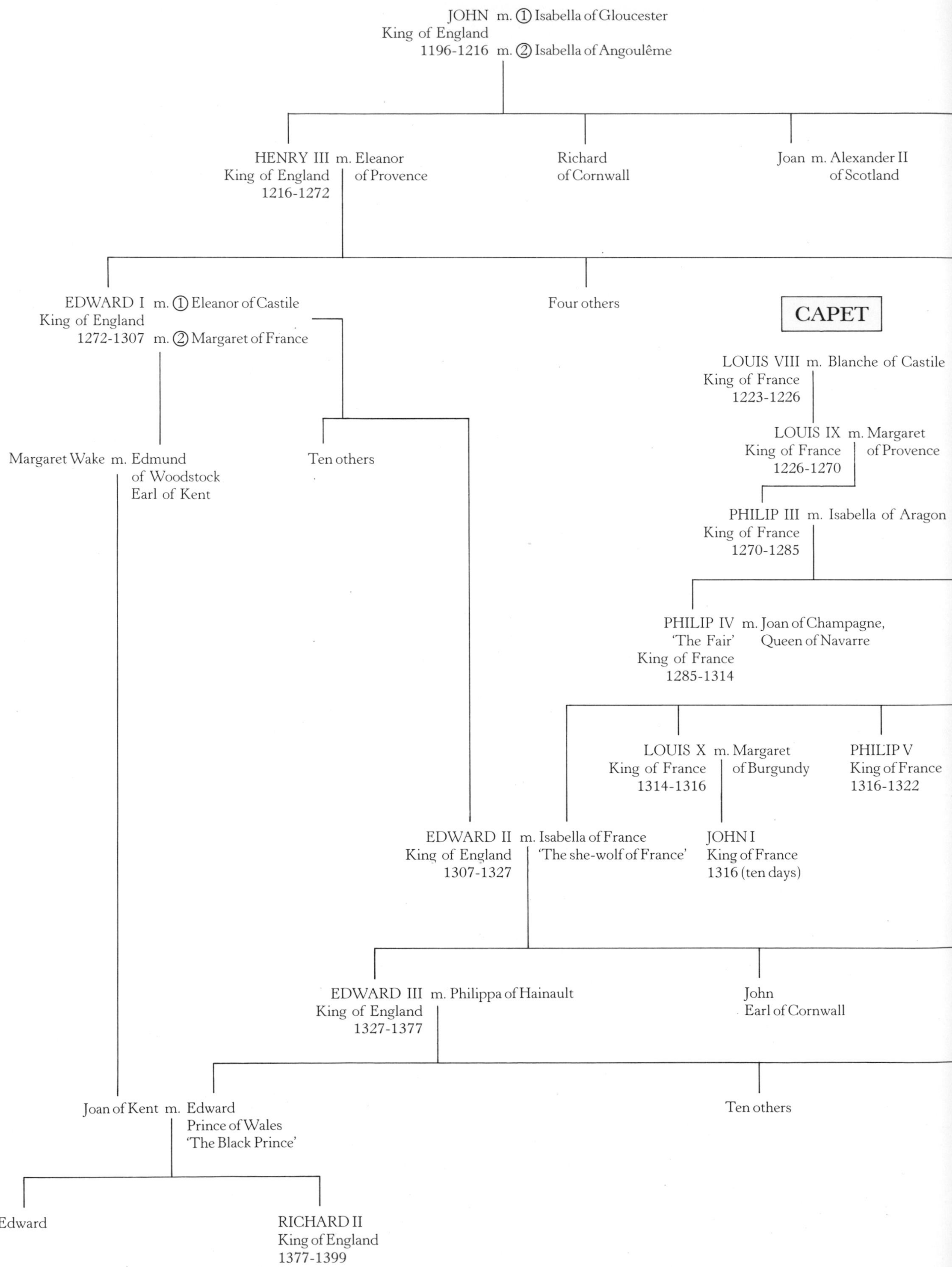

PLANTAGENET
JOHN m. ① Isabella of Gloucester
King of England
1196-1216 m. ② Isabella of Angoulême
HENRY III m. Eleanor of Provence
King of England
1216-1272
Richard of Cornwall
Joan m. Alexander II of Scotland
EDWARD I m. ① Eleanor of Castile
King of England
1272-1307 m. ② Margaret of France
Four others
CAPET
LOUIS VIII m. Blanche of Castile
King of France
1223-1226
LOUIS IX m. Margaret of Provence
King of France
1226-1270
Margaret Wake m. Edmund of Woodstock Earl of Kent
Ten others
PHILIP III m. Isabella of Aragon
King of France
1270-1285
PHILIP IV 'The Fair' m. Joan of Champagne, Queen of Navarre
King of France
1285-1314
LOUIS X m. Margaret of Burgundy
King of France
1314-1316
PHILIP V
King of France
1316-1322
EDWARD II m. Isabella of France 'The she-wolf of France'
King of England
1307-1327
JOHN I
King of France
1316 (ten days)
EDWARD III m. Philippa of Hainault
King of England
1327-1377
John Earl of Cornwall
Joan of Kent m. Edward Prince of Wales 'The Black Prince'
Ten others
Edward
RICHARD II
King of England
1377-1399

Kings of England, France and Scotland

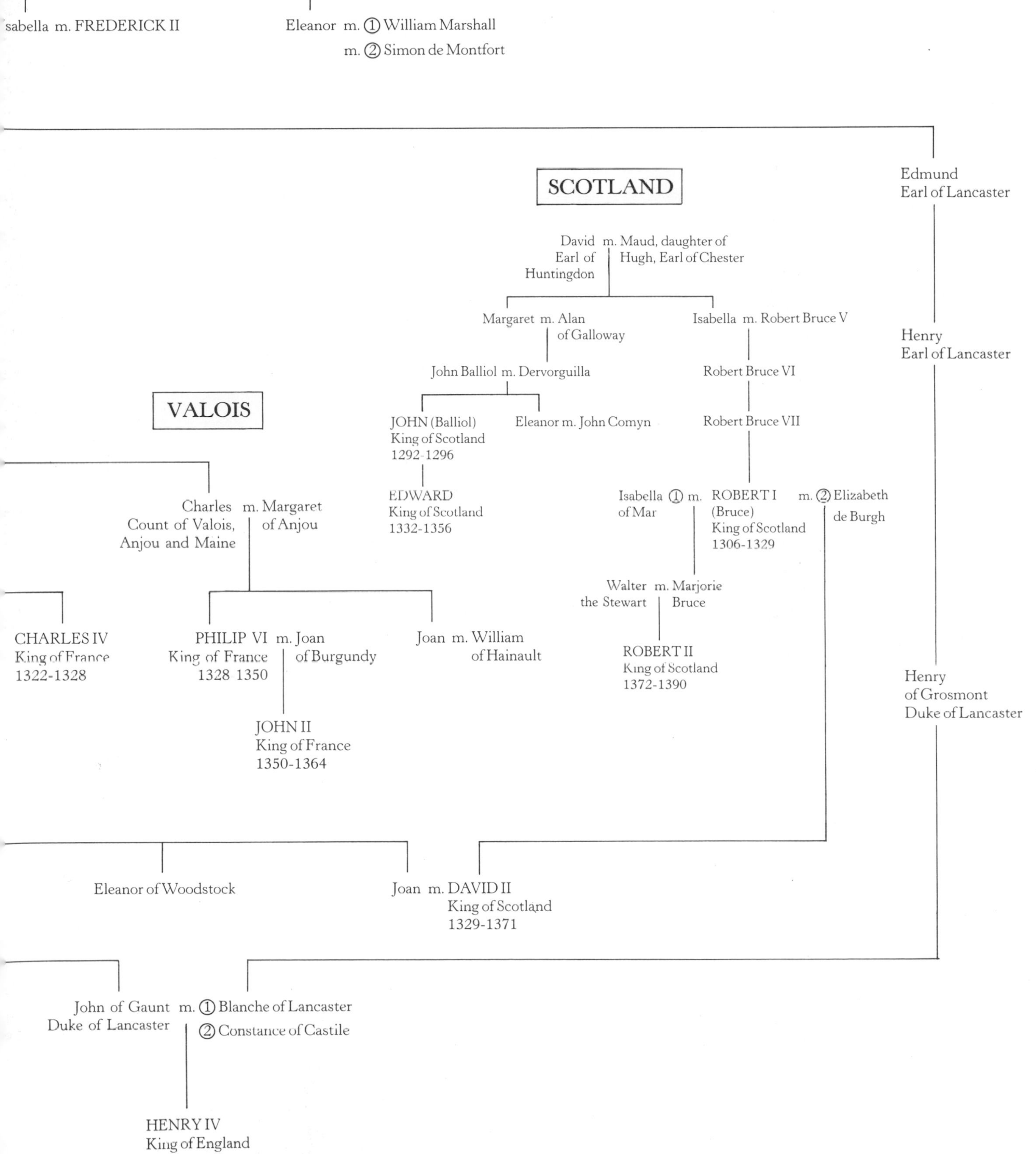

Part I

Henry III 1216–1272

Henry III came to the throne of England in 1216 when he was only nine years old. Compared with his brilliant contemporaries, King Louis IX of France and the Holy Roman Emperor Frederick II, Henry cut a dull figure as a king: he devoted much of his energy to pious and artistic activities and in particular to the lavish rebuilding of Westminster Abbey. Much of the routine work of government he left to his favourites – frequently foreign – provoking faction fighting at court, and finally causing his barons to impose reforms upon him from 1258. This, however, led to civil war which continued intermittently until 1265, when Simon de Montfort, earl of Leicester, leader of the barons who opposed the king, was killed at the battle of Evesham.

The events of Henry's momentous reign are vividly recounted by two St Albans chroniclers, Roger of Wendover and Matthew Paris, the pro-baronial Waverley Annals *describing the last dramatic years and the chivalrous* History of William Marshal *the first. The epitaph on King John, Henry III's father, by the anonymous 'Barnwell' annalist introduces the story.*

(Opposite: Henry III)

Laid low by illness, King John ended his days on 19 October after he had ruled for seventeen years, five months and four days. He was indeed a great prince but scarcely a happy one and, like Marius, he experienced the ups and downs of fortune. He was munificent and liberal to outsiders but a plunderer of his own people, trusting strangers rather than his subjects, wherefore he was eventually deserted by his own men and, in the end, little mourned.

When King John was buried, the great men came together in council, and resolved to send Thomas of Samford to Devizes, to bring from there the king's first-born son Henry and all those that were with him. William Marshal went ahead of them and rejoined them outside Malmesbury on the plain. Ralph de St Sanson, the prince's governor, was there, carrying him in his arms.

The child, who was well bred, greeted William Marshal and said to him, 'Greetings. I entrust myself to God and to you. May God help you to look after us well.' William Marshal replied, 'Sire, upon my soul, I shall neglect nothing to serve you faithfully so long as I have strength to do so.' All burst into tears, William Marshal like the rest. Then they set out again for Gloucester.

England and France in Henry III's reign

The young Henry III inherited a divided kingdom. His father, King John, had lost most of the Plantagenet lands in France; he also had forfeited the trust of most of the barons; and the future Louis VIII of France, with a strong following, looked set to take the English throne. But the child king became a focus of loyalty, and French support crumbled away, giving Henry a firm power base in his own realm.

In 1216 English power in France was relatively secure only in Gascony. Poitou was an unstable and divided area dominated by the powerful house of Lusignan, with

whose help Louis VIII of France overran the region in 1224–5. Henry made an inconclusive attempt to reassert his authority in 1230, and launched a fruitless expedition in 1242, which lost him Saintonge. Gascony now became increasingly unsettled. In 1253 a major revolt broke out under the leadership of Gaston de Béarn, which Henry put down with difficulty.

The treaty of Paris, ratified in 1259, was a successful attempt to settle the respective claims of the English and French kings to the former Plantagenet lands. Henry III surrendered his claims to Normandy, Anjou, Maine and Poitou and became Louis IX's vassal for Gascony. He was also given rights in the Périgord and the future reversion of Saintonge, the Agenais and Quercy.

There they deliberated whether to wait for Ranulf, earl of Chester, or to proceed without him. Some were for waiting, others advised them to crown the king immediately, for no one knew what the future held for him. The latter counsel won the day. Then someone asked who was to dub the king knight. 'Who indeed,' said someone, 'if not William Marshal, who among a thousand men deserves the honour more than the rest? It was he who girded the sword upon Henry II's son, the Young King. Not one of you rivals his greatness. It is he who ought to gird the sword upon this one and so he will have knighted two kings.'

All agreed to this. The child was dressed in royal robes made to his size: he looked a fine little knight. The great men who were present carried him to the monastery. Rich gifts were distributed when he was anointed and crowned. The legate Gualo, who represented Pope Honorius III, sang the Mass and crowned him King Henry III, assisted by the bishops who were assembled there.

When Henry was anointed and consecrated, and the service was over, the knights carried the child in their arms. A number of others lent a hand, who were not much help. He was carried to his chamber, where he was dressed in less heavy clothes. At this moment, just as the company was going to sit down at table, there came bad news.

A messenger, more foolish than wise, told William Marshal, in front of everybody, that his castle of Goodrich had been besieged the previous day and that his constable was asking him for help. William Marshal immediately dispatched knights, sergeants and crossbowmen.

Many considered that this event, on the very day of the coronation, was a bad omen.

The great men came to William Marshal and asked him to take upon himself the guardianship of the king. 'I cannot,' he replied. 'I have no longer the strength needed for such a charge. I am too old. You must give this responsibility to another. Wait until Ranulf, earl of Chester, arrives.' They left the matter at that for the night and each man went home.

The minority and ministers

NO Plantagenet king came to the throne in more difficult circumstances than Henry III, son of King John. In 1216, he was just over nine years old. Louis, son of Philip II, king of France, controlled the whole of eastern England, including London, and was recognized as king by the majority of English barons. It seemed that the Plantagenet dynasty was about to be swept away by the Capetian.

In this darkest hour the Plantagenet cause was kept alive by the papal legate Gualo, and by the barons and ministers who had remained loyal to King John. Amongst these, one man stood out: William Marshal, earl of Pembroke epitomizing the chivalric virtues of gallantry and loyalty. William Marshal was over 70, but still vigorous in mind and body. He became regent of the young king and his kingdom and, within a year, had carried the Plantagenet standard to victory over Louis. Henry was undisputed king.

Military victory was reinforced by political conciliation. Former rebels who professed allegiance to the young king were restored to their lands, and the political programme for which they had been fighting, Magna Carta, was conceded.

If King John had won the war with Louis and the barons, Magna Carta would have been ceremonially buried. As it was, William Marshal's government re-issued it in 1216 after Henry's coronation (in a form slightly different from the original in 1215), and in 1217 at the end of the war. There was then no going back. Henry

Above left *The head of William Marshal, first earl of Pembroke, from his effigy in the Temple Church, London.*

Above *The Earl Marshal rose to eminence through his prowess with lance and sword; here he unhorses Baldwin de Guisnes at a tournament in 1233.*

himself re-issued Magna Carta in 1225 – this version became the official text – and again in 1237 and 1253.

The early years of Henry's reign, therefore, formed a watershed in Plantagenet kingship. It was now limited by law; limited in its ability to exploit its traditional feudal sources of revenue; and limited in its freedom to act against people in an arbitrary fashion. Clause 28 of Magna Carta (still on the statute book), which stipulated that no free man was to be outlawed, exiled, imprisoned or deprived of his property save by judgement of his peers or by the law of the land, has rightly been seen as a foundation of English liberties and a bulwark against tyrannical rule.

When William Marshal died in May 1219, Henry III was still too young to govern for himself and the country was ruled by three men: the justiciar, Hubert de Burgh; the king's tutor, Peter des Roches, bishop of Winchester; and, until his withdrawal in 1221, Pandulf, the papal legate.

This central government faced one great problem: its own poverty and weakness. This was mainly because the king's castles, sheriffdoms and manors were controlled by men who had served King John and who claimed they could not be moved until the king reached his majority. Meanwhile, they siphoned off a good slice of the revenues.

This continued until the end of 1223, when Henry was declared of age (with certain restrictions); many castellans and sheriffs were then dismissed, on the orders of a faction led by Hubert de Burgh and Stephen Langton, archbishop of Canterbury.

The result was a bitter power struggle which lasted for the next ten years. Men who had been ousted from office soon found a leader in Peter des Roches, and in 1232 they ruined Hubert and returned to power. Two years later, Peter himself was disgraced. Although Henry's minority was brought completely to an end in January 1227, he remained under the influence of great ministers inherited from his father until 1234, when Hubert de Burgh and Peter des Roches finally quit the political stage. Only then did Henry III's personal rule begin.

These early factional struggles had a wider significance. Hubert de Burgh was an Englishman (his name Burgh is derived from Burgh next Aylsham in Norfolk); he was insular, conservative, cautious. Peter des Roches was a Poitevin; cosmopolitan, arrogant, autocratic. Many of the latter's allies were foreigners, like himself, whom King John had established in England.

In 1224, the greatest of these, the Norman Fawkes de Bréauté, had staged an ill-fated rebellion. As a result it was easy to depict the trouble-makers of Henry's early years as foreigners who conspired to disturb the peace and undermine English liberties. Because Fawkes de Bréauté's rebellion followed soon after the war between Henry's supporters and Louis of France, it increased the sense of English identity and resentment against foreigners. This was to be a backdrop to much of Henry's reign.

The next day after Mass, the earl of Chester arrived. He greeted King Henry III, who received his homage and that of the other barons. Many of those who came with the earl regarded it as unfitting that the others had not waited for him to arrive before crowning the king. But the earl silenced them by saying that they had done the right thing by proceeding without delay to the coronation. Then they all took counsel together and deliberated on the choice of to whom the guardianship of the king and the kingdom should be entrusted. 'By my faith,' said one, 'I see only William Marshal or Ranulf, earl of Chester.' 'In truth, my lords,' replied William Marshal, 'I cannot accept so exalted a mission. I am too weak. I am over eighty. But you, earl of Chester, make it your charge, and as long as I live, I will give you all the help I can.' 'No indeed, Marshal,' said the earl, 'you are so fine a man, so upright, so respected, so loved and so wise that you are considered one of the finest knights in the world. I say in all sincerity, it is you that ought to be chosen. I will serve you and will perform, as best I can, all the tasks you wish to command me.'

Then the papal legate Gualo took William Marshal aside into another room with Ranulf, earl of Chester, Peter des Roches, bishop of Winchester, and some of the great men, and they began to deliberate afresh. But they would never have managed to overcome the resistance of William Marshal had the legate not begged him to accept the regency for the remission and pardon of his sins. On this condition, he would grant him absolution from them before God. 'In God's name,' said William Marshal, 'if at this price I am absolved of my sins, this office suits me, and I will take it, though it weighs heavily upon me.'

The legate entrusted it to him, and the noble William Marshal received at the same time the king and the regency. He performed it well so long as he lived, but we lost him too soon for the well-being of England.

When William Marshal had taken charge of the kingdom, he spoke thus, 'My lords, behold this young and tender king. I could not undertake to lead him with me about the land. And I cannot stay in the same place, for I shall have to go to the Marches of the kingdom to protect them. That is why I ask you to name an upright man to whom the young king shall be entrusted.' 'Do as you please, sire,' said the legate, 'you will know how to put him into good hands.' Upon which William Marshal entrusted the child to Peter des Roches, bishop of Winchester.

When it became known that William Marshal had charge of the king and the kingdom, there was rejoicing. 'God protects us,' people said, 'for there is no one in England who would be capable of acquitting himself as well of this charge.'

William Marshal called into counsel the faithful friends whom he had consulted the previous day, and said to them, 'Advise me, for by the faith I owe you I see myself embarking upon a sea without either bottom or shore. May God come to my aid. They have entrusted to me an almost hopeless governorship. The child has no money and I am a man of great age.' Tears came into his eyes as he spoke, and the others wept too, out of pity.

'Yes,' said John de Erley, who had understood his way of thinking, 'you have undertaken a task that must be carried through at all costs. But when we reach the end, I tell you that, even putting things at their worst, only great honour can come of it. And as the worst possible outcome is so honourable, the most propitious will bring you both great honour and great joy. No man will ever have earned such glory on earth.'

'By God's sword,' said William Marshal, 'this advice is true and good; it goes so straight to my heart, that if everyone else abandoned the king, do you know what I would do? I would carry him on my shoulders step by step, from island to island, from country to country and I would not fail him, not even if it meant begging my bread.' 'You cannot say more, and God will be with you,' replied his friends.

'Now,' concluded William Marshal, 'let us go to bed, and there may God grant counsel and help, He who comes to the help of those who wish to do good and act loyally.'

Prince Louis, son of King Philip II of France, had in 1216 almost succeeded in wresting the English crown from Henry III's father, John. After John's death, his support from the English barons had fallen away and he retreated to France to recoup his strength.

1217

After an absence of seven weeks and five days, Prince Louis returned to England with a large and proud army. William Marshal was annoyed at his return, and he had all the castles he had taken from him dismantled.

When Louis learnt that the castles of which he thought himself master had surrendered he was displeased. Having assembled a large number of carters, sergeants, crossbowmen and ribalds, he went straight to Winchester. In a little while, he had restored the tower and the high walls with stone and mortar and had the breaches repaired. He left the count of Nevers on the spot, a cruel proud man, with a strong garrison. Subsequently he committed various excesses with which he has been reproached, but I do not want to talk about them.

On leaving Winchester, Louis divided his great army into two bodies. With one he went to besiege Dover, and he sent the other to Mountsorel, which the earls of Chester and Ferrers held under siege. These men, believing that Louis in person was descending upon them, raised the siege and retired to Nottingham. The French having relieved Mountsorel made their way to Lincoln, where they wanted to besiege the castle.

William Marshal, with a small force, followed the French army and rescued the castellan of Lincoln, Nicola de la Haye, and her forces, from the besiegers. The Barnwell annalist describes Prince Louis's reaction to this disastrous defeat.

Louis when he heard this left Dover and returned to London, whence he made no expeditions, nor undertook anything arduous. He then sent word to his friends overseas, requesting that they send him aid in his necessity.

Then the supporters of King Henry III, rising up everywhere, were able to prevail; having occupied territory wherever they went, and taken small fortresses, they came to London with a great force, as if to blockade Louis in the city.

Meanwhile, overseas, help was prepared with great effort and at great speed for Louis and the Londoners. The king's supporters were aware of this. They remained in the areas where the enemy was expected to land, and after having filled warships with men and arms, they kept continual watch.

What happened?

On 24 August, the whole enemy fleet joined battle with the king's men, not far from the Isle of Thanet. Many of their ships and some of the leaders of the French party were captured, but the rest were able to evade capture by flight; many of the lesser men were killed. Scattered in confusion, the enemy could not regroup.

From that day, the cause of the king flourished while that of Louis declined. Then, with the forces of the king gathering near London, Louis did not delay to make such peace as fortune offered.

On 12 September, terms were made, concerning the release of those who had been captured; concerning the evil customs which had been the cause of the war; and concerning the observance of the liberties which had been sought by the English nobles. A financial settlement was made for the expenses which Louis had incurred in the kingdom.

Louis was paid the enormous sum of 10,000 marks (nearly £7000), indicating the anxiety of the English barons that he should relinquish his claims and depart for France.

Louis was also absolved [for having taken up arms against Henry, a papal vassal] at Kingston upon Thames on 20 September by the papal legate Gualo, after taking an oath to stand by the judgement of the Church on pain of canonical sanctions.

Then, having handed over the fortifications which he was holding, Prince Louis received back those of his followers who were in chains.

At last, with part of the promised money, he returned to his own country on 29 September.

It was thought to be a miracle that the eldest son of the king of France, having come into England with such a large force of armed men, and having occupied such a large part of the kingdom with the support of so many magnates, should now so speedily be ejected from the kingdom without any hope of return.

After Louis had been absolved, the Londoners and many of the barons who had supported his cause followed his example and sued for peace. Having been reconciled with the king, they received back their lands. For it had been included in the peace terms made on 12 September that no one should be disinherited on account of the war, but that all should retain the position which they had enjoyed at its onset. This, however, was granted to the laity only.

The legate Gualo, reserving to himself the cases of all clergy, and especially those with benefices, now degraded them. All those who had been excommunicated he referred to the judgement of the pope. He left unpunished no one against whom he could find any grounds for accusation: who had openly given aid, counsel or approval to Prince Louis or his confederates, or who had not observed the sentences launched by the pope or the legate himself.

In 1219 William Marshal died, and was widely mourned. Pandulf, who had succeeded Gualo as papal legate in 1218, now played a major rôle in the administration of the realm.

1220

Pope Honorius III, in letters to the English Church, ordered that King Henry, the eldest son of King John, should be solemnly inducted into his kingdom for a second time, because his first coronation had been carried out without due and

The blossoming of cathedrals in Europe

THE 13th century, like the 12th, was an age of great cathedrals: massive and echoing stone edifices, whose windows were filled with richly coloured glass depicting scenes from the scriptures and lives of saints. Exteriors bristled with pinnacles and fretted gables, and enormous doors were surrounded by the carved figures of more saints and apostles.

A cathedral reflected a city's wealth and was very much a corporate enterprise. Gifts came from kings and princes; the windows of the north transept at Chartres were donated by Blanche of Castile. Many aisle windows at Chartres commemorate their donors, the various city trade guilds. And in the late 12th century, the bishop of Paris rather reluctantly refused the offer of a magnificent window for Notre-Dame from the prostitutes of the city.

Work started on the colossal High Gothic cathedrals of northern France – Chartres, Bourges, Reims, Amiens and Beauvais – between 1195 and 1225, after which, buildings in northern France became less gigantic. But the urge to emulate French High Gothic cathedrals spread. Henry III's Westminster Abbey reflected Reims. In Germany, Cologne's vast space and mass was based on Amiens. In Castile, the cathedrals of Burgos, Toledo and León remained architecturally close to their French sources.

Costs were high, and by the late 13th and early 14th centuries, enormous cathedrals were no longer being built in the north. Only the wealthy trading cities of the Mediterranean could support such enterprises, but even they often encountered difficulties. In the kingdom of Barcelona, there are four such High Gothic edifices: Palma de Majorca, begun in the late 13th century, but not finished until 1601; the cathedral at Barcelona, started in 1298 and under construction throughout the 14th century; the church of Santa Maria del Mar in the same city, 1329–83; and the immense cathedral of Gerona, begun in 1312 and limping to its completion in the 16th century.

In Italy, the cathedrals of Orvieto (1290–1425), Sienna and Florence were still based on the basilica shape, but were on a new scale. Florence, begun in 1296 by Arnulfo di Cambio, was so large that it took a century and a half to build. The Siennese also over-reached themselves. In 1339 they decided to expand their cathedral, using the existing, by no means insignificant, 13th-century building as the transept. It was a bad moment to choose. In 1348, the Black Death compounded financial insecurity, and only the new west front was ever built. Its isolated remains still stand, a sorry reminder of human *folie des grandeurs*.

Above *The Duomo, Sienna. High Gothic cathedrals, first built in northern France at the end of the 12th and beginning of the 13th centuries, were emulated in Italy as well as in England, Germany and Spain. The Duomo, like other Italian cathedrals, was based on the early Christian basilica shape.*

These reflected the wealth and civic pride of the cities in which they were built. In Sienna, during the 14th century, the citizens decided to enlarge their cathedral but, because of a combination of lack of money and the Black Death only the new west front was built.

Right *Stained glass window in Chartres Cathedral, depicting Prince Louis of France.*

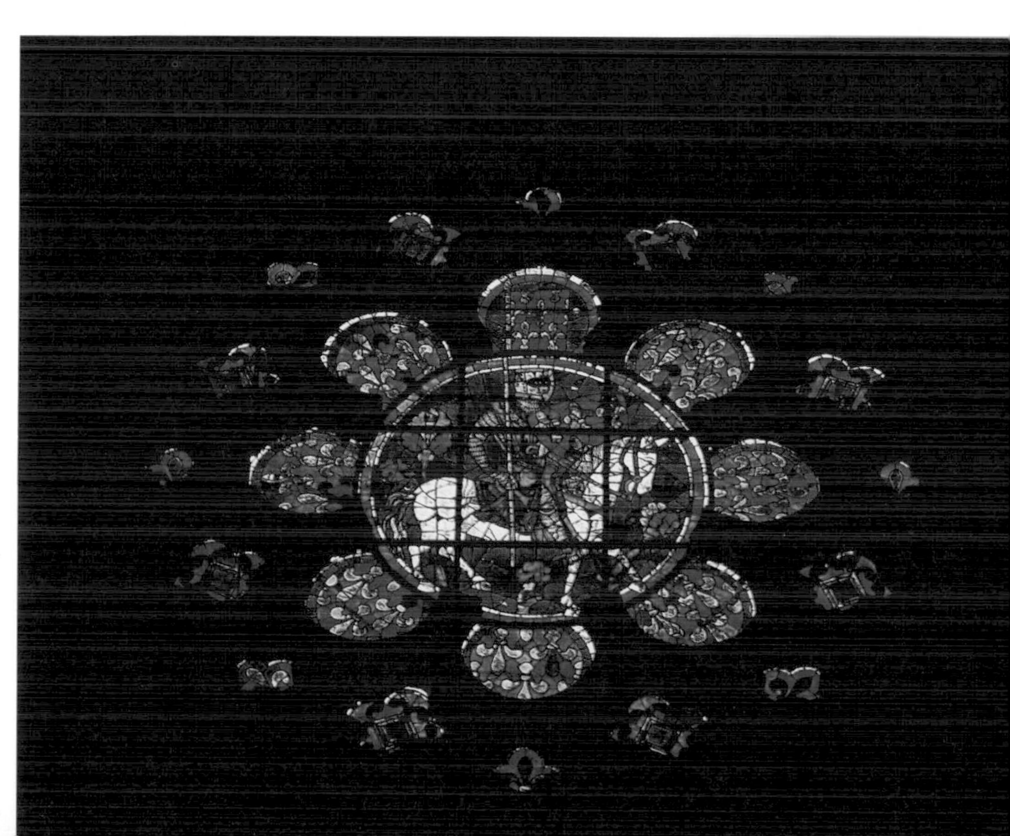

Left *Orvieto Cathedral in Italy. It stands in a walled city overlooking a plain, and was built to commemorate the miracle of Bolsena. Each of the triangles represents a scene in the life of the Virgin. The circular rose window is surrounded by statues of the apostles and Old Testament prophets. The lower facades contain low relief carvings from the Old and New Testaments.*

Right *Toledo Cathedral in Spain where many of the Gothic characteristics developed in France can be found.*

Below *The interior of Gerona Cathedral in Spain, exhibiting the classic features of a Gothic cathedral.*

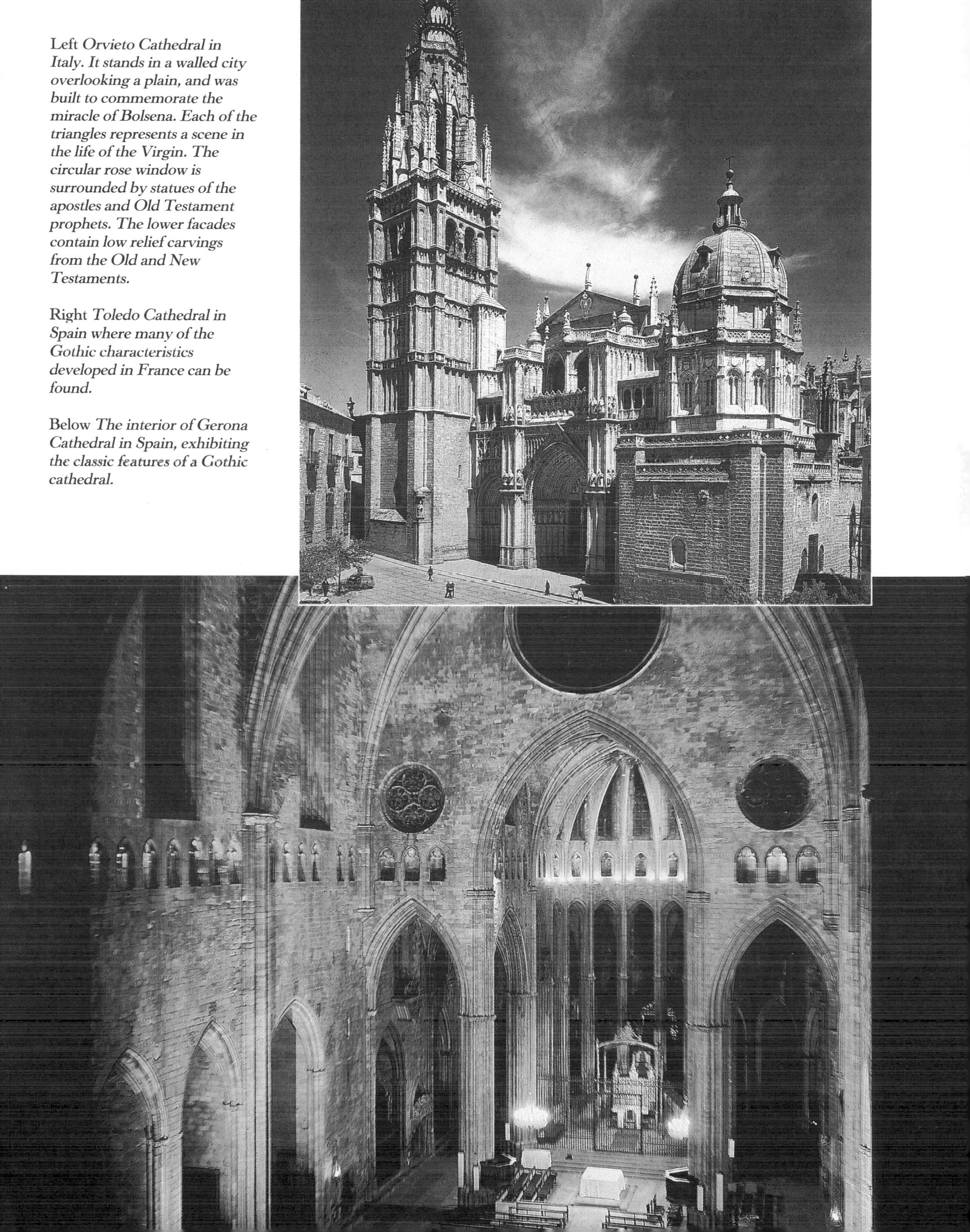

proper solemnity, on account of the disturbances and internal divisions of the country, and also in a different place than was customary.

Stephen Langton, archbishop of Canterbury, who held the king in great affection for his innocence, was much delighted with this order and, together with the legate Pandulf, he named a day when the papal mandate should be put into effect, and when he himself might fulfil the duty which he had undertaken towards the king.

When the day had been chosen, namely 17 May, it was announced throughout the kingdom. The prelates of the Church and nobles were warned that they should gather at London, without excuse and with due reverence for the king, to bring the ceremonies to completion.

On the day appointed, Stephen, archbishop of Canterbury, in the presence of Pandulf the legate, assisted by many other prelates of the Church, and together with many of the magnates of the realm, in the abbey church of Westminster, made King Henry III swear an oath that he would defend the Church of God and would protect the peace of clergy and people and the good laws of the land.

At this time the king had not completed the thirteenth year of his life. The coronation was accomplished in such a great spirit of peace and munificence, that the older members of the nobility asserted that none of his predecessors had been crowned in such harmony and tranquillity.

1224

Henry III, king of England, when he had reached seventeen years of age, in order that he might take the affairs of the realm into his own hands, took back into his own control many castles which for a long time had been held by both foreigners and natives of England, for he held these people in suspicion, fearing that they might do him great harm if their power as holders of castles endured any longer, as afterwards proved to be the case.

One of these men, the freebooting Fawkes de Bréauté, who had fought for King John, refused to relinquish his castles to King Henry; but his rebellion was overcome by Stephen Langton, archbishop of Canterbury, and Hubert de Burgh, the justiciar of England. Roger of Wendover, a monk of St Albans, records the firm measures enacted against libidinous priests.

1225

In that year, a decree went out from the archbishop of Canterbury and his suffragan bishops:

"The concubines of priests and clerks who are in Holy Orders and who have church livings, shall be denied burial in consecrated ground unless they have completely mended their ways, or have done penance so earnestly that they deserved proper burial.

"These keepers of concubines shall not receive the kiss of peace, moreover, nor receive consecrated bread in church for as long as they keep such women either in their houses or openly elsewhere.

"If the women bear children, they are not to be purified after childbirth unless they have given sufficient assurances to the archdeacon or his official that they will go before the next meeting of the chapter to make satisfaction.

"Those priests in whose parishes such concubines tarry shall be suspended if they do not disclose the fact to the archdeacon, and undergo heavy penance before such a suspension may be lifted.

"Any woman who can be proved to have known a priest carnally shall undergo solemn public penance, as if she had been convicted of adultery, even if she is unmarried. A married woman guilty of this shall be punished for a double adultery in case such an offence, unpunished, should encourage other opportunities for lawbreaking."

1226

On 3 October, a friar called Francis, who is credited with having been the founder and master of his order the Franciscans, departed this life at Rome, in a miraculous manner.

King Henry and his rule

THE only surviving description of Henry III's appearance, taken by Rishange from the Chronicle of Nicholas Trevet, portrays the king as being of medium height and strong build, with a drooping eyelid hiding part of the pupil. Henry was probably much the same height as his father John (five feet six and a half inches), since his coffin in Westminster Abbey is the same length as John's.

He lived to be 65, a considerable age for the time, proof that his constitution was sound.

For Henry, the duties of kingship were summed up in his coronation oath of 1220, which pledged him to maintain peace, dispense justice and uphold the rights of the crown. He remained a product of the early years of his reign, when royal authority was weak and when memories of the civil war of 1215–17, which had nearly destroyed the Plantagenets, were fresh. At home, therefore, Henry's basic aim was to live in peace and, to that end, he tried to conciliate his barons, even allowing them to develop their local power at the expense of his own.

Abroad, Henry was more ambitious, launching schemes to regain the Plantagenet lands in France (he invaded Brittany in 1230 and Poitou in 1242 – both fruitlessly), and in the 1250s, to install his young son Edmund as king of Sicily. But he could raise neither adequate finances nor the support of his barons, which he needed for any effective action; and to most of his subjects, such unrealistic notions were further proof of his 'simplicity'.

The fact was that Henry temperamentally was more suited to the peaceful style of post-Magna Carta kingship. Not for him his father's hectic travelling and energetic government. In 1244, Matthew Paris noted that the king preferred the 'delight and rest' of his palace of Westminster to a campaign in Wales. Henry yearned for an easy life. He was indifferent to hunting and tournaments, antipathetic to the rigours of campaigns and soldiering. He liked to spend comfortable weeks, sometimes months, at his favourite palaces, within a few days' travelling distance of each other in the home counties: Westminster, Windsor, Winchester, Clarendon, Marlborough and (the furthest north) Woodstock.

Like all Plantagenets, Henry had a fierce temper. However, it was easily appeased and descriptions of his meetings with Matthew Paris show that he was accessible, affable, courteous and sympathetic. The king's piety brought him widespread respect. He gave alms on a grand scale – feeding 500 paupers every day in the 1240s – and also every day, was said to hear Mass four times. From 1245 onwards, he spent vast sums of money rebuilding Westminster Abbey in honour of his patron saint, Edward the Confessor.

Above *Windsor Castle, one of Henry III's principal residences after his marriage in 1236. He began a series of improvements over the next 20 years that were to turn it into one of the finest castles in Europe. These included a new set of royal apartments east of the old hall, and a new chapel dedicated to St Edward.*

Right *Henry III crossing the Channel to visit his dominions in France.*

It was popularly believed that the Confessor had ruled in peace, and for many years Henry was able to follow his example. Political tension, however, was always near the surface, partly because of the king's personality. The Osney Abbey chronicler described him as *simplex*, a difficult word to translate precisely: at one extreme, it could mean honest or straightforward, at the other, plain stupid. In Henry's case the pendulum swung to both extremes, but usually settled somewhere between the two, possibly at naïvety. Henry, in short, found it difficult to calculate the effects of his actions and was unable to discern what was possible and what was not. In political terms, this lack of judgement was sufficient to nullify his many good qualities.

Francis was well known because of his distinguished noble birth, and yet he shone brighter by far on account of his honest life. Having led a normal childhood, he began to meditate more and more often on the changeability of the allurements of this life and of temporal matters, and to think incessantly of how those things which flow away in time are as nothing. This he had perceived in the literary and theological studies he had pursued since an early age and in which he was extremely well versed. It was an idea which led him to despise the instability of perishable matters and to yearn with all his might for the Kingdom of Heaven.

In order to achieve the aim he had set for himself, Francis renounced his paternal inheritance, which was by no means modest, with all its secular trappings. He put on a cowl and a hair shirt, took off his shoes, and tortured his flesh with nightly vigils and fasting. To adopt voluntary poverty, he declared that he would hold no possessions of his own, nor would he take any bodily sustenance, apart from what he might receive as alms from the faithful in the name of charity. If, by chance, anything remained after he had taken the most meagre nourishment, he would keep nothing back for the next day, but give it to the poor.

Francis slept in his clothes by night, used rushes for a mattress and placed a rock under his head for a pillow, content with only the hair shirt which he wore during the day as a blanket. Thus he travelled barefoot in accordance with the Gospel, and embracing the apostolic life, he fulfilled the duty of preaching on Sundays and festivals in parish churches and at other gatherings of the faithful. He was able to impress his words on his audience all the more easily because he stood dissociated from fleshly lust and drunken greed.

In order to carry out his salutary purpose, Francis, a true man of God, drew up a series of articles, covering these and other principles, which are most rigorously followed by the friars of the Franciscan Order to this day. He presented them in writing to Pope Innocent III, who was sitting in the Consistory at Rome, and sought confirmation of his petition from the pope, which he obtained.

Priests and their concubines

THE struggle to enforce celibacy on the English clergy, which reached its height during Henry III's reign, was not easily won – if it was ever won at all. Although there had been decrees against priestly marriage since the 5th century, they had been largely ignored in Anglo-Saxon England; and even after the Norman Conquest, efforts to enforce them were widely regarded as hopelessly utopian and likely to result in unbridled vice.

Parish priests' lives were not markedly different from those of their farming parishioners. They traditionally had custody of the village bull and other uncastrated animals, and were recognized as being much like other men. Gerald of Wales, writing in the early 13th century, assumed, with some disapproval, that village priests would be married, or at least keep a female 'hearth-mate', 'who kindles his fire but puts out his virtue, filling his wretched house with babies, cradles, nurses and midwives'.

Gerald was perhaps thinking of his native Wales, where married priests were the rule rather than the exception. But clerical marriages also died hard in remoter parts of England, sometimes producing dynasties which passed on a parish from priestly father to priestly son for generations, spurring popes and bishops into ever more frequent and thunderous denunciations of clerical liaisons. By 1250, legally married priests were becoming rare. Instead, many of the parish clergy (whom Bishop Grosseteste of Lincoln described as 'utterly sensual, given over to adultery, fornication and incest') turned to less hallowed arrangements. Their companions were known politely as 'concubines' or 'hearth-mates', and more vulgarly as 'priests' mares'.

Covert relationships like these were often marriages in all but name, and were more difficult to stamp out, as an official visit of Kentish parishes in 1293 demonstrated. Of 20 parishes visited, nearly half contained priests illicitly living with women, one of whom fled from the investigators with his heavily pregnant companion. Most were chaplains and lesser clergy, but the worst offender was the vicar of West Hythe. When his first partner died, after bearing him 'ever so many children', he took up with 'a certain Chima Tukkyld, whom he often consorts with in a hut or in ditches'. The vicar was dismissed, while Chima was whipped thrice round the market place and thrice round the church.

Punishments for erring clerics could be severe – an inveterate Sussex offender was sent on hazardous penitential pilgrimages to Rome, Spain and Germany – but sentences on their partners were usually much harsher. A Worcestershire parson, for instance, got away with fasting and public confession, but his mistress suffered 18 public birchings.

According to a tale by the early 14th-century poet Robert Mannyng, the consort of a priest was forbidden Christian burial, and her corpse was the devil's undoubted perquisite: even when it was tied down by her dutiful sons, the fiend carried it off. The ceaseless opprobrium heaped on priests' concubines must have done as much as bishops' decrees to discourage unofficial unions, ensuring that (in Mannyng's words):

'Shame it is everywhere
To be called a priest's mare.'

Below ***The Exeter puzzle jug showing bishops disporting themselves***

So Francis dedicated himself and his new order to the duty of preaching, throughout Italy and other lands, but especially in Rome. The people of Rome, however, being hostile to all goodness, so despised the preaching of the man of God that they would not listen to him, nor heed his holy exhortations.

After several days of this, Francis rebuked them sternly for their hardness of heart: 'I grieve deeply,' he said, 'at your wretchedness, for not only do you scorn me, Christ's servant, but truly you scorn Him in me. To confound you, I shall go to preach Christ to the brute beasts and the birds of the air, so that hearing God's words of salvation they may hearken and obey.'

Leaving the city, he found on the outskirts carrion crows, birds of prey, magpies and birds of many other kinds, and he said to them: 'I command you, in the name of Jesus Christ whom the Jews crucified, to come to me and to hear the Word of God, in the name of Him who created you and delivered you from the Flood in Noah's ark.' At his command, the whole flock of birds settled round him and fell silent. For half a day, without stirring, they listened to the words of the man of God, watching him intently as he preached.

When these extraordinary events had been repeated for three days in succession, and had become known to the people of Rome and to visitors to the city, the clergy and a great crowd of people came out to bring the holy man back, with deep veneration. His fame began to spread widely throughout Italy, and within a short time the Franciscan Order, devoted to preaching, spread throughout the world.

At length the hour came for Francis to leave this world and go to Christ, to receive reward for his labours. Fifteen days before his death, wounds pouring blood appeared on his hands and feet, just such as were seen on the Saviour of the world as he hung upon the Cross. His side also appeared so open, and so bespattered with blood, that even the innermost secret places of his heart were plain to see.

What more can I say?

Crowds of men and women flocked to marvel at this wondrous sight, among them some cardinals.

Then Francis gave up his soul to his Creator. When he was dead, no marks of the wounds remained, neither in his side nor in his hands and feet.

This holy man was buried in his own chapel at Assisi. Pope Innocent III entered him in the calendar of saints in 1228, and proclaimed that the day of his burial should be celebrated as his feast.

In the same year, the Holy Roman Emperor Frederick II, who had already fallen foul of the pope, Gregory IX, incurred anathemas and excommunication for abandoning his crusade to Palestine in its early stages, due to illness.

1228

At that time, the pope, Gregory IX, was deeply troubled by the intention of Emperor Frederick II, rebellious and excommunicated as he was, to resume his plans to travel to the Holy Land. The pope despaired utterly of ever persuading Frederick to do penance or make satisfaction by which he might return to the fold of the Church. So he instructed this man, whom he found contumacious and disloyal, to lay aside his imperial pride and to substitute a son of peace and obedience in his place.

Frederick II nevertheless went to the Holy Land and successfully negotiated the return of Jerusalem to the crusaders. This outstanding success did nothing to placate Gregory IX.

1229

In that year, there came to England one Master Stephen, papal chaplain and messenger to the King of England. He was sent to collect the tithes that had been promised to the pope by the king's own ambassadors in Rome, in order to support the pope in his war against the Holy Roman Emperor Frederick II. The pope had learned much about the

Above *An altarpiece depicting the life of St Francis, painted by Bonaventura Berlinghiero in 1235. This was one of the first altarpieces to be dedicated to a saint.*

The little poor man: St Francis

NO medieval saint exerts a more universal appeal than St Francis of Assisi, the 'little poor man'. He did not merely preach a life of Christ-like simplicity, dedicated to the sick and poor and to love for all created things, he lived it himself. So many legends have grown up about him that the precise truth is sometimes hard to discern, but he seems to have been born at Assisi in 1181, the son of Pietro Bernadone, a prosperous Italian cloth merchant. Christened Giovanni, he was nicknamed Francesco – 'the Frenchman' – because of his passion for fashionable French songs and romances; and his extravagance, wit and stylish clothing made him the natural leader of

Assisi's gilded youth. At the age of about 20 he was captured in a skirmish with neighbouring Perugia, and spent a year as a prisoner of war. Subsequently he fell ill, mentally and physically. Then, at the age of 25, according to his biographer, Thomas of Celano, 'God suddenly decided to deal with him.'

Francis dated his conversion from the day he felt impelled to kiss a leper; previously he had been especially repulsed by the disfigurements of leprosy. Soon afterwards, praying in a dilapidated chapel, he heard the figure of Christ on a crucifix tell him to 'go and repair my church, which you see is in ruins'. This probably referred to the need for renewal in the Church as a whole, but with characteristic simplicity Francis took the command literally. He begged for stones to repair the chapel and sold some of his father's merchandise to raise funds. When his enraged parent demanded its restitution, he publicly returned not only the money but also his clothes, stripping himself naked in the town square of Assisi to symbolize his utter rejection of worldly ties. These exaggerated and dramatic gestures were typical of Francis, and do much to explain his appeal to peasants, nobles and churchmen alike.

His vocation became clear two years later, when he heard a priest read Christ's injunction to 'Go and preach . . . Provide no money for your purse, nor pack for your journey, neither two coats, nor shoes, nor yet a staff.' Kicking off his shoes, Francis at once obeyed to the letter. He and the few companions he had gathered about him refused even the common ownership of property, distributing their possessions among the poor and living entirely by begging as they went on their missionary journeys. They were following an impulse already widespread in contemporary southern Europe, where pious laymen like the 'Poor Men of Lyon' and the Italian 'Humiliati' already embraced lives of evangelical poverty. These groups were regarded as heretics. Francis, however, who insisted on rigid orthodoxy and submission to the Church's guidance, gained the pope's authorization and blessing for his preaching in 1210.

The first years of the Friars Minor – the 'lesser brothers' as they named themselves – were far from easy. But their numbers grew apace, and the legends illustrating St Francis's love for all creation such as his preaching to the birds or subduing a ravening wolf, date from this period. An early biographer even describes him taking worms from the road, lest they be crushed by travellers. In 1219, Francis journeyed to the Holy Land, where he fearlessly confronted a Saracen sultan but failed to convert him.

By now, tension was growing between the uncompromisingly idealistic Francis, with his impatience of rules and worldly learning, and the more practical men among his followers, who favoured greater institutionalization along the lines of existing religious orders. Francis

Opposite above ***The church of S Damiano. It was here that St Francis heard the call from God, 'to rebuild the house that was falling into ruins'.***

Opposite ***St Francis as he is most often remembered, preaching to the birds.***

Above ***A Life of St Francis by Giotto.***

increasingly retired from the world, and, in 1224, miraculously received the 'stigmata', or marks of Christ's crucifixion, on his hands, feet and side. When he died two years later, blind and pain-racked but still singing for joy, he was already revered as a saint.

Although the Franciscans, Friars Minor, or 'grey friars' – so called from their homespun habits – had been constituted as a regular order in 1223, they remained devoted to evangelical poverty, and spread rapidly throughout Europe. In 1224 a party of nine landed at Dover, where they were arrested as vagabonds. Within six months, however, they had founded friaries at Canterbury, London and Oxford – the ecclesiastical, civil and intellectual capitals of England. Unlike seclusion-loving monks, these 'servants of Christ in the world' deliberately sought out centres of population, and were established in most large English towns, generally in the poorest areas, by 1240. Their initial popular impact was enormous, and for the many years that they retained their founder's ideals, the 'lesser brothers' exercised a revitalizing influence on medieval Christendom.

emperor that was detestable and contrary to Christian law; and he took care to publicize this in apostolic letters sent to different parts of the world.

In the first place, Gregory IX pronounced against the emperor for having entered the Church of the Holy Sepulchre at Jerusalem on the feast of the Annunciation of the Blessed Virgin Mary, although he was excommunicated, and for having crowned himself there by his own hand before the high altar. Sitting down again thus crowned, like a bishop, Frederick II had there preached to the people, defending his wickedness and challenging the Roman Church, which he accused of having proceeded unjustly against him.

Then he had left the church, followed by a crowd of hangers-on and, with not a single clergyman present, he had worn the crown all the way to the Hospitallers' house.

In his palace at Acre, Frederick had entertained the Saracens and provided Christian dancing girls to perform for them and, it was reported, to lie with them. What was more, no one but Frederick knew on what condition he had entered into his treaty with the sultan, but it seemed clear, at least from appearances, that he had greater respect for the law of the Saracens than for that of our own faith, for he followed many of their observances.

In addition, Frederick II had deprived the canons of the Holy Cross at Acre of the revenues which they should have received from the port there. He had also pillaged the archbishopric of Nicosia in Cyprus, robbed the canons of the Holy Sepulchre of the offerings at the tomb, and he had taken the returns of the canons of the Holy Temple.

On Palm Sunday, Frederick II had had preachers thrown out of the pulpits where they were preaching, dishonourably and violently handled, and thrown into prison. On Passion Sunday, he had besieged the patriarch, the bishops of Winchester and Exeter, and the Templars in their houses, although when he had seen that he could not overcome the Templars, he had gone away confused.

Frederick II

ADMIRERS of Frederick of Hohenstaufen called him *'Stupor Mundi'* – the wonder of the world. His enemies, of whom he had many, had other names for him. The Italian Franciscan chronicler, Salimbene de Adam, reported that epithets from Revelations were used for him – 'the dragon' or 'the beast'. In his person, Frederick combined different traditions as well as different opinions. His father was Henry VI, king of Germany and Holy Roman Emperor; his mother was Constance, last representative of the Norman royal dynasty of Sicily.

Born near Ancona in 1194, Frederick was an orphan by the age of four, in the guardianship of Pope Innocent III. The empire was embroiled in a struggle between rival contenders – Otto IV and Philip of Swabia – and Sicily lay uneasily under papal rule, its various racial communities at each other's throats. Otto was, however, defeated at Bouvines in 1214.

In 1215 Frederick was crowned king at Aachen, on the marble throne of Charlemagne. In 1220, Pope Honorius III consented to crown him emperor at Rome. But despite this success, Germany – the heartland of the empire – was not, and could never be, the centre of his world; Frederick's main concern was to rebuild his dynasty's fortunes in the south of Italy, where he had grown up.

Sicily was the most sophisticated monarchy of its day. It lay on the borders of three worlds: the Latin West, the Moslem South and the Greek East. Arabs and Greeks peopled the suburbs of its capital, Palermo. At the great school of medicine at Salerno, the most advanced in the world, Greeks, Latins and Moslems studied and taught. Sicily's bureaucratic government employed Arab personnel and language, and its monarchy even bequeathed some Arab words to the English language; its chief officer of state was the *ammiratus ammiratorum*, the 'emir of emirs', from which the title 'admiral' comes.

In the palace of Palermo, Frederick could sit enthroned in the manner of a Byzantine emperor or an Islamic caliph, below coffered ceilings of Arab inspiration and Byzantine mosaics of gold and precious stones. Suppliants would prostrate themselves before him as before the eastern emperor. Like his predecessor, William II, he maintained a 'harem' of concubines and was screened from the common gaze.

Isolated in splendour, Frederick's mind too was remote from his contemporaries. He shocked Moslems and Christians alike by his scepticism. According to his great and unremitting enemy, Pope Gregory IX, Frederick is said to have asserted that 'the world has been deceived by three men, Jesus, Moses and Mohammed'. When the emperor went on crusade, the pope excommunicated him, suspecting his motives; even when Frederick recovered Jerusalem and was crowned in the Holy Sepulchre in 1229, Gregory did not relax the sentence until compelled to do so by force in 1230.

Frederick was ahead of his age in his thinking. Writing on falconry, he made the novel claim that his work was based on his own observation and experience, not on works of stale antiquity. But applying the same principle to his religion was inimical to the Church; so the pope declared that he was the Antichrist, the harbinger of the world's downfall and the Second Coming.

Frederick's imperial strategy was to subject the north of Italy and link his southern (Sicilian) and northern (German) kingdoms. To do so, he had to crush the power of the pope and that of the region's wealthy city states. The two formed natural allies: Gregory IX incited the cities to rebellion, and in 1237, Frederick began a monumental struggle to subdue them. Although Gregory died in 1241, and Frederick imposed his own candidate, Innocent IV, as his successor, the new pope soon proved just as intractable as the old. Having fled from Rome to Lyon, Innocent called a full council of the Church in 1245 and solemnly declared Frederick deposed. A league of Italian cities then inflicted a decisive defeat on Frederick's army at Vittoria in 1248, and in 1250, at Lucera, the emperor died, his schemes in ruins.

Frederick II was entombed next to his father and grandfather at Palermo Cathedral. He rests in a sarcophagus of porphyry, the imperial stone, in the robes of a Byzantine emperor.

Above *Frederick II's wedding to Henry III's sister Isabella.*

Below *Bejewelled tiara belonging to Frederick II's mother Constance, heiress of Sicily, and found in her tomb in Palermo.*

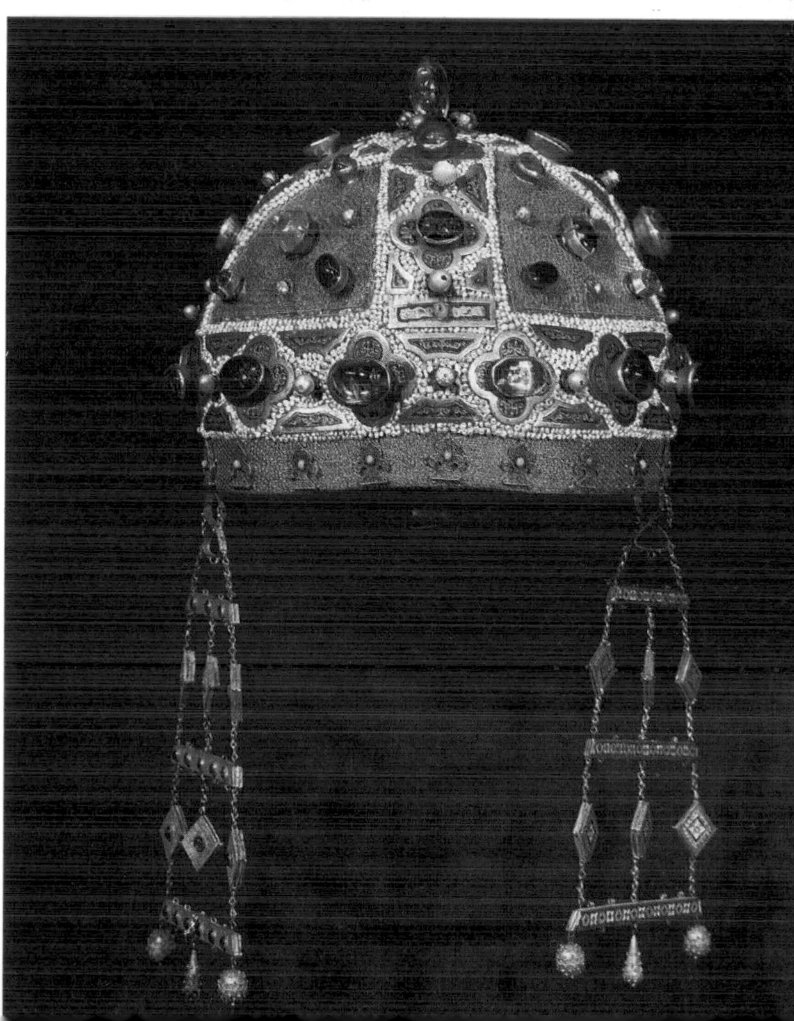

For these reasons, though others were not lacking, Pope Gregory IX counted as nothing what Frederick II achieved in the Holy Land and declared war against him. The pope asserted that it was just and necessary to the Christian faith that so determined a persecutor of the Church should be removed from exercising imperial authority; that the emperor was utterly execrable for having inflicted such oppression on his mother the Church; that he had occupied her forts, lands and possessions; and that, as a public enemy, he continued to occupy them.

In 1230, however, Frederick II and his forces returned to Italy, crushed the papal army which was threatening Sicily, one of his possessions, and persuaded the pope to lift his excommunication in return for a truce.

1230

That August, Pope Gregory IX and Emperor Frederick II came to an agreement. The emperor went to Rome and was absolved, all sentences touching on his imperial rights being fully revoked.

So the high priest and the most mighty emperor feasted together in the pontifical palace in Rome for three days on end, and all the cardinals and imperial magnates rejoiced at the concord so longed for and so suddenly confirmed.

By 1230, Hubert de Burgh, justiciar of England, had built up a major lordship on the Welsh Marches, threatening the local Welsh leaders. The most powerful, Llywelyn the Great, prince of Gwynedd, mounted a counter-offensive in 1231.

1231

In May, the Welsh burst forth from their dens like shrews from holes, raising fires everywhere. King Henry III sent Hubert de Burgh, justiciar of the realm, to repress their attacks.

No sooner had they heard of the king's departure, however, than the Welsh reverted to their pillaging and, infesting the provinces near Montgomery Castle, they laid them waste.

Papal taxation

THE pope's absolute monarchy (or plenitude of power) over every detail of ecclesiastical life developed during the later 12th century and reached its zenith during the long reign of Henry III. No longer simply spiritual leaders, popes had increasingly become the rulers and managers of a vast, centralized Church corporation, for which they needed an ever-growing bureaucracy – the 'Curia' or papal court. To finance this bureaucracy as well as to support their increasing intervention in the political affairs of Europe, they needed new and lucrative sources of income. Their exploitation of these sources provoked some of the fiercest controversies of the Middle Ages.

The clergy was a rich source of revenue, and the burden of taxation fell particularly heavily on Henry III's clerical subjects. As king of England, Henry ruled a realm which King John had surrendered to Rome in 1213, and which was therefore technically the pope's personal property. Henry was also grateful for papal support during his troubled minority, and so doubly disinclined to protect his clergy against papal exactions. The most direct of these was the papal income tax on churchmen's revenues. Although it had been instituted in 1199 as a once-only emergency levy, as the 13th century progressed, this tax was demanded with increasing frequency and at increasing rates.

The fees exacted for confirming senior churchmen in their offices were equally onerous. An abbot of St Albans had to pay the huge sum of £1700 to the Curia, including £800 for a private audience with the pope. Forced to borrow money from the pope's Italian bankers, he was then fined for condoning money-lending.

Papal provisions, which enabled popes to intrude their own candidates into ecclesiastical offices, were especially resented. At its worst the system could result in an absentee foreigner – generally an Italian member of the Curia – receiving the fees of an office he did not perform in a country he would never see. This practice drew howls of protest from chroniclers like Matthew Paris, who complained that absentee aliens were being granted English benefices worth over £40,000 a year. In 1231 it provoked armed resistance, led by an outraged Yorkshire squire who had twice seen Italians intruded into an office in his gift.

The modern view of papal provisions is not so damning. They mainly affected cathedral offices, which were in any case often given to absentee priests in royal or aristocratic service, and were nothing like so widespread as contemporaries believed. Moreover, many clerics who benefited from provisions were English, and were often

deservingly learned scholars in need of support. Candidates bombarded the pope with petitions – sometimes literally, as Clement VI complained, when he was hit by petitions wrapped round stones. Nevertheless, the system undoubtedly brought the papacy into disrepute and offended nationalist susceptibilities, fuelling the growing anti-papalism of the later Middle Ages.

Above *A richly ornamented statue of St Peter in the full regalia of pontiff. Much of the revenue that was raised by papal taxation went on embellishing the Curia, or papal court, which caused resentment in England among members of the English clergy.*

When the English soldiers who were defending that famous castle realized what was afoot, they set out to teach the Welsh a lesson. The English cut off their escape route, captured many and killed even more and when they presented their prisoners to the justiciar, he ordered them to be executed and their heads taken to Henry III.

This done, Llywelyn was furious and gathered a sizeable army with which he harried the lands and possessions of the barons on the Welsh borders. He spared neither church nor clergy, and those noble women and girls, who had sought the peace and safety of sanctuary, were burned along with the churches themselves.

When news of this horrific deed reached King Henry III's ears, he gathered an ample army at Oxford on 13 July. There, in his presence, the whole nobility of England, the priests and the people gathered. Then all the bishops and prelates of the Church struck with anathema Llywelyn and his associates, who had burned the churches.

After this, the king of England led his army to Hereford with all speed. At that point, Llywelyn had gathered his army not far from Montgomery, in a marshy water meadow right by the river bank, where he was preparing treacherous ambushes for the men of Montgomery Castle.

Llywelyn sent a monk from a neighbouring Cistercian abbey, Cwm Hir, to the castle, or so it is said. When the soldiers saw the monk coming, they went out to speak to him, and asked him what he had heard of Prince Llywelyn.

The monk replied that he had seen him with a little troop of followers in a meadow close by, where they were awaiting a larger number of men.

The soldiers asked the monk if their horses could safely cross the river and the meadow. To this, the monk replied: 'The bridge which used to carry travellers to the other side has been destroyed by Llywelyn who fears your attack. You, however, can go safely to cross the river and the meadow with your horses wherever you wish, to defeat or to scatter the Welsh who have only a few horses.'

Having heard this, Walter de Godardville, who trusted the false statements of the monk, ordered the soldiers and sergeants in Montgomery Castle to fly to arms, mount their horses and proceed quickly to the place. The Welsh saw them coming to attack and pretended to flee to a nearby wood. But the castle guards, pursuing them swiftly on horseback, sank up to the beasts' stomachs on the river bank and in the marsh of the meadow, especially those in front. Those following behind were forewarned and grieved deeply for their companions' fate.

Then the Welsh, aware that the enemy was going under, returned to assail them and they killed with great cruelty the soldiers and their horses as they wallowed in the mud. The struggle there was very grim, and many perished on both sides, but the Welsh were victorious. When news of this misfortune was intimated to the king of England, he descended swiftly and furiously on the abbey whose monk had betrayed the soldiers, and stripped its tithe barn of all its goods before burning it. Henry III ordered that the abbey itself be utterly despoiled and razed in a similar way, but the abbot paid two hundred pounds to the king to save the buildings which had been constructed with the greatest care, and in a little while, the king's anger abated.

1232

Llywelyn, prince of Wales, then began to sally over the borders in his usual fashion to ravage the lands of the English barons. Peter des Roches, bishop of Winchester, and other royal counsellors went to the king of England and told him that he was about to suffer a great affront to his royal dignity because the Welsh, despicable robbers, were roaming his lands and those of his barons with impunity; having devastated everything with fire, they left nothing standing.

To this, King Henry III replied: 'I have been informed by my treasurers that all the revenues of my exchequer are scarcely enough to provide me with the simplest food and clothes and the customary alms. So my poverty does not allow me to make expeditions for war.'

Right *Soldiers pillage a house after battle, taking all of value as legitimate plunder. In the many wars between the Welsh lords and the English, the villages of the Welsh Marches were under constant threat from such ravaging. It could take several years for a village to return to normality and make good the losses of manpower, crops and possessions.*

The warring Welsh

IN 13th-century England, the Welsh were traditionally seen as a barbarous people, ensconced in an inhospitable land on the very fringes of Christian civilization. English tolerance of their alien neighbours was further strained by a new assertiveness on the part of the Welsh, who displayed a resolve to unify themselves under the rule of a single prince. During the minority of Henry III, Prince Llywelyn ap Iorwerth (Llywelyn the Great) sought formal recognition of his status as the superior prince of Wales, but even though he had asserted his supremacy over the Welsh lords during King John's reign, Henry's counsellors would do nothing to undermine the king's traditional position as the sovereign of Wales.

After his death in 1240, his son Dafydd ap Llywelyn, Henry's nephew, was allowed to succeed only to Gwynedd, the territory in north Wales which Llywelyn had held by right. The other Welsh lords became, once more, the vassals of the king of England.

Dafydd died in 1246, without an heir, and by 1255 his nephew, Llywelyn ap Gruffudd, had asserted his sole power in Snowdonia (Gwynedd), the heartland of Welsh resistance. Then, taking advantage of the resentments Edward's officers had aroused in the lands east of the River Conwy, by tactlessly ignoring local customs, he extended his power into the wider Gwynedd of his great forebears. Soon after, Llywelyn established his supremacy over the lords of the other provinces of Wales and secured their feudal allegiance.

Matthew Paris praised his achievement and, in a stirring passage, conveyed his aversion to the prodigal young Edward and his despair at the incompetence of the government in England. The English, he wrote, were a wretched people prepared to concede their heritage to aliens, but the Welsh, proud of their descent from the Trojans, had risen in defence of their patrimony and achieved a unity such as had never been known before.

In 1258, Llywelyn assumed the title 'Prince of Wales'. However, he needed to secure a formal peace treaty with England, by which his position would be recognized by Henry. Although he might expect to profit from the dissensions in England as the barons' opposition to the king reached its height, his search for a treaty was hindered by influential magnates with land in the Welsh Marches who refused to make concessions to him.

Frustrated, Llywelyn eventually mounted a new offensive which carried his power deep into the Marches, and which led to active co-operation with Simon de Montfort. In 1267, two years after Montfort's defeat at Evesham, the treaty of Montgomery was sealed by Henry and Edward on the one hand, and Llywelyn on the other, recognizing Llywelyn's right to the title 'Prince of Wales', and to the allegiance of the lords of the principality of Wales.

During the next three years, it seemed that the legate's hopes might be fulfilled. In 1270, Edward departed on the Eighth Crusade, which, with his subsequent travels on the continent, kept him out of the realm for four years. Friction between Llywelyn and the lords of the Marches increased.

Roger Mortimer, whose lands and rights in the Welsh Marches had been diminished by the treaty of Montgomery, and who was a powerful influence in the court, proved to be an implacable enemy.

Llywelyn was also at risk within his own dominions. Faced with the need to raise money to further his political ambitions, he resorted to harsh methods of government which caused considerable disaffection – so much so that his brother Dafydd conspired, unsuccessfully, with one of his leading barons to kill him. When Edward returned to England as king in 1274, Mortimer and his fellow-regents reported that Llywelyn no longer commanded the support and respect of the Welsh.

The king's counsellors replied: 'If you are poor, blame yourself because you confer honours, wardships and dignities on the unworthy and alienate them from the treasury. You ought to be called king in name alone, not for riches of gold or silver. For your ancestors were kings splendid indeed, enriched with every glory of wealth, who gathered together priceless treasure not from other sources, but from the income and profits of the kingdom.'

So Henry III began to demand accounts of revenues and all matters pertaining to the well-being of his treasury from his sheriffs, bailiffs and other servants. Those who were convicted of fraud, he dismissed from their posts and detained to force them to ender all that they owed. He even took a thousand pounds of silver from Ralph, surnamed the Breton, the treasurer of his chamber, whom he dismissed from office, and replaced with a Poitevin, Peter de Rivaux.

At the same time, the king relieved the justiciar of England, Hubert de Burgh, of his duties, on the advice of Peter des Roches, bishop of Winchester. In his place, although in name only, the king appointed a soldier, Stephen of Seagrave. This was done on 29 July.

A few days later, the king, who was still feeling annoyed by the deposed Hubert, demanded an immediate account from him of the royal treasure paid into the exchequer and of the debts owed to the king from both his father's reign and his own.

Henry III demanded a report on all his demesnes in England, Wales, Ireland and Poitou [in France], and who was holding them or was in possession of them now. The king also wanted to know how well his peace was kept, not only amongst his own subjects in England, Ireland, Gascony and Poitou but also amongst aliens.

He wished to know what had been done about scutage, carucage, gifts, presents and profits of wardships, all pertaining to the Crown; and likewise concerning those marriages which had been placed in Hubert's charge by King John on his deathbed, and others handed over to him in Henry's reign.

English Gothic sculpture

THE west front of Wells Cathedral, built around 1220–30, is the quintessential English Gothic church façade. It forms a vast screen across the front of the church, completely concealing the internal divisions into nave and aisles. There is none of the French Gothic emphasis on towers and portals, and no rose window; just a great wall of elegant niches and quatrefoils filled with figures.

A Coronation of the Virgin, surrounded by angels, surmounts the small main door; a Last Judgement, with figures emerging hesitantly from their tombs at the sound of the Last Trumpet, extends across the upper levels: in between, two tiers of standing and seated saints gaze down with monumental impassivity. The quality of the carving coarsens slightly, especially in the upper reaches.

The finest sculpture in 13th-century England is the headless but exquisite figure in the retrochoir of Winchester Cathedral – probably depicting the virtue Fortitude before she was despoiled of the jewelled metal sword she once carried. The softness of her modelling, and the way she is caught in movement, suggest that the sculptor knew classical models; she treads lightly in her long flowing gown, which swirls around her feet with a softness which bears witness to the magnificent quality of early 13th-century English woollen cloth, as well as to the finesse of the sculptor.

The Winchester figure was intended to be seen at close quarters. The coarser Wells sculptures were not: they were part of a magnificent whole which came into its own during the great church processions. The liturgy used at Wells is known from the 13th-century Sarum Missal, which gives, in effect, the stage directions for events which had all the theatricality of the modern musical. Every year, as the elaborate Easter procession halted before the doors of the cathedral in remembrance of the Entry into Jerusalem, choir boys hidden in a wall passage just above the west door sang an antiphonal 'Gloria' through holes secreted between the sculpted angels flanking the Coronation of the Virgin, giving the impression that the very stones could sing.

Opposite top *The east front of Winchester Cathedral, seen from the town.*

Right and overleaf *The sculptured west front of Wells Cathedral. The detail shows carvings of the apostles and Old Testament prophets which form such a distinctive part of Gothic cathedrals.*

These were only the lighter charges for which the king demanded a defence. More serious charges followed, which alleged that Hubert de Burgh was guilty of treason.

The king also accused Hubert of having stolen from the treasury, a precious stone which had a power whereby its wearer could not be defeated in battle. These accusations, some true and some lies, had been suggested to the king by Hubert's rivals. Henry demanded that the man atone for his misdemeanours according to the judgement of the court.

Hubert de Burgh was locked up securely. Then, since he could see no other course, he demanded time to deliberate before he answered, asserting that these were grave and harsh charges placed before him by the king. The king, although perturbed, granted a brief respite until 14 September. Hubert, quite terrified, made his way to Merton Priory from the city of London. Thus, the man who had provoked the greatest dislike for himself amongst the English magnates, on account of the king's love for him and his exclusive control of the kingdom, was deserted by the king and his friends, alone and destitute of all consolation.

Hubert de Burgh next fled to Boisars chapel, from where he was taken by the king's men and imprisoned in the Tower of London.

A little later, Earl Richard, the king's brother, Earl Warenne, Earl Richard the Marshal and Earl William de Ferrers received Hubert with sureties, and in the custody of four of their knights, he was committed by the king to the castle at Devizes where he was to be kept under light guard.

At about the same time, on 12 November, terrible thunder was heard which continued for fifteen days on end and terrified many, especially the citizens of London who are particularly plagued by such weather, for if ever there is thunder anywhere in England, it occurs in London at the same time.

Then there ensued the most wretched strife between the king and his barons.

1233

By this time, Peter des Roches, bishop of Winchester, and his accomplices had provoked the hatred of the English people and the king's profound contempt equally. To wreak utter destruction, Peter summoned Poitevin troops, a few at a time, with whom he filled England, so that wherever the king went he was surrounded by them. Thus nothing happened in England unless Peter and his Poitevin crowd arranged it.

King Henry summoned all the earls and barons to a conference at Oxford on 24 June, but they did not want to do his bidding. For when they heard that many who would prey upon the realm were landing, a few at a time, with horses and arms, the magnates saw no hope for peace and let pass the day appointed for them to attend, announcing through solemn envoys that the king should rid himself of Peter des Roches, bishop of Winchester, and the other Poitevins without delay.

If not, they would, by common agreement of the whole realm, drive the king from the kingdom with his wicked counsellors and set about choosing a new king.

At this the king was thoroughly alarmed and his whole court with him. Then Peter des Roches, bishop of Winchester, advised the king to take up arms against his rebellious men, and to confer their lands and castles on the Poitevins, who would protect the kingdom of England from its traitors.

Henry III demanded hostages from those powerful nobles of whom he was suspicious, sending them written commands that by 1 August they were to render him so many men of such a rank, through whom they would remove all suspicion of rebellion from his mind.

Now Peter des Roches, bishop of Winchester, wished to secure the death of his fallen rival, Hubert de Burgh, who was held in chains at Devizes, by any means possible. So, without mentioning Hubert, but lured by the opportunity the power would give him for murder, he asked the king most eagerly for custody of Devizes Castle.

But Hubert, being warned of this by his friends at the royal court, expounded to two sergeants in the garrison at Devizes, men who had compassion for him in his misery, how they might save him from death.

When they considered that the time was ripe, at the first watch on the night of 29 September, when the castle guards were asleep, one of them kept a look-out while the other put the shackled Hubert on his shoulders, climbed from the tower with its guards, and carried him with due secrecy right through the castle. Coming to the main gate, the sergeant left through a little door and, with some difficulty, crossed the huge moat. When this sturdy traveller came to the parish church of the village, he did not put his burden down until, happy, he had reached the high altar.

On awaking, the castellans failed to find Hubert de Burgh in his accustomed place and they were extremely alarmed. They set out from the castle with lanterns, cudgels and arms, roaming everywhere until they heard reports that Hubert was in the church, freed from his shackles. Whereupon they rushed in there making a loud commotion, and found him before the altar bearing a crucifix in his hands. Viciously they snatched him, falling on him with fists and clubs alike, and they led him back to the castle where they subjected him to more severe imprisonment than previously.

But when these events reached the ears of Robert, bishop of Salisbury, he came to the castle with all speed and commanded the violators of the church that Hubert should be returned to the sanctuary and left exactly as they had found him.

The castellans, however, answered the bishop rudely and said that they would rather see Hubert hanged than themselves. When they refused to return him, the bishop excommunicated individually all who were holding Hubert or who had laid violent hands upon him, as was in his power to do. Then, accompanied by Roger, bishop of London, and some other bishops, the bishop of Salisbury went to the king and brought a formal plea in the royal presence concerning the injuries done to Hubert.

The bishops did not leave the king until he had guaranteed Hubert de Burgh's freedom. Thus on 18 October, reluctant though the king was, Hubert was sent back to the church.

In his anger, the king sent letters to the sheriff of the county, ordering him to besiege the church until Hubert died of starvation. But Hubert de Burgh, once justiciar of England, was abducted from the church at Devizes by armed men and, once he had been dressed as befits a knight, he was escorted to Wales at daybreak and on 30 October, he joined the king's enemies.

1234

The king set out for Gloucester and there Edmund of Abingdon, archbishop of Canterbury, came to him along with the other bishops who had been sent as envoys to Llywelyn. They informed the king of the nature of the agreement they had made with the Welsh prince, namely, that above all, the king should be reconciled with those noblemen with whom Llywelyn was allied, and who had been driven out of the kingdom on wicked advice. When this had been done, the said pact would be confirmed more fully.

Then the king, who longed for peace at any price, had all the exiles summoned by letter to appear at Gloucester on 28 May for a council, there to receive in full his pardon and their hereditary estates. Setting aside all mistrust, they were to come under safe conduct from the archbishop and the bishops.

So, through the mediation of the archbishop and the bishops, there came to the king's peace Hubert de Burgh, former justiciar of England and all who had been exiled with him or because of him. The king received these men with the kiss of peace, and returned all their rightful possessions to them on that day.

In that same year, which was the third barren year on end, fatal sickness and famine raged everywhere. These disasters arose, no doubt, as much from the price of sin as through the inclement weather and the widespread crop failure.

1235

In February of that year, two Templars came to Westminster, accompanied by knights and other solemn messengers. They were sent by Emperor Frederick II to the king of England, and bore letters from him sealed with gold, in which he requested the hand of King Henry III's sister, Isabella, in marriage.

The king of England was extremely interested in this idea and discussed it for three days on end with the nobles and bishops of the kingdom. Having carefully weighed the matter up, they declared unanimously that Isabella should be given to the emperor, and thus on 27 February, they reported their conclusion and their consent to the marriage.

When the envoys asked to see Isabella, the king sent faithful deputies to the Tower of London where his sister lived, carefully protected. They were to bring her into the royal presence with due reverence and show her to the messengers of the emperor, a beautiful girl in her twenty-first year, distinguished by her maidenhood, and properly bedecked with the accustomed trappings of royalty.

The ambassadors were pleased with the girl and judged her fitting in every way to be an imperial bride. They offered her a betrothal ring on the emperor's behalf, and when they had placed it on her finger, they shouted together: 'Long live the empress!' Then, after the delegates had informed the emperor of their deeds, Frederick II sent the archbishop of Cologne and the duke of Louvain to England with an escort of high-ranking nobles, who were to accompany the empress to him with all honour for the consummation of the marriage.

The preparations for that wedding were so lavish that they seemed to exceed all the riches of the kingdom. For the sake of the empress's dignity, her crown was most skilfully crafted from the purest gold and studded with precious stones. On it were sculpted the four kings of England who were confessors and martyrs, and to whom King Henry had especially commended the care of his sister's soul.

In her festal robes, which were made of silk and wool, and also of linen of different hues, decked out in all the dignity that befits an empress, Isabella shone out so that it was impossible to tell which of all her many adornments would most induce love in the emperor's heart.

In addition to all this, her bed, with its silk covers and gaily coloured mattresses, different hangings and draperies sewn from the most delicate muslin, stood so splendidly that its softness actively invited those seeking repose to sweet sleep. All the vessels sent, whether for wine or for food, were cast in completely unalloyed silver and gold and, what seemed almost superfluous to everyone, even the cooking pots, large and small, were of the finest silver. The task of organizing and looking after all this was delegated to court servants, who were to serve the empress and her train in regal fashion.

Exalted by these and many other honours from the king, and laden with gifts, Isabella was entrusted to the charge of William, bishop of Exeter, and Ralph, the king's steward, and to other nobles of her household, aristocratic ladies-in-waiting and high-born pages who were all versed in courtly manners and suitable to serve and escort an empress.

When all the arrangements were made, the king held a solemn celebration at Westminster on 6 May, with the archbishop of Cologne and the emperor's other messengers present. The next day, they set out on their journey, accompanied by the king and a huge escort of earls and barons.

The king had procured for his sister a host of well-bred horses of docile temperament which were most distinctive with their coats of different shades and appropriate for the empress's honour, because they would carry their riders gently, without stumbling. They were harnessed in fine tackle, their saddles gilded and wonderfully crafted, with gilded reins and ornamental breastplates, so that the steeds were as splendid as their knights.

When the troop had passed through Rochester and had paused at Faversham Abbey, they then

The literature of aspiration

IN 13th-century England, a man was considered of little account unless he spoke French, the language of elegant conversation; and the ideal form to follow was the continental French spoken at court. The mass of the gentry could manage only Anglo-Norman, derided by one chronicler as the 'French of Marlborough', although their ambitions for self-improvement are reflected in the popularity of a rhyming French vocabularly book in the 1250s. Most of the people would have understood very little French or Latin (the language of the Church), yet the English language had already absorbed many elements from the French.

'Romance' is used to denote literature written in French and also, in a more limited sense, to describe a particular genre of literature. Highly popular with 13th-century noble and knightly classes, its most obvious characteristic is its emphasis on individuals rather than groups. The feelings and aspirations of the main characters are minutely analysed. The most celebrated work of these romances is the unfinished *Roman de la Rose*, a poetic allegory that epitomizes courtly love and which was initially composed in the 1230s by William de Lorris. In it, the personification of love reigns over a garden in which a youthful hero seeks a rose guarded by symbolic obstacles to true love. Contemporary readers doubtless interpreted the poem as referring to human love, although it is equally effective as an allegory of spiritual love.

There were other, more materialistic themes. The *History of William Marshal* (*c.*1225), a stirring verse biography of a landless knight who rose to become regent of England, emphasizes chivalric conduct and values but allows the real problems of government and finance to intrude. By contrast *Guy of Warwick* (*c.*1240), a fictional chronicle of a successful military career crowned by an advantageous marriage, was typical of romances designed to bestow respectability on parvenu families.

Works which described a life of rags to riches appealed to the knightly class, as did tales of King Arthur's court, where the legendary Round Table blurred discrepancies of wealth and status. In this literary world, a country knight could easily imagine that he was the social equal of a great earl.

The most influential work of the 13th century was, however, a continuation of the *Roman de la Rose*. Written in about 1270 by Jean de Meung, it reflects a very different and at times satirical attitude to religion and the world. The outdated conventions of courtly love which were so strongly emphasized in the first part of the romance are rejected and, instead, nature is celebrated. Inspired by the intellectual milieu of Paris University, the second part of the poem expresses the supreme optimism of theologians and of the secular nobility.

Jean de Meung believed that nature was the work of God and was in conformity with His will, and that it had designed sexual intercourse for the propagation of the species. He believed that the created world was good and that happiness was possible and desirable on this side of heaven. The rose became the symbol of the victory of God, nature and mankind over death.

Above ***William de Lorris composing verse.***

Below ***An illustration from the*** **Roman de la Rose** ***manuscript.***

The emperor had the effrontery to refuse, however, saying that the causes of his actions were clearly grounded in reason. At this the pope, in the presence of many cardinals, as if he had already cast Frederick II down from his peak of imperial power, excommunicated him in a blast of blazing fury, 'consigning him to Satan' [1 Cor. 5[5]], to be held captive in dreadful death. This he did on Palm Sunday, 20 March.

1241

The Holy Cross was brought to the kingdom of France through the careful arrangements, with Christ's help, of Louis IX, king of France, and his mother, Blanche of Castile. The enormous sum of twenty-five thousand pounds was paid by Louis to the Saracens of Damietta for the Holy Cross.

The king of France ordered a chapel to be built in Paris near his palace, to be called the Sainte-Chapelle, marvellously beautiful and a fitting receptacle for this treasure, which he later deposited there with due honour. Besides this, the king kept in this magnificent chapel Christ's cloak, the spear (that is, the spearhead), the sponge and countless other relics. This is why Pope Gregory IX granted forty days' indulgence to all those going to Paris to pray in the chapel.

That same year, the king of England, Henry III, ordered a shrine of pure gold and precious stones to be made in London by selected goldsmiths, to hold the relics of St Edward the Confessor. It was skilfully wrought at the king's expense, and although the materials were very precious, yet, as the poet says: 'the workmanship outshone the stuff it used' [Ovid, *Metamorphoses*, II, 5].

Henry III was well aware of Louis IX's pious activities, and was impressed by reports of their scale and magnificence. But Louis was seen by Henry as a major rival. In 1242, Henry mounted an invasion of Poitou, which he claimed as his own hereditary possession. The campaign was a failure, and Henry had to make a humiliating retreat from Louis' army into his duchy of Gascony – a region which was itself to pose him many problems during the next few years.

The Sainte-Chapelle and the Rayonnant style

BY the 1230s it was clear that the vast High Gothic cathedrals of northern France were too big for their own good. Beauvais, the largest of them all, took nearly 60 years to build, and then all but fell down in 1284. As if in reaction, a new architecture, smaller, often intimate in scale, and elegant and rich in detail, emerged in the Paris of Blanche of Castile and the young St Louis.

The first building in this new Rayonnant style – the name deriving from the rose windows which are a characteristic detail – was the abbey church of Saint-Denis. Ironically, it largely replaced Abbot Suger's famous church which, a hundred years earlier, had seen the birth of Gothic. The use of bar tracery, another typical feature, was derived from Reims, but above all, the extent of the windows at Saint-Denis was new. The entire upper wall is a sheet of glass, held together by an elegant and increasingly complex web of stone tracery.

The Rayonnant style achieved rapid and widespread popularity. Unlike High Gothic, it was eminently suitable for small churches: a lesser abbey or parish church could acquire an immediate veneer of fashionable Parisian elegance by the mere insertion of a traceried window, easily copied from pattern books.

The style also appealed to private patrons. In 1239, at enormous expense, Louis IX acquired a relic of the Crown of Thorns from the bankrupt King Baldwin of Jerusalem, to which he added, in 1241, part of the True Cross and other relics (some of dubious authenticity). To house this precious collection he built the Sainte-Chapelle, a lavish new chapel in his Paris palace.

Like most palace chapels, the Sainte-Chapelle has two distinct levels. The main chapel, above, is like a giant gold and enamel reliquary turned outside in, with low arcaded side walls, richly painted and gilded. The arcade capitals are sculpted with strikingly naturalistic vines and roses, and fine life-size figures of the apostles line the walls and flank the central reliquary for the Crown of Thorns. Every surface is warmed and softened by the light which streams in through enormous stained glass windows. They are supported by a mere webbing of masonry shafts and trefoils, deceptively fragile in appearance, so that the walls of the upper chapel appear to be made of coloured glass, like an enormous gaudy greenhouse.

Right ***The upper chapel of the Sainte-Chapelle. It was reserved for the royal family. In the lower chapel stood the rest of the household.***

1243

Let it not be thought that at this period the world was free from many widespread turmoils. Strife was in the air between the Franciscans and the Dominicans, to the amazement of many, for both orders had apparently chosen to follow a life of perfection, poverty and hardship.

The Dominicans, or Friars Preachers, maintained that theirs was the older order, and that this entitled them to greater respect. Their attire, they said, was more seemly; by their preaching they had acquired their well-deserved name and function, and they claimed they were more truly stamped with apostolic worth.

The Franciscans retorted that, for the Lord's sake, they had chosen a stricter and humbler way of life, worthier because it was holier. Brothers could, and should, leave the Dominican Order and come to them, moving across, as it were, from a lower to a higher, stricter order.

The Dominicans flatly contradicted this, saying that although the Franciscans went about barefoot, clad in cheap habits, with bits of rope for girdles, their order did not prohibit the eating of meat and other luxury foods, even in public, which was forbidden to the Dominicans. So the Dominicans should not fly to the Franciscans as stricter and better, but rather the other way round.

Between these two orders, a grave and terrible dissension arose. Moreover, because the friars were men of education and scholarship, this was very dangerous for the whole Church, a sign that a day of reckoning was near at hand. Sadly, it is significant that over a period of more than three or four hundred years, the monastic order never saw such a rapid and headlong fall as that of these two orders of friars.

For scarcely twenty-four years after their inception, they were erecting their first houses in England. Within the high walls of costly buildings, growing larger daily, they set out priceless treasures, shamelessly overstepping the bounds of poverty, the foundation of their profession.

When great and affluent men lay dying, the friars would be in urgent attendance, greedy for gain, to the loss and detriment of the clergy.

They would wring out confessions and secret wills, recommending only themselves and their order, to the exclusion of all others, so that a Christian man could not believe in his own salvation unless he were guided by the advice of the Franciscans or the Dominicans.

Assiduous in the pursuit of privilege, they became counsellors, chamberlains and treasurers at royal and noble courts, groomsmen and speechmakers at weddings, and executive agents of the pope's exorbitant taxes.

1246

In the course of this year, a monstrous and unheard-of sexual deviation occurred in the diocese of Lincoln, to the amazement of all.

A good-looking noblewoman of free birth, the wife of a rich man, and a mother, impregnated another woman of similar background, and in some weird and wonderful way became a father.

When this pair had produced two sons, with another infant on the way, the mother, overcome with repugnance at the unnaturalness of their crime, made a charge against them both in public, and forced the other woman to open confession. She, in a disgusting attempt to minimize her guilt, shamelessly accused her own mother, saying that she had practised the same vice.

The Bible, in the Gloss on the passage in Genesis 'male and female created He them' [Gen. 1^{27}], makes mention of such things. It says that there are people called androgynes (that is, some sort of hermaphrodite), from the Greek *aner* man, and *gune* woman, thus called because they both take the active as well as the passive rôle in sexual intercourse, and both have the power to give birth and beget in turn.

Such people have a deservedly abhorrent and filthy reputation.

The watchdogs of God

SAINT Dominic, founder of the order which was to become the medieval Church's most effective weapon against heresy, was born in Castile in about 1172. A churchman from an early age, his life was one of conventional and undramatic if austere piety, marked from the outset by a burning desire to convert unbelievers by effective preaching. In 1206 he embarked on a mission to the Languedoc in southern France, the chief stronghold of the Cathars. These 'pure ones' – also called Albigensians from their centre at Albi – followed a pre-Christian dualist doctrine, probably influenced by eastern sects. They proclaimed the total separation of spirit and physical matter, the first being created by God and the second by the devil. The world and all it contained was therefore irretrievably evil, and man's only salvation lay in a rigid spirituality that rejected marriage, possessions and all animal foods produced through procreation.

Earlier Catholic missionaries had made little headway against the heretics. Dominic therefore decided to adopt a life of even greater simplicity than theirs, while disproving their doctrines by carefully reasoned arguments. In 1217 (possibly after meeting St Francis) he founded his 'Order of Friars Preachers'. Although the followers of both Francis and Dominic were vowed to evangelical poverty, the Dominicans differed considerably from the Franciscans, reflecting the contrast between Dominic, the intellectual organizer and unrelenting fighter against heresy, and the inspired, romantic Francis, who taught by Christ-like example. Punningly nicknamed '*domini canes*', or watchdogs of God, the Dominicans became the shock troops of the attack on dissent, and the instruments of the notorious Inquisition.

This was formally established in 1233, some 12 years after Dominic's death. The savage and sordid 'Albigensian Crusade' – when land-grabbing north Frenchmen exultingly and indiscriminately massacred Cathars and southern Catholics, crying out that 'God would know his own' – had failed to rid the Languedoc of heresy. Employing methods later favoured by totalitarian secret police, Dominican friars rigorously interrogated anyone suspected of even the slightest connection with heretics, forcing children to testify against parents and wives against husbands. Failure to co-operate was itself evidence of guilt. Unrepentant or relapsed heretics were burnt alive, without the 'mercy' of strangling at the stake, while penitents were often imprisoned for life, their property confiscated and their houses turned into dungheaps. The bodies of those retrospectively convicted after death were dug up and burnt. So effective did such terror tactics prove that heresy rapidly declined in the Languedoc.

There was no Inquisition in England, where the Dominican 'black friars' excelled principally as preachers, diplomats and chaplains to the great. Every king of England from Henry III to Richard II employed one of these formidable 'watchdogs of God' as his confessor.

Below ***A tribunal of the Dominican Inquisition interrogating heretics. No defence witnesses were allowed.***

Overleaf ***St Dominic by Fra Angelico.***

Kinsman mourned for kinsman, friend for friend. Lovely women lost their bloom, garlands of flowers were flung on to the rubbish heap. Songs were silenced, music forbidden, and every expression of happiness dissolved in woe. But the worst aspect of all was that people accused the Lord of injustice, and the faith of many began to waver.

Even Venice, the noblest of cities, as well as many of the half-Christian cities of Italy, would have fallen away from the faith without the moral support of the bishops.

At about this time, Emperor Frederick II died, greatest of earthly princes. This man, the wonder of the world, an amazing revolutionary, died contrite and humble, absolved from his sentence, and in the habit of a Cistercian monk.

His death took place on 13 December, lending meaning and significance to an earthquake which coincided with it.

The death of the emperor extinguished any hope the French might have had that he might rescue their king. But he left a generous will, compensating churches to which he had caused loss or injury. His death was kept secret for several days, so that his enemies should not start rejoicing, but it was made public on 26 December.

Salimbene gives a fuller account of Emperor Frederick II's character.

Emperor Frederick II died in a small city called Fiorentino, ten miles from Lucera in central Italy. He could not immediately be taken for burial to Palermo, where the tombs of the kings of Sicily are, because his corpse gave off such a foul stench that they were forced to bury him [temporarily] on the spot.

It must be remembered that Frederick II took delight in being at odds almost constantly with the Church, which he attacked on many occasions, although it was the Church which had nourished him, defended him and raised him to power. He had no faith in God, but was a crafty man, cunning, avaricious, lustful and wicked.

Venice

DURING the 13th and 14th centuries, two great maritime republics, Venice and Genoa, were battling for control of the Mediterranean. Pisa, once a potential rival, had been crushed between Genoa and the rising power of Florence. Eventually, in 1380, Venice defeated the Genoese at Chioggia, and emerged into the Renaissance as undisputed queen of the Mediterranean. Floating loose in marshy swamps, with close, if not necessarily friendly, links with Constantinople, Venice was almost an outpost of the East, and an emporium where merchants from the chilly north-west of Europe could purchase eastern exotica, silks and spices.

Artistically, too, Venice looked to the East, principally to Byzantium. St Mark's Basilica is largely 11th century, but the mosaics glimmering in its many domes are the work of 13th-century Byzantine artists. Greek goldsmiths used the old-fashioned *cloisonné* technique to produce enamels, creating glorious colours, limpid yet saturated; the enamels are held by strips of gold welded on to the gold base panel, and the patterns are stiff and hieratic. Only Greek artists were using this technique at this time; in western Europe, it had been superseded by *champlevé*, where the enamelled hollows were carved out of the base panel, rather like engraving. It allowed the artist to draw with great freedom and subtlety, though this tended to be at the expense of jewelled brilliance of colour.

The Venetians rejected artistic enterprise in favour of conspicuous wealth, and the finest of the Byzantine enamelled panels, some made in Venice, some stolen from Constantinople in 1204, were set on gold and surrounded with gems, in the immense altar retable, the Pala d'Oro, in St Mark's. Enlarged in 1209, and reset more elaborately still in 1345, it remains a gloriously unashamed monument to greed, theft and worldly things.

Opposite top ***The Doge's Palace, or Palazzo Ducale, centre of government for the Venetian republic and residence of its elected leader. It clearly absorbs Gothic, Islamic and Byzantine styles, which reflect Venice's wide-ranging eastern trading empire and the wealth this brought to the city.***

Right ***The Pala d'Oro, retable in St Mark's Basilica. It was created in Constantinople in 976 and brought to Venice in 1105. The enamel panels are bound with gold and silver, studded with precious stones and pearls.***

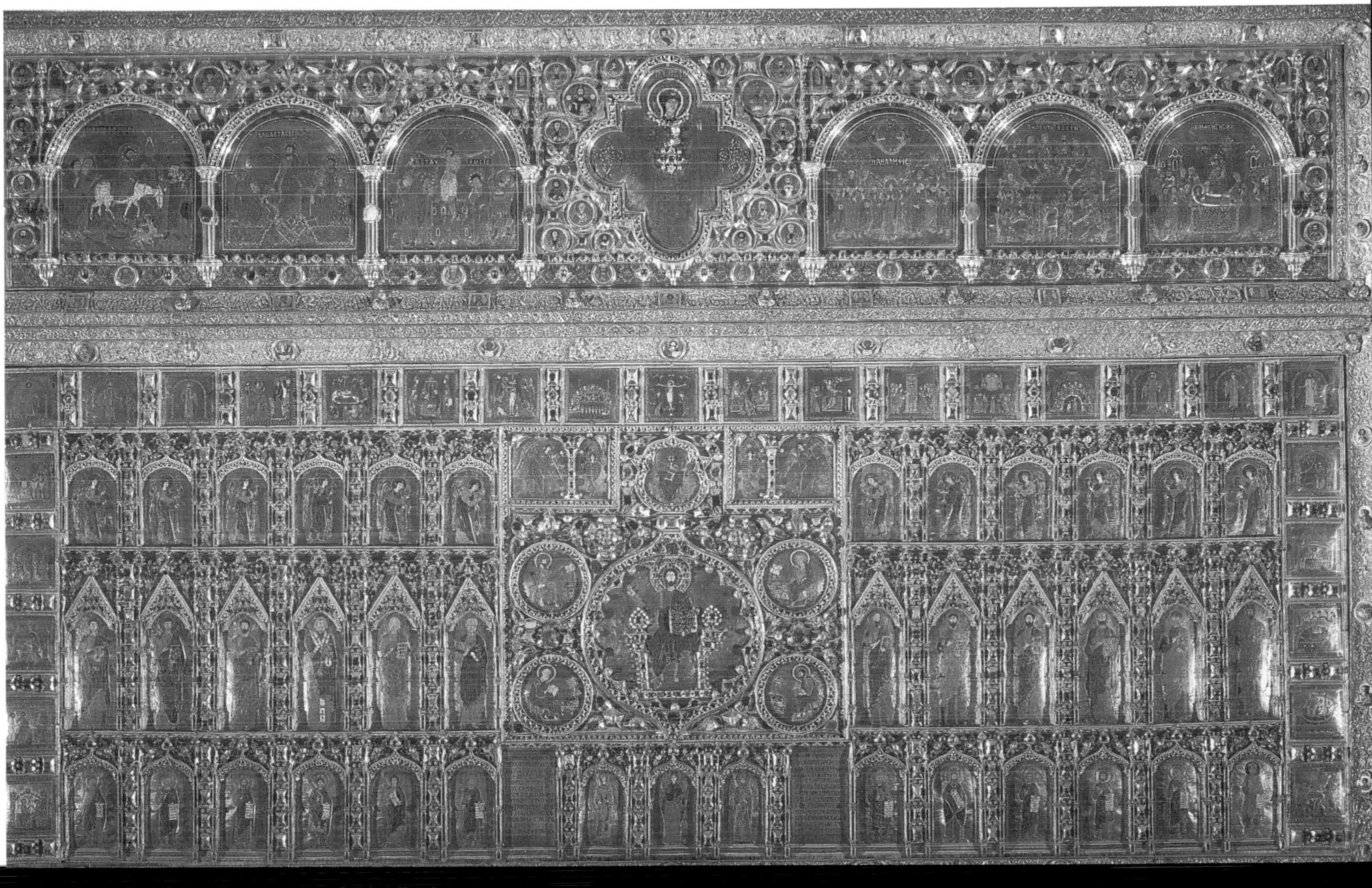

The king of England gave orders that his eldest son's wife, should be received with the utmost honour and respect, especially in London, with processions, illuminations, bells, singing and every conceivable demonstration of ceremonial rejoicing. The citizens of London went out to meet her dressed up in their best clothes.

When the royal daughter-in-law arrived at the residence allotted to her, she found it furnished with silken hangings and tapestries – they had even been laid on the floor. The Spaniards had done this, perhaps following the custom of their country, but the excess of luxury caused muttering and jeering among the people.

Serious-minded and sensible folk, with an eye to the future, sighed inwardly, weighing up in detail the extravagant welcomes King Henry III kept lavishing on so many foreigners. Everyone considered the great show put on for the benefit of the Spaniards impressive, even stunning, and no wonder. But the English, therefore, lamented the fact that, in the eyes of their own king, they themselves appeared to be the least important of all nations.

In a vain attempt to impress his subjects, Henry III spent enormous sums of money on his major obsession: the rebuilding and embellishment of Westminster Abbey in honour of St Edward the Confessor. The works, however, ran into financial difficulties, as these royal orders reveal.

Philip Lovel, treasurer, and Edward of Westminster are ordered, with money from the king's treasury or elsewhere from money owed to the king, to recall the workmen of the church of Westminster who, as the king is informed, have left, so that the aforesaid work may proceed at its due speed. For it is necessary that it should be consecrated at the latest on 13 October [1255].

1256

Because the masons and other workmen at Westminster want, so the king has heard, to leave for lack of money, Philip Lovel, the king's treasurer, is ordered to examine carefully the debts

Marco Polo and his travels

WHEN the 17-year-old Marco Polo set out for Cathay (China) in 1271, he was neither the first nor the only European to go there. What distinguished Marco from others was that he left an account of his experiences, the *Description of the World*, which he dictated while serving time as a prisoner-of-war in Genoa in the 1290s.

China was the source of silk, the most highly prized luxury textile, and of fine porcelain, and had attracted travellers for centuries. The 'silk roads' across central Asia to the Black Sea had been well known in Roman times, when merchants had contacts with both China and India, but trading links were disrupted after the Moslem conquests in Asia during the 7th and 8th centuries. The expansion of European trade from the later 11th century led to an increased demand for eastern luxury goods, especially spices from the Nicobar Islands in the Indian Ocean, often known as the 'spice islands'. In the 13th century, this trade was carried in the ships of the Italian maritime cities, particularly Venice and Genoa, who were fierce and often violent rivals.

The opportunity to challenge the Moslem stranglehold over the overland trade routes was a result of the Mongol conquests of the 13th century, when this nomadic people from deepest Asia created an empire which extended from Korea to the borders of Germany.

For a time the West hoped they would become Christians and eradicate Islam, but the Mongols were defeated by the Islamic Mamelukes in 1260 before either wish could be fulfilled.

However for the first time in six centuries, Europeans could travel overland to China in relative security, and it was this that Niccolo and Maffeo Polo, Marco's father and uncle, leading Venetian merchants, exploited. Their inspiration was not love of adventure, but hope of commercial advantage. Marco travelled in their company on his famous journey, leaving Venice in 1271. The Polo brothers had already paid one prolonged visit to China, when they had been permitted to leave only on the condition that they return with Christian missionaries. But it was 1275 before the Venetian caravan eventually reached the court of Kublai Khan, a successor of Genghis Khan, at Peking; and they arrived without the friars who had accompanied them to preach to the Mongol leader, for they had lost heart on the way and turned back.

China was more advanced than Europe, with a sophisticated technology which had already invented printing and gunpowder, and with a complex mercantile organization using banks, credit and paper money. Profiting from the support of Kublai Khan, the Polo brothers set to work as merchants, assembling goods for caravans to the west.

Marco, in his book, tells how he learned the Mongol language and entered the Chinese civil service, where he quickly attracted the attention of the Great Khan, who was always eager to employ able foreigners. Later, Marco recounts, he became a 'privy counsellor' and was entrusted with a number of important missions: he reported on Burma after 1287, and later went to Ceylon to buy the Buddha's tooth, the most important relic in Asia. But not all of Marco's reminiscences are accurate. His claim that the Polos were present at the siege of Xiangyang (1267–73) in the Sung empire (southern China), and that their knowledge of siege weapons brought it to a satisfactory conclusion cannot be true; nor can Marco have been governor of Yangchow for three years.

After 15 years in the service of Kublai, the Polos desired to leave for home, but the Khan refused permission. Only his death made it possible for them to escape and to return to Venice after 21 years.

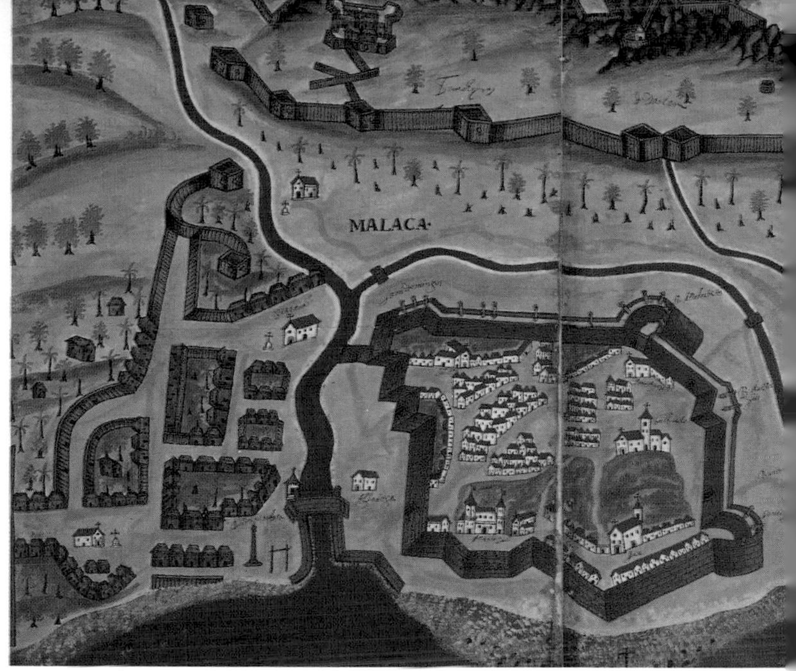

Above *Plan of Malacca (Malay Peninsula), an important trading post for the Spice Islands.*

Below *Trading ship from India lands its cargo at Ormuz (Iran).*

On 9 March, a number of masters of arts from the university of Oxford, about nine of them, came to the king at St Albans, in St Oswin's chapel, and lodged a plea against Henry Lexington, bishop of Lincoln. He was, they complained, trying to weaken the rights of scholars, in defiance of the ancient and accepted statutes of the university.

The same day one of the brothers, the present writer in fact, had a more private word with the king, and said: 'My lord, for God's sake have a care for the Church – it is already very insecure. The university of Paris, nurse and teacher of so many holy prelates, is in great turmoil. I am very much afraid that, if Oxford goes the same way at the same time, the whole Church will come to grief, since Oxford ranks only second as a school of the Church, or is indeed rather a very foundation of the Church.' The king answered: 'God forbid that such a thing should happen, especially in my time.'

A day was set at the approaching parliament for the bishop of Lincoln, Henry Lexington, chancellor of the university, to reply, so that, when both sides had stated their cases, some agreement might be reached.

In 1258, Henry III persuaded Pope Alexander IV to commute a promise he had made to go on crusade to the Holy Land, to an undertaking to capture Sicily, held by Manfred of Hohenstaufen, illegitimate son of Frederick II and papal enemy. Henry accepted the crown of Sicily for his second son, Edmund, and demanded large sums of money from the English barons and clergy to finance his 'crusade'. The barons, led by Simon de Montfort, earl of Leicester, Richard of Clare, earl of Gloucester and Hertford, and others, resolved to agree only on condition that Henry reform his government and administration according to a plan which they had drawn up.

1258

As the days slipped by before the parliament, due to be held at Oxford on 11 June [to discuss taxation and administrative reforms], formal

The first universities

AT the beginning of the 13th century, ambitious and well-connected Englishmen in search of education usually went abroad to one of the great European universities, such as Paris or Bologna. No English institution could provide teaching of a comparable range or level. As late as the 1230s, Thomas Cantilupe (later bishop of Hereford), the son of a great royal minister, and therefore given the best education money could buy, went to Paris and then to Orléans.

Less wealthy scholars, however, had to seek out one of several hundred schools, connected with cathedrals or monasteries, in English provincial towns. Oxford was the only one to offer an education in any way approaching that found abroad. By the early 13th century, Oxford was organized, very much like Paris, as a 'university' – a corporate association of teachers (the masters). By 1214 the masters had elected their own head, their chancellor, as they still do today.

The curriculum was also similar to that found at Paris.

Above left ***Modern Oxford, England's oldest university; it was established in the early 13th century.***

Above ***Merton College, founded by Walter of Merton. A graduate of Oxford, he was a bishop, and chancellor of England.***

Scholars, who could be as young as 14, attended an initial arts course, the *trivium*, lasting five years, which comprised logic, rhetoric and Latin grammar. On completing this, the student became a bachelor of arts and could take the more advanced *quadrivium* (usually a three-year course) in astronomy, arithmetic, geometry and music for his mastership in arts which licensed him to teach. Only then could he undertake the higher studies of canon and civil law, philosophy, medicine and theology.

Several factors contributed to give Oxford its preeminence. The bishop of Lincoln, its nominal overlord, was a remote figure, and the university was therefore free from petty restrictions. Unlike Cambridge, about which little is known in the 13th century other than that it existed, it was strategically placed in the central south of England. Oxford's reputation was advanced by a series of famous teachers of whom the greatest was Robert Grosseteste, who lectured at the university between about 1207 and 1235, and was elected its chancellor, before leaving to become bishop of Lincoln.

In 1255, Thomas Cantilupe returned to Oxford to complete the studies he had started at Paris and Orléans. His decision marked 'the coming of age of the university as a centre of learning comparable to Paris'. By this time, Oxford boasted well over a thousand students who lodged with the burgesses of the town or lived in halls owned by the masters. When in the second half of the century, a master, Walter of Durham, a graduate, Walter of Merton, and a great baron, John of Balliol and his wife Dervorguilla, made bequests to provide permanent support for small numbers of students, the result was the foundation of the university colleges, Merton and Balliol. Like Thomas Cantilupe, Walter of Merton became chancellor of England and a bishop. Oxford was now providing education for men destined for the highest positions in Church and state.

A council of fifteen barons now took control of the administration of the kingdom, under the leadership of Hugh Bigod, justiciar, and of his brother Roger, earl of Norfolk.

Negotiations were also continued with Louis IX of France to resolve English claims to Poitou and other French territories.

1259

On 9 February, the nobles of England gathered in London, as they had previously arranged. Simon de Montfort, earl of Leicester, came to this council. His long absence in France had been a cause of concern in England, for no one knew what had happened to him overseas. A confidential representative from the king of France, the dean of Bourges, was also present.

At this council there was a good deal of discussion about the question at issue between Henry III, king of England, and Louis IX, king of France, as to what had been done and decided in that matter overseas.

Within a short time, on 14 February, a peace treaty was drawn up and settled in London, dependent on both parties agreeing without argument to abide by what had been arranged by their special formal envoys, which would be more fully set out in due course.

By the treaty of Paris, ratified in October 1259, and negotiated by Peter, count of Savoy, and Simon de Montfort, earl of Leicester, Henry III gave up his claims to Normandy, Maine, Anjou and Poitou. However, Louis IX acknowledged Henry's lordship over Gascony – for which Henry paid homage – and made him a peer of France.

John, lord of Joinville, who knew Louis well and who wrote his biography in the early fourteenth century, notes the reservations with which Louis's barons greeted the treaty, despite their admiration for their saintly king.

In making peace with the king of England, King Louis acted against the advice of his council, who had said to him: 'It seems to us that Your Majesty is needlessly throwing away the land you are giving

Gascony: an English stronghold

THE possession of the duchy of Gascony by the kings of England was a relic of the great Plantagenet dominions collected together in the 12th century. In 1152 the future King Henry II had married Eleanor of Aquitaine, from whom he received the duchy of Aquitaine, which comprised Poitou and all the provinces from the Loire to the Pyrenees, including what became known as Gascony.

These possessions were part of a collection of territories including Normandy, Anjou, Brittany and the kingdom of England. Although the Plantagenets behaved as if they were independent, all their French lands save Gascony were held as fiefs of the king of France, and, as a result, in 1203–4, Philip II was able to deprive Henry II's son John of most of his vast French domains. Philip's campaign, and one by Louis VIII in 1224, left Henry III in effective control of only the Channel Islands and Gascony.

The English-held territories in France had always been a source of friction between the kings of England and France. Henry III, true to the traditions of his ancestors, continued to call himself 'king of England, duke of Normandy, duke of Aquitaine, and count of Anjou', and even launched a military campaign from Gascony in 1242–3, with negligible results. Gascony itself was profoundly loyal to the English crown, principally because of the lucrative trade in wine between its chief town, Bordeaux, and England. Henry ruled mainly through local Gascon officials until 1248, when he sent Simon de Montfort to govern the duchy. Simon's heavy-handedness provoked general rebellion, and in 1254 Henry's son Edward was put in to replace him. Gascony, however, continued to be restive. This, coupled with apparently unending disputes with the French monarchy about the precise locations of the duchy's frontiers, and his emerging troubles with the English barons, probably influenced Henry to seek a settlement of Gascony's status with Louis IX. The result was the treaty of Paris, finalized in 1259.

Its essence was that Henry agreed to abandon his claims to Normandy, Maine, Touraine, Anjou and Poitou, and accepted that he held the previously entirely independent Gascony as a fief of the French crown. In return, he was given substantial sums of money and rights in the dioceses of Périgueux, Limoges and Cahors, together with the promise that after the death of Alphonse of Poitiers, Louis IX's brother, he would receive some of his lands: the Agenais, Quercy and Saintonge. The treaty, agreed amidst great pomp and ceremony, was an honest attempt to find a diplomatic solution to a permanent sore in relations between the two kings, and led to a kind of peace between the two kingdoms until 1293.

At the time, however, critics in both countries accused their rulers of giving up too much, and difficulties in applying the terms soon built up acute tensions in south-west France. The king of France started to intervene in the duchy's law and administration in breach of local custom, and although Alphonse of Poitiers died in 1271, the English crown did not receive the Agenais until 1279 or Saintonge until 1289, at which time it abandoned its claim to Quercy altogether. Deep resentment against both the French and the English kings grew up on the Gascon borders and disputes between the two jurisdictions were to provide the catalyst for future conflicts between England and France.

Above *The wine trade was instrumental in keeping Gascony loyal to the English Crown.*

Below *Henry III landing in Aquitaine with his retinue.*

Above *Louis IX administering justice to his subjects. Despite the harsh execution pictured above, Louis IX was a fair and benign ruler. He expanded the role played by the monarchy in hearing appeals against other courts and strongly encouraged the use of Roman law in judicial practice. He also proved an effective ruler, curbing the endemic feudal wars, redistributing the tax burden more equitably and simplifying the administration.*

Left *Louis IX departing on a crusade with his assembled army. He felt strongly that the Holy Land should be under Christian rule.*

Right *A page from an illuminated manuscript depicting scenes from the religious life of Louis IX, also known as St Louis for his piety and asceticism. He can be seen washing the feet of the poor, collecting relics of the saints, being whipped by a monk in penance, donating food to a monastery and studying the Bible with the aid of a teacher.*

At that hour, the moon was visible in the west, with both horns pointing downwards to the earth. The great circular rainbow with the sun at the centre was seen again at mid-day the following day, 31 May, but this time did not last so long.

On 24 August, a great parliament assembled at Kenilworth; there, Henry III granted to the barons their ancient charter, and sought the grant of a tenth for three years from the whole English Church.

The response of the gathering was that first a peace settlement between the king and the disinherited should be reached, and that they would give the king their answer about the grant after that. The legate gave his support to this reply, and the king agreed willingly.

This settlement, the Dictum of Kenilworth, which defined the terms on which the disinherited could receive back their lands, did not meet with widespread acceptance amongst the rebels.

1267

On 8 April, Gilbert of Clare, earl of Gloucester, tricked his way into the city of London. The legate Ottobuono was then residing in the Tower of London, where he celebrated Easter. The disinherited had flocked to him as their protector and remained there with him.

News of these events provoked the king to send orders to the earl of Gloucester to leave the city, adding that unless he did so, the king himself would come thither and would strive to retrieve by force everything which had been wrested from him. Henry III then moved to Windsor, where he gathered an army of one hundred and nine standards, and set out for London on 5 May. They halted at Stratford Langthorne, while negotiations for a peace settlement were conducted.

Finally, on 6 June, Gilbert of Clare came to terms with the king and handed over the city of London. Then, at the instance of Earl Gilbert and the other earls and barons, many of the disinherited were reconciled with the king.

1268

A thunderclap was heard at Winchester on 12 January, followed by lightning and hail, just after the celebration of High Mass.

Despite all his troubles, Henry III's devotion to Westminster Abbey and to St Edward the Confessor never flagged. A royal account of 1268 reveals some of the details of his expenditure.

And in heavy timber, boards, beams of both oak and alder, hurdles, laths, withies, grease, glue, and in certain small necessaries for the same works, with carriage, ninety-two pounds and six shillings.

And in lead, iron, steel, charcoal, and firewood for making ironwork; in locks, ropes, glass, wax, pitch, and other things necessary for glass windows and for making cement, and canvas for closing the windows of the same church, with carriage, one hundred and fifty-three pounds, fifteen shillings and eleven pence.

And in tiles, tile-pins, litter, reeds and straw bought for covering the tower of the same church, which has been begun, and the walls of the aforesaid works; and for several of the king's buildings, with carriage, eight pounds, eleven shillings and two pence.

Total expenditure, two thousand, four hundred and twenty-one pounds, nineteen shillings and four pence. They owe two shillings and two pence.

The author of the Waverley Annals *notes the ceremonial celebrations in 1269, when the body of St Edward the Confessor was translated to its new shrine at Westminster.*

1269

In this year, the body of St Edward, the glorious king and confessor, was translated from its old shrine in Westminster Abbey to a new one, built at King Henry's direction. On the day, 13 October, at which the king had planned to wear his crown, there was a great gathering of bishops, earls, barons, abbots, priors and many others.

Henry III and Westminster Abbey

WESTMINSTER Abbey was Henry III's attempt to beat Louis IX and the French at their own architectural game. Although Henry did not visit Paris until 1254, he must have heard glowing reports of the glories of the French Gothic cathedrals and the Sainte-Chapelle, begun entirely at Louis' expense in 1241. In 1245, inspired to rival the generosity of his royal cousin, Henry declared that he would take on full financial responsibility for building a new fashionable church at Westminster, to replace the church built by St Edward the Confessor two centuries earlier. The design had to be sufficiently imposing to fit England's coronation and royal burial church, and Henry also clearly intended it to be a giant reliquary, like the Sainte-Chapelle. Fortunately, in view of the king's unsteady financial position, Westminster Abbey already had its own precious relic in the body of its founder, St Edward the Confessor, who had been canonized in 1161. The Plantagenets could claim descent from Edward's family (through Henry I's queen, Matilda, the niece of Edgar Aetheling); and Henry seems to have conceived a deep personal attachment to the only saint the family could call their own.

Although Westminster enshrined and celebrated an English saint, it was as cosmopolitan as Henry could make it. He commissioned an Italian, Pietro Oderisi, an expert in Cosmati work (i.e. setting small tesserae of coloured marble or semi-precious stones into marble sheets) to work on the base of St Edward's shrine, on his own tomb, and on the choir pavement.

He also sent masons to France to learn French stone-cutting techniques. The first architect, Henry de Reynes, had undoubtedly, as his name implies, worked at Reims Cathedral, although it is uncertain if he was English or French. Certainly, the abbey bears eloquent witness to the ascendancy of French architecture in the 13th century. The vaults, for example, are higher than those of any other English Gothic church, and are supported by flying buttresses, while chapels radiate from the aisle at the east end of the abbey, in marked contrast to the usual English square choirs and retrochoirs. Bar tracery was used in all the windows and, unlike the other French notions described above, had an immediate and far-reaching effect on church architecture in England.

Top ***The king consults his master masons.***

Right ***The vaulting in Westminster Abbey.***

Above *Westminster Abbey; the view from the choir, looking above the screen to the high vaulting.*

Right *An elegantly painted panel from a diptych in Westminster Abbey, gilded with gold leaf and inlaid with precious stones.*

Opposite *A floor tile from the chapter house, bearing the three lions of the Plantagenet crest.*

Part II

Edward I 1272–1307

Edward I was, in his outlook and behaviour, quite unlike his father Henry III. A strong leader, he was viewed with respect and fear throughout England; yet his devotion to his first queen, Eleanor of Castile, whom he married in 1254, was striking.

He was renowned for dispensing good justice, and the great series of statutes he made – tackling a wide range of grievances – is a monument to his reign. His military skills were considerable and frequently exercised – in the conquest of Wales, the subjugation of the Scots (hence his nickname 'the hammer of the Scots'), and in wars to defend his duchy of Gascony against the king of France, Philip IV the Fair. The costliness of these offensives produced serious financial problems, but Edward weathered the storms. News of his death in 1307 was greeted with dismay.

The first years of Edward's reign are described by William Rishanger, a monk of St Albans, and in the work of Thomas Wykes, a canon of Osney Abbey near Oxford. The story is continued in the Worcester annals; in the businesslike chronicles by Bartholomew Cotton, a monk of Norwich; and in the anonymous Flowers of History, *written at Westminster Abbey. All these authors are southern in their outlook, but the Augustinian Walter of Guisborough relates events from a northern perspective.*

(Opposite: Edward I)

Edward, first-born son of King Henry III by Eleanor, daughter of the count of Savoy, succeeded his father on the throne at the age of thirty-four.

He was skilful in the conduct of affairs of state, and was from boyhood dedicated to the practice of arms, for which he won a world-wide reputation surpassing that of any other Christian prince of his time. He was elegant in appearance, being a head taller than average in stature.

In boyhood, his hair was silvery-blond in colour; in his youth, it began to turn from fair to dark, while in old age it became a magnificent swan-like white. His forehead was broad, and the rest of his features were regular, except that his left eyelid drooped, which gave him a resemblance to his father.

Despite a lisp, he was not lacking in eloquence when persuasive arguments were needed. His long arms were in proportion to his supple body; no man was ever endowed with greater muscular strength for wielding a sword. His breast swelled above his stomach, and the length of his legs ensured that he was never dislodged from his seat by the galloping and jumping of horses.

During the night on which he died, Thomas appeared in a dream to his cousin, the count of Aquino, dressed in his Dominican habit. Thomas handed a sealed letter to the sleeping count, who woke soon afterwards, and, finding himself holding this letter, called to his attendant to bring a light. When the count opened the letter, he found inscribed in golden characters, surpassing any human calligraphy: 'Today I am made a doctor in Jerusalem.' Keeping the letter carefully, he sent messengers to enquire after Thomas's health, and learned that he had departed this life on the very night of his appearance to the count.

During this year, a terrible disease [called murrain] attacked the sheep flocks of England, which were wiped out everywhere by this disastrous pestilence. It raged for the next twenty-five years, and spread to every village in the land. This plague, hitherto unknown in this country, was widely believed to have taken hold when a wealthy merchant from somewhere in France had landed in Northumberland, bringing with him a diseased sheep from Spain, which infected the entire English sheep population, whose numbers were double those of the country's cattle.

For the English, however, this was a year of rejoicing, because of Edward's coronation.

The Augustinian chronicler Thomas Wykes gives a well-informed description of the coronation of King Edward I.

On Thursday 2 August, Edward I, king of England, returned from France to await at last the day of his coronation, preparations for which required the greatest possible care, as befits a royal occasion.

On Saturday 18 August, the new king entered London, which had been lavishly decorated. Not only the citizens of London, but all the nobles of the realm had come there to greet him, clerics and laymen together, all of whom had assembled in answer to the royal summons, partly because of the uniqueness of the spectacle, but more in order to render homage to their king, forming an innumerable throng from all parts of the kingdom.

Neither the pen nor the human tongue can describe the decorations of the city and the finery of its citizens, which had been zealously and cleverly devised without thought of the cost in order to glorify the king.

The following day, which was Sunday 19 August, the king was anointed by Robert Kilwardby, archbishop of Canterbury, in the presence of all the bishops of the realm, as was proper. The archbishop of York was not permitted to be present at the coronation, as a result of the petty squabble over the carrying of his cross which had embroiled the two archbishops for a long time, and had cost a lot of energy.

The king took up the crown and shone in glory before the peers of his realm. Also present, besides the citizens of London and of other towns and cities from all parts of the kingdom – who had vied with one another in bedecking themselves in a variety of rich clothes – was a large throng of earls, barons and knights, similarly decked out.

The city itself, which is deservedly called the capital of our realm, gleamed with silks and cloth woven with gold. I shall not mention the feast which both amazed and delighted the people gathered from all around. Nor should I pass over in silence how the queen, Eleanor of Castile, like the king, shone radiantly, glorious in her regal crown.

1275

Two weeks after Easter, a celebrated and solemn session of parliament was held at Westminster, where all the leaders of the kingdom had gathered, both secular and religious. This being his first parliament, the king wished, as was right, to win the goodwill of his people and to give new force to laws that had become ineffective, either through the weakness of his predecessors or because of disorder within the kingdom.

Assisted by the advice of loyal jurists, King Edward I drew up new statutes that were not only in accord with justice, but most necessary to the kingdom. He also had them promulgated widely so that

Thomas Aquinas, the dumb ox

SAINT Thomas Aquinas, the great medieval theologian and philosopher known as 'the universal teacher', was born near Naples in about 1225. A younger son of the count of Aquino, and intended for high office in the Church, Thomas was accordingly sent to school at the famous Benedictine monastery of Monte Cassino at the age of five. In his teens he studied at the University of Naples, where he secretly joined the Dominican friars, the new intellectual order vowed to evangelical poverty. His aristocratic relations, outraged, had him kidnapped and imprisoned in the family castle. For over a year they tried every means to make him renounce his vows, even smuggling a beautiful prostitute into his bedroom. Thomas immediately chased her out with a flaming brand. From then on he was blessed with permanent freedom from sexual temptation – although his earliest biographer records that 'he always shunned women . . . as a man avoids snakes'.

Thomas's family relented, and in 1248 the young theologian went to study under Albertus Magnus at Cologne, where he began a lifetime's work of reconciling the philosophy of the Greek thinker Aristotle to Christian theology. Massively built, slow-moving and amiably taciturn, he was nicknamed 'the dumb ox' by his fellow students. When he did speak, his brilliance was so apparent that Albertus prophesied 'This dumb ox will fill the whole world with his bellowing'. In 1252, he began to teach theology at the University of Paris, then the intellectual powerhouse of Europe, and in 1256 was admitted as a professor.

Thomas left Paris in 1259, and spent the next decade working in Italy, where he completed *Summa contra Gentiles*, a manual for missionaries sent to convert learned Jews and Moslems. Because the latter did not accept the Scriptures, he based his arguments on 'natural reason, to which all men are forced to assent'. He also wrote several still-popular hymns, including *Pange lingua* and *Laude Sion*, and appears to have invented the verse form – though not the dubious contents – of the limerick.

In 1267 he started his great *Summa Theologiae*, a textbook for beginners in theology. This stupendous work, which even in its unfinished state runs to over two million words (and 60 volumes in the most recent edition), exemplifies Thomas's extraordinary industry: he habitually dictated to three or four secretaries, and was said to be capable of composing Latin prose even in his sleep.

The textbook, which deals comprehensively with theories about God, Creation, the nature of existence and the Christian sacraments, was still being written in 1273, when an increasingly abstracted Thomas had a mysterious vision while saying Mass. After that he refused to dictate another word, declaring: 'I cannot, because all that I have written now seems like straw, compared with what I have seen revealed to me.' Three months later he died.

Thomas's works were at first regarded as dangerously innovative, and even after his canonization in 1323 his reputation grew comparatively slowly. It was only in the 19th century that St Thomas was recognized as the principal theologian of the Catholic Church and – even by non-Christians – the most brilliant thinker of the Middle Ages.

Above ***Even by non-Christians, Thomas Aquinas is widely regarded as being one of the Middle Ages most brilliant thinkers. His great work,*** **Summa Theologiae,** ***is unfinished but, even so, consists of more than two million words. He was canonized 50 years after his death. This portrait by Ghirlandaio is in S Maria Novella, Florence.***

they would be duly observed by future generations. Thus the king united the hearts of the people in their sincere and boundless affection for him.

On 11 September, an earthquake struck England. It was strongest in the cities of London, Canterbury and Winchester and along the south coast. In the north, the shock was felt too, but less severely.

Edward I summoned all the barons of the realm to Westminster on 13 October, where he held a long debate with them. After appealing to them, the king compelled each and every layman and cleric in the kingdom, whether willingly or not, to grant to him one fifteenth of his temporal wealth. This would enable Edward to recover the vast sums which he had spent in Syria, and, by payments, to lessen the demands of his creditors. However, the bishops replied saying that they would summon the clergy and then communicate to the king what they could determine.

In the same parliament, a significant discussion took place that it would be shameful not to mention. After due consideration, a new law was imposed upon Jews living in England, for they were enemies of the Cross and they burdened Catholic Christians with intolerably heavy rates of interest. Henceforth, Jews were not to loan any money at interest, but should provide their means of life by the toil of their own hands and by lawful business.

1276

In early February, Gaston de Béarn [had his case heard by King Philip III of France and] was sent to England. According to the pledge which he had made earlier, he surrendered freely to King Edward I, submitting himself and all his lands in Gascony to the king's will. Edward promptly locked him up in the castle at Winchester. Then, appointing keepers for all Gaston's lands and castles, he sent them to Gascony without delay.

Gaston de Béarn was set free again in 1277, and after another hearing of his case in the French parlement, was reconciled with Edward I in 1279.

1277

In January, the king of England sent a large army to the Welsh Marches in order to fortify those lands which Llywelyn, prince of Wales, having abjured his loyalty to the king, had frequently devastated, and to compel the prince to abandon his usual unruly behaviour.

This was achieved, and the royal army stayed on until the following May, stoutly defending the territory.

At that time the king of England wanted to encourage the army that had been sent to the Welsh Marches as much as possible by being present in person. Accordingly, he assembled all the forces of his kingdom and set off for that region.

On 24 June, he was in the Chester area. Since between Chester and Llywelyn's territory there lies a forest so broad and dense that the king's forces were unable to pass through it without risk, a considerable area of the forest was cleared or cut down, leaving a broad way into Prince Llywelyn's land for the king and his men. Through this gap they entered in triumph the region that had been encroached upon in the raids.

Edward I immediately began the construction of two castles, heavily fortified to suit the broad terrain, on the banks of the River Clwyd, which is daily washed by the tide, in order to provide secure quarters for himself and his men. One of the castles was called Flint, the other Rhuddlan.

The King stayed on in that area with his forces until 11 November, making frequent attacks on the Welsh lands. So constrained were the Welsh inhabitants, that as their food supplies ran short, they were forced unwillingly to retreat to their last major stronghold, Snowdonia, with no further thoughts of resistance or rebellion.

Sturdy sailors from the Cinque Ports with a large fleet of ships, landed on the island near to Snowdonia called Anglesey and seized it in triumph; whereupon Prince Llywelyn, by now

Above *Conway Castle. **The outer walls, almost a mile in circumference, enclosed a royal residence.***

Edward I's Welsh castles

THE most impressive series of medieval fortifications in Britain, Edward I's Welsh strongholds display the art of castle-building at its highest point of development. Each a masterpiece in its own right, collectively they represent a programme of fortress construction unparalleled in scale since the days of imperial Rome, and one which strained the resources of an entire nation. Their cost was immense – some £100,000 – at a time when the average labourer earned less than £2 a year. To raise them, Edward recruited a vast army of workmen, masons and craftsmen from virtually every county in England.

Their purpose was to ensure the permanent subjugation of the last and most obdurate outpost of Welsh independence: the mountainous principality of Gwynedd. Edward I ringed the conquered territory with no less than ten great new royal fortresses, backed up by 12 lesser strongholds. All but one of the major castles was accessible to shipping, so that they could be supplied by sea in time of siege. Edward attached newly founded fortified towns to five of them, 'planted' with English settlers attacted by tax concessions and trading privileges. These formed a reservoir of supplies and loyal manpower, and also speeded the anglicization of Wales.

The overseer of the project, the Savoyard architect Master James of St George, incorporated the latest developments in military engineering into his castles. Instead of relying, like earlier fortresses, on a single central strongpoint (or 'keep') – which could become a death trap – the new castles had high enclosure walls studded with massive projecting towers. From these the defenders could sweep the approaches with archery fire, and cover the intervening wall-tops if these fell to an attacker. Each tower could hold out alone, and in many of the castles (including Rhuddlan, Harlech and Beaumaris), pairs of towers were linked to form powerful gatehouses. What had been the weakest point of a fortress – its entrance – became its strongest feature.

At Harlech and Beaumaris – respectively the most dramatically sited and the most technically perfect of the castles – Master James raised one circuit of towered walls within another. The outer defences were lower than the inner ones and commanded by their fire. 'Concentric' fortresses like these were virtually impregnable: Harlech later became 'the castle of lost causes', the last British stronghold of beleaguered Lancastrians and Cavaliers. The great castles of Conwy and Caernarvon were built as royal residences and Caernarvon in particular reflects this concept: its polygonal towers and horizontally banded walls imitate the defences of imperial Constantinople, while its 'eagle tower' recalls legends of ancient Welsh heroes from whom Edward claimed spiritual descent. Edward brought his queen here, to bear the son – the future Edward II – who would be proclaimed the first 'prince of Wales' at Caernarvon. Wales has been under English rule ever since – in great measure because of the effectiveness of Edward's castle-building.

Above *Harlech stands as a fighting fortress some 200 feet above the old sea level. Its walls and towers are in ruins but almost at full height.*

Left *Rhuddlan was the first of Master James's Welsh castles. Queen Eleanor built a fishpond in the courtyard surrounded by seats for her ladies, and the yard itself was laid with 6000 turves.*

Below *Beaumaris, the last of Edward's Welsh castles to be built.*

bewildered and cowed, acting swiftly of necessity, submitted himself and his land to royal authority.

Having achieved his purpose, Edward I returned to England taking with him, in accordance with the terms of their agreement, the prince of Wales, who accompanied him to London at Christmas.

There, in the presence of Edward I and many of the nobles of the realm, Llywelyn rendered homage to the king of England. He swore an oath in respect of himself and the nobility of his land that he would hold all his territory in fief from the king of England his lord for as long as he lived, and that every year he would pay a sum of money in return for the island of Anglesey, which the king handed back to him in fief.

In addition, legal documents were drawn up between them to the effect that Llywelyn would not recognize any heir other than the king. When all this was completed, he returned to Wales under royal safe conduct.

1278

King Edward I heard that Prince Llywelyn intended to repudiate the allegiance he had recently pledged; it was furthermore reported to him on credible authority that the prince had refused to attend the royal parliament that had been held in London three weeks after Easter. In order to ascertain whether Llywelyn had indeed broken the pact by which he had earlier been bound, and had matched his words with deeds, the king set off for the Welsh Marches on 1 August, accompanied by a very small escort of knights.

Prince Llywelyn, lest he might be accused of prevarication or of breaking the agreement, went to greet King Edward I as his lord when he reached the Marches, and paid him all due honour.

Now that the pact between the king of England and Prince Llywelyn had been renewed, the latter made a most advantageous marriage to Eleanor de Montfort, daughter of the late earl of Leicester, Simon de Montfort, a match the prince had been seeking for some time.

Edward's conquest of Wales

'GLORY to God in the highest, peace on earth to men of goodwill, a triumph to the English . . . and to the Welsh everlasting extermination.' These sentiments, expressed by an excited royal clerk when he learnt of the death of Llywelyn ap Gruffudd, prince of Wales, in 1282, were echoed by other commentators who celebrated what they regarded as Edward I's subjugation of the Welsh. But the king himself had always been careful to count the Welsh among his subjects. He had regarded Llywelyn, even at the height of his power, as prince of all Wales, as no more than 'one of the greatest among the other magnates of my kingdom'.

The king's first Welsh campaign in 1277 was mounted to bring this rebellious vassal to heel. The conflict was not the inevitable outcome of a personal antagonism between the two men. Disagreements over land holding and castle-building had arisen between Llywelyn and Edward's administrators before Edward's return from the Holy Land in 1274. But when Edward provided a refuge in England for the Welsh barons – including Llywelyn's own brother, Dafydd – who had plotted against Llywelyn's life, the prince's attitude hardened. Edward in turn was disturbed by Llywelyn's decision to marry Eleanor de Montfort; he believed that the marriage would 'scatter the seeds which had grown from the malice which her father had sown'. Edward was also concerned by the more recent intrigues of Guy and Amaury, the sons of Simon de Montfort, who were still at liberty in Europe. The king arranged for Eleanor, who had married Llywelyn by proxy in France, and her brother Amaury, to be captured at sea in 1275, on their way from France to Wales. Negotiations between prince and king were deadlocked when Edward insisted that Llywelyn should fulfil his feudal obligation and pay homage: Llywelyn maintained that he would do so only on specified conditions, such as the release of Eleanor. These were unacceptable to the king, and Llywelyn was formally condemned in parliament as a rebel against the Crown. By the summer of 1277, having been deserted by his vassals, Llywelyn surrendered to the might of Edward's army.

The king seemed bent on disinheriting Llywelyn completely, but an agreement negotiated at Aberconwy allowed the prince to retain Snowdonia for his lifetime, provided he recognized the hereditary right of his younger brother Dafydd to a share of Snowdonia; while Llywelyn lived, Dafydd would hold a lordship in the land east of the Conwy. Dafydd was resentful that his earlier adherence to the king was not rewarded more generously, a resentment deepened by his friction with royal officers who administered the land which bordered upon his own.

The war of 1282 was instigated by Dafydd rather than Llywelyn, who, despite his grievances, preferred more politic solutions, perhaps influenced by his wife. Llywelyn and Eleanor were formally married on a resplendent occasion in Worcester Cathedral on St Edward's Day 1278, with Edward I's consent and at his expense. When Dafydd rose in rebellion at Easter 1282, Eleanor was with child, and Llywelyn – who hoped for a male heir to his princely status and political aspirations – did not join him until June, when his wife died giving birth to a daughter. His active participation in the Welsh movement brought it great strength; it was late autumn before Edward was in a position to attack Snowdonia.

The conflict was further postponed when John Pecham, archbishop of Canterbury, intervened. From his accession in 1279, he had tried to bring the Welsh Church into line with the English, and his ill-considered criticisms of Llywelyn and his strident condemnations of the Welsh for their moral failings had caused considerable bad feeling. But he was courteously received by Llywelyn, and discussions were held over three days, in November 1282. Llywelyn invoked the Trojan origins of the Welsh people, to be countered by Pecham's denunciation of the moral degradation of those very forebears whom the Welsh held in such esteem. Further negotiation was impossible and Edward declared war on the Welsh.

Llywelyn, hoping to revive Welsh resistance in the south, moved to Builth, where he died in combat on 11 December 1282. His severed head was taken to the king at Rhuddlan and then displayed at the Tower of London. English chroniclers describe the derision with which it was greeted by the London crowd. The Welsh poet Gruffudd ab yr Ynad Coch composed a magnificent elegy in which he described the tragedy as a cosmic disaster.

Edward completed the conquest of Wales in 1283. Dafydd, finally captured in his last stronghold in Snowdonia, was convicted of treason. He was hanged and drawn, and his quarters despatched to four English cities. Llywelyn's lands were 'united and annexed to the crown of England' and brought directly under the English royal administration. The king consolidated his conquest by constructing a group of mighty castles, including Caernarvon, Conwy, Harlech and later Beaumaris, designed by Master James of St George, his Savoyard architect.

Edward was a statesmanlike ruler, but the harsher aspects of his administration provoked a major rebellion in 1294–5. His Welsh enterprises cost him dearly and contributed to the financial and ultimately political difficulties he encountered in his later years. Within Wales, he acted prudently after 1294–5, cultivating influential men. Their allegiance was to be an asset to his son Edward, born at Caernarvon in 1284.

Above *The head of Llywelyn, carved in stone. Prince of Wales until his death in battle in 1282, he was the country's last independent ruler. After his death his title was given to the English sovereign's eldest son.*

Right *The execution of Llywelyn. Londoners jeered at his severed head when it was displayed at the Tower of London; a Welsh poet described his death as a 'cosmic disaster'.*

Amid considerable rejoicing, Prince Llywelyn married Eleanor with the king's consent on 13 October in the city of Worcester, where a large number of the nobles of the realm had been summoned.

At that time, the king of England saw clearly that his coinage was being rendered worthless by excessive clipping on the part of Jews in England who [at the parliament of 1275] had been forbidden to lend money at interest, to such an extent that it was not reaching half its due weight. Edward I was also aware that foreign merchants were visiting England with their goods less frequently than usual on account of the debasement of the coin, and that goods of all kinds were vastly more expensive.

In order to make good the loss to his kingdom, Edward I took the wise advice of noblemen and counsellors and, telling few people in advance, decreed that the perfidious Jews who were clipping coins be arrested in all the cities and boroughs of England. The king had them put in custody and shackled them, and, when all the wealth that had been acquired illegally had been transferred without appeal to the royal treasury, he ordered that they be detained further for punishment. Since it was quite evident that such a crime could not have been committed without the complicity of Christians, after a short time King Edward I arrested, with almost unbelievable speed and surprise, all the goldsmiths in the kingdom and several other individuals who, as a result of the accusations of Jews or of some other likely conjecture, came under suspicion of being partners or accomplices of the clippers, or purchasers.

After Christmas the king appointed wise and prudent men in his kingdom as justices, and decreed that they should interrogate the Jews and Christians about the coin clipping, so that the guilty would be punished and the innocent set free.

The justices condemned to be hanged very many Jews who had been convicted of clipping; they similarly sentenced some Christians, albeit few, who had committed the same crime or who were accomplices. After sworn inquests had been held with local juries, the goldsmiths and almost all the other suspects escaped the death penalty – rightly or wrongly I know not.

1279

On 25 January, Pope Nicholas III exercised his full authority conferring the see of Canterbury upon John Pecham, a Franciscan friar and a supremely learned man then dwelling at the papal court. For some time the Franciscan refused, but he was finally consecrated, unwillingly it was said, on 12 March. He was to set out for England on a convenient date.

In early May, King Edward I crossed over to France to take possession of the county of Ponthieu which he was claiming on the basis of the hereditary right of his queen, Eleanor of Castile. When he had successfully completed his business and all had paid him homage, he returned to England before 24 June. John Pecham, newly appointed archbishop of Canterbury, arrived shortly before him.

During the same period, Edward I had proclaimed an edict throughout England, to the effect that clipped money should no longer be circulated, nor should anyone be forced to accept it. In addition, he designated a small number of places in the kingdom, in towns and cities, where the money could be exchanged. For each pound of the non-current coin, an extra sixteen pennies were to be paid for the exchange, and people would receive one pound of unclipped coin. On 21 May, the regulation of clipped coin came into force and indeed within a short time no one would consider accepting it.

At the same time a statute [the statute of Mortmain] was widely proclaimed in England which the king had had drawn up on the advice and with the general assent of his nobles. According to this statute, in the future no one could sell lands, revenues or possessions to the clergy nor make a donation of them, nor was it permitted that any cleric should receive or accept from any secular person lands, revenues or possessions by deed of gift, collation or purchase.

Law and dis-order

THE first two decades of Edward I's reign witnessed a great surge of governmental energy. The king started in 1274 by instigating country-wide investigations into the usurpation of royal rights and lands following the civil war of the 1260s, and into abuses by local officials – the largest such undertaking since the Domesday survey nearly 200 years earlier. As in 1086, the information was provided by sworn juries of local men, and recorded in rolls which were later called the 'Hundred Rolls' after the local government districts, or hundreds, that they covered.

As a result of this survey, the first statute of Westminster was enacted in parliament in 1275; its many detailed clauses tried to deal with the abuses the investigations had revealed. From 1278 proceedings were held before royal justices in the counties against lords who were thought to have usurped royal jurisdiction. When they were asked 'by what warrant' (*quo warranto*) they held these rights, many could not provide documentary evidence to support their claims, and in 1290 the government had to agree to accept as valid, claims which had been continuously exercised since Richard I's accession in 1189. The agreement was embodied in a statute and came towards the end of a period in which there was a great proliferation of statute law in parliament.

Although Edward has been called 'the English Justinian' as a result, after the 6th-century emperor who reduced Roman law to a uniform code, the title is misleading. Edward and his ministers had no intention of codifying the law. Rather, legal points were clarified and grievances – of landlords, merchants or the king himself – were dealt with. The king is unlikely to have been concerned with the details in the statutes, which were drawn up by administrators like Robert Burnell, his chancellor, and judges like Ralph of Hengham.

In 1285 the government attempted to improve peace-keeping by stipulating that all men over the age of 15 should hold specified arms and be ready to use them, under official direction, to maintain law and order. Two years later, in 1287, keepers of the peace were appointed in the counties to supervise this militia. However, there was no improvement in order and, on the contrary, after 1294, in the prevailing atmosphere of war, lawlessness in the countryside increased. New commissions of justices were therefore appointed in 1304–5 to deal with offenders. Their sessions were known as 'trailbaston' enquiries, after the gangs of men armed with staves who terrorized the population. Many were soldiers who had fought for the king in his wars against the Welsh, Scots and French, and were now sheltering in his forests: Edward's wars outside England finally disrupted life within the country.

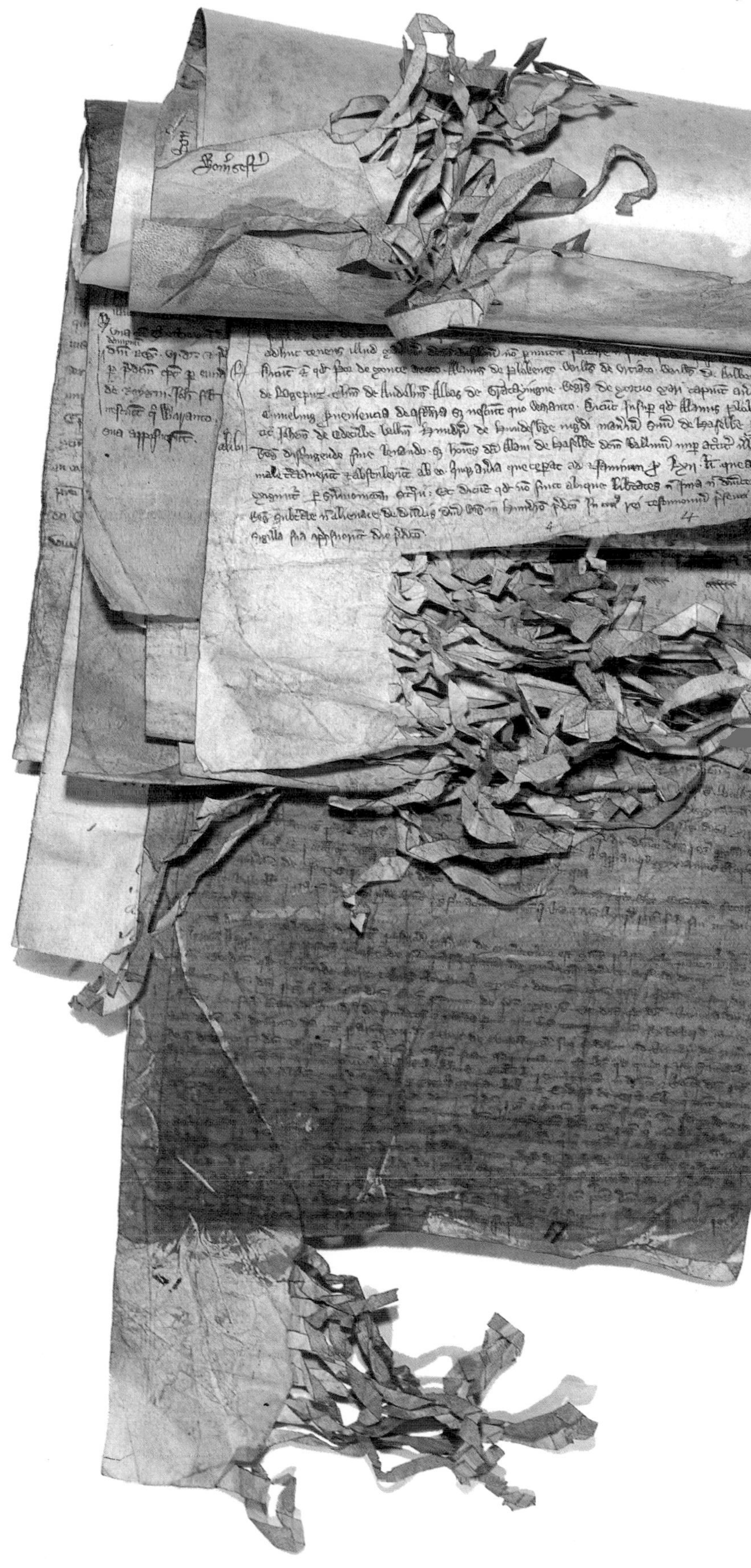

Above ***The Somerset roll; one of the Hundred Rolls from the royal enquiry into landholding, carried out during 1279. It was more detailed and thorough than any survey since Domesday Book.***

The Worcester chronicler provides valuable information about Edward I's Welsh wars, as well as showing a typical annalist's preoccupation with natural phenomena such as extremes of weather.

1281

From Christmas until early February 1282 there was bitter frost and heavy snow, the like of which even the old and the aged of that day had not experienced before in England. The five arches of London Bridge, and many other bridges besides, collapsed under the pressure of the ice.

The River Thames was frozen solid all the way from Lambeth to the king's palace at Westminster, and people were able to walk across without getting their feet wet. Fish died in the ponds and birds starved to death in the woods and fields.

1282

In this the tenth year of King Edward's reign, at dead of night on Palm Sunday [21 March], Llywelyn, prince of Wales, and David, his brother, invested Rhuddlan and Flint with a large army, and demolished any other royal strongholds which they were able to overrun.

At Hawarden, the Welsh forces captured Roger Clifford, a noble and renowned knight, whom they sent wounded and in chains to Snowdonia, after they had killed most of the garrison and, with no warning, had slaughtered in their beds both the young and the old, women and children alike. They then devastated a large area of the Marches.

Scarcely able to believe reports of these events. Edward I dispatched the barons of the exchequer and the justices of the king's bench to Shrewsbury to enforce the laws of the realm; he himself assembled an army and subdued Wales east of Snowdonia.

To the earls, barons and others, including numerous Gascons and Basques sent from overseas and who had supported him loyally, he granted many of the lands which came into his hands, to be held by them and their heirs forever.

As his next step, the king oversaw the construction of a large bridge made of boats across the tidal stretch of the River Conway, not far from Snowdonia. Subsequently, when some of the king's knights crossed this on a sortie, they were thrown into panic by the approach of a large and menacing band of Welshmen. In an unsuccessful attempt to retreat to the island of Anglesey, the knights drowned ignominiously.

The Welsh, attributing this not to misfortune but to a miracle, urged their prince to act boldly and without fear, since, according to the prophecy of Merlin, he would soon be crowned with the diadem of Brutus.

So Llywelyn collected a large force and came down to the lowlands, leaving his brother David in the mountains.

Edmund, heir of the late Roger Mortimer, lord of Wigmore, with a company of Marchers, fell upon Llywelyn's men, of whom they killed a large number without any losses of their own.

In this skirmish Prince Llywelyn's head was cut off. It was taken to London and displayed for a long time, crowned with ivy, on a stake at the Tower, where many years earlier Llywelyn's father, Gruffydd, had fallen and died of a broken neck.

The Welsh, alarmed and confused following the death of their prince, surrendered all the strongholds in Snowdonia to King Edward I.

Rishanger recounts two conflicting epitaphs to the prince of Wales.

Two monks wrote verses in memory of Llywelyn. One, a Welshman, wrote thus:

> Here lies the scourge of England,
>   Snowdonia's guardian sure,
> Llywelyn, prince of Wales,
>   In character most pure.
> Of modern kings the jewel,
>   Of kings long past the flower,
> For kings to come a pattern,
>   Radiant in lawful power.

The English monk wrote as follows:

Here lies the prince of errors,
  A traitor and a thief,
A flaring, flaming firebrand,
  The malefactors' chief.
The wild Welsh evil genius,
  Who sought the good to kill,
Dregs of the faithless Trojans,
  And source of every ill.

And so the king, having gained the upper hand, subdued nearly the whole of Wales. A long period of peace followed.

The Worcester annalist describes the rising against Angevin rule in Sicily known as the 'Sicilian Vespers'.

Charles of Anjou, king of Apulia, Calabria and Sicily, lost the greater part of Sicily in the spring [1282] after the Sicilians rose against him and many of his people were killed in a surprise attack by Peter III, king of Aragon. Peter III claimed these realms by hereditary right because he had married Constance, the daughter of Manfred [Frederick II's son], whom the Roman Church had deprived of the kingdoms.

Ignoring papal prohibitions, the two rival kings reached an agreement that each should bring one hundred knights to the plains outside Bordeaux on a day to be named, there to fight [a tournament] for the kingdoms. When the day came, however, the agreement was ineffective, because Charles brought too many knights to the encounter.

1283

On 28 March, the king of England's officials went armed and on horseback to every place where they reckoned that they would find money which had been collected for the tenth for the Holy Land. Any such money which they found, they carried off – but they found none here, in Worcester Priory.

On 9 May, a convocation of all the leading churchmen of the province of Canterbury was held in London. The archbishop and his suffragans promised the king (who was still in Wales) a specified sum of money, to be raised among themselves, but the religious orders and the secular clergy, already much burdened, refused to co-operate in this.

On 25 November, having subjugated Wales totally, the king came to Worcester to visit the shrine of St Wulfstan, whom he held in particular devotion.

A nobleman by the name of John Giffard granted land outside the walls of the city of Oxford, with other estates, to support thirteen monks of his choice from Gloucester Abbey, because he wished that Benedictine monks should offer prayers perpetually for his soul and that of his late wife, Matilda Longespée.

King Edward I directed that a mighty castle be built at Conway, at the foot of Mount Snowdon. David, brother of the recently beheaded Llywelyn, prince of Wales, was captured by the king's men, together with his wife, his two sons and his seven daughters, and was tried subsequently by the magnates of England. He was a fomenter of evil, a most vicious tormentor of the English and deceiver of his own race, an ungrateful traitor and a war-monger.

The death of a traitor is indeed shameful! David was dragged at a horse's tail through the streets of Shrewsbury, then hanged and finally decapitated. Afterwards, his body was hacked into four portions, his heart and intestines were burned, and his head was taken to London, to be displayed on a stake at the Tower, next to his brother's head. The four quarters of his headless corpse were despatched to Bristol, Northampton, York and Winchester.

A large piece of the Cross of Our Lord, called 'Croizneth' in the Welsh language, was among many famous relics handed over to King Edward I.

The crown of the renowned Arthur, once king of Britain, was also given to King Edward, along with other jewels. Thus, the glory of the Welsh people, reluctant subjects to the laws of England, passed by God's providence into English hands.

1284

On 24 April at Caernarvon, the queen, Eleanor of Castile, gave birth to a son who was named Edward after his father.

1285

Pope Martin IV died on 28 March, and was succeeded by Honorius IV.

King Edward arranged for his daughter Mary, together with thirteen other girls, to take the veil at Amesbury on 15 August.

On 8 September, the king created forty-four knights at Winchester. He ordered, also, that all his statutes be observed strictly throughout England, and he raised a scutage from the whole realm.

On 5 October, King Philip III of France died, and was buried at Saint-Denis near Paris. At around the same time, it was reported that French forces had lost an estimated fifteen thousand men in action against the excommunicated Peter III, king of Aragon.

On 10 November, King Peter of Aragon perished, still bound by the sentence of excommunication which he had incurred for invading the kingdom of Sicily without the approval of the pope and the Roman Church. While he lay under this sentence, it was an offence knowingly or intentionally to speak of him as king.

Bartholomew Cotton's English History, *although a chronicle of central political developments, gives information about local events in the area round Norwich, where it was compiled.*

Having subdued Wales, Edward, king of England, returned to London after Easter (1285). On the following Friday he made a solemn procession on foot from the Tower of London to Westminster, together with Queen Eleanor and all the magnates of the land, and with fourteen bishops. The archbishop of Canterbury, carried the cross which the king had captured in Wales.

A chance to live

QUEEN Eleanor of Castile was about 50 when she died of malarial complications in 1290, after a life devoted to travel and pregnancies. Blessed with an unusually happy marriage to Edward I, she had accompanied his progresses through England, France, Spain and the Holy Land – where she wailed so loudly when he was wounded by a Moslem assassin's poisoned dagger that the surgeons ordered her from the room – and was still travelling with him when she took to her deathbed.

In the intervals of this journeying, she had borne him 16 children, nine of whom died either at birth or in infancy. Her favourite son, Alfonso, lived only 12 years. Of the six survivors, the future Edward II had a robust constitution, which resisted his enemies' attempts to cause his 'natural' death by starvation, ill-treatment and deliberate infection. Four of the five surviving daughters died in their thirties or forties, and only Mary (a nun) lived to be as old as her mother. By comparison with other Plantagenets, Eleanor's offspring seem to have been particularly unfortunate: Henry III's five children all reached adulthood, as did all four of Edward II's and seven of Edward III's 12.

Less is known about humbler families, especially peasants and labourers – since records of their lives are sparse and unreliable. Certainly, child mortality among the poor was high, especially in years when harvests were bad, as during the disastrous famines of 1314–21. Even at the best of times, almost 50 per cent of children were likely to die before reaching 20.

Before puberty girls had a better chance of survival than boys because they were naturally stronger; but from then on the position was drastically reversed. Death in or immediately after childbirth reaped a terrible harvest among young and middle-aged women, raising their mortality rate well above that of their male contemporaries. The chances of survival undoubtedly varied with class: although expensive 'medical' care may have done as much harm as good, the wives of better-off men were at least properly nourished before the ordeal of childbirth.

All kinds of factors affected a man's life expectancy, quite apart from disease. Among the poor, the commonest killers were probably hard work and short rations. In 1245 an average 20-year-old labourer on the Winchester estates could expect to live only another 24 years. Clerics lived longer (the average age of Christ Church Canterbury monks when they died was 51), as did nobles and landowners – provided they escaped hunting accidents and the hazards of war. Henry III, Edward I and Edward III all survived well into their sixties, like about a fifth of their subjects.

Above *Caernavon was home and garden as well as fortress. Eleanor built a garden there, and its military importance was softened by its use as a royal family residence. Nonetheless life was precarious even for the king's children, and their record of early deaths may have been partly caused by continual travelling and frequent exposure to new infections and diseases.*

Below *Death was such a familiar figure to medieval illustrators that these details from an extraordinary calendar of death is perhaps not so surprising.*

Children die (below left); a mother and her newborn child die (below), and (far below), cattle 'give up the ghost' and die.

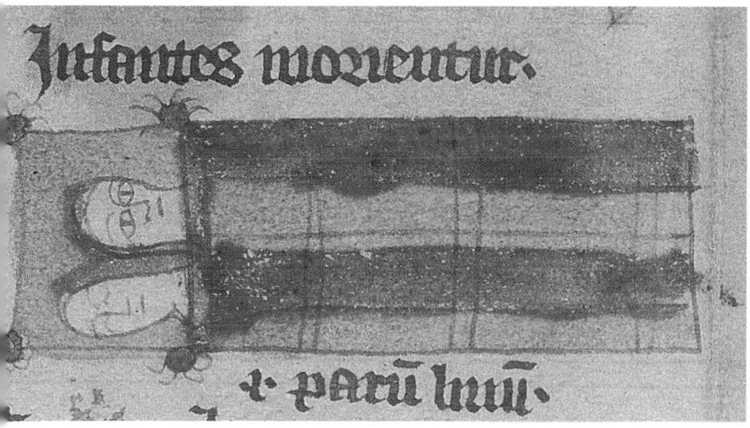

On that same day the king held a parliament at Westminster which lasted for seven weeks. In this parliament he instituted many new laws and knighted many of the sons of nobles. He also confirmed many of the charters of his ancestors, the kings of England.

In the same year, at Winchester, Edward issued new statutes against thieves, brigands, receivers and concealers of malefactors, and also concerning the keeping of watches throughout the whole countryside, townships and villages, and the cutting away of woods in the vicinity of the king's highway. He also forbade henceforth the holding of pleas on Sundays, and the holding of markets and fairs in the burial grounds of churches.

1287

On Sunday 21 December, a great tempest arose in the middle of the night. On the following Wednesday there was a great inundation of the land by the sea.

In the course of this flood and this great storm, two hundred men were drowned in Horsey, Waxham, Martham, Hickling and other neighbouring villages.

In the town of Yarmouth a hundred men were drowned, while in Great Yarmouth sixty feet of the stone wall of the cemetery collapsed under pressure of the sea flood. The wall of the priory was flattened to the ground and the river rose so high that it reached the high altar of the church.

In the same year at full moon, the moon appeared to be yellow, red and also various other colours; also at the same time, two suns were visible.

1289

At this time Thomas of Wayland, the Chief Justice of the Common Pleas in the royal court, was arrested by order of the king on account of the terrible crimes and murders which had been perpetrated by his men. He escaped from custody, however, and took refuge with the Franciscans at

Brides of Christ

'DO not wear a haircloth or hedgehog skins, and do not beat yourselves with these things, or with a scourge of leather thongs. Do not cause yourselves to bleed with holly or briars without the leave of your confessor, and do not at any one time flagellate yourselves too much. When you have let blood do nothing that is irksome for three days, but talk with other maidens and divert yourselves together with instructive tales. Because no man sees you, and you do not see any man, be content with your clothese whether they be black or white: only see that they are plain, warm and well made. Beware of pride, ambition, presumption, envy, sloth, wrath, of hyprocrisy, of a gloomy countenance, of sitting too long at the parlour window, of scornful laughter, of dropping crumbs, of spilling ale, of letting things grow mouldy, rotten or rusty. Keep no animals, my sisters, except a cat.'

These instructions for female hermits come from the anonymous *Ancren Riwle*, written in the early 13th century, but popular throughout the later Middle Ages. Their blending of spiritual and practical advice was characteristic of what the religious life had to offer to women at this time.

Right ***Mass in a convent. The abbess holds the crozier. Another nun, with a large bunch of keys at her wrist, is the cellarer.***

Below ***Franciscan nuns, called 'Poor Clares' after their foundress, at table, while a nun reads to them.***

The age of profession to the nun's vows was 16, but it was considered normal practice, particularly in aristocractic circles, for girls to enter convents when they were still children. Edward I's daughter, Mary, was only seven years old when she was sent to Amesbury Priory, in Wiltshire, to become a Benedictine nun.

Between 1216 and 1350, orders of nuns reached a peak of popularity and prosperity in England, with about 256 convents, containing about 3,300 nuns and their sister orders of canonesses – compared with about 14,000 monks, canons and friars. Most nunneries were small priories; of the 19 great abbeys, most were Benedictine and most were south of the Thames. Their inhabitants were a mixture of saintly, spiritual women who had joined because of their vocations, and those, such as widows seeking a suitable retirement home, whose motives were more practical.

Charges of immorality in nunneries were relatively rare, but sometimes dramatic. In 1351 the poor but aristocratic priory of Cannington, Somerset, was visited by commissioners of the bishop of Bath and Wells, who described it as little better than a brothel. Two of the nuns, Maud Pelham and Alice Northlode, were accustomed to hold long, suspicious meetings with two chaplains who were supposed to be ministering to their spiritual needs.

A third nun, Joan Trimlet, 'was found with child, but not by the Holy Ghost.'

The world intruded occasionally on even the most strictly cloistered nuns, sometimes violently. In 1304 the canonesses of Goring priory, Oxfordshire, were disturbed when some men-at-arms rode their horses into the church, defiling it with hoofprints and dung. The men were in search of Isabella of Kent, a married woman staying in the convent, whom they pursued to the top of the belfry and then dragged away.

Babwell near Bury St Edmunds. Here he assumed the habit of the friars, asserting that he had been a subdeacon before his first marriage. The king ordered that the place be guarded, and he appointed the knight Robert Malet as warder. Malet allowed no one to converse with Thomas, nor to bring him anything in the way of food. So Thomas lived on vegetables and herbs in the manner of beasts.

1290

The king held his Christmas court [at the end of 1289] in London. He was attended there by earls, barons and by nearly all the magnates of England, and he held his parliament beginning on 14 January.

On Friday 20 January, Thomas of Wayland, dressed in secular clothing, having abandoned the habit of the Franciscan friars, came to parliament. On Sunday 22 January he was placed under strict guard in the Tower of London. Other justices were also imprisoned with him, because they had given false judgements and had falsified the records of the royal courts. All these justices were fined by the king: so peace was restored between them, but he removed them from his service, and Thomas of Wayland went into exile abroad.

That year, autumn began so late, because the crops were behind, that on 10 August, scarcely any type of crop was ready for reaping.

At this time an edict went out from the king throughout England that after 1 November, no Jews should remain in the land upon pain of death, and that if any Jew were to be found there subsequently, he should be beheaded.

Many of them, crossing overseas, were drowned together with their books, through the guile and trickery of the sailors [of the Cinque Ports]. These sailors also practised piracy, and they kept for themselves any gold or silver, or anything else in the way of treasure which their passengers had with them. For this slaughter, many of the sailors were arrested and imprisoned by the king, and suffered the death penalty which they so richly deserved.

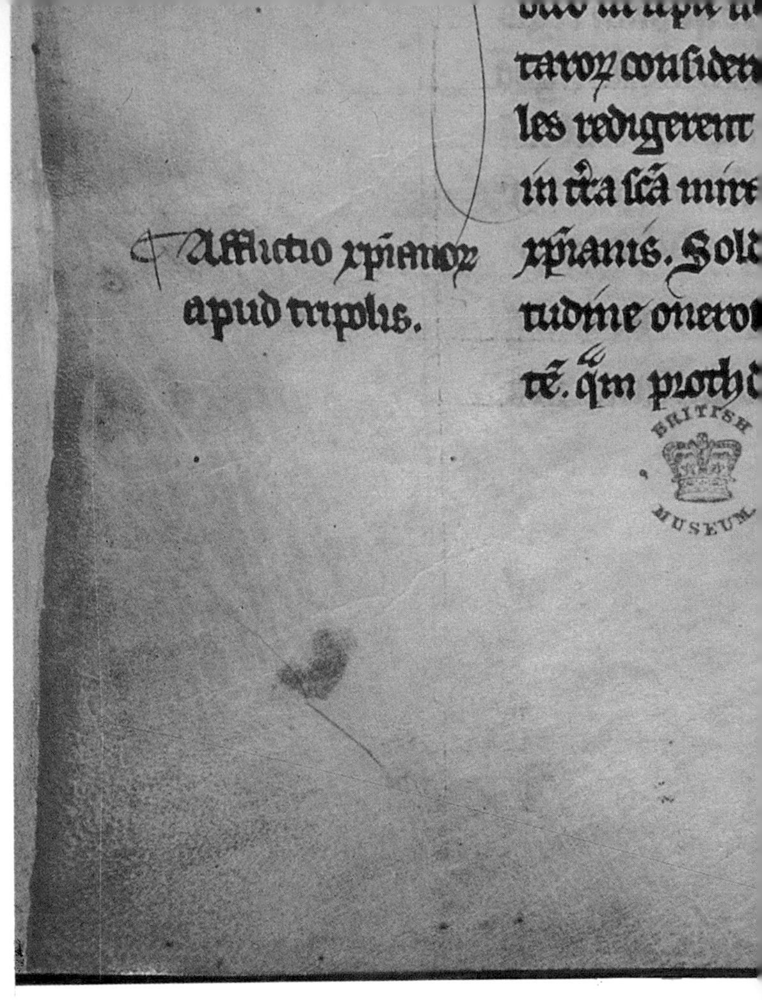

The exchequer of the Jews

'NO Jew shall remain in England, unless he perform the service of the King: and immediately any Jew shall be born, he shall serve Us in some manner.' So declared Henry III in 1253, defining the sole function – in government eyes – of 13th-century English Jews: to provide the king with cash, in the form of taxes and compulsory gifts or 'tallages'. It was tacitly understood that they would meet his needs from the proceeds of lending money to his subjects at interest. Although usury was strictly forbidden to Christians by the laws of Church and state, Christian monarchs did not scruple to profit from it at second hand; a department of government, 'the exchequer of the Jews', existed to keep careful record of their transactions, so that the king knew exactly how much he could extort from them.

The Jews were not merely the king's financial agents. They were also literally his physical property, prized for their business expertise and treated rather like valuable milch-cows. They could be lent, given or mortgaged to royal favourites for exploitation. At the beginning of the 13th century, nearly a seventh of the king's income was provided by the heavy taxes levied on the Jews from the cradle to the grave – and beyond: the Crown was entitled to confiscate a dead Jew's entire property, on the hypocritical grounds that it had been acquired by 'sinful

Above Jews were compelled to wear two strips of yellow cloth, six inches long and three inches wide – a precursor of Hitler's yellow star of David.

activities'. In practice, the heir was allowed sufficient funds to continue in business, and so to keep cash flowing into the royal coffers. For the same purpose, Jews were 'privileged' to pursue their debts through the royal law courts. Equally important, 'the king's Jews' could expect royal protection against attacks by Christians.

Because they enabled the king to raise money without consulting his subjects, the Jews were particularly disliked by baronial opponents of the Crown. Moreover, in the increasingly paranoid religious atmosphere of the 13th century, they were attacked as 'enemies of Christ' and subjected to a host of anti-Semitic regulations. Forced to wear a distinguishing 'badge of shame', they were forbidden to eat with Christians, employ Christian servants or enter churches. At Easter, when anti-Jewish fervour was at its height, they were prohibited from leaving their homes.

The Church did not hesitate to exploit the darker strain of anti-Semitism apparent in periodic 'discoveries' that Jews had ritually murdered Christian children: the fires of prejudice were kept aglow at the shrines of St William of Norwich and Little St Hugh of Lincoln, both allegedly infant victims of Jewish conspiracies.

The downfall of 'the king's Jews' was brought about by the king himself, rather than his subjects' prejudice, and resulted from royal policies which destroyed their livelihood while exploiting them without mercy. In 1269, already impoverished by grossly excessive taxation, they were relegated to the status of pawnbrokers, able to accept only movable personal property and not land as security for loans. Then, at the beginning of Edward I's reign in 1275, they were forbidden to lend money at interest; and at the same time effectively prevented from becoming merchants. Jews who traded illegally in silver from 'clipped' coins were brutally punished; nearly 300 were hanged in 1279. Yet they continued to be heavily taxed, until it became clear they could pay no more.

On 18 July 1290 – the fast of the ninth of Ab in the Jewish calendar, and the anniversary of the Roman destruction of Jerusalem – Edward decreed that all Jews be expelled from England. He seized the property they left behind, and took over the debts still due to them. The expulsion was carried out with comparative humanity and outgoing Jews were assiduously protected from attack: seamen who abandoned a cargo of refugees to drown on a sandbank were themselves taken and executed.

The first wholesale banishment of the Jews during the medieval period, Edward's action was a portent for the future. His example was followed by France in 1306, and, with savage thoroughness, by Spain during the 1490s.

When these events had taken place and the kingdom of Scotland had been placed in the king of England's power, Edward I installed his own garrisons in the castles and towns, and returned south, appointing as the date for his return the feast of All Saints the following year.

1292

When King Edward I returned north, to Berwick upon Tweed on 1 November, he ordained that fifty distinguished Scotsmen who were experts in the law should be appointed as arbiters. These men were appointed, and the king added to their number thirty Englishmen whom he had chosen. He made them swear to consider the claims of all the candidates and to bring the business of the Scottish succession to a satisfactory conclusion.

They awarded the right to succeed to the Scottish throne to John Balliol, since he claimed it by descent from the eldest daughter [of David, earl of Huntingdon].

The king of England approved this decision, and handed over to John Balliol the kingdom of Scotland with complete power, saving the homage and fealty due to him.

On 30 November, the feast of St Andrew, John Balliol was made king of Scotland in the usual Scottish manner.

At the monastery of Scone there was a huge stone set in the church near the high altar, hollow and shaped in the form of a round seat: it was the custom for future kings to be placed on it, as it were, in the manner of a coronation.

The task of enthroning the new king of Scotland in this manner belonged by hereditary right to the earl of Fife. The king had to swear that he would rule justly, defend the holy mother Church and his subjects, and would make good laws and maintain those already in force until his death. When the new king was thus placed on the stone of Scone, a solemn Mass was celebrated, and the king remained seated on the stone except during the elevation of the Host.

Bruce or Balliol?

IN 1290, the eight-year-old Margaret, queen of Scots, fell ill on her way from Norway to Scotland, and died. The throne of Scotland was open to whoever could successfully prosecute a claim to it.

There were 13 claimants in the 'Great Cause', all of whom agreed to submit to Edward I's judgement: the king of England had a reputation as a legalist – and the power and influence to make a decision stick. Two Anglo-Scottish barons emerged as the main contenders: John Balliol, who appealed to feudal law, and claimed direct descent through the female line; and Robert Bruce, who argued from 'imperial' law that he, as the next surviving male descendant of David I, should succeed.

After lengthy pleadings and consultations with lawyers, Scottish barons and churchmen, Edward pronounced in favour of Balliol, who, as King John, swore fealty. However, he was soon caught between the demands of Edward I and a growing mood of national resentment. His hand forced by his principal counsellors, John defied Edward.

Edward I invaded, forced John to abdicate in 1296, and proceeded to rule the country directly. Many of the Scottish leaders, backed by the 'community of the realm', did not acknowledge the abdication and Scotland's government was continued independently in King John's name. The resistance was successful at first, but eight years later, in 1304, Edward suppressed the last vestiges of the popular rising. Its charismatic leader, William Wallace, was hunted down with single-minded vindictiveness, captured, and taken to London. He was given a show-trial, and executed with full contemporary barbarity.

Most Scottish barons had made their peace with Edward by this time. Robert Bruce, earl of Carrick, the grandson of the 1290 claimant, was one of them; he submitted to the king of England in the hope that his claim might be reviewed. But his adherence was short-lived. Scotland was no longer an independent kingdom, but a subject land under Edward's firm and direct rule, and, to overthrow the English yoke, Bruce decided to prosecute his own claim to the throne. The support of John Comyn, head of a family with a long tradition of opposition to England, was essential to Bruce's plans, and the two men met in Greyfriars Church, Dumfries, in February 1306. However, to Comyn, as to many Scots, John Balliol was still the lawful king, and Bruce failed to win him over. Bruce and his supporters murdered Comyn, and mobilized support with a rapidity which suggests advance planning. On 25 March 1306 Bruce was crowned king in the abbey church at Scone.

Although King Robert was excommunicated for murdering Comyn, he had the robust backing of the Scottish Church, whose long fight for independence from the see of York had given ecclesiastics a head start in developing patriotic fervour. Throughout the long-running wars of independence, Scottish churchmen were in the forefront of the struggle, whether framing eloquent propaganda documents such as the Declaration of Arbroath, or simply swinging a ceremonial mace.

At this stage, however, there was no support for Bruce from the wider 'community of the realm' (or, at least, from the barons who mattered). The new king was soundly defeated by the English forces, and his family and friends were nearly exterminated. Robert himself went into hiding; and at the end of 1306, it looked as though his rising, like the one led by Wallace, had also been suppressed.

Robert's remarkable recovery is the stuff of fairy-tales rather than of history. In early 1307, he returned to his family power-base in Galloway, and began rallying support. This time, his campaign against the English was waged with the guerilla tactics at which he was to prove unsurpassed. When, in July 1307, Edward I died in pursuit of the Scottish king, the tide turned in Robert's favour.

Below ***Drawings of John Balliol (left) and Robert Bruce (right), each grasping the flag of Scotland. A domestic instance of family support is the coat of arms embroidered on each wife's dress.***

On 26 December, John Balliol, king of Scotland, paid homage to Edward I, king of England, at Newcastle upon Tyne. The king of England handed over to John all his rights, whole and unharmed, together with all the castles that belonged to him, and then returned to the south.

Edward I and his subjects now faced problems with the French, as Bartholomew Cotton relates.

1293

Sailors from the kingdom of England gathered together in great numbers in order to do battle with the sailors from Normandy. Their aim was to protect themselves from the Normans so that they might be able to sail without fear on business and commerce.

On 13 June the Normans in great arrogance, with many soldiers and one hundred and eighty ships, were able to draw near to the English ships since the wind was in their favour.

But with a change in the wind, the mariners from England and Bayonne struck back; and although they were very few to fight against such a great multitude, by means of great valour and as if by some miracle, the English defeated the Normans, burning some of their ships, and sinking or capturing others.

1294

This year the king of England gave back all his lands in Gascony and other regions to Philip IV, the king of France [since 1285], but before he did so, Philip promised faithfully and by oath taken in the presence of many of the nobles of France, in particular the duke of Burgundy and the archbishop of Reims, that after forty days he would restore all these lands into the possession of the king of England without retaining any.

There was even some preliminary discussion concerning a proposal that the king of England should marry Blanche, the sister of the king of France, and that he should receive back the said lands as her marriage portion.

A day was fixed in the fortnight after Easter for the king of England and the king of France to meet at Amiens and settle their disagreements, and for the king of England and Blanche to contract their marriage. It was also promised that the king of England should have safe conduct on his journey there.

Before Easter, however, it was reported to Edward I that Blanche, the sister of the king of France, would not have him as a husband. Edward would have been tricked if he had gone to the meeting at Amiens, as was brought clearly to light by subsequent events. For this reason the king of England did not attend the meeting.

In the same year Philip IV, angry because the king of England would not come to Amiens, and because he was therefore not able to put into effect his plot against Edward, returned to Paris.

The parlement then gathered in Paris. The king of France, seeing that he already had the lands of Edward I in his hands, but that all the military strength of the king of England lay outside Gascony and these lands at this time, Philip scorned his oath to restore them to Edward after forty days. Instead he procured a judgement depriving Edward not only of Gascony but of all his French dominions.

He even had it decreed publicly that Edward should be captured because he was an enemy of France and of all the French people.

In June, Edward I held his parliament in London over the course of a few days. There it was granted and provided that the king should go overseas with his army to recover and defend those of his lands which were now in the power of the king of France.

The men of the Cinque Ports and other seamen were empowered to guard the sea and to capture their enemies, including all ships from Sluys and Flanders, and any sailing from Sluys to Gascony. William Leyburn was made admiral of all the men of the Cinque Ports and of all other mariners and seamen within the rule of the king of England.

Philip the Fair

Above *Philip, shown here as larger and higher than his nobles, greatly increased the power and influence of the French throne.*

BERNARD Saisset, bishop of Pamiers, wrote of Philip IV: 'The king of France is like an owl, the most beautiful of birds, but worth nothing. He is the most handsome of men but he stares fixedly in silence. He is neither man nor beast, he is a statue.' By contrast William de Nogaret, the king's leading adviser from 1303 to 1313, portrayed Philip as 'full of grace, charity, piety and mercy, always following truth and justice, never a detraction in his mouth, fervent in the faith, religious in his life, building basilicas and engaging in works of piety'.

Philip was indeed outwardly pious: his donations to the Church outstripped even those of his grandfather Louis IX, in whose memory many of them were made. In 1297 Louis was declared a saint by Pope Boniface VIII and Philip showed great devotion to his cult. But Louis' canonization took effect at the height of Philip's first great dispute with Boniface over clerical taxation – and although much deserved, was conceded by the pope for largely political reasons. In 1301 another dispute broke out which ended only when in 1303 William de Nogaret and his followers sacked the papal palace at Anagni and frightened Boniface to death. Philip was subsequently, in 1314, able to suppress the mighty order of the Templars and take over many of their lands and moneys for himself – virtually unopposed by Pope Clement V.

Philip's unprecedented dealings with the Church scandalized and horrified contemporaries. Although his counsellors have often been blamed, it is probable that the king himself directed events and remained firmly in control throughout, his belief in the power of the French monarchy far outweighing any religious considerations.

Philip was an effective and successful king. Under his rule (1285–1314) France reached its medieval apogee of power and prestige. He became preoccupied with reducing the authority of Edward I of England in Gascony: in 1294 a costly war broke out between them – the Scots allying with Philip – and continued until 1303. Little was resolved by the peace negotiations, but the marriage of Isabella, Philip's daughter, to the future Edward II was arranged. Philip also tried to reduce Guy of Dampierre, count of Flanders, who sided with Edward, to obedience. Philip's army was heavily defeated by the Flemish townsmen in 1302, but later in his reign he managed to take over several Flemish castellanies from Guy's successor, Robert of Béthune.

Philip also extended royal authority in the other great French lordships such as Burgundy; he called great national assemblies to back some of his more dubious actions such as his treatment of the Church; and his administrators brought about major developments in government, finance and law. But his reign ended badly: his attempts to raise ever-greater sums of money produced baronial opposition, and the wives of two of his sons were accused of adulterous liaisons and cast into prison. Despite these setbacks, he is remembered as one of the great rulers of France.

Later in that year, commissioners were sent under letters patent from King Edward I into every county in England, to examine all the treasures deposited in religious houses, hospitals and colleges of whatever order.

Arriving in the counties assigned to them, the commissioners made many knights and two freemen from each hundred swear on the Holy Scriptures that none of them would reveal anything said to them in secret.

Then they sent to each house nominated persons, or at least one individual who would, on the same day at the same hour, place the treasures under their seals in the name of the king.

This was done throughout the whole kingdom on the same day and at the same hour.

1295

In this year, Philip IV, king of France, gathered together those skilled in carpentry, and he had them build many ships and galleys so that he could fight England and her mariners.

In April, King Edward I went to Wales with his army and captured the island of Anglesey. The Welsh allowed him to enter the island with his army without resistance, and afterwards they all came to make peace with him and he received them kindly. Then the king returned to England.

About 1 August, it is said, eighty ships and five galleys from Yarmouth and the adjoining coastal regions set sail for Normandy. There, along a stretch of coastline eight miles long and three miles wide, they burned villages, killed many men, and seized much gold, silver, animals and other things, then returned to England with great joy.

Around the same time, six hundred ships and thirty galleys set sail from France and landed at Dover, where they set to looting and killed ten men. Coming to the priory in Dover, they carried off the church ornaments and many of the goods of the monastery, and killed one aged monk who was lying in the infirmary.

Galleys, keels and cogs

FOURTEENTH-century English chronicles and records mention a great variety of ships – among them galleys, dromonds, keels, snakes, busses, balingers, nefs, hulks and cogs. Although it is not always easy to know exactly what these vessels looked like, it is clear that they fell into two main categories: sailing ships and multi-oared galleys, which could also hoist a sail when necessary. The former were the most numerous in English waters, so galleys were likely to belong to foreigners, very possibly pirates or enemy raiders. French and Genoese galleys, capable of manoeuvring with their oars in flat calms, wrought havoc among the south coast ports from 1337, at the outset of the Hundred Years War. In more peaceful periods, swift Italian galleys brought spices to England from the Mediterranean.

Galleys were essentially Mediterranean craft, and were ill-equipped for the battering of rougher northern seas. The comparatively few English galleys were exclusively warships. They were propelled by up to 140 double-banked oars, and shipyard accounts list expensive 'German boards' and Scots fir, Spanish iron for anchors and fittings, and 50-foot English oaks for main timbers: 24 Norfolk women, each paid 2d. a day, spent a fortnight stitching a galley's unwieldy single sail.

Most English ships, however, served as merchantmen in peacetime and were hired or commandeered by the Crown for war. Single-masted, they looked very much like Viking longships, except for the raised 'castles' at bow and stern. These battlemented and brightly painted platforms, designed to protect archers and crossbowmen, may have been attached only in wartime. However, even peaceful trading was hazardous, and they were probably permanent fixtures. Ships like these were called 'keels' or (echoing their Viking origins) 'snakes', and in the Viking tradition were steered by a large paddle projecting from the right-hand (or 'stearboard') side of the ship, which therefore docked on the left (or 'port') side.

During the early 14th century, keels were gradually superseded by 'cogs', which were probably developed by the German merchants of the Hanseatic League. With their straight, slanting bows and central stern-post rudder, cogs were stronger and more stable than the curved-prowed, paddle-steered vessels they replaced. Their deeper draught gave them greater carrying capacity; high, flattened sides made them more easily defensible against boarders; and loftier castles gave their fighting men a vital height advantage over lesser craft. Cogs were the dominant warships and favourite merchantmen of the 14th century; in 1340 Edward III directed the English naval victory at Sluys from his great 'Cog Thomas'.

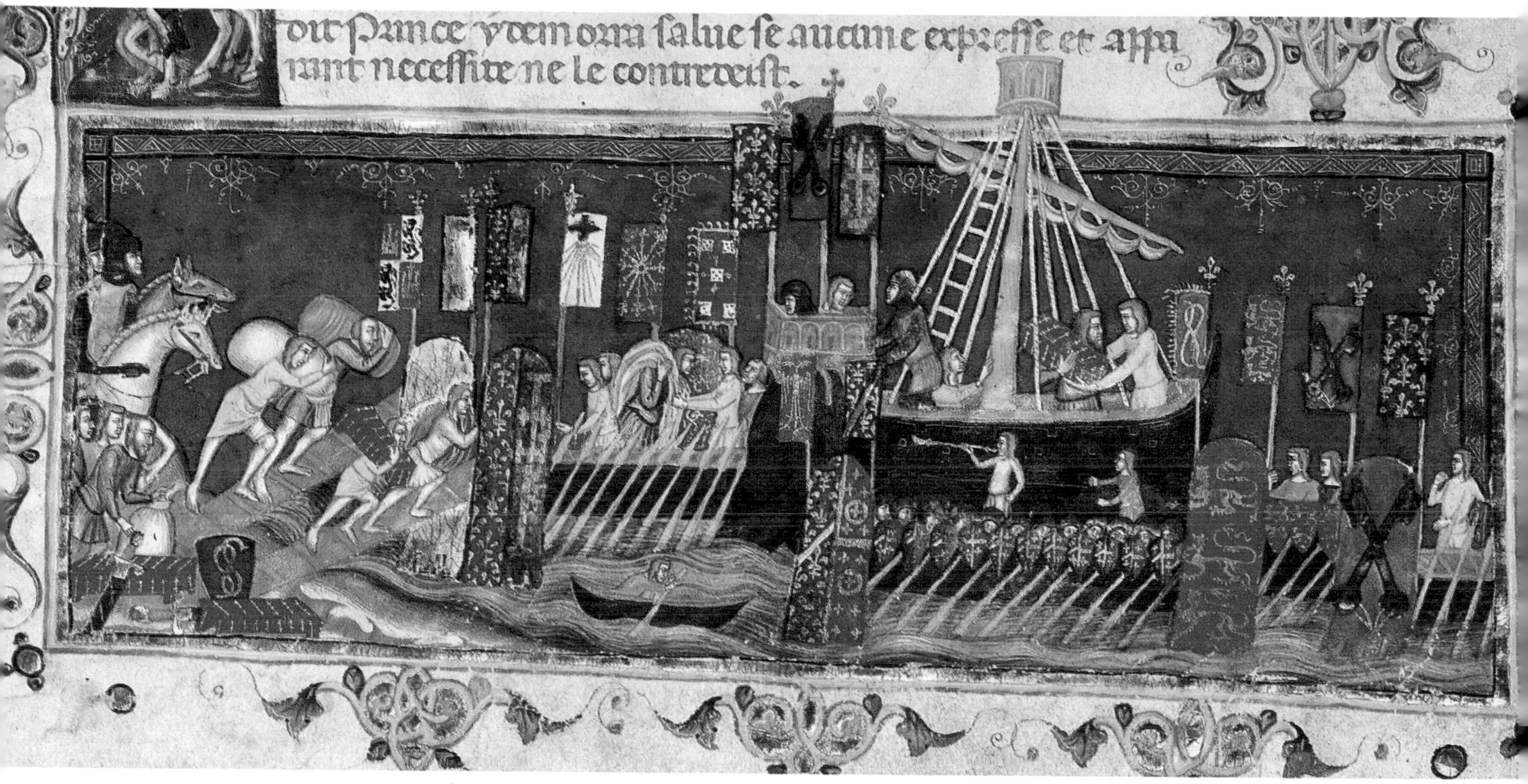

Above *With limited and difficult land transport for bulk goods, ships were vital for sea and river access, and often adapted for specialized cargo.*

Below *Manoeuvering was difficult when ships were loaded down with heavily armoured troops; once battle was joined, it was usually sheer brute force of individuals which won the day.*

When the French sailors wished to return to their ships, people from the neighbouring countryside or from the town killed many of them.

The rest, abandoning what they had seized, returned to their ships in great confusion.

On about 29 August, men from France came to Winchelsea with seven hundred ships and fifty galleys and tried to enter the port. It just so happened that at that time there were in the port eighty ships from Yarmouth and the neighbouring regions. When they saw these, the French, stricken by fear, did not dare to enter the port.

Those from Yarmouth, together with their allies, embarked on their ships and galleys and launched a fierce attack on the French ships, causing them to sail away in retreat. But when they pursued the French over the sea, the French, observing the small size of the English fleet, dropped anchor and waited for them. The English, seeing this, did not dare to proceed but on the following night entered the port of Sandwich.

In the same year, King Edward I ordered by writ that no one was to take duck eggs.

The king sent instructions to all his sheriffs ordering that they should make enquiries concerning all who had land worth forty pounds or more, and to warn such men to be prepared, when they should receive orders from the king, to accompany him on his expedition to Gascony for a period of three weeks.

On Sunday 27 November the prelates, earls and barons, the proctors of the clergy and agents representing religious communities gathered together, and the king asked them for a subsidy to finance the war. At first he met with resistance, but after a few days the laity granted an eleventh part of their goods; the royal towns, boroughs and ancient demesnes of the king conceded a seventh part. The prelates and clergy, however, resisted for many days, despite the threats, weariness and many expenses which they sustained whilst staying in London. At length, giving in, they conceded a tenth part of their goods.

Taxes for axes

DURING the 1290s the general confidence of the first two decades of Edward's reign was replaced by an atmosphere of uncertainty and tension. War with Scotland broke out in 1296, but the king's major problems arose from his efforts to retain Gascony, the last substantial remaining portion of the Plantagenets' continental lands, against the predatory attentions of Philip IV of France.

As duke of Aquitaine, Edward had held Gascony since 1254 – and paid an extended visit there from 1286 to 1289. A war erupted between English and Norman sailors in 1293, during which Edward temporarily handed Gascony over to Philip. The king of France used his position as overlord to confiscate the duchy. In response, Edward sent forces to Gascony and organized a coalition of allies in the Low Countries and Germany, paying them to attack the French from the north.

The fighting in Gascony was inconclusive, and in 1297 Edward mounted an expedition to Flanders to help his allies. The English barons, led by the earls of Norfolk and Hereford, the marshal and constable of England, refused to take part despite royal threats, and the king dismissed them from their offices. He also tried to force all men with an income of £20 a year or over to serve in his army. Unsuccessful in this attempt, he was able to take only a small force, consisting largely of his household knights, to Flanders. By 1297, the strain of paying for the war with Gascony through taxation and other levies had aroused opposition, and not only from the barons.

Up until 1294 the taxes on lay subjects – the subsidies, levied with the assent of parliament – had been collected only occasionally; there were three in the first 20 years of Edward's reign. From 1294 to 1297 there was a new one each year. The clergy had also been heavily taxed, often under protest, during this period and in 1296 their opposition was stiffened when Pope Boniface VIII forbade churchmen to pay taxes to the king. Led by Robert Winchelsea, archbishop of Canterbury, they refused to pay a new levy in 1297, until virtually forced to do so when the king withdrew his protection and impounded their property.

The population at large was severely affected during the war years when the scope of the king's right of prise, which had enabled him to requisition supplies for his household, was extended to supply his entire army. In theory goods were paid for, but in practice official corruption, or lack of ready cash, often meant that no payment was made. Wool merchants, and, indirectly, the wool producers, were suffering from the '*maltote*' – an export tax of 40s. per sack of wool. It had been imposed in

1294 and was still in force in 1297, when the king twice seized wool from the producers without payment to sell for cash. As a result of all these royal exactions, there was widespread anger and discontent throughout the land. The king needed desperately to obtain his people's consent for financing his wars.

The defeat of the English by the Scots at Stirling Bridge, in September 1297, reunited Edward and his subjects and led to an agreement between the opposition led by Norfolk and Hereford and the king's ministers: the 'Confirmation of the Charters', confirming Magna Carta and the Charter of the Forest (which regulated forest laws and customs). In a separate but associated document, the Crown conceded that in future, subsidies and prises would not be taken without agreement, and that the *maltote* would be abolished. Edward agreed to the concessions, and in 1298 sent justices round the country to enquire into administrative malpractices during the period of war – a token of good faith.

Above *Edward was waging war on several fronts and was getting desperate for money. Wool traders were the worst affected by his 'maltote'.*

Walter of Guisborough describes an additional problem which King Edward I faced: the gradual worsening of relations between the English and the Scots.

The Scots, a restless, fickle and unstable people, started a rebellion against the king of England, believing that they might throw off the yoke of servitude.

The king of England sent letters to John Balliol, king of Scotland, asking him to send a proportion of the finest part of his army to fight in Edward's war against France. But the Scots, having entered into a treaty with Philip IV, king of France, raised their horns and prepared for battle. They said that neither their king nor they themselves were in any way bound to the king of England, and that they had no obligation to obey his wishes or commands.

Edward I then invaded Scotland and captured Berwick upon Tweed. Earl Warenne inflicted a severe defeat on the Scots at Dunbar.

1296

The initiative and morale of the Scots were weakened by the English victory at Dunbar.

After several days the king of England went on to the castle at Roxburgh. The steward of Scotland had held it for a long time, but when Edward I arrived he surrendered it at once, on condition of safety in life and limb, lands and chattels. Fifteen thousand Welshmen joined the king there, and he quickly sent back to England about the same number of worn-out English soldiers.

After strengthening the castle at Roxburgh, Edward I set out with his whole army towards the castle of the maidens, which in English is called Edinburgh. He besieged it for eight days and assaulted it heavily by using wooden siege-engines which he had brought there in large numbers. The garrison surrendered and were granted their lives. The king of England then went on to Stirling and found the castle there empty with no one to resist him, for the garrison had fled in fear.

Afterwards, King Edward I set out towards Perth, where, on 24 June, he created new knights amid great solemnity.

He stayed there for several days, and messengers came to him there on behalf of the king of Scotland asking for peace, a thing from which only recently King John had shrunk.

After various negotiations and discussions, peace was made on the following terms: the king of Scotland was to resign his kingdom, and he and his nobles were to surrender themselves to the will of the king of England with no limiting conditions.

The Scots carried this out, and surrendered themselves to the king of England's will. King John himself gave his son, Edward Balliol, as a hostage, and renounced the kingdom of Scotland.

Edward I returned to Berwick upon Tweed by way of Scone, and gave orders that the stone, on which the kings of Scotland used to be enthroned as their equivalent of coronation; should be removed and transported to London, as a sign that the kingdom had been renounced and conquered. Edward held parliament for many days at Berwick upon Tweed, where the nobles of Scotland and Galloway came to him, and he accepted their homage and allegiance.

1297

During that year, the treacherous Scots started a rebellion as follows.

Earl Warenne, to whom the king had entrusted the care and protection of the whole kingdom of Scotland, as his own deputy, complained about the dreadful climate there, and said he could not remain there without damage to his health. So he went to live in England, albeit in the north, and was only half-hearted in his pursuit of exiled Scots there, which was the source and origin of our troubles thereafter.

Moreover, King Edward I's treasurer in Scotland, Hugh of Cressingham, a pompous, arrogant man, hoarded money and did not build the stone

The Stone of Scone

Above The Stone of Scone, under the throne in Westminster Abbey, is said to have come from Tara in Ireland.

THE ceremony of coronation and anointing emphasized the divine and imperial attributes which made kings different from great lords. Yet no king of Scotland was crowned and anointed until 1331; the coveted honour could be bestowed only by the papacy, which preferred not to antagonize the kings of England.

Instead, largely pre-Christian rites were emphasized at the inauguration of a king of Scotland. At Scone, a sacred spot from early times, an ancient ceremony of enthronement and investiture, the swearing of fealty, and the recitation of the king's genealogy, was held.

Alexander III's inauguration in 1249 featured the primitive and patent imagery of fertility: the king was marrying the land, and was enthroned on a stone, on top of a cairn. Some early customs had probably fallen into disuse. In old Irish practice, for instance, a mare might be killed and boiled up, and the king would eat its flesh and bathe in and drink the liquor, in token of his marriage to the earth-goddess.

The inauguration of kings of Scotland took place not in the abbey church of Scone, but on the moot (i.e. meeting) hill outside it, and the 'Stone of Destiny' on which they were enthroned was carried from the church for the occasion.

The stone is said to have been brought from Tara, the seat of the High Kings of Ireland, and was regarded with veneration.

In 1296, Edward I went on a relic-collecting expedition to deprive the Scots of their regalia and spiritual treasures. His men removed what they believed to be the stone, taking it to Westminster Abbey, where it lies under the throne on which English monarchs are crowned. Its return was an issue in Anglo-Scottish negotiations until well into the 14th century. However, in 1329 the papacy had granted the privilege of coronation with all its ceremonial to the Scots, and the stone became less vital to the status of Scottish kingship. But it was – and still is – a matter of national pride.

wall which the king had ordered to be constructed over the new moat at Berwick upon Tweed, which resulted in our defeat.

On the king's orders, his justiciar, William of Ormesby, banished all those who refused to swear fealty to the king.

There was an outlawed brigand, William Wallace, who had been banished by him many times. This man, who was now a fugitive on the loose, gathered together all the Scottish exiles, making himself their leader, and they grew into a considerable force. Indeed, Wallace was strengthened by such an immense following that the whole population looked to him as leader and head. The magnates' entire households were on his side. As for the magnates themselves, although their bodies were present, their hearts were far away.

1297 saw a major emergency in Flanders, the principal market for England's wool exports. Edward I took a costly army across the Channel to help Count Guy of Flanders fight Philip IV of France; but he was only able to hold the king of France to a truce in 1298. The dispute with Philip over Gascony was, moreover, still unresolved.

Now that the king was ready for the crossing to Flanders. He put Earl Warenne in charge of all military forces in the county of Yorkshire from the Trent to Scotland, and ordered him to go with all speed to crush the insolence of the Scots and punish the ringleaders as they deserved.

Thus provoked, the English could not endure this situation any longer, and marched armed towards Stirling.

On 10 September Earl Warenne ordered that everyone should be prepared to cross Stirling bridge the next morning.

Meanwhile, two Dominican friars were sent to the Scottish army, which was hiding with the brigand William Wallace on another part of the mountain above the monastery of Cambuskenneth, to find out whether the Scots were willing to accept the peace which they were being offered.

The brigand replied: 'Give this answer to your people. We have not come in search of peace, but to do battle in order to free ourselves and liberate our kingdom. So let them come up to meet us if they wish, and they will find us prepared against their very beards.'

The English army, cut in two at the bridge, suffered a severe and costly defeat.

In that day's battle the king's treasurer, Hugh of Cressingham, fell, killed by the Scottish spearmen: the man who had in the past slashed so many men with the sword of his tongue in his judgements, was himself slain by the sword of the wicked.

The Scots flayed his body and divided the skin into tiny pieces, not for relics but as an insult.

After this shocking start to the war, the Scots took courage, and English hearts were plunged into confusion. The English soldiers who had remained in Berwick upon Tweed justly feared for their lives and abandoned the place, so that the people had no leader or protector.

When they invaded the town shortly afterwards, the Scots found it as empty as though it had been swept clean. The English kept possession of the castle, however, and fortified it.

Edward I, who was still in Flanders, had now to make certain concessions to his magnates, as Bartholomew Cotton relates.

In the same year on 30 September, the archbishop of Canterbury, Robert Winchelsey, bishops, prelates, clergy, earls, barons, many knights, and proctors of counties and cities assembled in London. After much and varied discussion, Prince Edward, the king's son, and all the king's council conceded that the charter of liberties of the kingdom of England [Magna Carta], together with the Charter of the Forest should be granted and confirmed anew.

[On 9 October] Edward I, king of England, and Philip IV the Fair, king of France, agreed to make a truce.

The strategy that failed

THE attempts of Edward I and his son to gain control over Scotland gave rise to long and savage wars. The outcome turned, to a great extent, on the possession of Scotland's castles and fortified towns. At the outset of the fighting in 1296, Edward's first action was to storm the inadequately defended border town of Berwick upon Tweed, slaughtering the inhabitants almost to a man. Less than six months later, after over-running Scotland, he took care that all the country's fortresses should be 'stuffed with Englishmen'. By garrisoning vital strong-points like Edinburgh and Stirling, he could command the main routes through Scotland, but it soon became clear that this did not give him control over the whole nation. Instead, the English generally occupied the castles while the Scots dominated the countryside between them.

When the Scots temporarily gained the upper hand – as they did under William Wallace in 1297–8 – they were unable to dislodge the invaders from all their fortresses. When they did manage to acquire a castle, they were rarely able to keep it: Edward's military expertise and superior financial resources enabled him to bring all the latest refinements of siegecraft into play.

Neither side was able to achieve final victory until a new Scottish leader, Robert Bruce, emerged in 1306, and with him a new war strategy. Abandoning conventional methods, the Scots tried to starve the enemy out by applying a 'scorched earth' policy, and made all-out efforts to capture the English strongholds. Their weapons were the rope ladder and the cunning ruse – like the daring night escalade of Edinburgh Castle rock in 1314, or the farmer's cart used to jam open the gates of Linlithgow. When the fortresses were taken, they were systematically reduced to rubble, for fear that, as Robert Bruce declared, 'the English afterwards might lord it over our land by holding our castles'.

Above *The empty plain near Berwick (top) bears no apparent scars from the battle in 1296, pictured above. Edward's army slaughtered most of the inhabitants of Berwick.*

This strategy was a success, and by 1318 Bruce had ousted the invaders from Scotland and retaken Berwick. The English, now ruled by Edward II, found the tables turned on them as Scottish raiders penetrated almost to the gates of York, devastating everything in their path. A new type of fortification developed as a result: a simple stone tower in which a border squire and his family could take refuge until the hit-and-run raiders had passed, while his cattle took their chance in the surrounding stockaded 'peel'. Hundreds of these 'peel towers' still stand along both sides of the Anglo-Scottish border – the legacy of the bitter wars which Edward I began, and which were to drag on for nearly three centuries.

At about that time, Edward I had all the wool in the kingdom of England taken, promising that he would pay for it as soon as he was able. This was largely the reason why the magnates rose against the king.

On 10 October, in the presence of Edward the king's son, the earls, barons and magnates, Magna Carta was recited, together with the Charter of the Forest. Because the king remitted all rancour against the earls and barons, the confirmations of the charters were sealed with the great seal of the king on 5 November at Ghent. The charters were then handed over to the custody of Robert Winchelsey, archbishop of Canterbury. Thus a good state of peace was re-established between the king and his earls and magnates, and they then discussed the expedition against the Scots.

Blessed be God in all things. Amen.

The Flowers of History *was composed by an anonymous monk at Westminster Abbey, much of whose information was gleaned at first hand. He records events leading to the end of Edward's reign.*

1298

As King Edward I arrived at Westminster, having returned from Flanders on 29 March, a terrible fire broke out in the smaller hall of the palace. The strong wind whipped up the flames until they touched the roof, and then they devoured the building of the abbey next door.

The king moved up to York, and sent his barons of the exchequer and justices of the bench there, for he was to hold a parliament with the nobles of the land in June. Then he set out again, surrounded by a large troop of earls and knights, because he was anxious to put down the rebellious Scots.

And so, on 22 July, in the fields near Falkirk, they joined in terrible battle. Immediately the Scots fell, routed. About two hundred knights and forty thousand foot-soldiers or more were slain.

The golden fleece

WOOL accounted for half the wealth of England in the 13th century, as it had already done for at least two centuries. The stimulus for the wool trade came from Flanders, whose powerful counts had in the 11th century imposed a long period of peace on the region. With peace came prosperity and a rise in population: food shortages resulted and many Flemings emigrated. Others moved to the burgeoning Flemish cities, where they worked in the region's rising industry, cloth manufacture. There were rival demands for wool from the city-states of northern Italy, and English wool production expanded to meet both markets. As early as 1194 England grazed around six million sheep, and produced up to 50,000 sacks of wool a year. Expansion continued throughout the 13th century, and peaked during Edward I's reign, when London was exporting 14,500 sacks a year.

The fleeces were produced by two breeds of sheep: smaller upland animals yielded a short, curly wool suitable for making high-class cloth, while the long, lank wool of lowland sheep was used for worsted and serge. The wolds and uplands of England were therefore valuable land: by 1203 the monasteries of Margam and Llantarnam in south Wales were meticulous in their division of the pasturage rights in the Glamorgan and Gwent uplands. Both abbeys were Cistercian houses. This order had established itself in wastelands, away from the wealth and temptation of the world, but by the 13th century these very wastes were sources of wealth.

Cistercian houses accounted for 66 out of the 185 wool-producing monasteries listed in the 1290s by an

Italian merchant, Francesco Balducci Pegolotti. Fountains, in Yorkshire, produced the most sacks: 74. The Welsh Cistercian abbeys of Tintern and Dore sold their wool for the best price: £18.13s.4d. a sack.

The monks tended their flocks with the utmost care. Sheep were washed and clipped, treated with salves made of tar and grease, and housed in clean, dry folds. Flocks infested with diseases like the 'murrain', 'rot' and 'scab', all of which decimated the sheep population in 1250, were isolated. After shearing (which was women's work), the wool was delivered to contractors to be carded, baled and packed before being carted to the ports.

The aristocracy was not slow to exploit this lucrative trade and barons invested heavily in their flocks. The duchy of Lancaster controlled three great sheep 'ranches': two in Yorkshire, administered from the duchy's offices at Pontefract and Pickering, and another in Derbyshire's Peak District.

The king's efforts to milk some of the profits of the wool trade angered his noblemen and was politically dangerous. In the 1270s Edward I had established a regular export duty – 'the Great Custom' – of 7s.6d. on a sack of wool. Between 1294 and 1297, when he tried to raise it to 40s. on every sack exported, to help finance his war with France, England was brought to the brink of civil war.

There were two reasons for this reaction. People feared that the king intended the new duty – known as the 'maltote' (unjust tax) – to be permanent, and that the export duty would be passed on to the producers by the exporters, who would recover their profits by offering them lower prices. The king had to back down, but his successors, particularly Edward III, continued to levy 'maltotes' until bought off by parliament in 1350.

Royal interference on such a scale was the death of the Flemish trade. It forced prices up and drove the Flemish cloth manufacturers out of business. In the end the industry moved to Brabant and Holland. English entrepreneurs realized that the low price of wool in the home market meant that cloth could be made much more cheaply in England than abroad, and that the prices of foreign manufacturers could be undercut. The result was the decline of the wool trade, but the rise of the English cloth industry.

Above left *The art of weaving was essential to any household: woollen cloth was needed by everyone and for every purpose from coarse, thick blankets which were used under saddles to sheer woollen gauze for royal dresses and nightgowns. Carding, spinning and weaving were domestic skills before weaving became a professional occupation. Many delightful illustrations indicate that these activities were lightened by the pleasures of companionship; most show groups of women working together. With the change in taxation, women became part of the trading chain, making cloth for sale; weaving declined as an aristocratic household chore.*

Right *Bales of wool were shipped from inland pastures to towns and cities where merchants paid well for the best quality. Wool cloth became a staple product, more important, perhaps, than any other single commodity. The benefits the wool trade brought to many communities can still be seen in the richly endowed churches of East Anglia.*

On 28 June, the peace agreement between the kings of England and France, which had not yet been completely settled, was finalised by Pope Boniface VIII in Rome.

In the same year, at the supplication of Philip IV, king of France, Pope Boniface canonised the king's grandfather, Louis IX, on account of his resplendent miracles and outstanding merits. On 31 August, St Louis's relics were translated at Saint-Denis amid great festivity.

On 30 November there were earth tremors at Rome which lasted for three days. Shortly afterwards, in England, there was one at dusk. A comet appeared in the north, giving out fiery beams to the east each evening after sunset for three days.

1299

Margaret, sister of Philip the Fair, king of France, set sail for Dover on 8 September and, with the pope's blessing, married Edward I, king of England, two days later at Canterbury.

The king celebrated Christmas at Westminster. He realized at that time that England was much corrupted by counterfeit coins called crokards and pollards. On 26 December, King Edward I declared that they were all to be destroyed forever. At this, the son of a mason, thinking of his father's work, wrote the rhyme:

'By you, our sterling is honourably maintained
Crokar put to flight and copper left unstained.'

1300

In January, King Philip IV of France invaded Flanders. Very strongly prepared, he occupied towns and villages and pursued Count Guy of Flanders and his sons with all determination. Count Guy was an old man, unfit for war, and he fled to Ghent, hoping that the town would prove impregnable. When his people, who were sometimes loyal to the king of England, and sometimes to their own count, saw what had happened, they abandoned their natural lord and pitifully surrendered to their principal enemy, the king of France.

Crockards and pollards

THE kings of England had controlled the manufacture and use of coins – silver pennies called sterling – since Anglo-Saxon times, and therefore had the power to strengthen the silver content or, occasionally, debase it to make a larger number of coins and thus a quick profit for themselves. Between these recoinages, the stock deteriorated: it became worn and the edges were clipped. The latter was a serious offence for which a number of people were hanged in 1278.

The last recoinage before Edward I came to the throne had been in 1247, 25 years earlier, and the stock was in poor condition at the start of his reign. Between 1279 and 1281 about half a million pounds' worth of pennies were called in and reminted, mostly at the mints in London and Canterbury. New coins were introduced: the groat (worth 4d.), the halfpenny and the farthing. The Crown benefited financially, but not by debasing the coinage; instead it made a standard charge to cover costs plus a further levy of silver as a 'profit of lordship'. As a result of this recoinage, nearly £20,000 borrowed from Italian merchants to finance the Welsh war of 1277 was repaid.

Because English money was of good quality, it became profitable to bring slightly inferior foreign coin into England and to pass it off as English money: similar in general appearance to the English penny, it might easily be accepted by mistake. By 1284, it was necessary to issue a statute forbidding the use of coins other than sterling. The same statute also listed foreign coins that could easily be mistaken for English currency, and it helped to stem the inflow of foreign silver.

In 1294, the French debased their currency in order to pay for their war with England. Edward's subsidies to his allies in the Low Countries meant that large amounts of silver coin left England. The quality of what remained was low and prices rose as a result. 'Crockards' and 'pollards', minted in the Low Countries, circulated widely in England after the army's return from Flanders in 1298. Although they looked like English pennies, they were of lower purity, and threatened to undermine the economy.

'Crockard' comes from the Anglo-Saxon 'croket', a circlet worn by dukes and counts which was depicted on the coins of these rulers in the Low Countries. On a 'pollard', an imitation coin issued by lords, counts and even bishops and abbots, the head on the obverse of the coin was bare ('poll', old English for head).

In 1299 the government forbade the export of English coins and plate and prohibited the use of foreign coins for commercial transactions in England. It devalued crockards and pollards and then, between 1300 and 1302, called them in and reminted the silver. The quality of the

English coinage was restored and the government made a profit of nearly £11,000. Reminting of foreign silver continued until Edward's death in 1307, as the wool trade brought continental silver into England, and the amount of money in circulation increased as a result.

Above *English silver penny and impostors: the crockard, the pollard and an imitation sterling. Control of currency was a major problem, particularly as war demanded the movements of large sums of money to the continent. A penny would buy over 8 loaves of bread or half a chicken; the average daily wage for a labourer was ¼d.*

Below *A groat, farthing and a halfpenny. The groat was valued at 4d. and the farthing ¼d.*

In that year, King Edward I of England wintered in Scotland. Pope Boniface VIII sent messages to him through the archbishop of Canterbury that he was not to disturb the peace of the Scots, who were commended to papal protection. When King Edward I heard this, he returned to England.

1301

In January, the nobles were summoned to a parliament at Lincoln, where the barons complained of the robberies and other injuries done on all sides by the king's servants.

At last the renewals of Magna Carta and the Charter of the Forest were issued: the king put his seal to them and they were carried to every county of England.

In the same parliament, the king bestowed the principality of Wales and the earldom of Chester on his son Edward.

It was the first time that the king's eldest son had received the title of Prince of Wales.

Then the king and the magnates, acting as one, composed a fine letter to Pope Boniface VIII, sealed with a hundred seals, beseeching him to protect the right that the English had always enjoyed in the kingdom of Scotland, and to disregard the false claims of the Scots.

A dispute broke out between Philip IV, king of France, and Pope Boniface VIII, each of whom was sure of his own powers. For the pope told the envoy of the king of France: 'We have power of both kinds [spiritual and secular].'

The other replied on behalf of his master: 'Indeed, my lord, but yours is in words and ours real.'

Immediately Pope Boniface VIII's wrath was kindled and he swore that he would move heaven and earth against the king of France.

It was the king of France who came off best: his followers later sacked the papal palace at Anagni.

From Rome to Avignon

THE death of Pope Nicholas IV in 1292 was followed by an election conclave held at Rome and then Perugia which lasted an astonishing 27 months. The cardinals who supported the candidate of the powerful Roman Colonna family battled with those who favoured the interests of the masterful Charles II, king of Naples, and of the king of France, Philip IV, his second cousin. Neither faction gained the upper hand. In 1268–71, when a conclave had been similarly undecided, the cardinals had been locked in the papal palace at Viterbo by the citizens and threatened with starvation: in 1294, however, such measures were avoided by the choice of a compromise candidate, the renowned but eccentric octogenarian hermit Pietro Morrone.

Famed as a healer, ascetic, and organizer of monks, Pietro was living in a secluded grotto on Mount Morrone in the kingdom of Naples, and accepted the papal office with extreme reluctance. As Pope Celestine V his acts were naïve, confused and highly favourable to King Charles II of Naples. Elected in July 1294, he abdicated in December – largely on the advice of Cardinal Benedetto Caetani, who was chosen as his successor almost immediately and took the name of Boniface VIII. Celestine longed to return to his mountain retreat, but Boniface, fearing a schism, kept him in captivity. When the old man carried out a daring escape he was recaptured and strictly confined; and when he died in prison in 1296 rumours of foul play by Boniface began to circulate.

Boniface VIII was the antithesis of Celestine: a masterful, impulsive but highly sophisticated administrator whose ambition was to dominate the political life of western Europe. He soon came into conflict with the kings of France and England over papal government, taxation and justice. In 1296 he tried to prevent Philip IV of France from raising money from the Church to finance his military campaigns. Philip, however, forbade the export of any money from France – thus greatly depleting the papal coffers – and Boniface capitulated in 1297. Despite this setback, he staged triumphal celebrations to mark the year 1300.

One of Boniface's most celebrated proclamations was that 'it is necessary for salvation for every human creature to be subject to the Roman pontiff'. This was issued in 1302, at the height of his second great dispute with Philip IV about the extent of papal authority in France. Philip's advisers circulated lurid, obscene and fantastic allegations about the pope: he was a sodomite; he had silver images of himself erected in churches; he had a private demon as a counsellor. In September 1303 Philip IV's adviser William de Nogaret and Sciarra Colonna, at the head of a band of mercenaries, stormed and sacked the papal palace at Anagni. Terrified, Boniface fled to Rome and died shortly afterwards.

Boniface's weak and short-lived successor, Benedict XI (1303–4) was conciliatory towards the king of France, while the former archbishop of Bordeaux, who became Clement V (1305–14), was virtually Philip IV's puppet. Racked by ill-health and terrified of the resurgent Colonna family in Rome, in 1309 Clement settled with the papal court at Avignon, just outside the borders of France. Although his successors planned to return to Italy, the Curia remained at Avignon almost continuously until 1403. The great fortress-like papal palace, started in 1336, still dominates the city.

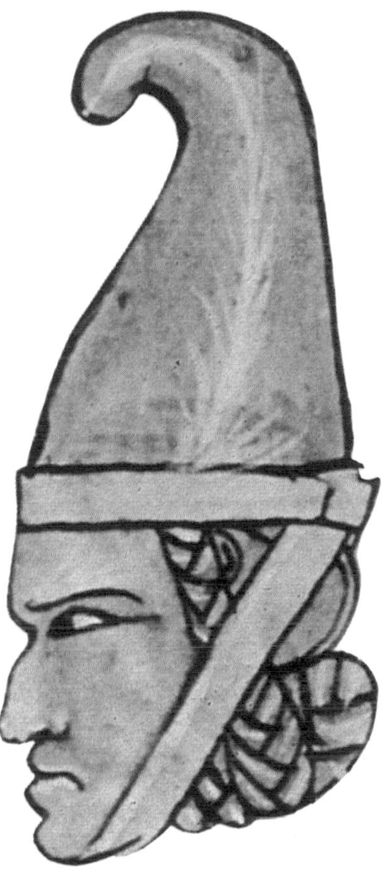

Left *A medieval map of Rome, personified as a grieving widow in the absence of her beloved papal community.*

Above *Boniface's portrait shows a man of dominating authority, ambitious for worldly power, rather than a spiritual healer. Although he reigned as pope for only ten years, his interest in intrigue and political use of the Church's position can be seen as an interesting preview of the attitudes of the Renaissance popes a few centuries later.*

1302

After Christmas had been solemnly observed, King Edward I took advice in secret at Westminster, and sent distinguished messengers to France to intimate to the king of France what conclusions he had reached concerning the truce, war, and peace.

1303

On 31 May, the much longed-for peace between the kingdoms was published, first in France and then in England. Accordingly, Gascony was restored to the king of England with all the rights and liberties that he had enjoyed there [in 1294] before war broke out.

That year, Edward I, king of England, triumphant over the attacks of his enemies, invaded Scotland to punish the insolence of the Scots, who had strayed shamefully from their allegiance to him when they had killed his liege men whom he had sent there to keep the king's peace.

While these events were taking place in Scotland, on 7 September, at the very same time that Pope Boniface was robbed in the city of Anagni in Campania, King Edward's treasury in England was robbed by a single thief.

Pope Boniface VIII died on 12 October, and was buried the next day in St Peter's church in Rome, in a magnificent tomb he had prepared for himself while still alive. The day after he had been buried, the cardinals met and elected the bishop of Ostia, a Dominican friar, who was consecrated pope ten days later, and called Benedict XI.

That year, King Edward I spent the winter in Scotland at Dunfermline Abbey, and miraculously, just as David was when surrounded by the Ziphites, he was neither harmed by the Scots nor betrayed.

1304

In February, the nobles of the kingdom of Scotland, earls and barons alike, submitted themselves and their possessions to the king of England,

Dante, poet of history

CERTAIN events in the lives of most major artists seem to give a new impetus to their intellectual and creative development. For Dante, this occurred in late 1301, when he was exiled from his beloved Florence.

His banishment was directly linked to the defeat of the White Guelfs (the political grouping with which Dante was aligned) by their opponents within the city, the Black Guelfs, who had engineered a seizure of power with the help of the papacy and of the French prince, Charles of Valois, the third son of Philip the Fair of France. The victory of the Blacks, which brought to a close a long period of internal strife in Florence, but which also curtailed its freedom as an independent city-state, was decisive.

Dante was never again to return to his native land. For the next 20 years, until his death in 1321, he was often on the move, finding shelter in a number of cities and courts of northern Italy. There is even a suggestion – quite without substance – that he wandered as far as Oxford.

Dante was born in 1265 into a well-established noble family, and by his early twenties had proved himself a writer of note, developing, together with other young poets, a novel kind of love lyric, the 'sweet new style', which emphasized in a highly refined language the spiritual qualities and internal effects of love. The supreme achievement of this poetic movement was Dante's own *Vita Nuova* (*c.*1294), written in Florence, which, in stylized poetry and prose, recounted the exemplary story of his love for Beatrice. It does not ultimately matter whether Dante's account is based on fact or whether his Beatrice is the Beatrice Portinari of history. Rather, the work is important because it took the European medieval courtly love tradition in radically new directions. Most significantly, it established for the first time how prodigious were Dante's artistic gifts.

Although his exile was a great personal tragedy, it was fundamental in broadening and refining his art and ideology. The result was a complex and all-embracing philosophy of history.

Dante believed that God had organized the flow of history in such a manner as to help humanity achieve salvation after death. Human beings, in their turn, had the duty to ensure that they did not offend against God's will. Sin, which they found so attractive, was an ungrateful attack against this divine process. However, according to Dante, God, in his kindness, had established two universal authorities on earth, each with its own clearly marked sphere of responsibility, to help humanity keep away from sin: the papacy to look after its spiritual needs, and the empire to dispense justice and to maintain peace

between different groups and geo-political entities. In his day, Dante argued that this divine scheme was under particular threat, since popes involved themselves in secular matters and few heeded imperial authority; instead, like Boniface VIII in his conflicts with Philip the Fair, they were driven only by personal greed.

The *Divine Comedy* should be read against this view of history. It purports to be the true account of a journey Dante made in the spring of 1300 through the three regions of the afterlife – Hell, Purgatory and Paradise – after which the poem's three principal parts are named. Dante further claimed that his journey had a precise reason. In the light of contemporary corruption, God had chosen him, like the prophets of old, to act as one of His messengers. By recounting all that he had seen and learned in the afterlife, Dante was to remind humanity of its responsibilities towards the divine, stressing in particular that our condition after death – eternal suffering or glory – was the direct result of our earthly lives. Real people and historical events – and, ultimately, the whole of creation – were considered in relation to what Dante claimed to be God's providential plan of history.

Above *Dante can be recognized in this painting by his crown of laurel leaves and the book of poetry in his hand. He is pictured standing in the centre of his beloved Florence, the Cathedral on the right.* The Divine Comedy *has inspired artists of every nationality who have re-interpreted Dante's vision of Hell and Paradise.*

Although the *Divine Comedy* can be considered a magnificent synthesis of life and ideas in the Middle Ages, its true importance, as with the *Vita Nuova*, lies in its poetry. To depict the whole of reality, Dante invented a flexible and linguistically all-inclusive style which could deal with things as diverse as obscenity and theology and, in doing this, challenged the view that particular topics should be treated in appropriate established styles. The stylistic and thematic breadth of Dante's poem calls into question, and transcends, such artificial boundaries, and the astonishing 'modernity' of his artistic solutions is one of the main reasons why the *Comedy* continues to fascinate.

for they realized that fire, and not peace, was spreading everywhere. In his great mercy, King Edward I admitted them to his grace.

After Edward I, that most fortunate of kings, had passed through certain areas of Scotland, and all the most important nobles of the kingdom of Scotland had been disarmed, even then there remained one mighty castle to reduce, namely Stirling. Once the king had arrived there, he promptly laid siege to this very strong fortress with its high walls, built on a solid rock next to the sea shore.

One day during the siege, something not merely unusual but even miraculous happened to the king of England. While he was riding repeatedly round the castle, unarmed, someone hurled a javelin, called in English a springald, from a sling in a tower. It struck between Edward I's legs, neither touching his flesh, nor even wounding his feet. Immediately, this was held to be a miracle. For not once, but a hundred times, weapons directed at him fell to his right and to his left, never harming him but frequently wounding those around him.

When the siege had lasted ninety days, the besieged saw another engine being raised, this time higher than the castle walls. And since they knew that what was available for their sustenance inside the castle had been used up, they came out of the castle on 20 July, and approached the king of England in the manner of caught thieves, without belts or shoes, ashes on their heads, carrying the cords of traitors around their hands and necks, knowing full well what they deserved. But the king was moved to pity by their groans and lamentations, and 'mercy triumphed over judgement' [cf James 2[13]]. He ordered them to be taken and imprisoned in different castles in England, killing none of them nor condemning them utterly. Thus this great war came to a close.

The king celebrated Christmas at Lincoln, where he refreshed his earls and knights with huge banquets for many days, extolling their virtues thoroughly through his herald. Rewarding them with suitable gifts and commending them for their labours, Edward I sent them home contented.

1305

On 25 March, King Edward I and his magnates assembled at Westminster to give thanks to God and St Edward the Confessor for the king's triumph over the Scots.

Around the same time, an inquiry was proclaimed by writ which was called 'trailbaston' in English. It was designed to deal with those who encroach on the land of others and then, fearing their complaints, dispose of the land or goods to someone more powerful.

Numerous justices were appointed to act upon this writ throughout England. So strictly did this punishment proceed that a father would not spare his own son but chastise him reprovingly. Many went into voluntary exile, so great was their fear; and through flight and fines, the treasury grew richer.

In early August, that Scot, William Wallace, a runaway from righteousness, a robber, a committer of sacrilege, an arsonist and a murderer, more cruel than Herod and more debauched in his insanity than Nero, gathered an army of Scots against the king of England at Falkirk. Seeing that he could not resist so strong an army as that of the English, he said to the Scots, 'See, I have brought you to the ring. Now hop or skip as best you can.' Then he fled from the field, leaving his people to perish by the sword.

In time, this man of Belial was captured by Edward's men after committing innumerable outrages, and was brought to London for trial, for the king wished to judge him in person.

On 23 August, William Wallace was condemned by the nobles of England to die a most cruel, yet fully deserved death. He was dragged through the streets of London attached to horses' tails as far as a very high gibbet built especially for him. He was hanged in a noose, and then cut down when semi-conscious. His genitals were cut off, his entrails gouged out and burnt in a fire. Finally, he was beheaded and his body cut in four. His head was impaled on a stake on London

Bridge and his quartered limbs conveyed to parts of Scotland. See the end of a merciless man, mercilessly punished!

On 15 September, a royal council was convened at the New Temple, attended by bishops, earls and barons, Scottish as well as English. For twenty days they deliberated over the pact to be made with the king of Scotland: how it could be made better, firmer and deeper, from the point of view of the Scots as well as the English, and how perfect peace and most excellent tranquillity could be well established in perpetuity.

By the decree and assent of both sides, justiciars and clerks were deputed to act two by two both north and south of the Forth, to keep the peace in their native regions, decide lawsuits and settle fights. Then the Scottish bishops, abbots, earls and barons swore for themselves and their heirs and for all in Scotland, now and in the future, to abide by the agreement. This was sworn on the Body of Christ, the Gospels and relics, at the manor of Sheen, by the River Thames.

Rejoicing, therefore, in the hope of a firm and lasting pact with Scotland, King Edward I of England dealt mercifully with the Scots, so that those that were to redeem their misdemeanours by payment to the king of the annual value of their lands for set terms of years, were allowed to prolong the time of reckoning, after consideration had been given to their condition and status.

After this, the Scots were given licence to leave, and returned to their own homes swiftly, with due honour.

That year, there was terrible blight and mildew and drought during the summer, with the result that hay was in short supply almost everywhere, farm animals died of hunger, and excessive heat oppressed men, with the sun in both Leo and Libra.

Then the growing and the young, the rich and the poor were laid prostrate by smallpox and pustules and spotted by a freckly scabies. Many young men and women died as a result.

Winter followed suddenly, oppressing the people with its bitter cold. The frost and frozen snow lasted from 15 December to 25 January.

The fish in the pools, the birds in the woods and the beasts in the fields all died. The icy breath of the wind whistled and blew rain for three days on end.

1306

Just when people thought they had escaped the winter, the air gathered up into clouds again, and the harsh east wind blew back the frost, which lasted from 13 February to 13 April.

Soon afterwards, there arose the disturbance of a new war in Scotland. For the earl of Carrick, Robert Bruce, gathered some other nobles at first secretly and then openly, and told them, 'You know how the people wanted to crown my father king [of Scots], but the cunning of the king of England had it otherwise. If you crown me king, I will lead you to war and free this kingdom and its people from the English yoke.'

Guisborough reveals more of Robert Bruce's plans to seize the throne of Scotland.

Robert Bruce greatly feared John Comyn, earl of Badenoch, who was a powerful man in Scotland and loyal to the king of England. Bruce knew that John Comyn might stand in the way of his scheme, so he sent to him as a trick two of his brothers, Thomas and Nigel Bruce, to ask whether Comyn would agree to come to see him at Dumfries to discuss with him matters which affected them both.

Suspecting nothing, John Comyn came to see him, with only a few men. In the cloister of the Franciscan friars they greeted each other with a kiss but it was not the kiss of peace.

Their conversation appeared friendly until Bruce's tone and expression changed, and he reproached Comyn for his treachery in having made accusations against Bruce to the king of England, and of having made Bruce's position more difficult.

When Comyn tried to pacify him and defend himself, Bruce refused to listen. Instead, as he had plotted, he kicked him and struck him with his sword, then departed. Bruce's men pursued Comyn, struck him down in the church on the paved floor in front of the altar, and left him there for dead.

Robert Bruce went outside, and seeing John Comyn's fine warhorse standing there, he mounted it. His men too climbed on to their horses, and they set out towards Dumfries Castle and captured it. When news of what had happened became public, the Scots rushed to meet Robert Bruce.

After this event, some ill-wishers told Bruce that John Comyn was still alive, for the friars had carried him into the vestry to tend his wounds. The tyrant Bruce had him dragged out and killed on the steps of the high altar, so that his blood stained the altar table, and even the altar itself.

Robert Bruce then travelled through Scotland, occupying and fortifying Comyn's castles and devastating his lands, while the dead man's relatives fled from him, and all the English fled to their own country.

On 25 March, Robert Bruce had himself crowned king of Scotland at Scone, in the presence and with the consent of four bishops, five earls and the Scottish people.

The earl of Buchan's wife, who was the daughter of the earl of Fife, and who had the hereditary right to crown the new king, stole away from her husband, taking with her his warhorses, which he had left at home, so that she could perform this duty herself. This act angered her husband, who still remained faithful to the king of England.

In the same year she was caught, and her husband planned to kill her. But King Edward stopped him, and ordered that she should be placed in a wooden cage perched on the walls of Berwick Castle, so that she could be seen and recognized by passers-by. She remained like this for many days, with very little to eat.

In 1306, Edward I, before setting out for Scotland again, knighted a large number of young men in a magnificent ceremony at Westminster. The author of the Flowers of History *was there.*

Before 5 April, the king of England, Edward I, sent Aymer de Valence, earl of Pembroke, to Scotland with a band of armed men to extirpate the crowned man Robert Bruce and his fellow traitors, and to protect the king of England's people.

To increase the numbers that were to set out for Scotland, the king issued a public proclamation that as many as were knights by inheritance, and who had the wherewithal for campaigning, should appear at Westminster on 12 May, where each individual would be equipped, from the royal wardrobe, with every knightly accoutrement except a horse.

So it was that to the three hundred young men who assembled, sons of earls, barons and knights, were distributed purple satin, fine linen and robes sewn with the finest gold.

The royal palace of Westminster, though big, was too small for the great crowd that had gathered, so the apple trees at the New Temple were cut down and walls demolished, and pavilions and tents erected where the young men might adorn themselves with their golden robes.

That night in the Temple church, these esquires, or as many of them as the place would hold, kept vigil. But on the instructions of his father, Edward, prince of Wales, together with certain very noble aspirants to knighthood, kept his vigil in the abbey church at Westminster. So loud were the voices of those shouting for joy, and so great the clamour of trumpets and horns, that the rejoicing of the congregation could not be heard from one side of the choir to the other.

In the palace the next day, King Edward I girded his son with the sword belt of a knight and granted him the dukedom of Aquitaine. And thus Prince Edward was made a knight in the abbey church of Westminster, that he might make his companions resplendent likewise with knightly glory.

Rising living standards

IN England, the 13th century was an age of expansion – in population, wealth and education – and the aristocracy lived in a magnificent style unknown since Roman times. The barn-like halls of the 12th century gave way to mansions with numerous private chambers added to the upper end of the hall, closed to all but the lord, his wife and children: it was considered necessary to keep followers and servants at a distance. Greater and lesser kitchens, butteries, pantries and larders at the lower end of the hall indicated greater sophistication in the culinary arts.

Conditions inside these houses were no longer spartan. Windows were larger than before, and commonly glazed and shuttered. Walls were plastered, and wainscoted in pine or painted: Henry III favoured a colour scheme of green spangled with gold stars. Hangings and murals lent dignity to private chambers. Floors of the lord's dais and chambers were often tiled, and other areas were covered with mats or, more commonly, rushes. Carpets were laid on tables, not on floors. Lead or elm-wood pipes brought water to the kitchen, either from nearby springs or, in the case of a London town house, from conduits (or aqueducts). In castles, the 'garderobe', the predecessor of the water closet, debouched through lead funnels into vaulted pits which were emptied and cleansed by contractors.

Furniture was sparse, partly because most people still travelled extensively, touring their estates or following the court. The bed was the chief item of furniture, with a feather mattress and pillows supported on boards and thongs. Sheets and pillow-slips were made of fine linen, and coverlets of thick wool, or sometimes of fur-lined, heavy silk. Linen hangings kept out draughts and prying eyes. Great chests and coffers held clothes and plate, and benches and 'X' chairs had cushions for sitting on.

The hall's great table was polished, and, with its carpet covering replaced by a fine white cloth, was set with a glittering display of plate: gilded silver cups, ewers and bowls. Lower tables were laid with turned maple-wood bowls and cups.

The wealthy adorned themselves lavishly with rings, gold chains and gems – so much so that there was a private language of precious stones amongst the educated: the jasper was a token for 'faith', the carbuncle for 'suffering', and so on. An annual gift of a set of robes was part of a retainer's wages and great men, like the earls of Chester and Lincoln, employed master-tailors to buy and work the large quantities of cloth their households needed. Silk – from the East and Italy, particularly the city of Lucca – was affordable only by the very wealthy.

In 1297 one of Edward I's daughters gave him a dressing case for Christmas: a leather box containing a comb, a silver-gilt mirror and a silver bodkin. Mirrors were increasingly important in an age which was beginning to appreciate the ritual of the toilette. Glass mirrors, probably from Germany, were small, usually circular, carefully boxed in a carrying case – and expensive rarities. Most people had to be satisfied with polished steel or bronze disks.

Above *The first glass mirrors appeared 1278–81; a marked improvement on the polished metal mirrors in use until then.*

Below *A 14th-century French ivory mirror case.*

There was such a crush of people before the high altar that two knights died, several fainted and at least three had to be taken away and attended to.

Then two swans were brought before King Edward I in pomp and splendour, adorned with golden nets and gilded reeds, the most astounding sight to the onlookers. Having seen them, the king swore by the God of Heaven and by the swans that he wished to set out for Scotland and, whether he lived or died, to avenge the wrong done to the Holy Church, the death of John Comyn and the breach of faith by the Scots.

The oath was pledged by all the other magnates, who asserted with the king that they were ready to journey to Scotland both during his lifetime and after, under his son the prince, to fulfil his vow.

On 30 May, when all had been roused to courage, the young men saluted the king and left Westminster, men who were to appear before the king in Scotland on 8 July.

For the knighting of the king's son, the clergy and people ceded a thirtieth part of their goods to the king, and the merchants a twentieth.

Meanwhile, there began great strife between the English and the Scots to see which of the two was stronger. At last, on 25 June, Robert Bruce, the crowned man of Scotland, and his accomplices, all wearing linen shirts over their armour, joined battle at Methven with Aymer de Valence, earl of Pembroke.

On that day, many of the Scots who had allied themselves with the pseudo king perished by the sword; their names are not reported here lest the page become dirty with them.

Then the king of England arrived in Scotland with his son, the prince of Wales, and the nobles of his nation. Some Scots received him with due honour while others withdrew and many sought hiding places in the woods. The king's army ranged over the whole of Scotland, pursuing and capturing fugitives and killing many.

Kingship and chivalry

DESCRIBED as 'the best jouster in the whole world', Edward I won this reputation during the turbulent years of his youth, in tournaments and on crusade. When he became king he discouraged mock battles which might distract his followers from the serious business of warfare – but turned this perception of him to good political account.

Contemporary enthusiasm for chivalrous codes and practices was given a focus in glittering ceremonies at the royal court, where the cult of chivalry merged with and enhanced the image of monarchy.

King Arthur, a hero of the age, was associated with his Plantagenet successor in a number of well-publicised royal ceremonies. In 1278, at Glastonbury Abbey, the supposed tombs of Arthur and Queen Guinevere were opened in the presence of Edward, his queen and a host of English and foreign dignitaries. The 'royal' bones were disinterred and reburied, with full pomp.

In 1238, when Edward returned from his conquest of Wales, he brought many relics with him including part of the True Cross and, equally important, King Arthur's crown which was said to transfer the glory of the Welsh to the English. The next year, in 1284, the king celebrated the birth of his son, the future Edward II, with a great 'Round Table' at Caernarvon: ceremonies, tournaments, singing, dancing and feasting. It lasted for more than a week and drew its inspiration from the Arthurian legends.

The best-documented chivalrous ceremony of Edward's reign took place in 1306, when he prepared for his last Scottish campaign by knighting some 300 young men, including his son Edward. In part his motives were practical; he needed the fighting men and the money the exercise would produce. Tax raised for the knighting of the king's eldest son was particularly lucrative.

However, the event was also intended to be a great spectacle. The young men, all sons of nobles and knights, were magnificently apparelled at royal expense before keeping an overnight vigil in Westminster Abbey and other churches, after which Prince Edward, himself only just knighted, girded on their swords. These had been blessed as a sign of the sacramental nature of knighthood. Dubbing, however, was the crucial part of the ritual. A blow with the flat of the hand, it could be, and often was, performed in haste on the battlefield.

The climax of the ceremony in 1306 was a magnificent banquet at which roast swans, decorated with golden nets and gilded reeds, formed the centrepiece. These noble birds, much prized as food, belonged exclusively to the king, and Edward swore by them, as well as by God, that he would avenge himself upon the Scots.

Above *Outside of battle, knights won honour and practised their skills by taking part in tournaments.*

Below *A knight is ritually dressed and armed for battle; a servant binds on his spurs, while another adjusts his sword.*

While the king of England's vengeance was being wreaked from day to day upon those wicked people, thus defeated, that pestilential crowned man [Robert Bruce] fled to the mountains, fearful for his own safety.

In Edward I's last year a momentous marriage alliance between Edward prince of Wales and Isabella of France was arranged. The negotiations are described by Guisborough.

1307

In Lent, King Edward held a parliament at Carlisle. Thither, in great state, came Cardinal Peter of Spain, sent by the pope to finalize arrangements for the marriage which the late pope, Boniface VIII, had decreed should take place between Prince Edward, the son of the king of England, and Isabella, daughter of the king of France.

First, however, the cardinal undertook lengthy discussions and consultations concerning a peace settlement with Scotland.

In the end he and the other bishops who were with him donned their vestments and, having lit candles and rung bells, they pronounced most fearful excommunication on Robert Bruce and his adherents, as he was guilty of perjury and wicked disturbance of the common peace.

The next day, in Carlisle cathedral, the cardinal announced, in King Edward's presence and with his authorization, that the king of England, for his part was ready to fulfil all that the good shepherd Pope Boniface had ordained, provided that the king of France was willing likewise to fulfil his part of the arrangement.

The cardinal gave assurances that King Philip IV was well and truly ready so to do.

King Edward said: 'He has not yet restored Gascony to me fully, as the pope ordered. I am still not in possession of the castle of Mauléon, a strong and almost impregnable fortress. Let him return that, and I will do all that is required of me.'

To this, the cardinal replied: 'My lord, the king of France now has that castle in his hands. He has already paid substantial compensation to the knight who was holding it, and is ready to return the place to you in the near future.'

'We wish', said King Edward, 'to give this matter a little thought,' and he gave instructions that the cardinal should stay with him until the envoys whom the cardinal had sent should bring firm news from Philip IV about the castle. The cardinal remained there for two months, receiving courteous treatment.

Details of the marriage were subsequently settled, but Edward's problems were far from over. Robert Bruce came out of hiding and in May defeated an English army at Loudoun Hill in Ayrshire.

When he learned of the evil actions of the new king of Scots, King Edward sent orders to the magnates of the realm to meet him at Carlisle on 8 July, in battle array.

In the meantime, however, the king was so stricken with dysentery that no one, apart from the men of his chamber, was able to speak with him, and rumours spread among the people that the king was dead. Hearing of such tales, the king commanded that everything be made ready for an advance upon Scotland.

On 3 July, which was a Monday, he moved camp from Carlisle, over a distance of two miles. On the Tuesday, he rode another two miles, and on the Wednesday he rested.

On the Thursday, King Edward reached Burgh by Sands, and made arrangements to remain there the next day. It was his customary practice to remain in bed each day until the ninth hour.

On the Friday, when his men went to raise him up so that he might take some food, he breathed his last, there, in their hands.

The king's men concealed his death until his son and the magnates had arrived. Many who spread rumours of his demise were imprisoned.

The common tongue

Above *Earthworks are all that remain of Braybrooke Castle, where Lollards first issued standardized sermons in English.*

IN 1290 Edward I proclaimed that the king of France in his malice wished to eradicate the English language. This implied that the common tongue was a mark of nationhood; but took no account of the variations in the language as spoken from region to region.

At the beginning of the 13th century, the Suffolk congregation of Abbot Samson of Bury St Edmunds could scarcely understand the sermons he delivered in his Norfolk dialect; and, during the late 14th century, southern sailors shipwrecked on the Northumbrian coast were murdered because, when they asked in English for food, they were thought to be Frenchmen.

The 14th-century writer John Trevisa suggested a reason for these problems: because they stemmed from three different Germanic tribes, the English had three manners of speech; subsequent confusion arose from intermingling with Scandinavians and Normans, leading to strange garbling and chattering. Midlanders could understand both northerners and southerners, who were incomprehensible to each other.

In the post-Conquest period, English was the language of common speech, while French was used for administration and for polite and literate conversation. The displacement of Anglo-Saxon, the formalized language of the kings of Wessex, as an instrument of government, allowed regional dialects, never suppressed as spoken tongues, to re-emerge in written form.

The first great text in English, the *Ancren Riwle* (*c.*1220), an instructional manual for anchoresses (female hermits), was written in a West Midlands dialect which was obviously spoken by genteel ladies in the area of Wigmore. There is, however, no indication of a 'class accent' in late-medieval England. Differences in speech were regional rather than social; a northern or West Country lord might normally speak French, but when he did speak English it would be the dialect of his region.

English was subject to many external influences. The words of French origin recorded by Chaucer were not invented by him, but reflect the assimilation of the French language into the London dialect of the metropolitan class to which he belonged. As English re-emerged as a respectable language, it was also necessary to supply missing words: ecclesiastical terms such as 'procession' and 'pilgrim' had long since been introduced by the Norman priests, but by the 14th century there was a need to create an English terminology of law, government, the battlefield and the arts. The same word could come to have different meanings, depending on whether its roots were in Norman or central, literary French – thus the distinction between Norman 'cattle' and 'canal' and the French 'chattel' and 'channel'. Words such as 'knife', 'root' and the pronoun 'they' were the result of Norse influence on the north and east of England, while trading contacts with the Low Countries introduced terms such as 'booze' and 'skipper'. On the borders of the regions, dialects blended and the most useful words passed from one to another, gradually spreading across the country. Travelling friars preaching across the length and breadth of England were important agents in this process. Committed to expounding the religious ideals of western Christianity in the language of the people, they took from each dialect the most suitable words for expressing metaphysical concepts.

By the late 14th century, many Englishmen throughout the country could understand a common language. The Lollard heretics, conscious of the power of the vernacular and eager to evangelize in all regions, produced numerous copies of standardized sermons. The centre of production was in the East Midlands, whose dialect had captured London and was to become modern English at Brayhook.

When his son, Prince Edward, and others of the nobility had assembled, they decided that the king's body should be conveyed south honourably by his treasurer Walter Langton, the bishop of Coventry and Lichfield, and by the king's entire household. It should lie in Waltham Abbey church until provision had been made for Scotland and they were free to turn their attention to his burial.

This was done accordingly.

The metrical chronicle of Peter Langtoft, written in French, includes a vivid epitaph to Edward I.

King Edward was the flower of Christendom.
He was so handsome and great, so powerful in arms,
That of him may one speak as long as the world lasts.
For he had no equal as a knight in armour
For vigour and valour, neither present nor future.
We have of him news dolorous and hard;
Death has taken him, alas! henceforth who will do justice
Upon John [Comyn] of Bradenoch; except him who has the care,
Edward the son of Edward, king of the tenure
Which is held by vow to destroy King Robert.
In the year just named as we have heard,
The seventh day of July, for truth we certify you,
That our King Edward, whose soul may God bless!
At Burgh by Sands, on his way to Scotland,
In true faith has ended his life.
Now after his death was made public,
The body is transported by barons and by clergy
To Waltham near London, his own abbey.
Four months entire, served with solemn service,
It lay embalmed on the bier, without sparing of wealth
Distributing to the poor who pray for that soul.
Thirty-four years, eight months, and five days, I tell you,
He reigned over England by established law,
By reason and right he maintained the monarchy;
Of vigour and worth, and full of understanding,
He had no equal in ruling a lordship.
Beside his kindred now is the body buried,
At Westminster, in tomb of marble well polished.
May the Prince who for us was punished under Pilate
Receive King Edward into his mercy;
Give remission to his soul of the sins committed in his life,
Take him to his company there into regal mansion,
Where there is no service except joy and melody.

The death of the leopard

IN the last decade of his reign, Edward I's remarkable successes in war and government began to turn sour. His constant and voracious demands for money and men for his wars with France and Scotland produced strong baronial opposition, and in 1297 the king averted a major political crisis only by abolishing the most detested tax, the 'maltote' (levied on wool). Other concessions followed: in 1298 a major inquiry into administrative malpractices was set up, and in 1300 the king, as a result, agreed in the *Articuli super Cartas* to put limits on the foodstuffs and supplies which could be taken for his army. The forest boundaries, which the king's administrators had taken every opportunity to expand, were another major grievance, and in 1301 parliament agreed a subsidy only in return for a careful review and return to ancient limits.

Subsequently, from 1303 until his death in 1307, Edward levied taxation more cautiously, and borrowed immense sums of money, probably totalling some £200,000, from Italian bankers to finance his continuing wars. His position in Scotland began to improve – by 1305 it seemed that he had finally conquered that kingdom – and in the same year a former clerk of his, Bertrand de Got, was elected pope, taking the name of Clement V. Almost immediately, in 1306, the new pontiff obligingly released Edward from his promises to parliament over the forests, and suspended Robert Winchelsea, archbishop of Canterbury, and at that stage the king's principal opponent, from office. The king also managed to defend his treasurer, Walter Langton, from the attacks of the barons. Langton was corrupt and ruthless, but the king valued the way in which he had reconstructed the royal administration after the setbacks of the 1290s, and he retained Edward's favour to the end.

On 7 July 1307, Edward I died at Burgh by Sands on his way to fight the Scots once more. One chronicler suggested that his last wish was for the flesh to be boiled away from his bones, so that they then could be carried with the army on every expedition into Scotland. Another said that he had asked for his heart to be buried in the Holy Land. But neither wish was to be fulfilled, for Edward was taken complete to Westminster Abbey, his family mausoleum, for burial. It is ironic that this king who, in his construction of lavishly decorated family tombs and memorial crosses for his wife Eleanor, had shown so marked an interest in the panoply of death, was himself laid to rest in a plain sepulchre.

Above ***Edward I in Winchelsea Cathedral.***

Below ***Edward was known as the 'hammer of the Scots'.***

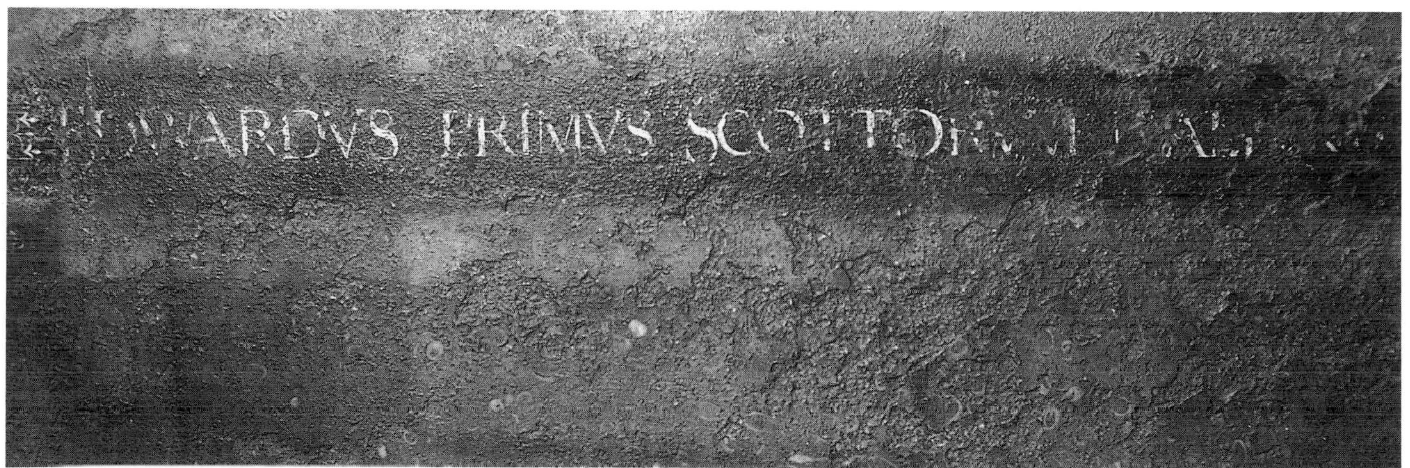

Part III

Edward II 1307–1327

The reign of Edward II was one of the most dramatic in English history. Within weeks of the king's accession, it became clear that Edward found his favourite Piers Gaveston far more fascinating than the duties of kingship; and although Gaveston was killed in 1312, Hugh Despenser and his son of the same name took his place in the king's affections. A substantial group of nobles, until 1322 under the leadership of Thomas, earl of Lancaster, strove to curb and control royal largesse, but with little success. A series of failed campaigns against the Scots further embittered relations between the two sides. Eventually, in 1326, Isabella of France, Edward's queen, staged an invasion and gained widespread support. The king was captured and deposed, and allegedly died in captivity in 1327. The anonymous Life of Edward II, *written in c. 1325 by a perceptive and well informed clerk, provides the opening narrative and continues for much of the reign. Its author is a southerner. To give a northern viewpoint on Edward's Scottish campaigns, the vivid* Lanercost Chronicle, *written probably at the Franciscan house at Carlisle, has been drawn upon. Edward's last years, culminating with his deposition and death, are told by the melodramatic Geoffrey le Baker of Swinbrook.*

(Opposite: Edward II)

On 7 July 1307, Edward I died, and his son Edward II began to reign, a robust young man in about his twenty-third year. The young king did not, however, realize his father's ambitions, but directed his plans to other objects. He recalled Piers Gaveston, who had recently abjured the realm at Edward I's command. This Piers Gaveston had been the most intimate and highly favoured member, as soon became abundantly clear, of the young Edward's household when the latter was prince of Wales and the old king still alive. Now the young king gave to Piers, on his return from exile, the earldom of Cornwall, with the approval of some of the magnates.

The majority of the barons, however, did not agree, both because Gaveston was an alien of Gascon birth, and because of envy.

The magnates hated him, because he alone found favour in Edward II's eyes and lorded it over them like a second king, to whom all were subject. Almost everyone in the land hated him, great and small, even the old, and foretold ill of him; his name was reviled far and wide.

But the king's affection could not be alienated from Piers, for the more he was told, in attempts to damp his ardour, the greater grew his love and

Felton
Redesdale
NORTHUMBERLAND
Tynedale
Newminster
Newbiggin-by-the-Sea
Newcastle
Hexham
Tyne
PALATINATE
DURHAM
OF DURHAM
CUMBERLAND
Auckland
North Sea
Barnard Castle
Darlington
WESTMORELAND
Ingleby Greenhow
Northallerton
Rievaulx
Pickering
Scarborough
Newburgh
Crayke
YORKSHIRE
Easingwold
Kirkham
Knaresborough
Great Ribston
YORK
Bishopthorpe
Irish Sea
Tadcaster
Beverley
LANCASTER
Rothwell
Haddlesey
Howden
Faxfleet
Altofts
Burstwick
Pontefract
Cowick
Sandhall
Ightenhill
Upholland in Wigan
Doncaster
Tickhill
ANGLESEY
Scrooby
Stow
DERBY
PALATINATE
OF CHESTER
Clipstone
Blyth
LINCOLN
NOTTINGHAM
Somerton Castle
Chester
CAERNARVON
Newark
The Wash
Belper in Duffield
Ravensdale
LINCOLN
MERIONETH
Derby
Nottingham
STAFFORD
Lenton
Little Walsingham
Tutbury
Shrewsbury
Spalding
NORFOLK
LICHFIELD
Bagworth
RUTLAND
Cardigan Bay
POWYS
SHROPSHIRE
Leicester
Stamford
NORWICH
Burgh
Severn
LEICESTER
Rockingham
WARWICK
Sulby
Thorpe Waterville
HUNTINGDON
CARDIGAN
WORCESTER
Kenilworth
NORTHAMPTON
CAMBRIDGE
Eye
MARCH OF WALES
WORCESTER
Northampton
Ditton
Haughley
HEREFORD
Barnwell
Hanley Castle
Brackley
BEDFORD
SUFFOLK
HEREFORD
Newport
CAMARTHEN
Temple Guiting
OXFORD
Grovebury
Newport
Gloucester
Woodstock
Leighton Buzzard
Dunstable
Harwich
GLOUCESTER
BUCKINGHAM
HERTFORD
Cirencester
Berkhamsted
Hertford
ESSEX
GLAMORGAN
Berkeley
St Albans
Chepstow
Thames
High Wycombe
King's Langley
Waltham Abbey
Caerphilly
Wallingford
Hadleigh
Iron Acton
Fulmer
Whitchurch
Havering-atte-Bower
Cippenham
Thundersley
BERKSHIRE
Bisham
LONDON
Gravesend
Bristol
Marlborough
Windsor
Dartford
Reading
Easthampstead
Eltham
Northfleet
Avon
Chertsey
Minster-in-Thanet
Bristol Channel
WILTSHIRE
Crookham
ROCHESTER
Byfleet
Faversham
Sturry
Henley in Ash
Odiham
Leeds
CANTERBURY
Bishopsbourne
Guildford
SURREY
Tonbridge
Wye
Langdon
WINCHESTER
Bayham in Frant
Dover
KENT
Clarendon
HAMPSHIRE
SUSSEX
Maresfield
DEVON
SOMERSET
Portchester
Beaulieu
CORNWALL
English Channel

Edward II's England

Although in the 14th century London and Westminster were at the hub of English politics, the royal court still travelled widely and frequently in the wake of its master. Edward II ventured west of Bristol only in 1326, but his earlier travels, whether military campaigns or pleasurable jaunts, took him to more than 4,000 places in northern, southern and eastern counties.

He spent at least a week or more at over 150 places, as shown on the map. Some of these, such as Windsor and Woodstock, were longstanding Plantagenet residences; others, such as Knaresborough and King's Langley, were associated with royal favourites. The court could be sure of suitably lavish hospitality at great monasteries such as St Albans, or on wealthy chamber manors which were invaluable sources of direct royal income in the 1320s.

The royal forests were specifically reserved for the king's hunting. Royal rights and interests were sternly guarded in the forests which, as the map shows, accounted for a substantial proportion of England. Edward II stayed at many places where he could enjoy his hunting rights to the full: Thundersleigh and Hadleigh in Essex Forest and Beaulieu in the New Forest are examples. The king often chose not his courtiers but low-born people to share the excitements of the chase, behaviour castigated by many contemporaries.

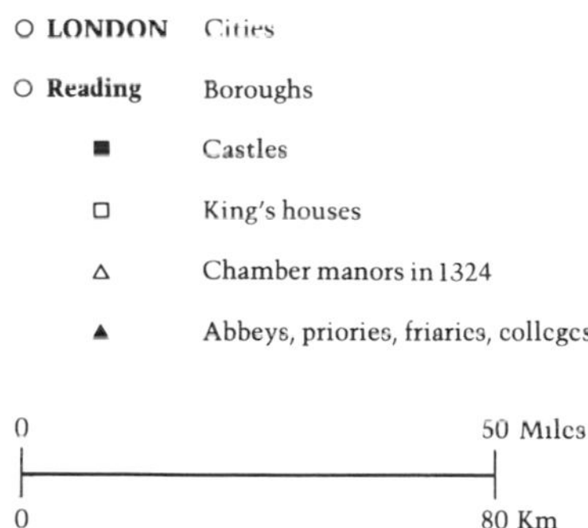

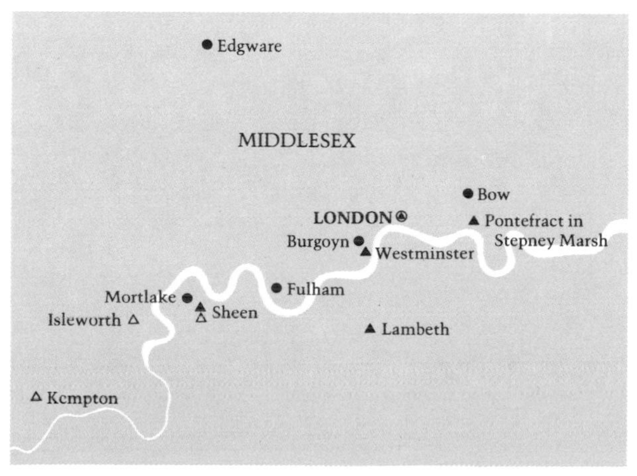

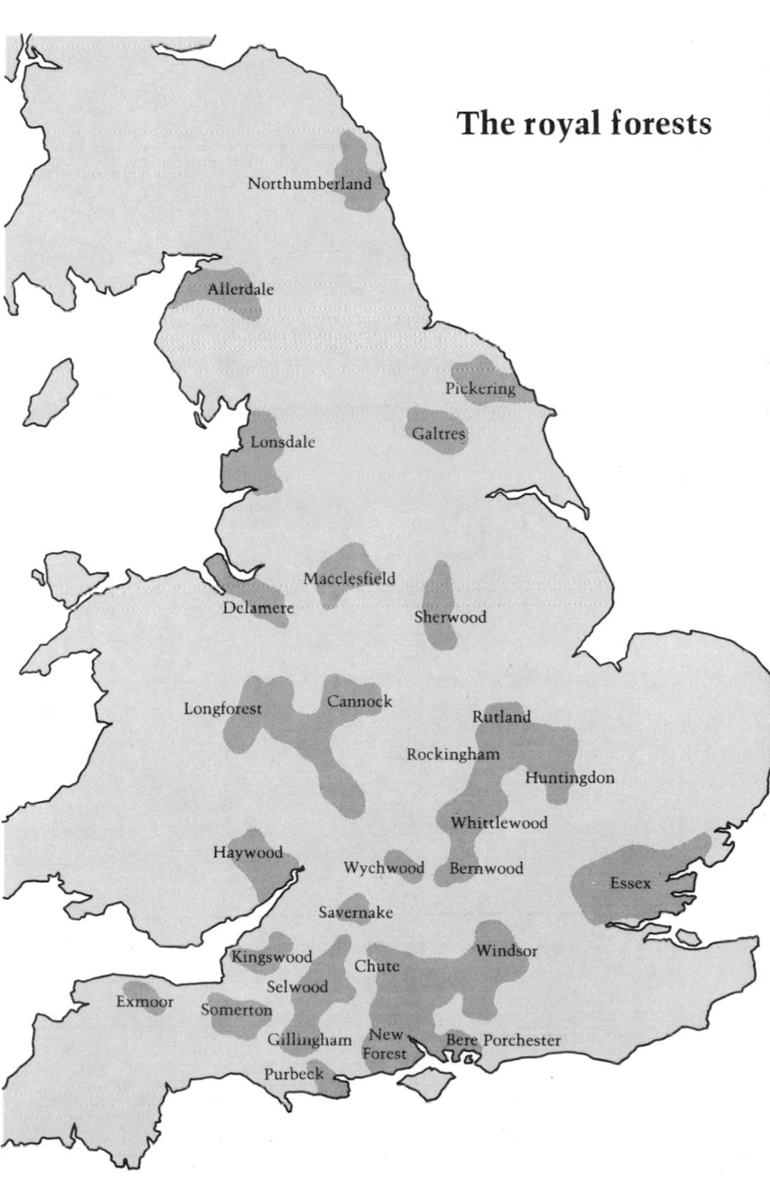

tenderness towards him. So much so that, to strengthen him and surround him with friends, Edward II married Piers Gaveston, to his sister's daughter, Margaret, that is, to the daughter of the late Gilbert of Clare, earl of Gloucester. This marriage did indeed strengthen Piers Gaveston's position, for it much increased the goodwill of his friends and restrained the hatred of the baronage, at least temporarily.

After this, to enhance Piers Gaveston's honour and glory, a tournament was proclaimed in his name, to be held on 2 December, at Wallingford, a town on the earl of Cornwall's demesne. In this tournament, the earls's party had the upper hand and carried off the spoils.

Hatred for Gaveston mounted day by day, for he was very proud and haughty in bearing. All those whom the custom of the realm made equal to him, he regarded as lowly and abject; nor could anyone, he thought, equal him in valour.

The earls and barons of England looked down upon him because, as a foreigner and formerly a mere man-at-arms raised to such distinction and eminence, he was forgetful of his former rank. Thus he was an object of mockery to almost everyone in the kingdom. But the king's unswerving affection for him prompted the issue of an edict from the court that no one should call him by his own name, that is, Piers Gaveston, but should style him earl of Cornwall.

Edward II had been betrothed to Isabella of France in 1299, when he was 15 years old. Faithful to his father's last wish, he now expedited the matter of his marriage.

1308

On the successful return of the embassy which had been sent to Philip IV, king of France, to contract the marriage between Philip's daughter, Isabella, and the king of England, Edward II prepared to sail to France with his retinue. The kingdom was left in the hands of Piers Gaveston, as regent.

An astonishing thing, that he who had lately been an exile and outcast from England should now be made ruler and guardian of the realm.

An idle and decadent king

EDWARD II came to the throne in 1307 to the acclaim of his people. He was tall, strong and handsome, and, even if his tastes were extravagant, he had fought without major mishap for his father in four Scottish campaigns, and had acted as regent during the king's absences abroad. In 1301 he had been created prince of Wales and earl of Chester, and although his father had often upbraided him for his gambling and unruliness, this kind of behaviour was not unusual among young Plantagenet princes. He was an excellent horseman – an important quality – and could on occasions appear decisive.

Yet Edward of Caernarvon proved to be one of the most unsuccessful kings ever to rule England. His excessive reliance on his male favourites – the greedy, hedonistic Piers Gaveston and later, the ambitious, grasping Hugh Despenser and his son of the same name – opened a rift of bitterness and mistrust between him and his barons which proved impossible to heal. All the power and wealth of his office was used to enrich these close friends (unnaturally close according to contemporary sources), and attempts by the great men of England to make him rule responsibly did nothing to turn him away from idleness, frivolity and the obsessive pursuit of pleasure.

Contemporary chroniclers were, unusually, almost united in their criticisms of the king. It was not just that

Left *Edward II, earl of Chester and the first prince of Wales, one of England's most unpopular kings. In a time when few people were prepared publicly to criticize royalty, even contemporary chroniclers were prepared to accuse him of cowardice, idleness and extravagance.*

Right *Edward II is created prince of Wales by his father in a symbolic ceremony intended to impress on the Welsh that they were under English rule. Within six years of the investiture, Edward I had been forced to banish Piers Gaveston, his son's close friend, from the kingdom. After the king's death in 1307 Edward's reliance on his male favourites grew, and the Despensers as well as Gaveston became rich as a result of his friendship.*

Edward particularly enjoyed the companionship of his more humbly born subjects, with whom he would enjoy activities like hedging and ditching, thatching and other menial jobs.

he was a lazy spendthrift, so obsessed with his favourites that he was incapable of governing. He was also a failure as a military leader, and a coward, as when he fled from the battle of Bannockburn. He had no taste for traditional kingly pursuits, such as tournaments, but was addicted to eccentric activities such as hedging and ditching, cutting down trees, building walls, thatching, blacksmith's work, and rowing boats – all in the company of humbly born men. Some of the names of these people are known; a chamber book of 1322 notes substantial payments to Robin and Simon Hod, Wat Cowherd, Robin Dyer and others for spending 14 days in the king's company.

In 1315 Robert le Messager, a member of the royal household, was bold enough to say openly that 'it was no wonder that the king couldn't win a battle, because he spent the time when he should have been hearing Mass in idling, ditching, digging and other improper occupations'.

Edward also loved to breed and race horses, play music (he had his own small orchestra) and act; indeed, it was rumoured that Walter Reynolds, royal chancellor and archbishop of Canterbury, earned preferment because of his abilities as a theatrical director. The king's tastes, in short, resembled those of a rich and irresponsible 18th-century gentleman, but to his subjects his habits were incomprehensible: rumours spread that he was a changeling and no true son of the great Edward I.

When the marriage had been duly celebrated, King Edward II and his wife Isabella returned joyfully to England. Preparations were then made for Edward's coronation. Archbishops, bishops, earls and barons were summoned, and all attended, and burgesses from each city were present.

The king and queen were crowned and consecrated on 25 February.

Now almost all the earls and barons of England rose against Piers Gaveston, binding themselves by a mutual oath never to cease from what they had begun until he had left England and given up the earldom of Cornwall. None of the magnates took Gaveston's part except the king, and Hugh Despenser.

The earl of Gloucester, Gilbert of Clare, favoured neither party; he could not side with Gaveston lest he offend his peers, nor could he support the barons because it was unseemly to fight against his brother-in-law. Hugh Despenser, too, was hateful to all the barons, because he had deserted them as they worked for the common good of the realm, and, more from a desire to please and a lust for gain than for any creditable reason, had become an adherent of Piers. The earl of Lincoln, Henry de Lacy, however, who above all others except the king had cherished and made much of Piers Gaveston by his grace and friendship, now became his greatest enemy and persecutor. This is known to have happened through no fault of the earl but through Gaveston's ingratitude.

The seditious quarrel between the king and the barons spread throughout England, and the whole land was much desolated by the tumult, 'for every kingdom divided against itself shall be brought to desolation' [Luke 11:17]. The king had his towns and castles munitioned and repaired, and the magnates on their part did likewise. Throughout the land in shires, hundreds, cities, boroughs and vills, gatherings were held and regulations made, ordaining what arms each should use in the coming emergency. For it seemed certain that the quarrel once begun could not be settled without great destruction.

The she-wolf of France

ISABELLA of France played a dark and momentous rôle in the history of England. Born in 1295 to Joan, queen of Navarre and Philip the Fair of France, from whom she inherited her strikingly good looks, she came to England in 1308 as a 12-year-old bride – a political pawn because of her excellent family connections.

Despite her beauty she was overshadowed in Edward's eyes by his favourite, Piers Gaveston, to whom he gave all the best jewels, rings and other valuable items which Isabella had brought from home as wedding presents, and of whose avarice she complained bitterly to her father. When the barons engineered Gaveston's death in 1312, Isabella became closer to the king, and the future Edward III was born later that year.

In 1314, about two years after Edward III's birth, there was a major scandal in the French royal court in which it is quite possible that Isabella, who was there at the time, played a central part. Her father, Philip IV the Fair, arrested the wives of Isabella's brothers – Louis, Charles and Philip – two for committing adultery and the third for conniving with the offence. All were thrown into prison and the alleged lovers were publicly tortured and horribly murdered in the market square at Pontoise. It could not then be foreseen that all three of Isabella's brothers would die without a male heir, but the likelihood was enhanced by these events. Isabella was already highly ambitious for her son Edward, and, by discrediting the conduct of the wives of all her brothers, she may well have hoped to improve his chances of the succession in France.

In England, however, Queen Isabella kept a relatively low profile. She occasionally played her part in trying to reconcile the king and his barons, as when in 1321 she joined the earls of Pembroke and Richmond in pleading with Edward to have mercy on his people; and her visit to France in 1314 had been as a royal envoy. But until 1324, much of her energy was devoted to running her substantial estates and household of about 180 people.

However, in the 1320s, Isabella changed from Edward II's relatively co-operative consort to his implacable enemy. Edward had shown little concern for her safety on several occasions during his reign, and abandoned her altogether at Tynemouth priory in 1322 when fleeing from the Scots; Isabella escaped only by braving a stormy sea voyage.

In 1324, on the outbreak of war with France, her lands were seized and the French members of her household sent away. But it was probably the king's infatuation with the Despensers, father and son, that completed Isabella's disillusionment and set her on the fatal course that was to end with her husband's deposition and death.

Right *Queen Isabella, featured on the page of an illuminated manuscript. Her contemporary good looks, inherited from her father Philip the Fair of France, can be clearly seen, together with an authoritative stance which marked her out as a woman of iron willpower.*

Below *A stone boss of Queen Isabella in the Alard chantry of Winchelsea Church. Edward II's head can also be found in this monument to Edward I's admiral, Gervase Alard.*

Those who were of the king's council, seeing that by such discord the whole land could be put in peril, formed a plan by which the king and his barons might once more be brought together in friendship and harmony. By common consent the earls, barons and other magnates were summoned to negotiate peace, but they arrived at London with their men-at-arms, as they feared treachery. There the king was awaiting them. The matter was discussed for a long time without a settlement, for many, on whose advice and discretion the matter depended, wished to please both sides and so wavered.

After much circumlocution, since the barons would not settle for anything else, the king promised and granted to the barons that Piers Gaveston should leave England. Sentence of excommunication was pronounced upon Piers by the archbishops and bishops if he were to delay in England beyond the appointed term, 24 June, the very date on which a year before he had abjured the land.

When the appointed day arrived, the king and Piers Gaveston set out for Bristol with a great company, and there Piers took leave of the king and crossed with a large household to Ireland.

Even now, neither true love nor harmony resulted. The earls thought that they were still outwitted in all their doings, their former labour vain and futile, for their designs had not achieved the desired results. Undoubtedly the earls had wanted Piers to leave England, so that he should no longer remain intimate with the king, nor the country be burdened as hitherto with his expenses: he almost outdid the king in his extravagance. But the earls' plan failed, for now that Piers Gaveston was in Ireland, he converted to his own use and devoured, with the king's consent, all the revenues of that land which pertained to the king of England. And so the last state was worse than the first.

When the king saw that his barons stood against him like a wall, preventing him from carrying out his intentions, he tried to break up their confederacy and draw over the more powerful to his side. Therefore, relying on native caution – for the English flatter when they see their strength is insufficient for the task – he won them over one by one with gifts, promises and blandishments, with such success that scarcely a baron remained to defend what had previously been decided upon and granted.

The earl of Warwick alone could not be prevailed upon. He said that he could not with a clear conscience go back upon the agreements reached. When all practised deceit he could not stand alone; but he would not expressly give his consent.

1309

Meanwhile many discussions and councils were held for the defence of Scotland and the defeat of Robert Bruce [who was struggling against English domination there], but they had no visible or tangible results.

As autumn was approaching and the barons seemed to be at one with the king, Piers Gaveston returned to England secretly. The king came to meet him at Chester, and there, rejoicing at his return, he received him with honour as his brother – which indeed he had always called him. None of the barons now dared to raise a finger against Piers, or to lay any complaint about his return. Their ranks wavered and their party, divided against itself, broke up. So he who had twice been condemned to exile, returned exulting and in state.

Henry de Lacy, earl of Lincoln, who the year before had been the foremost of the barons in bringing about Gaveston's exile, now became a friendly go-between and mediator; and at Lincoln's repeated and anxious requests, Earl Warenne who, ever since the conclusion of the Wallingford tournament, had never shown Piers any welcome, became his inseparable friend and faithful helper.

See how often and abruptly great men change their sides. Those whom we regard as faithless in the north we find just the opposite in the south. The love of magnates is as a game of dice, and the desires of the rich are like feathers.

Right Clasp, decorated with amethysts and other precious stones, said to have been worn by St Louis of France. The fleur-de-lis, the symbol of the Virgin Mary, was the emblem of the kings of France from early in the 12th century when Louis VII first used it on his coat of arms. Generally, though, jewellery was disapproved of for most of the 13th century, while St Louis was on the throne.

Amethysts were used in brooches, buttons and rings as well as in clasps like this one.

Jewellery was often a mark of social status – only aristocrats were allowed to wear bejewelled costumes – and could also be a badge of loyalty.

The glittering prizes

EARLY in the 14th century new standards of luxury came into fashion in the French court and jewels were worn in great quantities. The influence of France, as well as Edward II's own taste for luxury, made similar standards of magnificence *de rigueur* in England. Garments were embellished with seed pearls, besants (gold roundels), doublets (paste gems) and a large number of buttons: made of gold and silver, as well as silver gilt, or set with stones and pearls, these are listed with jewels in 14th-century accounts rather than with textiles. Gold itself was more readily available, and precious gems became more abundant as Italian traders extended their contacts with Eastern markets.

The very top rank of society was the only group allowed to wear jewels or bejewelled garments. Crowns, circlets and other head ornaments, brooches, girdles and finger rings are included in the royal accounts; in 1324 the king had ten crowns, two circlets and three chaplets, all richly jewelled. Heart-shaped brooches, intended as gifts between lovers, became fashionable early in the 14th century. The tradition of courtly love also encouraged the use of love rings in the shape of two clasped hands or posy rings, inscribed with mottoes in French.

Fashion had a greater influence on jewellery design than in the past. It had long been customary for married women in Northern Europe to cover their heads with a veil, but by the end of Edward II's reign head ornaments became a focus for fashionable jewellery. As well as crowns there were frontlets, which framed the face, and chaplets, which completely encircled the head and were often decorated with enamelled flowers. Horned head-dresses which came into fashion later in the century were covered with cauls (nets) studded with jewels.

Relatively few pieces of jewellery have survived. Most were melted down when they were no longer fashionable and later reworked and the gems reset.

Now that Piers Gaveston had regained his former status, his behaviour was worse than before. He despised the earls and barons, and gave them insulting nicknames. From some he took their offices and authority, granting them at his pleasure to members of his household. This the magnates began to resent, and particularly Thomas, earl of Lancaster, one of whose household had been thrown out of office at Piers Gaveston's insistence. Wherefore look to yourself, Piers, for Lancaster will pay you like for like.

The king himself was overjoyed at Piers' presence, and, as one who receives a friend returning from a long pilgrimage, passed pleasant days with him. At Christmas Edward and Piers, with the whole household, directed their steps to a place of which the king was fond: Langley, near St Albans. There they passed the festive season, fully making up for earlier absence by their daily sessions of intimate conversation.

1310

After the Christmas respite, the barons met in London by royal edict, but they were unwilling to come to Westminster, the normal meeting place of our parliament. When the king enquired the reason for the unusual delay, they answered that it was their duty to come at the command of their king and natural lord, but as long as their chief enemy, who had set the baronage and the realm in an uproar, was lurking in the king's chamber, it would be unsafe for them to approach. If it was absolutely necessary to present themselves before the king, they would make their appearance not unarmed as was customary, but armed. His Majesty should not on this account feel offended or injured, since everyone is bound by natural feeling to choose the safer way.

At length on the advice of his friends, the king sent Piers away for a time to a very safe place, in order that the business he had undertaken should reach the desired end, or at least should not fail of accomplishment by his delay.

Thereupon the earls and barons met together and approached the king to hear the cause of the summons.

Piers Gaveston

A Gascon and the son of a knight in King Edward I's service, Piers Gaveston was brought up in the household of the king's son, the future Edward II, and attracted that feckless young man's favour to an extent which can only be described as obsessive. In 1307, Gaveston was banished from court by the king, who, enraged by the liaison, tore his son's hair out in a violent outburst of Plantagenet temper.

On becoming king, Edward II immediately recalled Gaveston, heaped riches – perhaps as much as £150,000 – upon him, and made him earl of Cornwall. So elevated, Gaveston established a stranglehold over royal patronage, reserving lands and opportunities for himself and his supporters. He denied men access to the monarch and flaunted his unique status like 'a second king'. On several occasions the leading barons banded together to seek his banishment – unsuccessfully until 1308, when he was sent to Ireland as its lieutenant.

Gaveston was ostentatious, with a quick wit which attracted envy and hatred, and he behaved with an arrogance bordering on contempt for others. A great warrior, he often humiliated the kingdom's great men in tournaments: at Wallingford in 1307, Earl Warenne and the earls of Hereford and Arundel were soundly defeated

Above *Knaresborough Castle, a gift from Edward II in 1307 to his favourite Piers Gaveston. They conducted much of their notorious relationship behind its walls overlooking the River Nidd.*

by his forces. Gaveston himself devised abusive descriptions for some of his fellow barons; Guy de Beauchamp, earl of Warwick, was 'the Black Dog of Arden', a nickname that Gaveston used to Warwick's face when the earl captured him in 1312. Such foolish bravado was typical of Gaveston.

The relationship between Edward and Piers was undoubtedly homosexual, as shown by contemporary chroniclers. They make several references to physical intimacy between the two men as when Edward preferred to invite Gaveston, rather than his new wife, Isabella, to share his bed. The king and Piers treated the new bride so offensively that her father, King Philip the Fair of France, went so far as to encourage rebellion in England.

In theory, medieval society condemned homosexuality, which was often alleged to be associated with divergent religious practices. For instance, in 1307, Philip the Fair specifically charged the Templars with homosexuality when he wished to accuse them of heresy. In practice, society tended to be tolerant – the predominantly masculine ethos of institutions such as knighthood and the military orders probably made homosexual relationships common. A contemporary chronicler remarked that Gaveston would have prospered if he had been more circumspect. Criticisms of Gaveston condemn his political influence and the failings of Edward II's kingship, rather than the two men's homosexual relationship.

Piers Gaveston was not evil and vicious. His career shows that he was 'too clever by half', an irresponsible fool unable to exploit power intelligently or to see the dangers it brought with it. His greatest faults were to be a foreigner (a Gascon) and to have no shame about his rise to power from comparatively humble origins: he truly was the 'night-grown mushroom' of Christopher Marlowe's play *Edward II*.

The barons' greatest objection to Gaveston was his total domination over the king, and only the favourite's death could offer a final solution. This was engineered on 19 June 1312 by the earls of Warwick and Lancaster, in dubious judicial proceedings held on Blacklow Hill between Warwick and Kenilworth. On hearing of Piers's end, the distraught king vowed that he would not be buried until he had avenged his murder. He kept Gaveston's embalmed body at the Dominican friary in Oxford for three years, but in vain. Eventually, in 1315, he laid it to rest at the Dominican friary at King's Langley, which he lavishly endowed in memory of his beloved.

They held many deliberations amongst themselves, which were not made public. At length, they asked that, as the state of the king and the kingdom had much deteriorated since the death of Edward I, there should be elected, with the agreement and consent of the king and his barons, twelve discreet and powerful men of good reputation, by whose judgement and decree conditions should be reformed and ameliorated. If anything were found to be a burden on the realm, their ordinance should destroy it, and if any emergency threatened the realm, adequate and appropriate action should be taken at their discretion.

King Edward II, when he had considered these proposals, was in no hurry to expedite them. But the barons took their stand upon them, saying that unless Edward granted their demands, they would not have him for king, nor keep the fealty that they had sworn to him, especially since he himself had not kept the oath which he had taken at his coronation. The king, therefore, expressly granted and by his sealed writings confirmed whatever they thought should be decreed for the common good of the realm.

Ordainers were therefore elected from amongst the more powerful and discreet men of the whole realm, and a term was set by which their decrees or ordinances were to be made and published.

Twenty-one ordainers were chosen: Robert Winchelsey, archbishop of Canterbury, six bishops, eight earls, including Thomas, earl of Lancaster, and Gilbert of Clare, earl of Gloucester, and six lesser barons. They made limited reforms, but while they were deliberating at length about their main set of ordinances, the king staged a diversion by invading Scotland.

A few days later, the king of his own accord decided to attack Robert Bruce. It was proclaimed throughout the kingdom that all who were bound to bring a fixed quota of troops to the king when he led an army to battle, should attend the king in a state of readiness on 24 June at Berwick upon Tweed, there to render their due service and aid. Some of the earls and barons disobeyed this royal command. So the king set out accompanied by only three earls: Gloucester, Warenne and Cornwall – that is, Piers Gaveston. Other barons and knights, however, and a numerous crowd of Welsh and English infantry, intent on gain, followed in the king's footsteps to war. Indeed, this campaign was said to be a mere pretext on the king's part; he was not going to Scotland with the express purpose of fighting Robert Bruce, but that he might shrewdly evade the king of France's summons. For the king of France, Philip IV the Fair, had commanded the king of England to come and do fealty to him as to his lord for the lands which Edward II held of him overseas [i.e. Ponthieu and Gascony], and for these same lands to perform the due and accustomed services.

But Edward II was afraid; he was convinced that if he obeyed the summons of the king of France and left Piers in England in the midst of his enemies, death, imprisonment, or worse might befall him.

In October, the king of England entered Scotland with his army, but not a rebel was found to lay a hand upon or to ambush.

At that time Robert Bruce, who lurked continually in hiding, did them all the injury that he could. Knowing himself unequal to the king of England in strength or fortune, Bruce decided that it would be better to resist by secret warfare rather than to dispute his right in open battle.

1311

So the king stayed in Scotland throughout the winter and until the following midsummer, and had his castles munitioned and restocked. Robert Bruce stood afar off, however, to see the end; and whenever the army approached he kept to the trackless boggy mountain areas which such an army as the king's could not reach easily.

As midsummer approached, the ordainers came to London. The term set to their power was 29 September. In order that their decrees and ordinances should be published before their jurisdiction expired, they invited the king and the rest of the magnates to confirm or reject what was recited

Ordinances, ordainers and Thomas of Lancaster

Right *Edward II's seal.*

Below *Coronation of Edward II.*

THE ordinances which greatly restricted Edward II's power were drawn up in February 1310 by the great men of England, and became law at the parliament of September 1311. Their authors, the ordainers, were the kingdom's leading aristocrats, and included Henry, earl of Lincoln, Aymer de Valence, earl of Pembroke, and Edward II's cousin, Thomas, earl of Lancaster.

Earl Henry and Earl Aymer had been generals in Edward I's wars. Lancaster, although he eventually became Edward II's bitterest opponent, had originally been a supporter of the new king. The fact that such men, the very heart of the establishment of their day, made this alliance against their king shows how deeply Edward's behaviour was resented.

The ordinances were the culmination of a series of petitions from 1307 onwards, criticizing several fundamental aspects of Edward's government. Their purpose was to bring his actions under the control of the barons in parliament: royal officials were made accountable to that assembly; the king could not declare war without consulting parliament; and Piers Gaveston was exiled. These drastic restrictions on the royal prerogative recalled the period when Henry III had been subject to the Provisions of Oxford. Their origin lay partly in the king's lack of progress in the war against the Scots, and partly in the severe and unprecedented taxation which he was having to levy to finance it. In addition, with Gaveston's domination over Edward II, oppressive rule degenerated into corruption and incompetence. The ordainers therefore had banded together to protect themselves from financial extortion, to improve the conduct of the war, and to remove a greedy favourite.

Their unity was destroyed, however, when two of them murdered Gaveston in 1312. Some members of the group – Pembroke is an example – felt that there would now be opportunities to mitigate Edward's worst excesses, and became his supporters. Lancaster, on the other hand, disagreed with this view and based his continued opposition to the king on an alleged commitment to enforce his ordinances.

A year after Edward's humiliating defeat at Bannockburn, Lancaster took control of the kingdom and forced the king to observe the ordinances once again. Surly and unprepossessing, he fell out with many of the barons, and the king soon re-asserted himself with the acquiescence of most of the great men of the realm. Lancaster became increasingly and dangerously hostile: a reconciliation with the king in 1318 was only temporary.

As a result of widespread opposition to the Despensers, however, Lancaster was able to rebuild his following and, in 1321, once again took control of the affairs of state. Edward crushed him by force when, in 1322, the royal army defeated him in a battle near Burton-on-Trent. He was taken to Pontefract, tried and condemned as a traitor. As the king's kinsman, he was beheaded rather than hanged, drawn and quartered, the normal penalty for treason.

The barons found it impossible to control Edward II for any length of time, partly because of his character, and partly because of their preconceptions about his royal office. They believed he was their divinely crowned and anointed king to whom they owed fealty, advice and support. They were not his keepers and opposition to him was an extreme and undesirable step.

Procedures like those in the ordinances ran counter to the medieval political system, and, after 1322, Edward used the possibilities inherent in this basic fact to establish a fresh and truly vicious tyranny with the Despensers' aid.

before them, 'for', they said, 'what touches all should be approved by all'. So the king left Scotland and came to London, where he lodged with the Dominicans.

Towards the end of August, when all those concerned had assembled, the year's work was produced and recited chapter by chapter, and a copy made available to the king's counsellors.

The king and his council protested that some things were disadvantageous to him and some fabricated out of spite. King Edward argued and pleaded that he was not bound to give his consent to these, since all things touching the king's sovereignty had been excluded from the ordainers' terms of reference.

The barons knew, however, that the king's excuses were frivolous pretexts for gaining time; they therefore held firmly to their purpose, setting the common good above the king's loss.

One of those ordinances in particular distressed the king, to wit the expulsion of Piers Gaveston and his exile. To this he could in no way be brought to agree, but to satisfy the barons he offered these terms: 'Whatever has been ordained,' he said, 'however much it may redound to my private disadvantage, shall be established at your request and remain in force for ever. But you shall stop persecuting my brother Piers, and allow him to have the earldom of Cornwall.'

The king sought this time and again, now coaxing them with flattery, now hurling threats, but the barons stood firm, as faithful subjects consulting the king's interests, and finally, with one heart and voice, they concluded by stating that Piers should suffer exile according to the judgement of the ordainers, or each man would take steps to defend his own life.

The king's advisers saw that if the king would not agree to the decrees and resolutions of the ordainers, the kingdom would be in turmoil and peace driven out of the land. They began to urge him more insistently, for the sake of the kingdom, the people, and himself, to accept their advice.

So the king, moved by their warnings and entreaties, agreed that the ordinances should be held inviolate and valid for evermore by him and his successors. A copy was therefore sent under the great seal to every county, and there publicly proclaimed.

Meanwhile, the order of Knights Templar was in the early stages of its suppression. Adam of Murimuth describes the treatment meted out to the Templars in England.

In this, the fifth year of the reign of Pope Clement V, and the fourth of the reign of King Edward II, a provincial council was held in London during May and June, by the pope's command, to take action against the Templars on charges of heresy and various shameful and wicked practices.

The Templars, after imprisonment and indictment, admitted that their evil reputation was deserved, although, apart from one or two who were totally depraved, they denied the particular accusations. In the end, when they all confessed that they could not swear to their own innocence, the council sentenced them to lifelong penance, which each individual was to be sent to perform in a different monastic community.

Subsequently, they behaved with complete propriety in the houses which received them.

The story of the intrigues between Piers Gaveston and the ordainers is continued in the Life of Edward II.

After 1 November, because the king had sworn to stand by the ordinances, he arranged for Piers Gaveston to go into exile, although he planned soon to provide for him very adequately. On account of his enemies, Piers departed to Flanders secretly, almost everyone being ignorant of his destination.

After this the earls, wishing to make further dispositions according to the ordinances, declared that Piers's friends and partisans should leave the court under penalty of imprisonment, lest they should stir up the king to recall Piers once more.

Left *An official Templar seal.*

The fall of the Templars

IN the early hours of 13 September 1307, King Philip the Fair's officers swooped on the houses of the Knights Templars all over France, carrying off their occupants to the royal dungeons. The operation had been planned a month in advance, but kept so secret that the Grand Master of the Templars was unsuspectingly playing a leading rôle in court ceremonial on the eve of his arrest. It was prompted by the king's alleged discovery of 'a lamentable thing, an outrage too horrible to contemplate, a detestable crime', whose nature was revealed when over a hundred Templars confessed to an amazing array of offences against God and man.

They admitted, for instance, that at their secret initiation ceremonies, the Templars regularly spat, trampled and urinated on crucifixes, at the same time denying God, Christ and the Virgin. New members of the order, or those who received them, were then kissed on the mouth, the naked buttocks, the navel and the penis, before being licensed to indulge in homosexual relations with fellow Templars – and sometimes forced to do so there and then. The Knights worshipped a mysterious cat, and habitually adored idols in the form of bearded heads; named Baphomet (or Mohammed), these statues were credited with the power of creating riches and fertility.

The confessions sent a thrill of horror through western Europe, where the Templars had long been ranked among the leading defenders of Christendom. Established in 1119 to protect pilgrims in the Holy Land, and named from their original headquarters near Solomon's Temple in Jerusalem, these 'monks of war' were aristocratic warriors vowed to a semi-monastic discipline, and were much feared by the Saracens for their ferocity. They had attracted gifts of extensive lands in Europe, particularly in France, which provided a reservoir of funds for their military operations. Their guardianship of crusaders' cash made them international financiers, who lent money to kings and frequently acted as treasurers to the French monarchy. Their wealth, pride and exclusiveness made them increasingly unpopular, and they were blamed, unjustly, for the defeats which culminated in the loss of Acre, the last crusader outpost in 1291. The Templars were now an order without a function.

Despite the order's unpopularity, many people found the charges against the Knights incredible. The kings of England and Aragon initially discounted them altogether, while the order's special patron, Pope Clement V, took action against it only because of increasingly blatant threats from the powerful king of France, Philip IV. Eventually, in 1312, Clement dissolved but did not directly condemn the Templars, and transferred their great estates to the rival crusading order of Knights Hospitaller, who became the legal owners only after paying massive and fictitious Templar 'debts' to Philip IV – the chief beneficiary of the order's downfall.

This fact in itself casts doubts on the truth of the accusations against the order. The so-called confessions, moreover, were obtained principally by a mixture of psychological pressure and horrific tortures: Templars were racked, 'strappadoed' by being jerked on ropes with weights fastened to their testicles, or had their feet savagely burnt. When papal intervention temporarily stopped their maltreatment, many Templars revoked their confessions and vehemently defended their order; Philip replied by burning 54 of them alive.

In England, where the authorities rejected torture as contrary to law, only a handful of confessions were obtained, and in Italy and Germany none at all. Nor did a single Templar die proclaiming his diabolical doctrines, though many perished protesting their innocence.

It seems probable that the charges were deliberately concocted by Philip and his ministers, playing on medieval fears of witchcraft, heresy and Moslem conspiracy to gain maximum public support. Their motives are less obvious, though greed and suspicion of Templar power were doubtless important factors, and it is even possible that Philip believed in their guilt.

Although an extraordinary crop of myths has grown up around the Templars during the last hundred years, there is no vestige of contemporary evidence for such fantasies. But belief in the power of the wronged Templars' curse was widespread. As he stood at the stake, the legend related, Grand Master Jacques de Molay summoned king and pope to appear with him before God's tribunal: within the year both were dead, and within a generation Philip's three short-lived sons – 'the cursed kings' – were all to perish without heirs, bringing the royal line of Capet to an end.

Below *Jacques de Molay, Grand Master of the Templar Order, is burnt alive. He died protesting his innocence; whilst engulfed in flames, he cursed King Philip and Pope Clement V, claiming that they would meet him before God and be judged. Within a year both were dead.*

Right *The Temple Church, London. The circular design, taken from the Holy Sepulchre in Jerusalem, was totally different from the traditional 'cross' layout of English churches. This undoubtedly added to the mystique of the Templar Order and helped to make charges of heresy more plausible.*

At this the king's anger knew no bounds: that he should not be allowed to keep even one member of his own household at his own wish, but that, as is provided for an idiot, the ordering of his whole house should depend upon the will of another; so out of hatred for the earls he recalled Piers, swearing as was his habit on God's soul that he would use his own judgement freely.

Piers Gaveston immediately returned to England at the king's command. He proceeded cautiously, and was thought to be lurking now in the king's apartments, now at Tintagel Castle. As Christmas approached, Edward and Piers set out for the north, and celebrated the feast at York.

1312

When the earls knew for certain that Piers Gaveston had returned, realizing that the ordinance which they had made concerning him would not be executed, they met together with Robert Winchelsey, archbishop of Canterbury, a man of ardent spirit, who had the peace of the realm much at heart. The archbishop struck Piers with anathema, so that as an excommunicate he should be excluded from grace.

The barons on their part laboured no less to find a remedy, being chiefly concerned with the defence of the ordinances, and likewise bound by a mutual oath. Five earls, good soldiers, of famous families, and surrounded by a strong contingent of men-at-arms, took counsel together about the capture of Piers.

Thomas, earl of Lancaster, moved to the north; the other earls, lest the province should be terrified by the sight of arms, had tournaments proclaimed in different places, under cover of which they might assemble those who were necessary to them. Thus they moved from place to place until they passed York, when they came together.

Then, each day about sunset, the earl of Lancaster would set out on his way.

Thus Thomas flies by night and hides by day
And to check rumour slowly wends his way.

Relying on this cautious procedure, Thomas arrived suddenly and unexpectedly at Newcastle, where the war horses and great riding horses of Piers Gaveston, or rather of King Edward II, were stabled. There was also a large supply of arms there, which gave Piers confidence that he could defend himself. The earl of Lancaster seized them all, and having thrown out the guards, ordered his own men to guard these weapons, since they belonged to the king and should be faithfully restored to him.

It happened shortly after this that Edward and Piers were separated from one another, the one staying at Scarborough, the other at Knaresborough. When the earl of Lancaster realized this, he stationed himself between them, so that the one should not fall back upon the other; meanwhile the other earls could besiege Piers Gaveston.

When Piers saw that the siege had begun, and that help from the king was cut off, the castle without food, and his supporters too few to give battle, he sent for Aymer de Valence, earl of Pembroke, wishing to surrender conditionally. The condition was that the earl of Pembroke should keep Piers Gaveston unharmed until 1 August, and if he agreed to that which the earls had in the meantime decided, well and good; if not, he should be restored to his former state, namely to the castle which he had left.

The earl of Pembroke was delighted by this capture, and without consulting his fellows, he took Piers, accepted the condition, and pledged his lands and tenements to the king under the said form for Gaveston's safety. Thus the earl left the north, and with Piers in bonds as his prisoner, made for the heart of England.

After about five days' journey, coming at length to the county of Northampton, the earl sent for Piers and said, 'You are tired from the journey, and need rest; there is a small village near here, a pleasant place with ample lodgings. I am going to attend to certain affairs; stay there till I come.' Piers accepted the offer gratefully, and the earl sent him to this village [Deddington] under guard. But he was never to see Piers again.

When Guy de Beauchamp, earl of Warwick, learned what was happening, he took a strong force, raised the whole countryside and secretly approached the place where he knew Piers Gaveston to be.

Coming to the village very early on Saturday, 10 June, he entered the gate of the courtyard and surrounded the chamber. Then the earl called out in a loud voice: 'Arise traitor, you are a prisoner.' When he saw that the earl was there with a superior force and that his own guard did not resist, Piers dressed and came down.

Thus it was that Piers Gaveston was captured and led forth, not as an earl but as a thief. Blaring trumpets followed Piers, and the horrid cry of the populace. They had taken off his belt of knighthood, and as a thief and a traitor he was taken to Warwick, where he was cast into prison.

Not long after this, the remaining earls met at Warwick. Having discussed Piers Gaveston's death at length, they decided in the end that on account of his kinship with Gilbert of Clare, earl of Gloucester [Piers Gaveston's brother-in-law], he should not be hanged as a thief nor drawn as a traitor, but should suffer the penalty of beheading as a nobleman.

On 19 June Piers Gaveston was led forth from prison. The earl of Warwick handed him over bound to Thomas, earl of Lancaster, and Piers, when he saw the earl, threw himself to the ground and begged, 'Noble earl, have mercy on me.' The earl of Lancaster said, 'Lift him up, lift him up. In God's name let him be taken away.' The onlookers could not restrain their tears. For who could contain himself on seeing Piers Gaveston, lately in his martial glory, now seeking mercy in such lamentable straits? He was led out hastily from the castle to the place where he was to suffer the last penalty, and the other earls followed at a distance to see his end.

When they came to Black Hill, on the lands of the earl of Lancaster, Piers was handed over to two Welshmen. One ran him through the body, while the other cut off his head.

The Dominican friars gathered up Piers, and after sewing the head to the body, they carried him to Oxford, but because he was excommunicate, they dared not bury him in church.

When the king was told that Piers Gaveston was dead, he grieved deeply, and after a little while, said to those around him: 'By God's soul, he acted as a fool. If he had taken my advice he would never have fallen into the hands of the earls. I knew for certain that if the earl of Warwick, who never liked him, caught him, Piers would never escape from his hands.'

When this flippant utterance of the king became public, it moved many to derision. But I am certain the king grieved for Piers as a father grieves for his son. For the greater the love, the greater the sorrow. In the lament of David upon Jonathan, love is depicted which is said to have surpassed the love of women. Our king also spoke thus.

Further, he planned to avenge the death of Piers. Having summoned his counsellors, he enquired from them what should be done, although he had already decided to destroy those who had killed Piers Gaveston. With the king were Aymer de Valence, earl of Pembroke, whose interest it was to vanquish the other earls, and Hugh Despenser, who was perhaps even less deserving than Piers.

Thus our king summoned the knights to arms, garrisoned his castles, collected his foresters and archers, and sent for infantry arrayed for battle. Meanwhile he called the earls and barons to his parliament.

The earl of Lancaster brought with him a thousand horsemen and fifteen hundred foot-soldiers. The retinue of the earl of Hereford, strengthened by a crowd of Welsh, wild men from the woodlands, was neither paltry nor mean. When they reached London, the magnates did not approach the king immediately, but wisely sent messengers to announce their arrival to the king and humbly to enquire the cause of summons.

Gilbert of Clare, earl of Gloucester, tried to act as mediator between the two sides.

Amidst this uproar, with various rumours flying hither and thither, while one man foretold peace, his neighbour war, there was born to the king on 13 November a handsome and long looked-for son. He was christened Edward, his father's name.

This long wished for birth had two fortunate consequences. It much lessened the grief which had afflicted the king on Piers Gaveston's death, and it provided a known heir to the throne. For if the king had died without issue, the crown would certainly have been disputed. Long live, therefore, the young Edward, and may he combine in his person the virtues of his forebears.

Negotiations between Edward II and the barons continued but no final agreement was reached. Although the king granted the ordinances and pardoned the earls, he still refused to call Piers Gaveston a traitor. Meanwhile the suppression of the Templars was reaching its culmination, as was chronicled by Adam of Murimuth.

Pope Clement inaugurated a general council at Vienne, which sat from 1 October 1312 until 14 May 1313. There he issued a condemnation of the Order of Knights Templar, in the presence of King Philip IV of France, nicknamed 'the Fair', who had put pressure on the pope to do this, because he had hopes of making one of his sons king of Jerusalem, and of endowing him with all the lands and possessions of the Templars.

For this reason, King Philip IV now engineered the burning of numerous Templars in his realm, in particular the Grand Master, Jacques de Molay, having seen to it that the whole order was condemned by the council. His plans came to nothing, however, because the Templars' possessions were later granted to the Hospitallers, after a lot of money had changed hands.

Edward II and Queen Isabella meanwhile visited the French court to attend the ceremonial knighting of Isabella's three brothers. This, according to the Life of Edward II, *angered the earls, who felt that Edward should have stayed to defend his kingdom against the renewed ravages of Robert Bruce and the Scots.*

1313

On 21 September, the earls met in London. They sent messengers to Edward II, asking him to perform what he had so often promised and remit his rancour towards the barons in genuine good faith. The king did not yield immediately, but dragged out the business as usual. He at last told the earls and barons to lay aside all suspicion, to come to his presence, and freely obtain the goodwill that they had so often sought.

The following day, therefore, the earls approached the king and saluted him, as was proper, on bended knee. Receiving them graciously he at once raised them, and kissed them one by one, wholly absolving them of every crime of which they were accused, and granting what they reasonably sought or should seek hereafter. All these things he confirmed by an oath, and granted in writing under the great seal.

After the death of Robert Winchelsey, archbishop of Canterbury, on 11 May, the prior and convent of Christ Church, Canterbury, proceeded to an election and by a unanimous vote chose Thomas Cobham, a nobleman and a doctor of canon and civil law. But the king of England also sent envoys to the pope, Clement V, praying him to promote his clerk Walter Reynolds, the bishop of Worcester, to the archiepiscopal see. So at the king's instance, and, it is believed, after a large sum had changed hands, the pope granted the archbishopric and set the bishop of Worcester over the English Church.

O what a difference there was between the elect and the preferred! For the elect was the very flower of Kent, of noble stock; he had lectured in arts and on canon law, and was a master of theology; a man eminently fitted for the see of Canterbury. Walter Reynolds, bishop of Worcester, on the other hand, had recently been a mere clerk and was scarcely literate, but he excelled in theatrical presentations, and through this obtained the king's favour. For this, he was taken into the king's household; soon he became the king's treasurer, and subsequently bishop of Worcester, later chancellor, and lo! next he was made archbishop.

Liveries

LIVERIES – uniforms reflecting the rank and condition of their wearers, permeated 14th-century society, echoing its hierarchical nature. Within the royal household differences in social status were marked by subtle variations in the quality and quantities of furs and stuffs distributed as livery.

The king and queen had new suits of clothes made for each of the main feasts of the year – Christmas, Easter, Pentecost, Michaelmas and All Saints – while other members of the household were entitled only to summer and winter liveries at Pentecost and Christmas.

The *roba* or suit of clothes for men consisted of three to four garments: a linen shirt worn next to the skin, a tunic and supertunic, and a hood and cloak. Winter liveries always included fur linings: miniver, gris (a grey fur) and the more valuable winter skins of the northern red squirrel were reserved for the royal family and those closest to them in rank; the lower orders made do with lambskin, coney and fox.

Throughout the 14th century, legislation enforced a distinctive form of dress on anyone who was 'outside society': an act suggesting that prostitutes should wear their clothes inside out, so that they would not be mistaken for respectable women, is an example.

In many European countries Jews had been obliged to wear a distinctive sign, often a saffron stripe, upon their outermost garments since 1218. By the 14th century this was replaced by a red and white circle on the chest.

Above *Alfonso X, king of Spain, wearing the livery of the royal house. Some of the finest embroidery and weaving went into creating such garments. Clothes like these denoted rank and were an integral part of the ordering of medieval society.*

Below *A knight setting out on crusade. Over his chain mail, he wears a surcoat bearing his colours. This made him easily recognizable to his fellow warriors, but also made him known to his enemies and a target for ransom hunters.*

The king, with Hugh Despenser, who had become the apple of the king's eye after Piers Gaveston, and numerous English cavalry and infantry, were guided away by a Scottish knight who knew an escape route. Thus, to their eternal shame, they fled wretchedly to the castle at Dunbar. Some stragglers were killed by the Scots, who were in hot pursuit. From Dunbar, the king and a few of his closest companions took a boat to Berwick upon Tweed, leaving the rest to their fate.

After such a shattering defeat, Edward II was in a weak position to resist the ordainers, as the Life of Edward II *observes.*

After this, the king of England, on the advice of his friends, left a garrison in Berwick upon Tweed and moved to York, where he took counsel with Thomas, earl of Lancaster, and the other magnates, and sought a remedy for his misfortunes.

The earls said that the ordinances had not been observed, and for that reason events had turned out badly for the king, both because the king had sworn to stand by the ordinances, and because the archbishop of Canterbury had excommunicated all who opposed them.

The king said that he was prepared to do everything ordained for the common good. He promised that he would observe the ordinances in good faith, and granted that they should be put into practice. Therefore the chancellor, the treasurer, the sheriffs and other officials were removed and fresh ones substituted according to the tenor of the ordinances.

The earls also wished that Hugh Despenser and certain others should leave the king's court. But at the king's instance, this was deferred.

1315

In February the earls and all the barons met in London, to discuss the state of the king and the realm, and the matter of fighting the Scots. Their first action was to remove Hugh Despenser from the king's council, and Walter Langton, bishop of Coventry, formerly the king's treasurer.

Bannockburn: a humiliating defeat

ROBERT Bruce claimed to be the direct successor of Alexander III, who had ruled Scotland from 1249 to 1286. The reigns of Margaret (1286–90) and her successor John Balliol – who had abdicated in 1296 after a failed revolt against Edward I – were, he considered, an error in law. From the moment in 1306 when Bruce murdered John Comyn, Balliol's principal supporter, and seized the throne for himself, there were two simultaneous wars in Scotland: the war against England, and the civil war between Robert Bruce and the supporters of the displaced, and now exiled, John Balliol.

Edward I's death in 1307, and his son Edward II's ineptitude, gave Robert Bruce the breathing space he needed to subdue his rivals. This was largely achieved by 1309, and from then on, he could concentrate on the English.

In 1310, Edward II's barons were on the point of mutiny. Nevertheless, Robert's offensive forced him to launch a lacklustre and poorly financed campaign in southern Scotland. Scottish counter raids followed, and Robert Bruce wrought destruction as far south as Durham, exacting protection money on the way.

By stealth, and without siege engines, Bruce systematically recaptured most of the Scottish castles still in English hands. By spring 1314, only five major strongholds remained to be won, including Stirling, the strategic key to Scotland. In the summer of 1313, its beleaguered captain, Sir Philip Mowbray, had bought time by promising the Scots that if they would abandon their siege immediately, he would yield it to them at midsummer 1314 – unless the English had come to his aid before then.

This shamed Edward into taking a large army into Scotland and on to the Forth Valley plain near Stirling. The force, well equipped, and well trained, consisted essentially of cavalry. The Scottish host which met it was primarily an infantry army, adequately fed and in excellent spirits after its recent run of victories. The two sides were vastly different, but in many ways they were well matched.

On 23 June, the encounter began when Henry de Bohun charged alone against Robert Bruce. Robert sidestepped the levelled lance and de Bohun collected Bruce's axe in his brains.

That evening, the English made a tactical error, abandoning their position by the roadside for a field where they were hemmed in between the River Forth and the Bannock Burn. At daybreak, the Scottish army bore down on them, schiltrons bristling with spears, and crushed

Above *The lone statue of Robert Bruce surveys the scene of his victory over the English. It is still a symbol of Scottish national pride.*

them into the marshy ground. Panicking English troops tried to escape across the burn, and soon the stream was dammed with bodies.

The rout was completed by the Scottish guerillas and camp followers, who fell upon and massacred the English as they attempted to flee. Edward and his household were turned away from Stirling Castle by the pragmatic Mowbray, who fully intended to surrender to the Scots without further complications. With difficulty, Edward escaped to Dunbar, from where he took a boat, and ignominiously returned home.

A few months later, a parliament held near the Bannock Burn pronounced sentence of forfeiture on all within the kingdom who had not sworn loyalty to Robert Bruce: the Balliols and the Comyns, his principal opponents, were disinherited.

Robert had mastery over most of his kingdom after Bannockburn; only Berwick remained in English hands. But although the battle was a triumph of military strategy and a humiliating defeat for Edward II's army, it did not end the war. Scottish independence from England was established within Scotland – but English recognition of that fact did not follow.

Next they removed the unnecessary members of the royal household, who were said to be overburdensome to the king and to the land. This reduced the daily expenses of the king's household by ten pounds. After this, parliament began to discuss matters peaceably and dragged on almost to the end of Lent.

Robert Bruce soon followed up his victory at Bannockburn by laying siege to the important border city of Carlisle. The Lanercost chronicler gives a vivid account of the Scottish attacks.

From 22 July, Robert Bruce with his entire army laid siege to Carlisle for ten days. Every day of the siege they attacked one of the city gates, and some days all three gates at once, but never without loss, for the defenders hurled down on them from the walls darts and arrows and spears in such profusion that the besiegers wondered whether stones were breeding inside the walls. On the fifth day of the siege, the Scots set up a machine near to Holy Trinity Church, to hurl stones at the wall and gate, but despite a continuous rain of stones they did little damage, killing only one man.

Inside the city, however, there were seven or eight similar machines, as well as other engines of war called 'springalds' [which hurl long darts], and slings on poles for throwing stones, all of which terrified and injured the besiegers.

Then the Scots built a 'belfry', a tower-like structure, considerably higher than the walls, but they never succeeded in bringing it up to the walls, because as they were transporting it on wheels across some wet and muddy ground, it sank under its own weight and could be pulled no further.

They set up long ladders, which they climbed under covering fire from a huge body of archers, whose rain of arrows prevented the defenders from putting their heads above the parapet.

But – God be praised! – the defenders found the strength to hurl the ladders away. Many of the besiegers were killed, wounded or captured, there or elsewhere around the walls, but only two Englishmen were killed throughout the siege.

After ten days, whether because they had news of the approach of English forces, or because they despaired of success, the Scots returned homewards in confusion, leaving their siege-engines behind them.

The years 1315 and 1316 witnessed exceptional weather conditions throughout western Europe. Torrential rains led to a ruined harvest, famine and widespread misery, as is graphically described in the Life of Edward II.

Certain portents show the hand of God was raised against us. For example, in the previous year, there was such heavy rain that men could scarcely harvest the corn or bring it safely to the barn.

In the present year worse happened. Floods of rain rotted almost all the seed, so that the prophecy of Isaiah seemed to be fulfilled, that 'ten acres of vineyard shall yield one little measure and thirty bushels of seed shall yield three bushels'. In many places the hay lay so long under water that it could neither be mown nor gathered. Sheep everywhere died and other animals were killed by a sudden plague.

1316

After Easter, the dearth of corn was much increased. Such a scarcity had not been seen in our time in England, nor heard of for a hundred years. A measure of wheat was sold in London and neighbouring places for forty pence, and in other less thickly populated parts of the country, thirty pence was a common price.

Indeed during this time of scarcity a great famine appeared, followed by a severe pestilence, of which many thousands died in different places. I have even heard it said by some that in Northumberland, dogs, horses and other unclean things were eaten. For there, on account of the frequent raids of the Scots, work is more irksome, as the accursed Scots despoil the people daily of their food.

By 1317, relations between Edward II and Thomas, earl of Lancaster, had become strained almost to breaking-point. However, a number of bishops

Pride of the table

MOST people in 14th-century England subsisted on a plain diet of bread, weak ale and potage – a thick stew made largely with cereals and pulses. Fish and fowl occasionally relieved the monotony of this fare, but meat was a rarity. Famine, caused by bad weather or failed harvests, was a constant threat which raised food prices to exorbitant levels and left the poor to starve.

In the *Nun's Priest's Tale* Chaucer writes of a poor widow who had no *sauce piquante* to spice her veal, or wine to drink, but lived on milk, bread, broiled bacon and the occasional egg.

The wealthy, by contrast, could choose from an astonishing array of dishes, both sweet and savoury, and 14th-century royal banquets might run to hundreds of courses. Elaborate confections served on these occasions included peacock that had been skinned and roasted, then had its feathers and begilded beak and claws replaced to lifelike effect. Pork meatballs were coated in batter and coloured green with herbs so that they looked like apples (*pommes dorées*). Dried dates, figs, prunes and almonds were stuck on a skewer, covered in batter and roasted to look like the entrails of wild boar, a hunter's delicacy. Such disguising of food was known as 'pride of the table', and although widely condemned remained popular for centuries.

Sauces were also popular. A green one, often eaten with the fish which was required fare on fast days (such as Fridays and in Lent), was prepared from herbs, bread-crumbs, vinegar, pepper and ginger. Frumenty, for meat and fish, consisted of wheat boiled in milk or water with herbs and spices. But the most versatile sauce of all was mustard, which accompanied meat, fish, fruit, vegetables, creams and puddings.

For the royal and noble table, fine wine was a necessity, and Gascony supplied a substantial proportion of the high quality red wine consumed in England. Ale was the poor man's staple, and was brewed and drunk in vast quantities, with cider and mead, sweetened with honey, to relieve the monotony.

Top left *A banquet in full flow, with servants bringing hot food to the table. Hundreds of courses could be served on occasions like this, with dishes including roast peacock, meatballs coloured to look like apples and dried fruit cooked in batter.*

Top right *A miller delivering flour. Bread was important in the 14th-century diet.*

Above *A monk buying fresh fish. Required fare on feast days, fish was eaten with various sauces, the most popular of which was mustard.*

and barons aimed to bring the idle king and the arrogant Lancaster to an agreement.

On 9 August 1318, the leaders of this moderate group met Thomas of Lancaster near Nottingham and sealed the treaty of Leake. This provided namely that the ordinances should be maintained, and that Lancaster and his associates should be pardoned their alleged offences. On 14 August, Lancaster met the king and their disagreements, too, were settled.

1318

When peace had been made between the king and Thomas, earl of Lancaster, the magnates took steps to promote peace and unity among the people. Discreet men of good reputation were assigned and appointed to each county, to hear and determine the complaints of the people. For the king's servants, with the authority of the state, had been robbing the simple and despoiling the innocent so that no one could finish any business without greasing the official palm. All such men were removed from office to allow the inquiry to proceed more freely.

1319

After Easter the magnates met the king at York, and agreed unanimously that all should muster in arms at Newcastle upon Tyne on 22 July. Then the king sent envoys to Scotland to claim the kingdom, offer peace, and allow safety in life and limb to Robert Bruce.

Bruce replied that he did not much care for the king of England's peace; the kingdom of Scotland was his both by hereditary right and by right of battle. Fortified by these titles, he protested that he neither ought to nor would acknowledge any superior or earthly lord.

The Lanercost chronicler describes the attempts to wreak vengeance on Robert Bruce.

That same year, King Edward II and Thomas, earl of Lancaster, invaded Scotland together on 15 August, and set about attacking Berwick upon Tweed with a large army.

Wine and wool

WOOL, said to be the best in Europe, was England's principal export during Edward II's reign. Most went to the great cloth-manufacturing towns of the Low Countries, but some was beginning to find its way overland to Italy. Many of England's other exports – fish, corn, cheese, hides and lead – went to Gascony, which, under English rule, devoted more and more of its land to the cultivation of vines: most of the resulting wine was shipped to England. England's imports were dominated by wine: indeed, more than 5 million gallons a year were drunk by people of all social classes, from the king to all but his poorest subjects – for anyone could buy a beakerful in a tavern. Most of the wine was brought in by

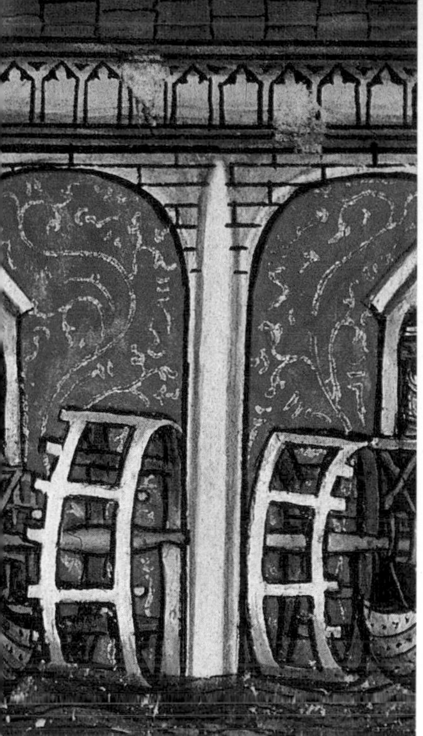

Above *Corn arrives by boat for grinding; coal is loaded aboard ship for export.*

Below *Imports from the world: wine from France, linen from the Low Countries, oil from Spain.*

the king's Gascon subjects, who travelled up and down the country selling it.

Other imports from France included woad, salt and Caen stone. Further south, Spain supplied oil, fruit, leather and iron. The Low Countries provided England with linen, herrings and Flanders tiles, while the Hanseatic League of north German towns sent ships from the Baltic carrying wax, furs, timber, tar and pitch. The Italians provided the greatest luxuries: silk, cotton and cloth of gold from Genoa, and, from Venice, costly eastern spices, sweet wines, sugar and dried fruit. Every year a fleet of Venetian ships – 'Flanders galleys' – set sail for the Low Countries laden with Mediterranean produce to sell in exchange for cloth. As was recorded in 1317, half of them in fact came to London.

Most internal English trade, mainly in food and everyday objects, was carried on at weekly markets and annual fairs. Markets attracted business from about 20 miles away, the greatest distance a man with a cart could travel in a day and still leave time to trade – and return home. Fairs provided the only opportunity for trading products from distant parts of the country, and often lasted for a week or more. Goods were transported the length and breadth of England by packhorse, cart – or boat where possible, particularly if they were heavy – and sometimes even on foot.

Meanwhile, Thomas Randolph, earl of Moray, and James Douglas, who dared not fight an open battle with the king and Lancaster, invaded England, seizing prisoners and cattle as far south as Boroughbridge. Hearing of their approach, the citizens of York, unknown local men led by William of Melton, archbishop of York, and the bishop of Ely, with numerous priests and clerics, including many from the monastic and mendicant orders, met the Scots in a skirmish at Myton-on-Swale, twelve miles north of York. Being inexperienced in warfare, they entered the fight strung out across the field, not in a unified force. The Scots, seeing them rush headlong into battle, raised a mighty clamour in order to terrify the English, who fled on hearing it.

The Scots leapt on to their horses and chased the English, slaughtering clergy and laity alike. About four thousand were slain, including the mayor of York; it was said that another thousand were drowned in the River Swale. But for nightfall, scarcely one Englishman would have survived.

Edward II then raised the siege of Berwick upon Tweed and turned for England, expecting to encounter the Scots. Learning of this, however, the Scots took their prisoners and the stolen cattle back to Scotland by the western route over Stainmoor and through Gilsland. King Edward II dismissed his army, having achieved nothing.

The author of the Life of Edward II *speculates as to why Edward abandoned his Scottish schemes.*

The earl of Lancaster was held to blame that the king had raised the siege of Berwick upon Tweed. It was commonly said that the earl had received forty thousand pounds from Robert Bruce to lend secret aid to him and his men.

O earl of Lancaster, whose wealth is so great, why for such a sum of money did you lose your reputation and name for constancy?

After this, Philip V, the new king of France [son of Philip IV and brother of Edward II's queen, Isabella], demanded homage from the king of England for the land of Gascony. Because this kind of service could only be performed in person, King Edward II entered upon a two year truce with the Scots, and so arranged to cross the Channel in the near future. The king of England did not make the truce so much because he was about to go overseas, as because when it was made, the Scots would desist from attacking his people, whom they used to plunder especially in winter.

1320

After the king's return, a great quarrel arose between some of the greater barons and Hugh Despenser the son, the king's friend and chamberlain. Hugh [whose father, Hugh Despenser, was a long-standing favourite of the king] had married the eldest of the three Gloucester heiresses, and almost all of Glamorgan had fallen to his share. He now exerted all his strength to gain control over the neighbouring lands.

Hugh Despenser the son further proposed that the land of Gower should be assigned to the royal treasury, because John Mowbray had entered it without the king's licence, although it was held from the king in chief. The king promoted Hugh's designs as far as he could. The earls opposed this, pointing out the general disadvantages and humbly petitioning King Edward II not to introduce a new law, contrary to long-established custom. But Hugh Despenser the son took no heed of the special law and customs of the Welsh March. He appeared to accuse the barons who cited them of talking treason.

Deeply moved by such abuse, the barons departed full of indignation. Meeting in Wales, they unanimously decided that Hugh Despenser the son must be pursued and utterly destroyed.

1321

Before they took action, the barons requested that the king dismiss Hugh Despenser the son, or to place him in custody, so that he could be put on trial on a certain day, when he might answer the charges against him; otherwise they would no longer have Edward as their king, but would utterly renounce their homage and fealty and

Art in Italy

THE artistic genius of Gothic Italy was in its sculpture as much as in its painting. This was partly because of the magnificent marble available for carving, of which probably the finest came from the quarries of Carrara, and partly because so many fine pieces of classical sculpture were available to copy, to emulate or simply to re-use.

By the early 13th century, Roman art was inspiring figure sculpture of rounded solidity and great realistic detail. The statue of Virgil, *c.*1215, at the Palazzo Ducale in Mantua, is a solid and realistic representation of a worthy university grammarian with his feet planted firmly on the ground. There is none of the spirituality, the sensitivity, the anxiety found in the faces of 13th-century French, English or German figures. In the second half of the 13th century, in the works of Nicola Pisano, solidity becomes weighty dignity, and realism becomes individuality and dramatic human emotion.

Sculpture was too expensive to cover the large walls of the 13th- and 14th-century churches. The grand and traditional solution was mosaic, still in wide use in the 13th century. But as the economy began to falter around 1300, the cheap alternative of paint became an ever more attractive proposition. In a magnificent series of fresco cycles in the church of S. Francesco at Assisi, the Arena Chapel in Padua, and Santa Croce in Florence, Giotto attempted in highly simplified form to transform the sculptural vision of Nicola Pisano into painting; indeed, in the Arena Chapel, figures painted in grisaille are set in illusionistic niches to simulate real sculpture. Often considered a herald of the massive perspectival style of Masaccio and the early Florentine Renaissance, Giotto was, in fact, a man of his time.

Giotto's sculpturalism was not the only possibility in late 13th-century Italian painting. The rich enamel-toned and gilded Byzantine tradition had a continuing charm for Italian painters. It was particularly appropriate for panel painting – fresco could not achieve the same saturated colour – and the Siennese Duccio (*c.*1250–1319) and the Florentine Cimabue (*c.*1240–1302) both worked within it. Simone Martini (1284–1344), whose work epitomizes the swaying elegance and golden Gothic beauty of Siennese art, was one of the most famous and cultivated artists of his day. He worked at Assisi as well as in his native Sienna, but in 1336 he went to Avignon, where he was the first artist ever paid to paint according to his fancy rather than to a commission. Martini formed a fast friendship with Petrarch, of whom he painted several portraits. The earliest known attempts to achieve specific likeness, all of them are lost.

Below ***A detail from the pulpit in Sienna Cathedral, carved by Nicola Pisano.***

Above *Giotto: St Francis preaching to the birds:*
Top right *Duccio: Maesta*
Below *Cimabue: Enthroned Madonna*
Below right *Martini: Guidoriccio da Fogliano.*

that Pembroke was faithless and fickle and that his help should be rejected. The king and his army set out towards Cirencester, and stayed there over Christmas.

1322

The king sent ahead a force of cavalry and infantry to prepare his crossing at Bridgnorth. But Roger Mortimer, lord of Wigmore, and his uncle Roger Mortimer of Chirk, offered resistance and made a serious attack upon the king. The king reached Shrewsbury in order to cross into the March. The barons there could have hindered his progress if they had wished, but the Mortimers would not agree to this, because Thomas, earl of Lancaster, had not come at the appointed day. The Mortimers were afraid to attempt any large-scale operation or to resist the king further without the earl's help. Then, seeing that the earl of Lancaster would not help them in their hour of need, the Mortimers deserted their allies, and threw themselves upon the king's mercy.

On leaving Shrewsbury, the king crossed to the March, and as no one opposed him, he took all the castles easily. When he reached Hereford, he upbraided Adam Orleton, the bishop of the place, for supporting the barons against their natural lord, and confiscated many of his goods by way of revenge.

The king sent the Mortimers to the Tower of London, where they were to remain, lest they should repent of what they had done and return to their baronial allies.

About this time, the Despensers, father and son, returned from exile. Their reconciliation and reception into the king's peace, at his mere will, was to be proclaimed in England. They returned to England, I say, because the king knew that they had been banished out of malice.

Emboldened by these successes, Edward II now marched north against Thomas, earl of Lancaster, who was by this time almost certainly in league with Robert Bruce and the Scots. Lancaster and the earl of Hereford retreated.

Sieges and stratagems

THERE were many ways of attacking a medieval fortress, and almost as many means of countering such attacks. The first step was to batter the walls with a variety of 'engines', the most common of which was the catapult or 'mangonel'; its throwing beam was hauled back with a windlass and powered by a twisted skein of sinews or, better still, of human hair. When released, the beam struck a massive cross-bar and hurled its missile: a stone, a pot of flaming 'Greek fire' or, occasionally, a dead horse (to infect the garrison) or a captured messenger – to show that all hope of relief was in vain.

The 'ballistas' or 'springalds' used by Edward II against Leeds Castle, Kent, in the siege of 1321, were essentially huge crossbows, which fired either stones or giant arrows, as did the primitive cannon which joined the besieger's arsenal in the mid-14th century. They were far more accurate than other siege engines, but because they were unreliable and difficult to transport, they were initially more useful to stationary defenders.

If battering was ineffective, it was sometimes possible to undermine the walls, particularly at vulnerable right-angled corners. Beginning some distance away (and if possible concealing their shaft), professional miners

Above *Leeds Castle, Kent. In 1321 it was besieged by Edward II, who used 'ballistas' against its inhabitants.*

burrowed beneath the defences, supporting their tunnel with wooden props. They then filled the mine with combustible materials – at Rochester in 1216, the fat of 40 pigs – and fired them, burning away the supports, collapsing the tunnel and, with luck, demolishing the wall above it. If a garrison knew, or suspected, that their position was being undermined, they could sometimes locate the underground workings by standing filled water jugs in different parts of the fortress and observing them when they vibrated. They could then sink a counter-mine from inside the fortress, and either slaughter the opposing diggers in hand-to-hand fighting, or flood their tunnel with water.

Castles surrounded by moats, or founded on solid rock, were virtually impervious to mining, and in these cases it was often necessary to storm the walls, using suicidally hazardous scaling ladders and perhaps a 'belfry' or 'malvoisin' (bad neighbour) – a wheeled tower whose uppermost platform was level with the wall top. The besiegers would also assault the wooden gate of the fortress, potentially its most vulnerable point, using, more often than not, an iron-headed battering ram swung from a framework covered with wet hides. These hides gave protection against 'firepots' that were dropped from above, along with javelins, stones, boiling oil, and what can only be described as boiling porridge, a scalding oatmeal mush, which stuck to besiegers' skins.

Once within the outer gate, the attackers might find themselves trapped in a passage between two portcullises, and showered with missiles from 'murder holes' in its roof.

The best way to avoid such horrors was to mount a surprise attack, a tactic much favoured by Edward II's Scottish guerilla opponents who generally lacked the resources for a formal siege. On a dark night in 1314, for example, Sir James (Black) Douglas's men donned co-whides and approached Roxburgh Castle on all fours, deceiving the watch until they were close enough to throw up their grapnelled scaling ladders.

A traitor within the walls was a still more effective weapon; but the most inexorable were hunger and thirst. All castles had wells, but if these ran dry (or were poisoned), the defenders ultimately had to surrender: a waterless French garrison which attempted to subsist on wine soon became incapable of resistance. Treachery or blockade, indeed, probably encompassed the downfall of more medieval fortresses than ever fell to siegecraft.

When the king's army reached Boroughbridge, where they intended to rest for a night, who should be there but Andrew Harclay, an active north-country soldier, already aware of the earl of Lancaster's flight. Fully apprised of the earl's plans, Harclay had speedily led some four thousand men to that place.

The earls were settling into their lodgings, when they learned that Andrew Harclay and his followers had come to destroy them utterly; so they left the town in two columns to meet their opponents.

The earl of Hereford crossed the bridge with his men-at-arms, but none of them was mounted, for the bridge was narrow and offered no path for horsemen in battle array. The earl of Lancaster and his knights made their way to the ford. But Harclay, like a prudent knight, had shrewdly stationed a force of men-at-arms opposite each crossing. The earl of Hereford attacked the enemy, but fell, badly wounded in the fighting, and died. Three or four knights were killed with him, and many returned to the town badly wounded. Others, trying to cross the ford, were cut up by a shower of arrows; but after the death of the earl of Hereford, their zeal for battle cooled, and they at once retreated.

The earl of Lancaster made a truce with Andrew Harclay until the morrow; and each returned to his lodging. That same night, the sheriff of York arrived with a large force to attack the king's enemies. Relying on his help, Andrew Harclay entered the town very early; he captured the earl of Lancaster and almost all the other knights and squires unwounded, led them off to York and imprisoned them.

Four or five days later, on coming to Pontefract, the king ordered that the earl of Lancaster be brought before him without delay.

The following day, the earl of Lancaster was led into the hall before the justices assigned for the purpose, and charged one by one with his crimes. To each charge a special penalty was attached, namely, that first he should be drawn, then hanged, and finally decapitated, but out of reverence for his royal blood, the penalty of drawing was remitted, as also that of hanging, and one punishment was decreed for all three.

The earl wished to speak in mitigation of his crimes, but the judges refused to hear him. So the earl said: 'This is indeed a powerful court, and great in authority, where no answer is heard nor any excuse admitted.'

Here was a sight indeed! To see the earl of Lancaster, lately the terror of the whole country, receiving judgement in his own castle and home. He was led forth from the castle of Pontefract, mounted on some worthless mule, to the place of execution.

Then the earl stretched forth his head as if in prayer, and the executioner cut off his head with two or three strokes.

The Lanercost chronicler provides a vivid depiction of Edward II's last – and once more, disastrous – expedition against the Scots.

On 1 August, the king of England came to Newcastle upon Tyne. Soon afterwards, he invaded Scotland with a mighty army, but the Scots, as usual, retreated, not daring to fight with him. However in early September, the English were forced to withdraw, partly by lack of supplies, partly because of illness in the army, which was ravaged by a type of dysentery.

As soon as the English had gone the king of Scots assembled a massive force and crossed the Solway Firth into England.

King Edward sent John, duke of Brittany, earl of Richmond, with a troop, to reconnoitre the Scots' position from a hill between the abbeys of Rievaulx and Byland. In fact, John and his troop came face to face with the Scots suddenly and without warning, and had to try to prevent them from climbing the narrow path up the hill by hurling rocks at them. But the enemy made a fierce, bold ascent, and captured many of them, including John of Brittany, although some escaped.

The king himself was then at Rievaulx Abbey. When news of the encounter reached him, he, who was always faint-hearted and unlucky in war, and who had been avoiding battle in Scotland out of fear, now took to flight even in England.

Leaving behind his silver vessels and other treasure in his haste to quit the monastery, King Edward II fled to York.

Shortly afterwards, the Scots arrived at Rievaulx. They carried off the king's valuables and despoiled the monastery, then set off across the wolds, taking John, earl of Richmond, with them. They laid waste the whole region, as far as Beverley, where the townspeople paid heavily to be spared from destruction.

In 1323, the Scots agreed to a 12-year truce with the English, and the next year, as the Life of Edward II *shows, were ready to discuss peace.*

1324

It was agreed by common consent that the parties should meet at York for negotiations. There the king of England met certain Scottish magnates who put forward demands that Scotland should be for ever free from every English exaction, and that by right of conquest and lordship, the whole land which they had perambulated should be free as far as the gates of York.

The Scots demanded that the royal stone [of Scone] should be restored to them, which Edward I had long ago taken from Scotland and placed at Westminster by the tomb of St Edward the Confessor. Robert Bruce proposed that his daughter should be joined in marriage with the king's son. Finally, the Scots wished that the promises of the nobles should be confirmed by the king of France, in the presence of the pope, so that a treaty of peace, strengthened by such authority, should never be broken.

When King Edward II heard the Scottish proposals he said: 'The Scots have come to us not to make peace but to seek opportunities for further discord and for unprovoked breaches of the truce. To grant these demands would be much to our loss, and they will return to their own country without satisfaction. For how without prejudice to our crown can we surrender the right we have in Scotland? We know that my father, Edward I, when Scotland was conquered, took with him the famous royal stone as a sign of victory: if we were to restore it, we should appear to be tossing aside the right thus acquired.'

The Scots were told, therefore, that the king did not approve their terms, nor could he be forced to make such an ignoble peace [although the truce continued to run].

Edward II's wish to make peace with the Scots stemmed in part from his anxieties about the duchy of Gascony, for which he had delayed doing homage to Charles IV, king of France, since 1322. A French force invaded Gascony in 1324, forcing a truce on its English defenders. Pope John XXII intervened and sent messengers to Paris; they suggested that Charles IV's sister, Queen Isabella of England, would be a suitable ambassador and peacemaker.

The events which followed are unfolded by the lively – if sometimes inventive – Geoffrey le Baker. Unlike the other chroniclers, he shows considerable sympathy for Edward II.

1325

Queen Isabella, the only sister of the king of France, Charles IV, at last saw the dear face of her beloved brother and embraced him, after a long separation. She was to act as intermediary between the two kings, her brother and her husband.

King Edward II, Isabella's husband, stayed in Kent throughout the spring and summer, so that it would be easy for messengers to pass swiftly between himself and his wife, while she was engaged in the negotiations in France, which were the purpose of her visit.

Finally, the French parlement decided that, if the king of England would surrender his claims to the duchy of Gascony and the county of Ponthieu to Prince Edward, his eldest son, the king of France for his part would accord full recognition to the young prince's claim to these territories, contenting himself with the sole condition that the prince should pay him homage in respect of those lands. In addition, Charles IV, king of France, sent letters patent and other letters concerning the safe conduct of the young prince, son of the king of England, who was to be sent to him.

There was much discussion among the English, both at London and at Dover, concerning the conditions specified by the French king. Some were of the opinion that King Edward II himself should make the journey across the Channel, for they felt that his son would be vulnerable to all manner of misfortunes if he were exposed to the wily and avaricious French without the protection of his father or his English companions. 'Who', they asked, 'will prevent the French king from marrying off the poor lad to some person of inferior birth, or assigning him some tutor or guardian of his own choosing?' Those who argued thus were indeed justified.

The two Despensers would not accept this, however, for they dared neither to cross the Channel with King Edward II nor to remain behind in England in his absence.

Thus the king of England granted by charter to his son Edward the duchy of Gascony and the county of Ponthieu, to be held by the prince and his heirs, the kings of England. He added a clause to the effect that if he were to survive his son, the lands would revert to his authority, for he was afraid that the other conditions of the charter might give an advantage to the king of France, if the latter could contrive to arrange a marriage for Prince Edward, or submit him to the authority of a tutor or guardian.

This was the proposal of the king, agreed by the clergy and the rest of the English nobility at Dover, on 9 September.

On the following Sunday the king's eldest son, Prince Edward, began his journey to France, accompanied by Walter Stapledon, bishop of Exeter, and a goodly number of other nobles.

The Decorated style

IN about 1300, England was suddenly in the van of architectural developments, rather than, as hitherto, struggling to keep abreast of France. Although it is true that the source of the English Decorated style was the tracery-dominated French Rayonnant of Saint-Denis and the Sainte-Chapelle, and English architects still went to France for inspiration, there was no more need to invite French architects like William of Sens at Canterbury, or Henry of Reyns at Westminster, for the major commissions. The architects of the Decorated style were strictly indigenous.

Two commissions from Edward I seem to have played a key rôle in its development: the two-level chapel of St Stephen at Westminster Palace – the English answer to the Sainte-Chapelle – begun in 1292; and the Eleanor Crosses, those touching memorials of a hard man for his beloved wife. Both the chapel and the crosses are distinguished by the highly imaginative handling of tracery and arch forms, including the introduction of double-curved or ogee arches. Gradually these were curved not in one plane but in two, extending forwards into the nodding ogees, which ripple along the walls of the Lady Chapel at Ely Cathedral.

At Exeter Cathedral, rebuilt, apart from its Norman towers, between about 1280 and 1360, window tracery reaches new levels of complexity, with patterns forming into nets and flowing flame-like shapes taking advantage of the double curve of the ogee. The vault, almost overladen with ribs, has an opulence that prefigures the fan vault.

The east end of Wells Cathedral, rebuilt in the early years of the 14th century, is another design of patterned surfaces, with elaborate tracery nets drawn across walls, vaults and windows; the octagonal Lady Chapel is pulled into an egg shape, and the whole cathedral is built to a geometrically complex plan.

The result is a building of strangely shifting vistas of slender shafts and cones of vaults like an Arthurian forest.

Between 1322 and 1342, the famous central tower at Ely also exploited the design possibilities of the octagon. The span was enormous – 65 feet – and the Ely octagon is an impressive engineering feat. Built in wood – the weight of stone could not have been sustained across that space – it is painted and gilded to imitate stone.

The choir of the Augustinian abbey (now cathedral) of Bristol is in striking contrast to these richly decorated buildings. Bristol is elegant and restrained; its spaces are open and of pristine clarity. A hall church, its aisles, with narrow transverse vaults, are the same height as the main nave. Both features are suggestive of the churches of

Above *The west door at Exeter Cathedral. The increased complexity of tracery work can be clearly seen. The tiny branches of stone work not so much support the masonry as fill in an exposed area of glass. In the carving beneath, a forest of arches ornament the wall space surrounding the door.*

Right *Interior view of the west front stained glass window. The impact of more stone limbs and smaller fragments of glass was to reduce the amount of light reaching the interior.*

Poitou and Gascony, perhaps reflecting Bristol's connection with these areas through the wine trade.

Bristol's elegance and restraint are recognizable influences on the two major works produced for Edward III: the upper levels of St Stephen's Chapel, and the choir and transepts of Gloucester Cathedral. Begun in about 1330, Gloucester was intended as a mausoleum for Edward II, built by his son. Because it was too expensive to dismantle the solidly built Norman choir, vast panelled skeins of tracery were stretched across the Norman walls. The Perpendicular style, the last Gothic transmutation of medieval England, was born.

The king and Hugh Despenser the son were captured and entrusted to the custody of Henry, earl of Leicester, on the authority of Adam Orleton, bishop of Hereford. The king was then taken to Kenilworth Castle, where he spent the winter in reasonably comfortable conditions as befits a king in captivity.

The queen was, at that time, at Hereford, together with the man who bore the main responsibility for her wicked plot, Adam Orleton, the so-called bishop of that town who was the general of her army.

Then Hugh Despenser the son was brought forth in chains, his eyes blazing terribly at this indignity, for he held no hope of being tried fairly according to the proper procedure.

And indeed, here, at Hereford, he was drawn, hanged, beheaded and cut into quarters. His head was sent to London Bridge and the four quarters of his body were sent forth to the four quarters of the kingdom.

1327

Many more had been killed according to the wishes of Queen Isabella, Adam Orleton, bishop of Hereford, and Roger Mortimer by the time they moved on to London. There, in January, in a parliament which they themselves had summoned – for no one dared oppose them – it was ordained and established that on behalf of the whole kingdom, three bishops, two earls, two abbots, four barons, two knights from each county of England, and two burgesses from each city, county, town and port, were to be sent to Kenilworth, where King Edward II was being held. John Stratford, bishop of Winchester, Adam Orleton, bishop of Hereford, and Henry Burghersh, bishop of Lincoln, together were the chief agents of the uprising.

The bishops of Winchester and Lincoln went on ahead to talk secretly with the king and his keeper Henry, earl of Leicester, trying to persuade him to pass on his crown to his eldest son, Prince Edward. Together, the three of them tried to

Crime, punishment and spectacle

WHEN Sir John le Breton, a Norfolk gentleman, found out that his daughter had a nocturnal assignation with Sir Godfrey Millers, a married man with grown children, he dealt with the matter very simply; as Sir Godfrey crept into the house he was met by the whole family, who strung him feet first from the rafters and castrated him.

This incident, in 1248, typifies the common image of medieval crime: abundant lawlessness, wanton savagery, and weak policing by central government. Sir John ended his days in exile as a result of his actions that night, but Henry III did little for the rule of law when he declared such behaviour to be illegal – except by husbands who caught men with their wives. The 13th and 14th centuries were rich in spectacular and bloody crimes, often unpunished, and the society which provided the backcloth for the tales of Robin Hood is easily seen as virtually ungovernable.

The reality was less grim. England was undoubtedly difficult to police; major crimes were committed in the course of political disputes; there were large numbers of itinerant poor, who provided plenty of larceny, robbery, cattle-rustling and horse-stealing. Some of these problems were fed by national affairs: the power-struggles under Henry III and Edward II allowed property to be seized under the guise of civil war, while the demobilization of the armies after Edward I's successful campaigns against Scotland and Wales let thousands of freebooters loose upon the civilian population.

No king was strong enough to exercise control over all the sources of disorder. But the mechanisms of law and order were there, and continued to function and develop, even during the most lawless of times such as Edward II's reign.

Petty crime was tried and punished through a comprehensive network of local courts, which operated regularly and according to well-established customary laws. Although these courts were mostly in the hands of the gentry or their deputies, the Crown took a direct interest in them, partly by regulation, partly by piecemeal takeover, and partly by providing rival courts under the jurisdiction of the sheriff.

The Crown also experimented with courts for trying serious crimes. Under Henry III, the eyre – a circuit by judges and administrators from Westminster, who reviewed and if necessary tried all the crime in a county since the previous visitation – was used to assert royal control throughout the country. When this institution

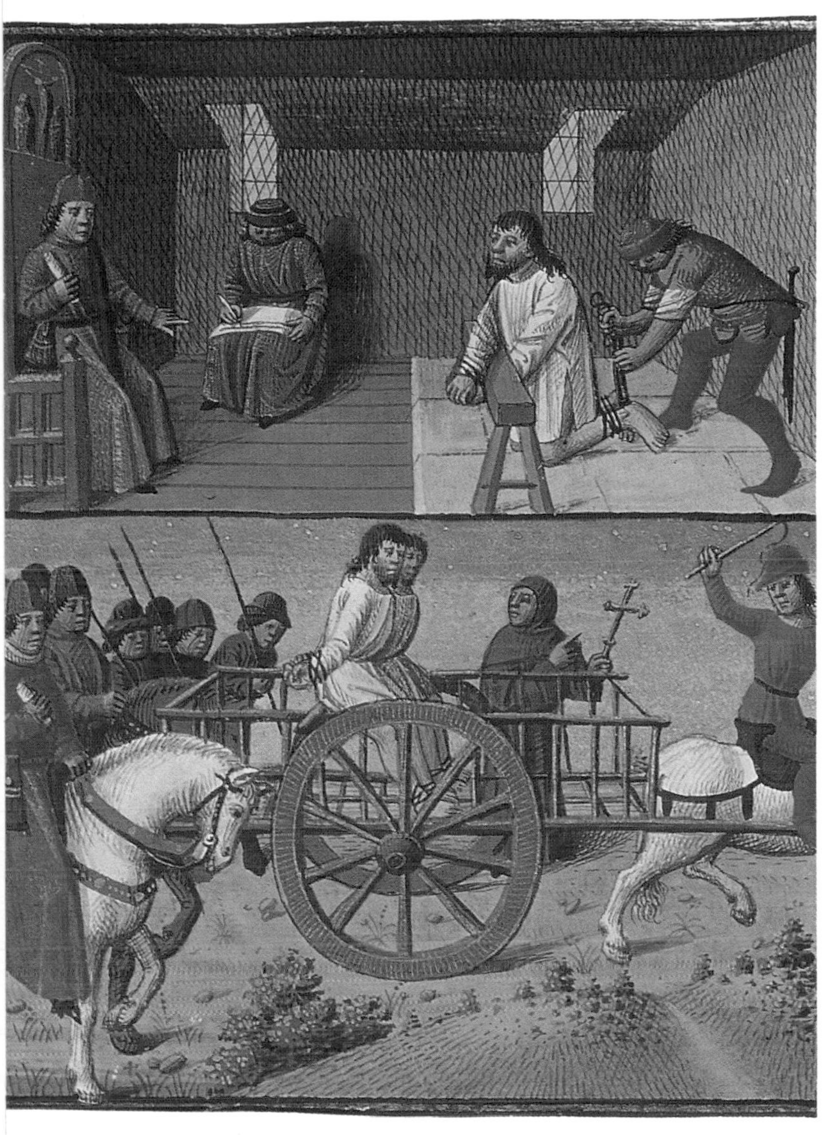

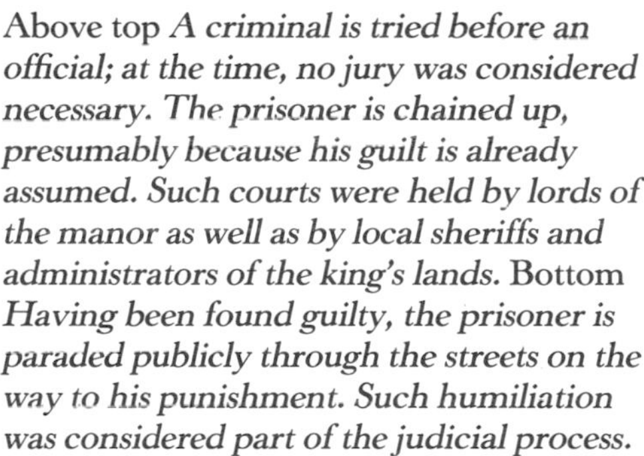

Above top *A criminal is tried before an official; at the time, no jury was considered necessary. The prisoner is chained up, presumably because his guilt is already assumed. Such courts were held by lords of the manor as well as by local sheriffs and administrators of the king's lands.* Bottom *Having been found guilty, the prisoner is paraded publicly through the streets on the way to his punishment. Such humiliation was considered part of the judicial process.*

Above *Hugh Despenser's execution was certainly not the comparatively humane beheading accorded to royal favourites. He was crowned with nettles, hanged from gallows 50 feet high, and his genitals were cut off and burnt in front of him to punish his heresy and sodomy. He was finally beheaded. As he went to his execution a catalogue of his crimes was recited. The venom of his executioners and their vilification of his crimes put them into a category of brutality exceptional even by the often inhumane standards of the Middle Ages.*

broke down under his successors, quarterly sessions (held by mostly lay magistrates from the county) were established to hear all offences and try the most serious ones, such as rape and homicide. Some such cases, however, were sent up to the justices of assize, central court judges travelling round the counties during their Easter and summer vacations. Quarter sessions and assizes survived without fundamental change for six centuries.

Indeed, those enemies of the Lord were skilled in devising ways to disguise Edward, lest any of his friends should be able to recognize him: they decided to shave not only his beard but his hair also. As they travelled along, they came upon a small ditch with running water. Here they ordered him to dismount that he might be shaved, causing him to sit upon a mole-hill, and a barber came to him with a basin full of cold water from the ditch. But Edward said to them, 'Whether you will or no, I shall have warm water to shave in.' And indeed, he at once began to weep profusely.

These things were told me by William Bishop, in the time after the great plague. He had seen them with his own eyes for he had been among those who took Edward to Berkeley.

Finally they arrived at Berkeley Castle, where, ever patient in the face of his misfortunes, the noble Edward was shut up like a hermit. He was robbed of his earthly kingdom and stripped bare like the blessed Job, not by his rivals but by his own wife, his servants and serving women.

Despoiled of his command, his honours, his goods, Edward II looked forward to the kingdom of Heaven. However, his wife, Isabella, was angered that his life which had become most hateful to her should be so prolonged. She asked advice of the bishop of Hereford, pretending that she had had a dreadful dream from which she feared, if it was true, that her husband would at some time be restored to his former dignity and would condemn her, as a traitress, to be burned or to perpetual slavery. The bishop of Hereford feared greatly for himself, just as Isabella did, if this should come to pass, conscious as he was that he was guilty of treason.

And so, letters were written to Edward's keepers, setting forth in vivid detail the false accusation that they had been too lenient with him and fed him on delicacies. Moreover, it was hinted that the death of Edward would cause these nobles no great displeasure, whether it were natural or violent. Concerning this point, the bishop of Hereford penned a message of double meaning:
Edwardum occidere nolite timere bonum est.

The art of cleanliness

ILLUSTRATIONS in 14th-century manuscripts depict figures with neatly done hair, and well trimmed beards, dressed in the height of contemporary fashion. For the rich, style and cleanliness were important in themselves and were also a tangible demonstration of power and sophistication.

Bath houses were important social centres, and had been for some 260 years in Southern Europe. Sophisticated baths were marble or other stone – an Eastern one was made from an Egyptian sarcophagus – but other, more portable versions, for one or more people, were made of wood, often in the shape of a tub formed of wooden staves held together with horizontal metal hoops.

Communal bathing in these baths was generally a social occasion, with food and drink to hand. Water was heated in large bronze cauldrons, over a log fire, and poured over the bather or bathers with bronze or pottery bowls.

Sponges were imported from the Mediterranean, and soap was made with olive oil. England was an important centre of production.

Perfumes or their equivalents were valued not only for their fragrance, but also because they were thought to have the power to ward off disease. They included ambergris, the secretion of the sperm whale, musk and other natural perfumes from plants and flowers. Rosewater, lavender, sandalwood and nutmeg were the most common. Rarer perfumes were worn round the neck in special containers, often pierced gold or silver spheres containing a sponge soaked in perfume. Small bottles made of rock crystal, generally obtained from Egypt or Syria, were also used.

Combs for the toilette were made of wood or bone, although beautifully carved examples in ivory were used to comb the hair of bishops or priests preparing to say Mass. These were usually rectangular with the teeth fretted out with a saw, and were often double sided. Mirrors were circular and made of highly polished steel or latin – a form of brass. They were contained in ivory cases, carved with scenes of courtly love, war and the chase.

There were also less sophisticated versions, in wood or stamped leather cases. Glass mirrors had recently been invented and only came into general use during the next century.

Cut-throat razors were used for shaving, some with flat oval shaped blades. Scissors – really small steel shears forged in one piece with a hooped top acting as a spring – were easily sharpened and could be employed to trim the hair and beard.

Dentistry was primitive. Although complicated techniques such as crowning and filling are discussed in contemporary medical texts, and many remedies are given for toothache, there was little attempt at preventing tooth decay, which must have been very common in the 14th century.

Top left *Detail from a 14th-century French ivory comb delicately carved with two lovers. Objects like these were highly prized possessions.*

Above *A public wash house. Apart from providing people with a place where they could get clean, public baths were also a meeting-place for friends to pass the hours. Baths were sometimes prescribed by doctors as part of a treatment.*

A 13th-century manuscript of Roger of Salerno's Chirurgia *shows a patient taking a bath under medical supervision. Bathers used wooden tubs, in some cases marble ones, with water heated near by. Soap was used; its principal ingredients were goats' tallow and beech ash, until they were replaced by olive oil.*

This saying may be resolved into two parts: the first consists of the first three words of the bishop's puzzle: *'Edwardum occidere nolite'* – 'Do not kill Edward!' – followed by the second three: *'timere bonum est'* – 'fear is a good thing.' Read thus, the message would not be construed as treason.

But those who received the message were aware of the true import of the bishop's communication. They construed the message thus: *'Edwardum occidere nolite timere'* – 'Do not fear to kill Edward!' – followed by *'bonum est'* – 'it is good!' Those who were guilty of evil, read the message as evil. Thus did that skilful trickster have recourse to a puzzle, for he knew that without his authority, Edward's keepers would not dare to carry out their cruel instructions and kill him, lest they should later be brought to trial for this crime.

The bishop of Hereford himself made careful provision that the authority which he gave might appear to mean the opposite of what he intended, but to have been misread by the thick-witted keepers who then took the life of an innocent man as a consequence of their own mistake. Taken in the contrary sense, his message made him safe from any accusation of treason. And indeed, events were to prove the bishop correct.

In the end, Edward's murderers, who had believed that the favour of Isabella and the slippery and deceitful bishop made them secure, found instead that these two were eager to take vengeance for the murder of their hostage, Edward.

The keepers were dumbfounded and did not know what to do. They showed the letters with the seals of Isabella, the bishop of Hereford and the other conspirators to prove that the latter had indeed given their consent.

The bishop did not deny the letter, agreeing that he and his accomplices had sent it, but he explained it as being perfectly innocent and loyal in its meaning. It was the keepers, he claimed, who had misinterpreted it and used it as authority for their own wicked deed. He so terrified them with his threats that they fled. So much for the letter of double meaning.

Edward II was welcomed kindly at the castle and treated well by Thomas Berkeley, lord of the estate. After receipt of the letter, however, Edward's torturers took control of the castle.

They gave orders that Thomas Berkeley was to have no contact with Edward. This caused him not only sadness but also shame for he was unable to do as he wished and as before had been his right. Sighing, he bade Edward farewell and removed to another of his estates.

Then began the most extreme part of Edward's persecution which was to continue until his death.

Firstly, he was shut up in a secure chamber, where he was tortured for many days until he was almost suffocated by the stench of corpses buried in a cellar hollowed out beneath. Carpenters, who one day were working near the window of his chamber, heard him, God's servant, as he lamented that this was the most extreme suffering that had ever befallen him.

But when his tyrannous warders perceived that the stench alone was not sufficient to kill him, they seized him on the night of 22 September as he lay sleeping in his room.

There, with cushions heavier than fifteen strong men could carry, they held him down, suffocating him.

Then they thrust a plumber's soldering iron, heated red hot, guided by a tube inserted into his bowels, and thus they burnt his innards and his vital organs. They feared lest, if he were to receive a wound in those parts of the body where men generally are wounded, it might be discovered by some man who honoured justice, and his torturers might be found guilty of manifest treason and made to suffer the consequent penalty.

As this brave knight was overcome, he shouted aloud so that many heard his cry both within and without the castle and knew it for the cry of a man who suffered violent death. Many in both the town and castle of Berkeley were moved to pity for Edward, and to watch and pray for his spirit as it departed this world.

Edward II's ultimate fate

IN April 1327 the deposed Edward II was taken away from Kenilworth Castle and imprisoned at Berkeley Castle, Gloucestershire, in the custody of Thomas, lord of Berkeley. Although two attempts were made to rescue him, the second in early September 1327, he died at Berkeley Castle in the same month. Adam of Murimuth, a contemporary, writes: 'Although many abbots, priors, knights and burgesses of Bristol and Gloucester were summoned to inspect the body whole – and thus looked at it superficially – it was widely rumoured that the king had been cunningly killed on the orders of John Maltravers and Thomas Gurney, his gaolers. Because of this, these two, and certain others, fled.'

On 21 September 1327 it was officially announced at the Lincoln parliament that Edward was dead, and on 21 December, a solemn funeral was held for him at Gloucester Abbey, where a flourishing cult soon grew up around his supposed remains. Most of Edward's contemporaries assumed that he had been murdered. The fact that Queen Isabella had had the heart removed from the corpse and placed it in a silver vase, which was later buried in her own coffin, was seen as an open announcement of apparent remorse. Yet no one was convicted of killing the king. Thomas, lord of Berkeley, had been absent when the death took place and was soon acquitted. Maltravers, who escaped a perfunctory trial by fleeing abroad in 1330, was pardoned some 20 years later and taken into Edward III's service.

In a letter written to Edward III, Manuel de Fieschi, a canon of York and high papal official who claimed to have met and confessed Edward II, gives an apparently well-founded account of how the king escaped from Berkeley Castle to wander across Europe, first as a fugitive, then as a hermit. 'Finally', de Fieschi writes, 'they sent Edward to Berkeley Castle. Later the attendant who guarded him told him: "Sire, Thomas Gurney and Simon Beresford have come to kill you, but if it pleases you I will give you my clothes so that you may escape." Edward, dressed in these clothes, crept out of his prison by night and reached the outermost door unchallenged because he was not recognized. Finding the porter asleep, he immediately killed him, took the keys of the door, opened it and escaped with his former guard.

'The knights who had come to kill Edward saw that he had gone and, fearing the queen's anger and terrified for their lives, they put the porter in a chest, having first cut out his heart. They presented the porter's heart and body to the wicked queen as if they were your father's, and the porter was buried at Gloucester as the body of the king.

'Edward and his companion were received at Corfe Castle by the castellan, Thomas, without the knowledge of his lord, John Maltravers, and the king remained secretly at Corfe for a year and a half. Later . . . he crossed to Ireland where he stayed for eight months, but he was afraid that he might be recognized there. Putting on the clothes of a hermit, he came back to England, went to Sandwich and crossed to Sluys, then travelled to Normandy . . . and on to Avignon. Here Edward gave a florin to a papal servant and sent a note to Pope John XXII.

'The pope summoned him and for more than 15 days kept him in secrecy and honour. Finally . . . Edward departed and went to Paris, then to Brabant, and then to Cologne to see the three kings and offer his devotions. He next crossed Germany and reached Milan, where he entered a hermitage at Milazzo Castle, staying there for two and a half years. Because this castle was involved in a war, he moved on to another hermitage near Cecima in the diocese of Pavia in Lombardy. And the king remained in this last hermitage for some two years, in seclusion, praying for us and for other sinners.'

However, no independent corroborative evidence for this story has ever been found.

Above *Edward II's cell, scene of his murder.*

Overleaf *Berkeley Castle, a formidable prison.*

So he whom the world hated, more even than it had hated the Lord Jesus Christ (who was hated above all others among the Jewish nation), this follower of Christ, was robbed of his kingdom, but received into the kingdom of the angels.

Queen Isabella and the bishop of Hereford now turned their attention to the punishment of the traitorous agents who had brought about the death of the good and noble Edward, that they themselves might appear innocent in thought and deed.

Thomas Gurney fled to Marseille, where he hid for three years until he was recognized and captured. But on the journey back to England, where he was to have received the punishment he deserved, he was beheaded at sea lest once back in England he made some accusation against the magnates, priests and other nobles. John Maltravers, however, remained for a long time in Germany, filled with penitence.

Queen Isabella triumphant

ON 24 September 1326 Isabella and her lover Roger Mortimer anchored at Orwell with their invasion fleet. Edward II tried to rally London to his defence, but, meeting with hostility, he panicked. On 2 October he left the capital for the last time and, equipped with the large sum of £30,000, fled desperately west, heading for Ireland and safety. A week later he was at Gloucester, and on 20 October he set sail from Chepstow, accompanied only by Hugh Despenser the younger and Robert Baldock, his chancellor. His household waited for the queen's arrival at Westbury near Bristol, its officials continuing to spend money and draw up the accounts as if nothing had happened.

Isabella and Mortimer were not far behind the king. On 26 October, in Bristol, they declared the young prince Edward keeper of the realm, and the next day the elder Hugh Despenser was brought to trial and hanged. The king had been blown ashore by contrary winds; forced to land at Cardiff on 25 October he set off for Caerphilly, probably in an attempt to shelter with some of the younger Hugh's under-tenants.

On 16 November the king and his handful of followers were captured near Neath by Henry, earl of Leicester, brother of the dead Thomas, earl of Lancaster. The younger Despenser was taken to Hereford, tried and cruelly executed. The great seal of the realm was taken away from Edward, who was led off by Leicester to Kenilworth Castle and captivity. The queen's hold on the realm seemed irreversible.

In January 1327 a great council met at Westminster, and, under the threat of mob violence from the citizens of London, who were passionate partisans of Isabella, it was agreed that Edward II was no longer king. A delegation was sent to Kenilworth, where Edward, weeping and begging for mercy, relinquished the throne, provided that his son succeeded him. This paved the way for Edward III's acceptance by the commons and his coronation on 1 February 1327.

Edward II was immortalized by the Elizabethan playwright Christopher Marlowe as the embodiment of evil, and, some four centuries later, the Victorian historian William Stubbs suggested that his reign had witnessed a major decline in English civilization and morals.

Edward II was singularly incompetent; but his feuding barons were motivated as much by personal jealousies as by a desire for the reform of the administration, and were more concerned by the use and misuse of royal patronage than fundamental constitutional principles.

Right *Gloucester Cathedral, burial place of the deposed Edward II. At the time of his death in 1327, Gloucester had yet to achieve the status of a cathedral, which was eventually granted in 1541.*

Below *Detail from the effigy on Edward II's tomb in the north ambulatory of Gloucester Cathedral. It was impressively carved in alabaster and mounted on a Purbeck marble base.*

Part IV

Edward III 1327–1377

The long reign of Edward III began unpropitiously with the deposition of his father, but, once he had attained his majority and had broken away from the tutelage of his mother, Isabella of France, the king was to earn great glory. He indulged his taste for warfare to the full – a taste shared with his equally bellicose son Edward the Black Prince – in the long conflict with the house of Valois over the throne of France. This, the Hundred Years War, broke out in 1337 and was not to be resolved until the end of the fifteenth century. Its early stages saw some major English victories, notably at Crécy (1346) and Poitiers (1356), and the emergence of a glittering cult of chivalry. But to the miseries of war were added, from 1348, the horrific effects of the Black Death. The lively chronicle of Geoffrey le Baker provides the main narrative, followed by the celebrated works of Froissart, a Hainaulter, and those of his compatriot Jean le Bel. Thomas Walsingham, a monk of St Albans, describes the last years of Edward III's reign.

(Opposite: Edward III)

After glorious King Edward II had given up his crown to his eldest son, Edward of Windsor, the noblemen and clergy of England at once received Edward, a lad of about fifteen years, pleasing to God and to the whole world, as his father's successor, in parliament in London.

And so, on 1 February, Prince Edward was crowned at Westminster by the archbishop of Canterbury, Walter Reynolds. This great ceremony was attended by many, foreigners as well as English, and in particular, the mercenaries of the queen-mother, Isabella, whom she herself invited from Hainault and Germany.

The new king received the crown which the most blessed confessor, St Edward, his predecessor, had worn. It was of vast size and a great weight but he bore it like a man, so that those who saw marvelled that such a slip of a lad, who had never worn a crown before, could manage to wear one of such size and weight.

1328

King Charles IV of France, the king of England's uncle and the brother of Isabella the queen-mother, went the way of all flesh. He was succeeded by Philip de Valois.

The start of the Hundred Years War

Most of the battles and campaigns in the Hundred Years War took place on French soil, but the northern Spanish kingdoms of Aragon and Castile had long been valued as potential allies by both the French and the English sovereigns. In 1366 the Black Prince, who was ruling as prince of Aquitaine, took advantage of a lull in the conflict with the Valois and agreed to go to the aid of King Peter the Cruel of Castile. Peter had been deposed by his half brother Henry of Trastamara backed by Bertrand du Guesclin, whose allegiance was to the French Crown. Control of Castile and its navy was at stake, and the Black Prince showed his military prowess to the full in his victory near Nájera in 1367. His levy of crushing taxes in Gascony to pay for his Spanish campaign stirred up considerable opposition, and a resumption of hostilities with the French king followed in 1368.

In 1337 Edward III laid claim to the French crown, and in 1339 staged his first campaign in France. His forces won many victories with the help of the Black Prince, notably at Poitiers in 1356, when the French king was captured, which led to the gains of the treaty of Brétigny in 1360. This gave Edward full sovereignty over Gascony, Poitou, the Agenais, Périgord, Quercy, the Limousin, Calais and Ponthieu. He in his turn dropped his claim to the French throne. The peace was shortlived however, and in 1369 the next round of the war began – with unhappy consequences for Edward.

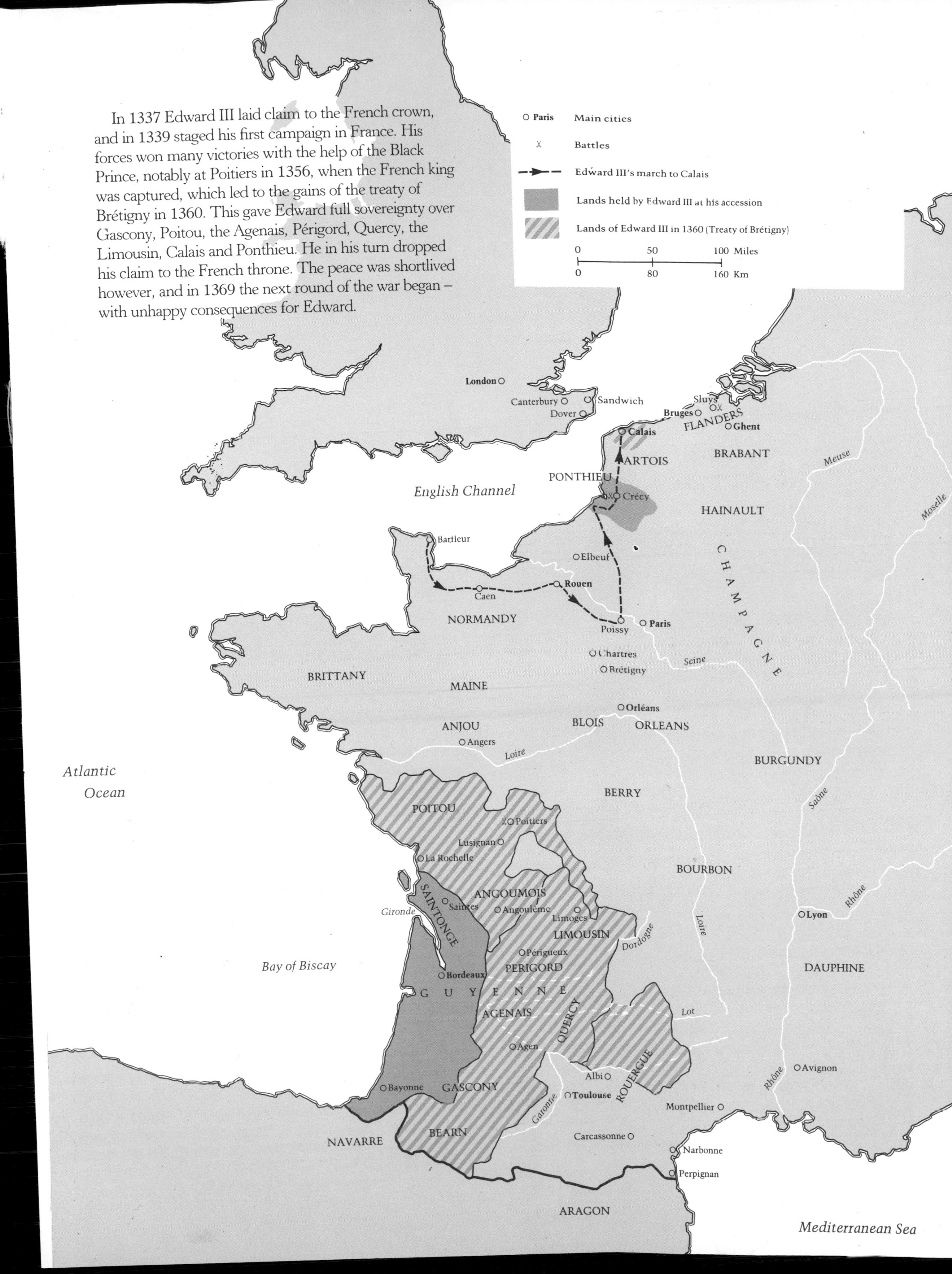

That year, a fortnight after Easter, when parliament had been held by King Edward III, a shameful peace was made between the English and the Scots.

It was agreed that David, the son of Robert Bruce, who had been adopted as king of the Scots, should marry Joanna, sister of Edward III, and with her should reign peacefully over Scotland in his own right. And indeed, this later came to pass.

In that same year, the young king of England, not ruling, nor yet well ruled, but under the evil influence of traitors, drew up a charter for Scotland whose significance and terms were not generally known. Furthermore, the charter by which the people of Scotland and their king, John Balliol, had made submission in perpetuity to the king of England, on behalf of themselves and those to come after them (in testimony of which the seal of the king of Scotland, with the seals of the magnates and prelates of that realm, had been appended to it), was brought forth on the end of a long spear, at Berwick upon Tweed, in the presence of the councils of both kingdoms, read out, revoked absolutely and burnt in the presence of all.

There, David Bruce was betrothed to the king of England's sister and crowned. On being dedicated at the altar, the child, who was suffering from diarrhoea, dirtied himself. At this, the Scotsman James Douglas said to his friends, 'I am afraid he will besmirch the whole kingdom of Scotland.' It was with reference to this event that blasphemers called him David 'drip-on-the-altar'.

Of all the kings of Scotland, David II was the first to be anointed king with holy oil at his coronation. The Scots, in a meeting of the parliament at York, requested that the great stone of Scone which lay beneath the king's throne next to the high altar in Westminster Abbey, bound with iron bonds to the foundations of the church, be handed over to them. It had been the custom for the kings of Scotland to be enthroned on this stone – for this reason it was called the royal stone of the Scots. They wished to be able to consecrate their king on this stone according to their ancient custom.

The king's council assented to their request and solemn envoys were sent to get the stone. However, the abbot of Westminster, when he had heard what the messengers had to say, wrote a letter to the king and his council to the effect that the stone had been brought from Scotland with great pains by the king's grandfather Edward I, and had been presented as an offering to his church. He could not and should not permit it to be removed from the church. With this reply, the messengers returned empty-handed to Scotland.

It was Isabella, the queen-dowager, together with Adam Orleton, bishop of Hereford, and Roger Mortimer among the English, and James Douglas among the Scots, who had desired and planned the marriage and all the other terms favourable to the Scots.

For Isabella, Adam Orleton and Roger Mortimer were fearful lest, after the death of Edward II, the king's father, they might find themselves the victims of just accusations and in need of the friendship of the Scots. So they treated the Scots favourably, in order that, if Edward III, the king of England, should die by some mishap, Roger Mortimer, with the help of the Scots, would usurp the kingdom and marry Isabella, the king's mother. For this reason, they caused Edmund of Woodstock, earl of Kent, the king's uncle and close friend, to be beheaded, so that King Edward III, like his father before him, would be bereft of all friends.

1330

In order to discover any supporters of Edward II, the late king of England, rumours were started by Isabella and Roger Mortimer that Edward II was living happily in Corfe Castle, but that he did not wish ever to be seen by day. To make this rumour sound convincing, dancing was arranged on the walls and towers of the castle on many evenings, and candles and flaming torches were carried, so that fools among the people might catch sight of them, and think that they betokened the pomp and ceremony of some great king guarded there.

The news spread through all England that the king's father was still alive. When he heard of this,

An education at arms

EDWARD III was just 14 years old when he was crowned on 1 February 1327. For three years he was king only in name, and remained firmly under the tutelage of his mother Queen Isabella and her lover Roger Mortimer, who had usurped royal authority.

The new regime was quick to make peace with France, conceding the Agenais, paying the massive sum of £60,000 as an inheritance due, and agreeing that the young Edward should do homage to the French king for all his continental lands.

Worse humiliation followed at the hands of the Scots. The campaign led by the young king against Robert Bruce was a total disaster, and in 1328 Bruce was able to dictate his terms in the treaty of Northampton, described as the 'Shameful Peace'. The English abandoned all they had fought for since the days of Edward I, and renounced his claims to overlordship over Scotland. These failures, and the earl of March's overweening arrogance and greed, hastened the break-up of the barons' coalition.

Opposition to Mortimer was led by Henry of Lancaster, who won the support of the king's uncles, the earls of Norfolk and Kent. In 1329 civil war was only narrowly averted by the mediation of the archbishop of Canterbury. With peace restored, Mortimer moved quickly to crush his enemies. The weak and foolish Edmund, earl of Kent, was the most vulnerable. He was tricked into believing that his brother Edward II was still alive and became involved in plots to secure his release. These were immediately reported to Mortimer, who accused the earl of treason and secured a conviction on his own confession.

Edward III was no longer a boy, however, but a man of nearly 18, a husband and the father of a son, the future Black Prince. Since becoming king he had experienced nothing but humiliation at the hands of Isabella and Mortimer. The judicial murder of Kent gave added urgency to the plans of Edward and his well-wishers to seize power from the over-mighty earl of March.

The trap was sprung in October 1330. Isabella and Mortimer were arrested by Edward and his men in Nottingham Castle. Isabella was firmly retired from public life at Castle Rising, while Mortimer was arrested and condemned to death. He was drawn through London to the Elms at Tyburn, and hanged.

Freed from his tutelage, the young king was now free to indulge his taste for military glory to the full in major campaigns against the Scots and the French.

Below *A carving of Queen Isabella on Bristol Cathedral.*

Edmund, earl of Kent, the late king's brother, sent a Dominican friar to Corfe to discover whether the story was true. This friar, however, who had hoped to bribe the door-keeper of the castle, was himself deceived. For he was taken into the door-keeper's chamber to lie concealed during the day, so that he might have the opportunity to see the man he sought when night came.

At nightfall, the friar was led into the great hall and instructed to put on the clothes of a layman so that he should not be noticed. There, he had the impression that he saw Edward II, the king's father, sitting down to a splendid feast. This he believed and this was what he told the earl of Kent on his return. The earl then swore an oath in the presence of certain people whom he should not have trusted, that he would make it his aim that his brother Edward II should be set free from the place where he was held prisoner.

In that same year, the third of his reign, at the request of those who hated his father, King Edward III held parliament at Winchester. There, at the instigation of the king's mother, Isabella, and Roger Mortimer, accusations were made against the King's uncle, the earl of Kent, and against many other nobles and members of the clergy, including the provincials of the Dominican and Carmelite orders. They were alleged to have conspired to free the king's father from prison and make him king again, although the plan was a fantastical impossibility.

The earl of Kent was beheaded as a consequence of his own admissions and the letters which were found about his person – but no confession or letter, however true, could be enough to justify such a punishment for a man of that rank. The provincials of the Dominicans and the Carmelites were sent into exile, but the bishop of London was sent away with a pardon.

The people of England regretted the death of the earl of Kent little, for the ways of his household servants were wicked. They travelled through the country seizing the possessions of the common folk at the king's price and giving in return little or no money.

On Friday 19 October, parliament co Nottingham, where Roger Mortimer, now ea March, shone with all too transient honour Isabella's chief adviser whose word was law to those assembled. No one dared to address him by name, but only by the title of earl of March.

Indeed, as the earl went about, he was accompanied by a greater band of courtiers than the king himself. He condescended to rise in the king's presence; when walking with the king, he would arrogantly walk at his side, never giving him precedence but sometimes, indeed, walking before him.

On one occasion, when one of King Edward III's servants was taking a house in the town for Henry, earl of Leicester and Lancaster, one of the king's kinsmen, the earl of March rebuked him sharply, asking who had made him so bold as to lodge an enemy of Queen Isabella's so near to her. The servant was, as a result, much frightened and assigned the earl of Leicester to a lodging a league outside the town.

A rumour began among the nobles and spread to the common people, for some were secretly saying that Mortimer, the lover of Queen Isabella and master of the king, was planning to destroy those of royal blood and himself usurp the throne.

This rumour brought great fear to the king and his friends, that is to say, William Montague, Edward de Bohun and others who had sworn to protect Edward III. They thought, and rightly, that it would be in the interests of the safety of the kingdom if Mortimer were to die.

They took counsel with Robert Eland, their sworn ally, who for many years had been a scout in Nottingham Castle and knew all its secret passages, asking him how the king and his friends might by night gain access to Queen Isabella's chamber from outside the castle without the knowledge of the door-keeper. The scout, by the light of torches, took the king along a secret underground passage which began at some distance from the castle and led to the kitchen and to the hall of the main tower, in which the queen had her lodging.

A man's hero

Above left *Edward's head and blazon.*

Above *King Arthur's round table.*

EDWARD III was one of the dominant personalities of his age, a man round whom legends gathered. Over six feet tall, he towered over his contemporaries literally as well as figuratively. For half a century his court was the most magnificent, his armies the most feared in western Europe. Yet in spite of his great reputation (or perhaps because of it) historians have found it difficult to assess his true character.

He was above all a man of action and passion, energetic, restless, generous to a fault, a lover of display and pageantry. The swashbuckling coup by which he seized power in 1330 set the tone for his reign, and for his great feats of arms on the fields of France. He was never happier than when leading his troops on campaign, or jousting and feasting with his knightly companions in arms. In short he was a new King Arthur, just as his subjects expected him to be.

It was Edward's good fortune, therefore, to be ideally suited by physique, temperament and taste for the role to which he had been born – unlike his unfortunate father Edward II. He was also lucky in his marriage to Queen Philippa, daughter of the count of Hainault, who bore him 12 children. Her calm good nature, gentleness and dignified tolerance of her husband's infidelities won her universal affection. After her death in 1369 Edward deteriorated rapidly into premature old age.

Edward was not just a pleasure-loving warrior. He was also a shrewd politician, keenly aware of the damage that the monarchy had suffered during his father's reign, and determined to re-establish its authority and prestige. He knew instinctively that political stability depended on maintaining good relations with the nobility. Successful military campaigns, tournaments and the chivalric orders of the Round Table and the Garter all strengthened the bonds between the king and his barons, establishing a common sense of purpose and companionship. His love of display and ostentation, too, was more than mere extravagance. Fine clothes, magnificent feasts and great building projects like Windsor Castle boosted the image of monarchy, emphasizing its splendour and wealth and, as a result, its authority and stability.

There may have been a darker side to Edward III's passions. He was notoriously licentious, and rumours circulated about his affair with the 'countess of Salisbury', probably Alice, wife of Edward Montague, younger brother of the earl of Salisbury. The chronicler Jean le Bel relates how the king brutally raped Alice, leaving her battered, bleeding and dishonoured.

Then the king's friends leapt from the passageway that ran under the earth and, with their swords drawn, made for the queen's bedchamber, which, through the grace of God, they found open. King Edward III, his weapon at the ready, kept watch for them outside the chamber of his enemies, lest his mother should see him.

They then found the queen, who was preparing herself for her night's rest, and the object of their search, the earl of March. They seized him and took him to the hall, while the queen cried out, 'My son, my son, have pity on gentle Mortimer!' For although she had not seen her son, she suspected his presence.

The king and his friends sent at once for the keys of the castle and took control of every lock in the place. However, this was all done secretly, in order that no one outside the castle should know what was going on, apart from those friendly to the king.

At dawn the following day, with a great hue and cry, they took Roger Mortimer and certain of his friends who had been captured with him to London, by way of Loughborough and Leicester.

In London, he was thrown into the Tower as once before, and on 29 November, while the parliament of England was sitting at Westminster, he was drawn and hanged.

With his death on the thieves' common gallows at Tyburn, there came to an end the civil wars which he had stirred up so frequently in his lifetime. He was condemned by his peers to the death he deserved, although he was not permitted to appear before them nor to speak in his own defence. The earl of March found himself used as he had used others, and was justly apportioned the same punishment as he himself had meted out.

In this same year, the fourth of King Edward III's reign, the king's first son, Edward of Woodstock [the Black Prince], was born on 15 June, at Woodstock. May God grant that I live to praise him and describe his great achievements when he captured the king of France.

In 1332, Edward Balliol, son of John Balliol, a former king of Scotland, raised a force of disinherited Scots and defeated the army of Robert Bruce's young son David II, king of Scots, who had succeeded his father in 1329. Edward Balliol was crowned king of Scotland at Scone in 1333, with the help of Edward III, but, as the Lanercost chronicler shows, David II sought help elsewhere.

1334

On 19 June, Edward Balliol, king of Scots, came to Newcastle upon Tyne and rendered homage to Edward III, king of England, for the kingdom of Scotland, to be held of him as overlord. Because the king of England had, at great expense, helped him to return to and to take possession of Scotland, the king of Scots granted the Scottish shires closest to the English March: Berwick, Roxburgh, Peebles and Dumfries, with the town of Haddington and the town and castle of Jedburgh, and the forests of Selkirk, Ettrick and Jedburgh, to be separated from the crown of Scotland and to be annexed to the crown of England in perpetuity.

David Bruce, whom the Scots had anointed as their king on 30 November 1331, had been sheltering in the strong fortress of Dumbarton. In the spring of 1334, he had sailed to France, where he performed homage to King Philip VI, so that he would hold Scotland from him as overlord, in return for which the king of France would help him to recover his kingdom from the hands of the king of England, Edward III, and the other king of Scots, Edward Balliol.

When reports of these developments reached Scotland, the number of Scots in revolt against Edward Balliol, their king, increased daily; by Michaelmas almost the whole of Scotland had risen, forcing Balliol to flee to Berwick upon Tweed which belonged to the king of England.

Upon receiving this news, Edward III set matters in train for an expedition to Scotland. He reached Newcastle upon Tyne by early November, and on 25 November he invaded Scotland. He advanced to Roxburgh, where he repaired the castle, for the use of himself and his garrison.

The battle for Scotland

Above *The battle of Neville's Cross; a diversionary action for the French which resulted in David II's capture.*

DAVID II was five years old when he succeeded his father as king of Scotland in 1329. The coronation was at Scone, and for the first time, a pope gave permission for a Scottish king to be formally crowned and anointed. In 1332, however, Edward Balliol, a pretender to the Scottish throne, defeated David's supporters near Perth and was himself crowned at Scone as Edward I of Scotland. David's supporters fought back, expelling him from the realm, but Balliol returned in 1333 with the full backing of the English king. Their forces overcame David's army at Halidon Hill, near Berwick upon Tweed.

Shortly afterwards, David was evacuated to France, a country with which the Scots had long had diplomatic and trading ties, and remained there for eight years while the war in Scotland dragged on.

David returned home in 1341. In 1346 the French called on him to fulfil his obligations under the treaty of Corbeil: in exchange for nebulous promises of support, the Scots had undertaken to invade England whenever the French king required and, as Edward III laid siege to Calais, the French called for such a campaign. A Scots force therefore crossed the border and headed for Durham, but was intercepted at Neville's Cross and was soundly defeated. David himself was wounded in the head by an arrow and was taken prisoner. Edward stood to win a king's ransom, but the Scots were unwilling to pay to have their king back, and, in 1352, Edward sent David to Scotland on parole to negotiate his own ransom.

Although there were rumours that David was obtaining his freedom by selling Scotland's independence, it is more likely that the terms he offered to a council at Scone were the maximum he had been prepared to concede: a hefty ransom, and the succession of one of Edward III's sons to the Scottish throne should David die childless. The terms were rejected and David returned to London.

In February 1356, Edward III embarked upon a campaign of destruction in southern Scotland. Later that year the Black Prince captured the French king at Poitiers, and the Scots, isolated, accepted his terms: a ten-year truce and a ransom of £66,000, payable in instalments.

In October 1357, David returned to Scotland, at liberty. It remained for the Scots to organize the collection of the ransom, a heavy and long-lasting burden on a war-weary land. David II's rule was strong and effective; he was vigorous in administering justice and imposing his will upon the Scots barons, many of whom remained reluctant to pay his ransom. Only two annual instalments were made over to the English king as agreed, and in 1377, when Edward III died, over a quarter of the total still remained unpaid.

1335

On 25 May, the king of England held a parliament at York and made arrangements for another expedition to Scotland. On 24 June, it was decided that he would lead a force into Scotland from Carlisle on 12 July, while King Edward [Balliol] of Scotland would invade from Berwick on the same day. So the two kings entered Scotland by different routes. They encountered no resistance, but progressed through the whole land, burning, looting and destroying crops.

Some of Edward III's forces, especially the Welsh, spared neither monks nor monasteries, but despoiled secular and regular clergy indiscriminately. Some sailors from Newcastle set fire to a large part of Dundee, including the Franciscan friars' dormitory and house of studies, from which they stole a large bell. They killed one brother, who had been a knight before entering the religious life – a fine and holy man. The bell they took to Newcastle, where they offered it for sale. It was purchased for ten marks by the Dominicans of Carlisle, who had no more right to buy it than the vendors had to sell it.

Eventually, confused and utterly powerless to resist the two kings, the Scots came to make peace, on 15 August.

Philip VI, king of France, continued to support David II's cause and, as le Baker relates, he threatened Edward III with war.

The French saw that the king of England and his parliament set little store by the letters of their master, Philip de Valois, although in them he had threatened that, unless the king of England made peace with Scotland, he would declare war on him.

Neglect of the threats contained in his letters seemed to Philip justification for making war upon this English kinsman of his, unfurling the fleur-de-lis against the man who was the rightful heir to the kingdom of France which he himself occupied. And so Philip VI, the tyrant of France, became puffed up with pride and fury and goaded the French to fight the English.

This was the beginning of a terrible war which Philip himself could not bring to an end, even though he was vanquished many times on land and at sea, and though the kings of Bohemia, Scotland and France were captured and killed and the blood of many Christians was spilt.

Tension between France and England mounted, and in 1337, Edward III secured a major coup – alliance with the powerful Holy Roman Emperor, Louis IV of Bavaria, and some of his vassals in Flanders and Holland. Philip VI had declared Gascony, Edward III's French duchy, forfeit to the French crown. Pope Benedict XII tried to mediate, but in 1339 Edward launched the opening campaign of the Hundred Years War.

1339

In the twelfth year of his reign, Edward III began his campaign against the tyrant of France, Philip VI, on 20 September.

At the head of a force of twelve thousand armed men, his standard flying, he rode forth into the Cambrésis, burning and laying waste towns and castles in the area.

One evening, at dusk, just as the shadows were gathering, Geoffrey le Scrope, one of the king of England's justices, led a French cardinal, Bertrand de Montfaucon, up into a great and lofty tower. There, indicating all the land in the direction of France to a distance of fifteen miles which had been put to the torch, Geoffrey le Scrope said to the cardinal, 'My lord, does it seem to you that the silken cord which runs around the edge of France is broken?' When he heard this, the cardinal, as if in a faint, fell and lay stretched out on the roof of the tower, overcome with grief and fear.

For five weeks, the king of England rode through the kingdom of France, using the same tactics, and every day his army laid waste as much of the countryside as it was able.

All the lands of Cambrai, Tournai, the Vermandois and Laon, apart from the walled towns, churches and castles, were completely devastated.

The first E.E.C.

IN April 1337 Edward III dispatched an embassy to the Low Countries, to win allies among the counts of Flanders and Hainault and other princes of northern Europe for the impending war against France. This diplomatic strategy was ultimately ruinous. It drew the English king into the complexities of imperial politics, humiliated him before his enemies, and, in four years, left him financially and politically bankrupt. It took all Edward's later military successes to redeem him from this, the worst mistake of his career.

In the 14th century the Holy Roman Empire extended from Brussels to Rome; it included most of the Netherlands and all of Germany between the Rhine and the Polish frontier, as well as Switzerland, Austria, and northern Italy. The emperor's authority was limited, but the prestige attached to his office was enormous; and because the title was elective rather than hereditary, it was open to fierce and often unscrupulous competition. The Emperor Louis IV of Bavaria (1314–46) spent most of his reign trying to overcome the problems caused by a disputed election. In the process he killed his rival, alienated his fellow-rulers in Germany, and was condemned as a heretic by three successive popes. Such were the political and religious controversies raging in the Empire at the outset of the Hundred Years War.

Edward III had no particular desire to be embroiled in these matters, but as his relations with Philip VI of France deteriorated in the 1330s, he became acutely aware of the need to build up a confederation of friendly states on the continent. Inevitably, he looked for support to his nearest neighbours across the North Sea. England had important historic and commercial links with the Netherlands, recently re-inforced by the marriages of Edward to Philippa of Hainault and of the English princess Eleanor to the count of Guelders. Edward hoped to exploit these ties in the diplomatic mission of 1337.

The English king's emissaries stayed at Valenciennes in Hainault, a convenient point from which to communicate with the princes of the Empire, and with the county of Flanders which, it was hoped, might renounce its allegiance to France and join the Plantagenet cause. Bribes were offered and the rulers of Hainault, Brabant, Guelders, Jülich, Cleves, Berg and Marck, as well as their neighbours the count palatine of the Rhine and the duke of Brandenburg, soon offered support. The Emperor Louis was won over with a promise of £60,000.

However, the imperial coalition soon became a liability. By the spring of 1338 Edward had run up obligations of some 276,000 to the German princes, and it soon became clear that the English exchequer did not have the resources to meet these debts. When Edward eventually organized an attack into northern France from Brabant, the princes' military assistance counted for little. The English army was driven back, and Edward's only answer was to offer still higher bribes. When there was no more money he was forced to pawn his crown and hand over English noblemen as hostages for his debts. He returned to England late in 1340, his plans for a great military adventure in ruins.

Neither side could afford to keep up the disastrous alliance, and although England retained contact with the Netherlands, the German confederation ceased to be significant in Edward's strategy against France. Later, in 1348, a group of princes hostile to Louis' successor Charles IV offered to elect the English king as emperor. But the suggestion was politely declined. Edward's involvement in Germany in 1337–41 had been a fiasco; not even the prospect of the imperial title could tempt him to repeat that error.

Above *The High Gothic cathedral of Cologne. The city's archbishop was one of the main supporters of the Holy Roman Emperor.*

When they saw the English army approaching, the inhabitants fled in terror. Indeed, no one dared to resist this advance, although the king of France had assembled his own great armies outside his walled cities, while he himself hid in the well fortified town of Saint-Quentin. Not once did he dare to venture outside the walls of his cities to defend the lands which he claimed were his against the king of England, while the latter always led his army in the field. Moreover, among the many slanders which everyone repeated about the French tyrant, someone attached the following to an arrow and shot it into the town of Saint-Quentin:

'If you're so strong, Valois, then what do you fear?
Don't hide away, show us your strength, come near.
You may be a flower, but you'll wilt if you stay in the dry.
With those coward's spots, you're more leopard than lion, say I.'

And playing on the king's name because he was called Philip de Valois, another made up the following verse:

'"Phi" is a blemish, "lippus" a stain;
Philippus is twice as bad again.'

However, when he heard that Edward's allies, the men of the county of Brabant, because food was in short supply and a harsh winter was approaching, had decided to retreat and were indeed retreating, the tyrant of France, Philip VI, decided to face the army of the king of England, who, awaiting him joyfully, recalled the men of Brabant.

Having received letters from the tyrant to the effect that he was willing to join battle, Edward III sent a message in return to say that he was willing to wait for Philip three days in the field.

And so, on the fourth day, the king of England waited in the appointed field for the king of France. The latter, however, would not come any closer than two miles distant. He then beat a shameful retreat to Paris, having broken the bridges and blocked the roads with cut-down trees and branches behind him, so that the king of England would be unable to follow in pursuit.

Above ***The king of England doing homage for Aquitaine and Ponthieu.***

Right ***Heavily armoured English troops embarking for France at the outset of the Hundred Years War.***

The longest war

THE Hundred Years War was only the final phase of a much longer struggle, which began when William the Conqueror, duke of Normandy, became king of England in 1066. The king of England held extensive lands in France and as the power of the French kings grew they became more determined to drive the English king into the sea. By 1250 the only substantial English possession left in France was the duchy of Aquitaine or Gascony, which was already exporting fine claret wine to England. Edward I only narrowly defeated an attempt by Philip the Fair to confiscate and conquer Gascony in the 1290s, and it soon became clear to Edward III in the 1330s that his cousin and adversary Philip VI was looking for any excuse to repeat the attempt.

The Hundred Year War, therefore, can be seen as a

civil war in France, a battle between the French king and his greatest vassal. By the 14th century, however, the struggle was increasingly taking on international dimensions. The Scots, fighting desperately for their independence against Edward III, found firm allies in France. In 1334 Philip VI insisted that there could be no settlement with England over Gascony unless the king of Scots' rights were guaranteed in the same treaty. For his part Edward III sought to cultivate support in the Low Countries, using an embargo on English wool exports to Flanders as a weapon to win an alliance with the wealthy cloth-making Flemish towns.

The final breach was caused by fear in England of a French invasion. In 1336 Philip VI planned an expedition across the narrow seas to assist the Scots, and sailed a huge fleet, ostensibly gathered for a crusade, to the Channel ports. Edward III prepared to meet the threat, securing a large war tax from a worried parliament, and in the following year the French made a pre-emptive strike by invading Gascony. The Hundred Years War had begun.

Edward III possessed a powerful weapon denied to his predecessors in the struggle with France: a claim to the French crown. The Capetian royal house, which had passed the French throne from father to son in unbroken line from 987, suddenly came to an end in 1328. The three sons of Philip the Fair had occupied the throne in succession and all died childless. The crown passed to Philip VI of Valois, cousin of the last three Capetians (and of Edward III).

Edward III was Philip the Fair's grandson through his mother Isabella of France, and, although he was in no position in 1328 to advance his title to the French throne – and claims through the female line were debarred by the parlement of Paris – in 1337, when Philip declared Gascony forfeit to the French Crown, Edward was able to trump his adversary's ace by asserting his hereditary right. In 1340 he formally laid claim to the kingdom of France and added the fleur-de-lis to his coat.

When he heard this news, the king of England followed the advice of his friends and retreated through Brabant to Hainault as his food supplies were running short. There, the English forces spent most of the winter.

In the meantime, Edward III contracted an important alliance with the Flemings, who made ready to swear every oath of obedience, homage and allegiance to him, provided that he would style himself king of France and bear arms with the emblem of the fleur-de-lis as a symbol of this. The Flemings dared not obey him on any other terms, on account of Pope Benedict XII's interdict which had been laid upon them were they ever to rebel against the king of France.

And so, on the advice of his council of nobles and his Flemish allies, Edward III agreed to assume the royal title and arms of France and took over the lordship of Flanders.

Thereafter the Flemings obeyed him in all things, as the conquering king of France.

Concerning the aforementioned title and arms, Philip VI made the following speech to some Englishmen who were sent to him as envoys:

"It does not displease us that our kinsman has chosen to bear the arms of England and of France quartered, for we freely permit that a poor knight bachelor kinsman of ours should carry a part of our royal crest. However, we are much disturbed that he should have chosen to call himself on his seal and in his letters, king of England before king of France, and that he should have chosen to place his own arms with the leopards rather than the fleur-de-lis in the first quarter of his shield, since it suggests that he considers the little island of England more to be honoured than the great kingdom of France."

When he heard this, John Shoreditch, a knight and messenger of the king of England, replied that his lord the king of England followed the custom of the men of his day and considered that the title and arms of his father's family should precede those of his mother's both in name and in law.

1340

Not long afterwards, in early February, Edward III returned to England, having sent the queen, Philippa of Hainault, who was expecting a child, to Ghent. He held parliament at Westminster where the laity made him a grant of every ninth fleece of wool, every ninth lamb and every ninth sheaf of grain of every variety. The clergy granted him a nineteenth of the same produce. The king of England then resolved, and proclaimed, that no Englishman should be subject to him as king of France.

King Edward III celebrated Pentecost at Ipswich, where he waited to sail back to Flanders. The king had intended to make his journey with only a few companions. However, when he heard a rumour that the French tyrant, Philip VI, had sent a great fleet of ships from Spain and almost all of the French fleet to prevent him from sailing, Edward summoned his own fleet from the Cinque Ports and elsewhere. Thus, with two hundred and sixty ships, great and small, he made a fortunate start to his journey to Flanders, with a following wind, on Thursday 22 June.

On the Friday, he saw the French fleet in the port of Blanckenberghe, all ready for battle and disposed like the ranks of an army camp. So, anchoring his ships off Sluys, at some distance from the shore, King Edward deliberated the best plan of action for a whole day.

However, early on the morning of 24 June, the French fleet separated into three sections and moved about a mile towards where the English fleet lay.

When he saw this, the king of England announced that they should wait no longer but arm themselves and be at the ready. In the early afternoon, with the wind and sun behind him and the current flowing so as to aid his attack, Edward III divided his fleet into three sections and delivered the longed-for attack upon the enemy.

A hail of iron, of bolts from crossbows, and of arrows from longbows, brought death to men in

Blood royal

FOR centuries the earldom was the sole heritable rank in England. By the 1300s, however, earldoms were in decline: from 23 in 1154 they had dwindled to a mere ten in 1337. The Crown's attitude towards creating earldoms was always strongly influenced by the need to provide for the younger males of the royal family. When the time came for Henry III to provide for his younger brother, Richard, the king had little alternative but to create an English earldom for him. This new earldom – Cornwall, has remained in the royal family ever since.

Henry's son and heir Edward, however, had no title. When he became King Edward I he created only three earldoms: his younger brother, Edmund Crouchback, became earl of Lancaster; and his two younger sons were created earls of Norfolk and Kent. When he died in 1307 most of the earldoms were held by his relatives. In complete reversal of his father's policy, Edward II gave his favourite, Piers Gaveston, the royal earldom of Cornwall when Richard's son died without heirs, and created the earldoms of Winchester and Carlisle for other favourites. All three were later executed and forfeited their titles.

During the 14th century the nobility of England began to recognise an elite amongst themselves. These were peers of the blood royal, descendants of the kings in the male line. In France such men were known as the 'princes of the fleur-de-lis'. There is no doubt that Edward III was following the French example in 1337 when he raised the earldom of Cornwall, held by his son Edward, the Black Prince, to a dukedom: the first in England. Previously, the French title of duke had been held only by the English kings as dukes of Normandy and Aquitaine. The lands of the duchy of Cornwall have provided an income for the king's son ever since (the title prince of Wales, first given to Edward I's oldest son, is purely honorary).

At the same time as he added this new tier to the English hierarchy, Edward III also expanded the next rank down by creating seven new earldoms; most of them went to young men, his own companions in arms.

Edward did not intend dukedoms to be reserved solely for the king's sons. In 1351 the earl of Lancaster, Henry of Grosmont was also raised to the new rank. He was one of Edward's greatest military commanders, and enormously wealthy, but would probably not have been so elevated if he had not been of the blood royal. Henry's son-in-law John, the king's third son, was created duke of Lancaster when Earl Henry died in 1362.

Top right *A French duke in heraldic regalia.*

Right *The quarterings of knights.*

their thousands. Those who were willing and daring enough, fought at close quarters with spears, axes and swords. Some hurled stones from the towers of the masts, thus killing many.

In short, it would be no distortion to say that this great naval battle was so fearful that he would have been a fool who dared to watch it even from a distance.

At first, the Spanish ships [of Philip VI's Castilian ally], because they were so great and so tall, withstood the attacks of the English; but eventually, after the French had been beaten and the first line of their fleet abandoned, the English were able to seize them.

The French ships were chained together so that their line could not be broken. Consequently, while a few of the English stood guard over the first of the abandoned lines, those on the other English ships turned their attention to the second line. Despite the great difficulty of the manoeuvre, they launched their attack. However, the French abandoned this line even more readily than the previous one. Indeed, the French, when they had left their ships, leapt overboard and for the most part drowned.

At dusk, when the first and second lines of the French fleet had been defeated, the English decided to rest from battle until morning, for it was growing dark and they were too tired to go on fighting.

During the night, the thirty French ships in the third battle line fled. One great ship, the *James* of Dieppe, attempted to drag with it a ship from Sandwich, which belonged to the prior of Christ Church, Canterbury; but the sailors on board, with the help of William Clinton, earl of Huntingdon, fought bravely to drive them off, the fight continuing throughout the night.

On the following day, when at last the English sailors had defeated the Normans, they found four hundred men dead on board the captured ship. Moreover, when day broke and they discovered the flight of the thirty French ships, King Edward

Victory at sea

WHEN Edward III attacked Sluys in Flanders on July 24 1340, his action resulted in the capture or destruction of practically the entire French fleet. Its admirals, more accustomed to fighting on land, had bunched their ships together in the mouth of the Zwin (against the advice of the Genoese commander) in three squadrons, the ships of each chained 'like a line of castles'. They were crammed with men, although few were experienced men-at-arms and crossbowmen.

The English fleet bore down on them after 9 o'clock with the advantages of wind, tide and sun behind them, arrayed so that each shipful of men-at-arms alternated with one of archers. The leading French squadron fought for three hours while English bowmen shot hails of arrows, seamen threw stones and quicklime from the mast-tops, and the battle between French and English men-at-arms raged to and fro across the ships. Many men on both sides drowned in their heavy armour before the two French admirals surrendered. Both were executed, and the wounded were thrown overboard by the English, who had suffered from French piracy and raiding.

The English then attacked the second and third squadrons. The struggle continued after darkness fell, by the light of burning French vessels. During the night 30 ships escaped, but this did not detract from the magnitude of Edward's first great triumph in the Hundred Years War. The invasion threat was removed and more than 200 vessels captured. So many French had drowned, it was said, that if fish could speak they would have learned French.

Both sides fought Sluys as a land battle, the normal naval tactic of the time. Most English ships were cogs, broad-beamed merchantment of 30–200 tons. High-sided and capacious, their wind resistance, primitive rudders and square sails made them unmanoeuvrable and ill-suited to war. While the French built proper war-galleys on the Mediterranean model in the arsenal at Rouen, Edward's 'royal navy' was embryonic, a handful of galleys and large cogs with 'castles' (fighting platforms) fore and aft. On the open sea they were to prove no match for the war-ships.

The ancient duty of the Cinque Ports to provide ships at their own expense was in decline as the ports silted up, so the 'king's ships' were augmented by the royal right to 'arrest' all English shipping in times of need. As a result, most ships in English fleets were requisitioned merchantmen, temporarily converted for war. The sailors' wages were paid by the king: ordinary seamen received 3d. a day, masters twice as much. Many vessels were provided in this way: over 700 for the campaign of Crécy and Calais, mainly from London, Southampton and the east coast ports.

This rudimentary system was cheap, but had its disadvantages. There was no question of England controlling the sea after Sluys – cogs could hold station for short periods only, in good weather – and before long French raids resumed. Local communities bore the burden of coastal defence.

While the war at sea went well for England, there was the chance of seizing profitable cargoes. But in the long run these gains were more than offset by commandeering ships for the navy: wages paid by the government did not balance lost profits from trade. Requisitioned ships often lay idle in port waiting for the troops they were to carry, their owners receiving little compensation for lost income. During Edward III's reign many individuals and communities complained that their ships were lost to the French and their livelihoods gone.

Above *Close action at the battle of Sluys.*

Below *A warship filled with soldiers.*

sent forty well armed ships in pursuit under the command of John Crabbe, whom the English considered of all their commanders to have the greatest skill in naval matters and most knowledge of the French ports.

Altogether, about two hundred French warships were captured on that occasion, and thirty barges. The number of the enemy killed or drowned exceeded twenty-five thousand. There were four thousand English dead, including four knights, one of whom I know not.

After a lull, hostilities between Edward III and Philip VI broke out once more over Brittany, but Edward III's campaign there in 1342–3 proved indecisive. Although Edward's able young commanders in Gascony, Henry, earl of Derby, and Walter Manny, gained a number of victories, the king of England decided to concentrate his next major efforts in Normandy.

1346

The king hastened his preparations for Normandy, while the fleet awaited him at Portsmouth and Porchester. There King Edward III waited from 1 June to 5 July for the wind to turn in his favour.

At last the fleet, with a thousand ships, pinnaces and carracks, set sail – and what a marvellous sight it was. The king's plans were kept secret. Even the masters of the ships were not told their destination before they left the harbour but were merely instructed to follow the admiral's orders. However, once they were at some distance from the shore, the king sent messengers from his ship to the other vessels. The helmsmen were instructed to follow their admiral, steering their ships in the direction of the port of Saint-Vaast-de-la-Hougue in Normandy.

At last, on 13 July, they put in at their destination. When they had landed, the king, standing on the shore, knighted his eldest son, Edward of Woodstock, and made him prince of Wales.

Burning and looting, the English army moved towards the Somme.

It was the evening of Friday 25 August, and the king was encamped on the bank of the Somme, when, over the river bank which the English had already crossed, came Philip VI, the French tyrant, and with him the kings of Bohemia and Majorca, with a vast army composed of eight great divisions.

The French shouted exultantly at the king of England and his men, and on both sides of the river soldiers waded into the shallows or stood on the banks and shook spears like jousters at a tournament.

The king of England sent messengers to the king of France offering him safe passage across the river by the ford and proposing that he select a place fit for a battle. But that coward, Philip de Valois, though he had previously threatened to pursue the king of England, was now unwilling to engage in battle and turned aside, as if to cross the river at some other point.

All night, Edward III waited for him. The following day, a Sunday, King Edward moved his army to the field of Crécy, where they came upon the king of France.

Edward III was ready for battle at any time; he placed the first division of his army under the command of the prince of Wales, his son; the command of the second he entrusted to another, while that of the third he kept for himself. He commended all to God and the Blessed Virgin Mary. Then, observing that all his foot soldiers were impatient for the enemy's attack, he kept the destriers and the coursers behind the lines, together with the supplies, in order to be ready to pursue any of the enemy who might flee.

The French banner, the 'oriflamme', flying on the right of the royal standard, was adorned with broad golden lilies.

In response to this, the king of England ordered that his standard be flown, on which was depicted a dragon wearing his arms, whence it was called the 'dragon', signifying that the ferocity of the leopard and the softness of the lilies had been transformed into the cruelty of the dragon.

Who pays?

BY 1340 Edward III had spent no less than £500,000 on the war with France, leaving himself with an unprecedented £300,000 in debts. The fiscal system was pushed to its limits in 1336: two grants of taxation were made by parliament, and a year later a tax was granted for more than one year. English merchants were given monopoly rights to buy and sell wool, with the king taking a slice of the anticipated profits. In 1340 the government resorted to a tax in kind: corn and wool was collected and sold off for cash.

Despite all these efforts Edward did not gather sufficient money for his plans and had to borrow from Italian merchant houses. It was the peasants, particularly in the east of England, who suffered most from the rigorous taxation, made all the more insufferable by the taking of requisitions for the army and a shortage of coin to pay with. A series of excellent harvests forced down the prices of grain and livestock, the staple living of the peasants, and reduced their capacity to pay tax. Those who did have to pay might be driven to sell their stock or seed-corn to raise the cash required, impoverishing themselves in the process. Those who could not pay simply left their tenements and took to the fields, leaving their homes behind to rot.

In 1340 at Cold Weston in Shropshire it was reported that all but two of the tenants had fled because of worries about paying a tax granted by parliament. Peasants who stayed on their land were threatened with imprisonment if they failed to contribute. Growing discontent gave rise to outright refusals which increased throughout the 1330s, and reached a peak during the freezing weather of early 1339.

Below ***Evading tax collectors was difficult.***

Thus arrayed, the battle lines stood facing each other on the field from dawn until dusk, the French ranks being constantly swollen with new arrivals. At last, towards sunset, after the soldiers had spent the whole day intimidating each other with war-like displays, the battle began, to the sound of trumpets, drums and pipes making a great racket, while the shouts of the French almost deafened the English.

It was the French crossbowmen who took the initiative, but their bolts hit none of the English, falling far short of them. The English archers, roused by the great noise of the crossbows, showered their opponents with arrows and put an end to the storm of crossbow bolts with a hail of arrows.

The English first prayed to the mother of God and marked the Lord's day with fasting, then within a short time, they dug many trenches in the ground in front of their first line of soldiers, each a foot deep and the same distance wide, so that, if the French cavalry were to come too close to them, God forbid, their horses would stumble when they came to the trenches.

Loud screams arose from the French crossbowmen trampled by the great horses, and from the knights' chargers who had been wounded with arrows, while the French ranks were thrown into further confusion by the stumbling of the horses. Many men fell as they fought with the English, wounded by axes, lances or sword, while many who had suffered no honourable war wound were simply crushed to death in the midst of their own numerous army.

In the heart of this ferocious battle, the noble-spirited Edward of Woodstock, King Edward III's eldest son, who was at that time sixteen years old, was showing the French his admirable bravery at the head of his division. He stabbed horses, killed knights, struck helmets, snapped lances, craftily parried blows, aided his men, defended himself, helped up fallen comrades, and encouraged all to good deeds by his own example. Nor did he cease from his noble efforts, until the enemy retired behind the mound of their dead.

The battle of Crécy

ON 26 August 1346, Edward III gave battle to a French army at Crécy, in his county of Ponthieu. He had set off from Portsmouth in early July with 15,000 men-at-arms and archers, originally bound for Gascony; but contrary winds drove his fleet to the Cotentin peninsula in Normandy. He accepted this as God's judgement. In the same spirit, when Edward fell and bloodied his nose as he disembarked, he turned this bad omen to good use and claimed that the land welcomed him.

The army moved inland and sacked Caen, then turned eastwards, spreading destruction. This enriched the English and weakened the French, showing them that their king could not protect them. His footsteps dogged by the French army, Edward crossed the Seine and the Somme into Ponthieu before turning to fight on home ground.

The king drew up his force, now numbering less than 10,000, on sloping ground. Before the army was a hedge strengthened by pits one foot deep. There were three divisions of dismounted men-at-arms and archers: the right, commanded by the 16-year-old Black Prince; the left under the earls of Northampton and Hereford; and the centre under the king himself. The bulk of the archers, on the wings, inclined forward to shoot at the advancing enemy from the sides. The king oversaw all from a windmill on a commanding height.

The time had at last come for the French to take revenge on the marauding English, and they had the confidence which comes from overwhelming strength. Genoese crossbowmen led the French advance, but their bowstrings were ruined by rain (the English bowmen kept theirs dry inside their helmets) and they were driven off by the English cannon.

The French cavalry then advanced into the 'valley of death' formed by the English army, riding down the Genoese who had preceded them. The hail of English arrows and the obstacles threw their attacks into confusion. John the Blind, king of Bohemia and an ally of the French king, died in the mêlée.

There were 15 French assaults, all pressed with the utmost bravery, but they could make no headway against such a strongly defended and narrow front. Throughout the battle the English maintained a strong discipline, and resisted the temptation to break ranks to take rich prisoners. The French finally admitted defeat and fled, leaving behind perhaps 4000 dead knights – no one counted the humbler corpses. Edward was now free to besiege the important port of Calais.

It was a shattering victory for tactics developed over the

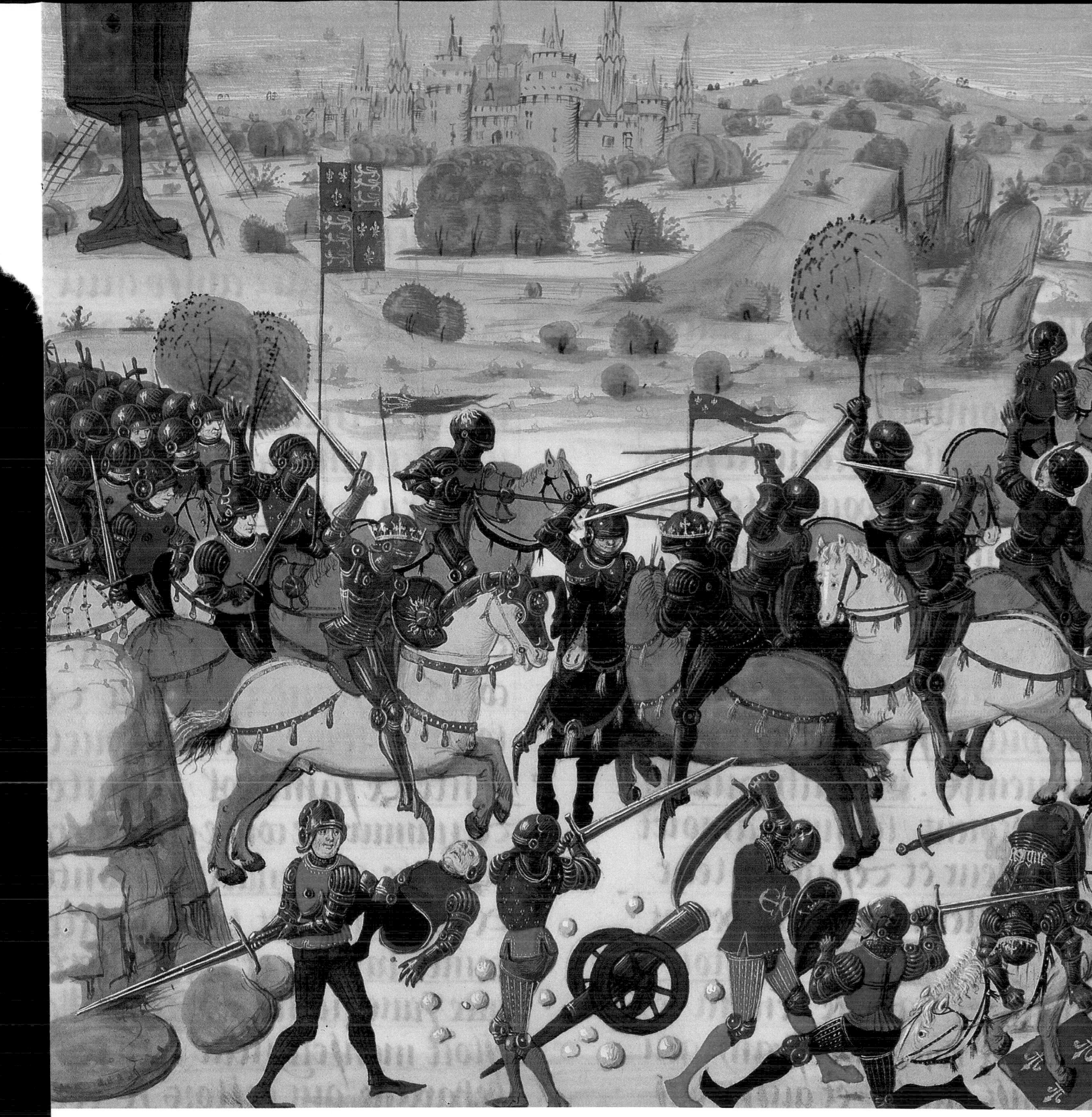

preceding decades, and taught the French a healthy regard for English fighting skills. Crécy is not as famous as the battle of Agincourt (1415) because it was not immortalised by Shakespeare. Yet it was the first in a succession of English victories over the French which extended over five centuries.

Above *The Battle of Crécy saw an innovation in battlefield tactics. The Black Prince made full use of archers to soften up a mounted frontal assault, followed by dismounted knights to attack the stranded horsemen. This strategy was to prove successful in subsequent engagements.*

From sunset until the early hours of the morning, Mars showed his grim face. During that time, the French three times provoked our men to battle and made fifteen hostile advances, but eventually they fled, defeated.

On the following day, the French returned, in four battle lines, as if nothing had befallen them. For a fourth time, they cried out solemnly to the English, before renewing the fight for the sixteenth time. After a long and fierce battle, the English compelled the enemy to retreat and pursued them as they withdrew. During this pursuit and the previous day's fighting, three thousand men met their death.

Early in the afternoon that Sunday, the two-day battle ended.

More than four thousand French knights and nobles died in the battle of Crécy. As for the other dead, no one took the trouble to count them. It was the arrogant ambition of those knights striving to outshine their fellows in capturing or defeating the king of England that was the cause of their downfall.

On the following day, a Requiem Mass was celebrated with other private masses, then the English forces set out for Calais. They at once surrounded the town with ramparts and laid siege to it, on 4 September.

While Edward III, by the grace of God, king of England and conqueror of France, was laying siege to the impregnable town of Calais, Philip VI, king of France, sent to David II, king of Scotland, a large number of Genoese and other mercenaries and instructed him, by means of a letter, to make a mighty attack on England, since the English soldiers and knights were absent. David II was to pillage and seize the English castles and fortresses (which he might keep and put to what use he pleased), so that the two of them might easily conquer all England together.

And so, on 9 October, King David II of Scotland invaded England with a Scottish force and the mercenaries sent him by the king of France, passing by Berwick upon Tweed, which was defended by the English.

Edward III's northern commanders rallied their armies against David II and, at Neville's Cross near Durham, decisively defeated and captured the Scottish king.

The siege of Calais meanwhile continued for almost a year until, in 1347, Philip VI withdrew with his army. Froissart gives a graphic description of the ceding of the town to the English.

After the departure of King Philip and his army, the people of Calais realized that the support on which they had been counting had failed them, and at the same time they were so weakened by hunger that the biggest and strongest among them could hardly stand.

So they took counsel together and decided it would be better to throw themselves on the mercy of the king of England, if they could not obtain better terms, than to die one by one of starvation; for hunger might drive many of them frantic and cost them their souls with their bodies. They so entreated the governor, Jean de Vienne, to negotiate that at last he consented. He went on to the battlements and signalled to those outside that he wished to talk with them. When King Edward heard of this, he immediately sent out Walter Manny and Ralph Basset. They came to Jean de Vienne and he said to them:

'My dear lords, you are very gallant knights with much experience of war, and you know that the king of France whom we serve sent us to this place to hold the town and castle for as long as our honour and his interests might require it. We have done everything in our power, but now our help has failed us and you are pressing us so hard that we have nothing left to eat. We must all die or go mad with hunger if the noble king whom you serve does not take pity on us. We beg you, in the kindness of your heart, to go back to the king of England and entreat him to spare us.'

'Indeed, yes,' said Walter Manny, 'I will do that willingly. And I sincerely hope he will listen to me, for it will go better with all of you if he does.'

Town life, city life

AT least ninety-five per cent of the English people lived in the country during the 14th century, and only London could compare with Europe's great cities. York, second city of the realm, had fewer than 8000 inhabitants; an average country town less than 500. Most towns developed at the crossing of ways, where a market would flourish. Houses clustered round the market place and the church – which was inevitably built close by – and straggled out along the streets which converged at the market.

Highway towns like these could never be defended. But other cities developed as administrative centres of counties, lordships or bishoprics. These grew up round the castle or cathedral, as at Ludlow or Hereford, or continued on a grid pattern established by the Romans, as at Chester or Chichester, and could be encircled by walls: over 100 towns, usually royal boroughs, had their own fortifications. Many were in a constant state of disrepair, but their importance was civic rather than military: they delineated the bounds, ensured that entry was only by the gates so that tolls could be collected, and deprived people living outside the walls, in the suburbs, of their civic rights.

Each trade was concentrated in its own quarter in larger towns, and in its own street in smaller ones. Skinners and dyers needed to be close to running water, while tanners or butchers were assigned areas where the noxious effects of their trade could least offend. Potters, smiths and other tradesmen who presented a serious fire risk might be banished to the suburbs. The trade and craft associations, or guilds, were recognized as self-governing in the early 14th century, when they were given the power to control admission to the freedom of the towns and cities. To take up this freedom, to practise a trade or craft and take part in town government, it was necessary to be the son of a freeman (or burgess), or complete an apprenticeship to one. The longer surviving guilds owned property which they held in trust for charitable purposes – usually to the benefit of their old or sick members – and often built their own halls.

Many boroughs had acquired extensive rights of self-government by the reign of Edward III. They elected their own officials, collected tolls from citizens to meet royal tax demands, used a municipal seal to authenticate documents, kept their own records and above all, owned corporate property. In 1373 Bristol became the first provincial city to be raised to the status of a county in its own right; it had its own sheriff and was free of all other jurisdictions.

Although provincial merchants rarely amassed fortunes on the scale of leading Londoners, many were wealthier than the local country gentry. In the larger cities and ports there was always a handful of merchants who were as rich as the nobility.

Below left ***The rich quarters of Florence were occupied by merchants and bankers.***

Below ***Carcassonne, a typical medieval fortified city.***

The two English knights went off, leaving Jean de Vienne standing on the battlements. King Edward was waiting for them at the entrance to his quarters, eager to have news of the state of Calais. His envoys bowed and went up to him and Walter Manny began:

'Sire, it appears that the captain of Calais and his companions in arms as well as the citizens would be quite ready to surrender the town and castle and everything in them to you, on the sole condition that they are allowed to leave unharmed.'

'Walter,' replied the king, 'there is not the slightest hope or prospect of my changing my mind.'

Walter Manny went closer to the king and reasoned with him, saying, to help the defenders of Calais: 'My lord, you may well be mistaken, and you are setting a bad example for us. Suppose one day you sent us to defend one of your fortresses, we should go less cheerfully if you have these people put to death, for then they would do the same to us if they had the chance.'

This argument did much to soften the king's heart, especially when most of his barons supported it. So he said: 'My lords, I do not want to be alone against you all. Walter, go back to Calais and tell its commander that this is the limit of my clemency: six of the principal citizens are to come out, with their heads and their feet bare, halters round their necks and the keys of the town and castle in their hands. With these six I shall do as I please, and the rest I will spare.'

Walter Manny went back to Calais to where Jean de Vienne was waiting and told him what the king had said.

Jean de Vienne left the battlements and went to the market-place, where he had the bells rung to summon the people together. They all came, men and women, eager to hear the news, though they were so weak with hunger that they could scarcely stand. Jean de Vienne quietly repeated all that had been said, telling them that nothing more could be hoped for and asking them to consult together and give their answer quickly. When he had finished speaking they began to cry out and weep so bitterly that their lamentations would have moved the stoniest heart. For a time they were unable to say anything in reply and Jean himself was so moved that he also was weeping.

At last the richest citizen of the town, Eustache de Saint-Pierre, stood up and said: 'Sirs, it would be a cruel and miserable thing to allow such a population as this to die, so long as some remedy can be found. To prevent such a misfortune I wish to be the first to come forward. I am willing to strip to my shirt, bare my head, put the rope round my neck, and deliver myself into the king of England's hands.'

When Eustache de Saint-Pierre had said this, his hearers were ready to worship him. Men and women flung themselves at his feet weeping bitterly. It was indeed a pitiful scene.

Then another greatly respected and wealthy citizen, who had two beautiful daughters, stood up and said that he would go with his friend Eustache de Saint-Pierre. His name was Jean d'Aire. A third, called Jacques de Wissant, who owned a rich family estate, offered to accompany them. Then his brother, Pierre de Wissant, and a fifth and a sixth, said they would go, too.

These six burghers stripped to their shirts and breeches there and then in the market-place, placed halters round their necks as had been stipulated and took the keys in their hands, each holding a bunch of them.

Jean de Vienne mounted a pony – for he could only walk with great difficulty – and led them to the gates. The men, women and children of Calais followed them weeping and wringing their hands. Jean de Vienne had the gate opened and closed behind him, so that he stood with the six burghers between it and the outer barriers. He went to where Walter Manny was waiting and said to him:

'Sir Walter, as the military commander of Calais and with the consent of the poor people of this

Above *The chief citizens of Calais kneeling before Edward III, handing over the keys to the city after their defeat.*

The siege of Calais

EDWARD'S victory at Crécy in August 1346 left him free to besiege Calais at the beginning of September. Standing at the point where the Channel is narrowest, the town was a nest of pirates who preyed on English shipping, and a vital base for future attempts to conquer France. It was not easy to take: for it was defended by a double wall with towers and ditches, strengthened by the marshy course of the Hem to the east and north; and as a port it could be victualled from the sea. Nonetheless, the governor Jean de Vienne expelled 1700 'useless mouths' at the start of the blockade – men, women and children too old or young to fight – to save food. It was customary to leave such people between the lines to starve, but on this occasion Edward was generous, feeding them and sending them away.

Edward decided the only way to take Calais was to starve it out. His preparations were meticulous. From England he called for men, cannon and ships: the army of 32,000 men that he raised was the largest of his reign.

To house this multitude during the winter he erected a town of wooden buildings around a central market place, where the Flemings came to sell food twice each week. The English amused themselves by raiding the country-side round Calais; and there were also challenges between chivalrous knights on each side. Meanwhile supplies were beginning to run low in the town. Five hundred more 'useless mouths' were expelled, but Edward's earlier gallantry gave way to frustration and they were not allowed through the lines. Jean de Vienne wrote to the king: 'everything is eaten up; dogs, cats and horses, and we have nothing left to subsist on, unless we eat each other'.

In Paris, Philip VI trusted in Calais' strength to resist during the winter and spring. He summoned an army in March 1347 but it was not ready to march until mid-July. Although Philip claimed to be eager to fight he had no such intention. On the night of 1 August he fled, leaving Calais to its fate.

The defenders had won the right to surrender with honour, but the English king, enraged at their 11-month resistance, determined to make an example of them. The governor and six leading citizens were forced to carry the keys of Calais to Edward, barefoot and hatless, halters around their necks. It may or may not be true that Queen Philippa, a moderating influence upon her hot-tempered husband, saved them from execution when, heavily pregnant, she knelt before the king and pleaded for their lives. Certainly, the town's citizens were expelled and replaced with Englishmen, and Calais became an English colony in France for nearly two centuries.

town, I deliver up to you these six burghers. I swear that they have been and are to this day the most honourable and prominent citizens of Calais, by reason of their personal characters, their wealth and their ancestry, and that they carry with them all the keys of the town and citadel. And I beg you, noble sir, to intercede with the king of England not to have these good men put to death'.

The barriers were then opened and Walter Manny led the six burghers to the king's quarters, while Jean de Vienne went back into the town.

At that time King Edward was in his chamber with a large company of earls, barons and knights. Hearing that the men of Calais were coming as he had ordered, he went out to the open space before his quarters, followed by his nobles and by great numbers of others who were curious to see them and learn what would happen to them. Even the queen of England, Philippa of Hainault, who was far advanced in pregnancy, went out with her lord the king. When Walter Manny arrived with the six burghers, he went up to the king and said: 'Sire, here is the deputation from Calais at your orders.'

King Edward kept quite silent and looked at them very fiercely, for he hated the people of Calais because of the losses they had inflicted on him at sea in the past.

The six burghers knelt down before him and, clasping their hands in supplication, said: 'Most noble lord and king, we surrender to you the keys of the town and the castle, to do with them as you will. We put ourselves as you see us entirely in your hands, in order to save the remaining inhabitants of Calais, who have already undergone great privations. We pray you by your generous heart to have mercy on us also.'

None of the brave men present, lords, knights or men-at-arms, could refrain from shedding tears of pity when they heard this.

It was indeed a moving to see men so humiliated and in such mortal danger. But the king continued to glare at them savagely, his heart so bursting with anger that he could not speak.

When at last he did, it was to order their heads to be struck off immediately.

All the nobles and knights who were there begged the king to have mercy, but he would not listen. Walter Manny spoke up for them: 'Noble sire, curb your anger. You have a reputation for royal clemency. Do not perform an act which might tarnish it and allow you to be spoken of dishonourably.'

At this the king ground his teeth and said: 'That is enough, Sir Walter, my mind is made up. Let the executioner be sent for. The people of Calais have killed so many of my men that it is right that these should die in their turn.'

Then the noble queen of England, pregnant as she was, humbly threw herself on her knees before the king and said, weeping: 'Ah, my dear lord, since I crossed the sea at great danger to myself, you know that I have never asked a single favour from you. But now I ask you in all humility, in the name of the Son of the Blessed Mary and by the love you bear me, to have mercy on these six men.'

The king remained silent for a time, looking at his gentle wife as she knelt in tears before him. His heart was softened, for he would not willingly have distressed her in the state she was in, and at last he said: 'My lady, I could wish you were anywhere else but here. Your appeal has so touched me that I cannot refuse it. So, although I do this against my will, here, take them. They are yours to do what you like with.'

The queen thanked him from the bottom of her heart, then rose to her feet and told the six burghers to rise also. She had the halters taken from their necks and led them into her apartment. They were given new clothes and an ample dinner. Then each was presented with six nobles and they were escorted safely through the English army and went to live in various towns in Picardy.

After the capture of Calais by the English, there was a lull in the conflict. As Geoffrey le Baker relates, the Black Death now began to take its toll on both sides.

A more than faithful queen

PHILIPPA, Edward III's queen, was the daughter of William count of Hainault, Holland and Zeeland. She and Edward were close in age and remained deeply attached throughout their long marriage, even though the king was not always faithful. Philippa was by no means beautiful, but she was warm-hearted, intelligent and physically hardy. She bore Edward 12 children, only three of whom died in infancy, and accompanied her husband on his campaigns. Two of her sons, Lionel of Antwerp and John of Gaunt, were born in her native Low Countries.

For the first time since Henry II, the king had a large family of sons growing to manhood. However, no greater contrast to that earlier Plantagenet family could be imagined. Unlike Henry's children, Edward III's sons remained on remarkably good terms with each other and, more importantly, with their father. A great deal of the credit for this happy family life is Philippa's.

The queen was an important moderating influence on her husband, who relied on her advice and encouragement. Deeply religious, she had a strongly developed sense of the responsibilities of kingship. She did not bring a host of relations or a large train of Hainaulters to England; instead, men of talent from the Low Countries, like the chronicler Jean Froissart, received a warm welcome at her court.

Early in Edward's reign she encouraged clothworkers from her own country to settle in Norwich and train Englishmen in cloth manufacture. The experiment prospered and from cloth she turned to coal, gaining permission from the king to exploit the mines on her Tynedale estates. Coals were soon being carried south from Newcastle as well as east to the Low Countries.

Philippa's greatest failing was her inability to handle her own finances. She was hopelessly extravagant, and although this benefited luxury trades in London, it was less than ideal for a country financing an expensive war. Edward finally abolished her separate household.

The queen's interest and concern for ordinary people made her beloved in a way few queens have been before or since. In 1369, nearly eight years after her death, the chancellor, in his address to parliament, said of her, 'Behold, lords, if any Christian king, or any other ruler in the world, has had so noble and gracious a lady as wife'.

Right ***A section of a pavement floor laid for Queen Philippa at one of her main residences, Clarendon Palace.***

1347

After the capture of Calais, the plague, which had gradually spread from the east, flared up in that region. All over the world, a great many people, both men and women, sickened and died. I shall tell more of this later.

Taking advantage of the opportunity offered by the outbreak of the plague, the French sent two cardinals as their representatives to the English to seek a truce which was to last from the fall of Calais to 11 June next year. Edward III granted their request, and the terms of the treaty were drawn up by the aforementioned cardinals and by two French nobles, the count of Eu and the lord of Tancarville, who had been taken prisoner by the English.

1349

In the twenty-third year of King Edward III's reign, the swiftly spreading plague, which had arisen in the east among the Turks and the Indians, infected the air men breathe and went on to ravage the Saracens, the Turks, the Syrians, the men of Palestine and then the Greeks, causing these peoples such terror that they decided to adopt the faith and sacraments of the Christian religion, for they heard that the Christians who lived across the Mediterranean had suffered much less from the fatal sickness than had their own people.

In the end, the plague spread from those regions to the lands beyond the Alps and thence to western France and Germany, bringing with it fearful disaster, until finally, seven years after it had arisen, it came to England.

First of all, it affected the harbour towns in Dorset, almost denuding the county of its inhabitants. Thence, it spread to Devon and Somerset, raging as far as Bristol so fiercely that the people of Gloucester refused entry to their area to any from Bristol, thinking that the breath of any living person who had been among those dying of this plague must have become infectious. But eventually it did reach Gloucester, then Oxford and, finally London.

Plague years

THE Black Death was the first and most catastrophic outbreak of the plague which was to menace western Europe periodically from the 14th to the 18th century. It first arrived in October 1347 from Constantinople with a Genoese fleet which docked at Messina in Sicily, and within three years it had spread throughout the continent.

A Gascon sailor who landed at the small port of Melcombe Regis in Dorset in June 1348 brought it to England, and its passage across the country was rapid and destructive. Where figures are available they suggest a horrifying death toll: over 50% of the inhabitants of Bristol and Winchester died and, overall, between two-fifths and one-third of Europe's population is thought to have perished.

The Black Death was carried in the bloodstream of the black rat and transmitted by its fleas, which attacked human beings. It could also be spread from person to person through the breath – a more virulent strain of the disease which was nearly always fatal. Its symptoms were (and still are) a high temperature and large swellings in the groin or arm pit. These might suppurate and give off a terrible stench. Death, if it was going to occur, came within two to five days.

The speed with which the Black Death spread has never been fully explained; fleas from animals other than rats may also have become sources of infection. At the time, some people believed that an infected person's stare could transmit the plague. More bizarre theories blamed over-eating or sex with an older woman. The traditional remedies of bleeding and laxatives were used, in order to balance the humours of the body, but with little success. Flight and prayer were also tried. Many saw the Black Death as a terrible punishment meted out by God upon a sinful mankind. There was mass religious hysteria in parts of Germany and France; bands of flagellants toured the countryside scourging themselves and singing hymns. Jews were massacred in cities throughout western Europe. Boccacio, in a highly coloured account of the effects of the plague in Florence, describes how all moral and legal restraint collapsed, property was held in common and imminent death was faced with unrestrained debauchery.

London, already a violent city, also suffered a moral decline. The chronicler Henry Knighton lamented that thieves and criminals had flocked there, and John of Reading commented on the increase in acts of sacrilege. At Rochester, according to the monk William Dene, 'the plague carried off so vast a multitude of people of both sexes that nobody could be found who would bear the corpses to the grave. Men and women carried their dead children and threw them into the common burial pits, the stench from which was so appalling that scarcely anyone dared even to walk beside them.' In Somerset, priests even refused to give the last rites to the dying for fear of contracting the disease. Some of these stories are clearly exaggerated, and although few communities can have escaped the plague, some areas were more severely afflicted than others.

When the Black Death gradually abated in 1350, the organization of society, the conditions under which land was held, and levels of wages and prices changed in its wake. So, too, did the way in which people thought: the collective wave of terror and dismay which had swept Europe left its mark on the art and literature of the later 14th century.

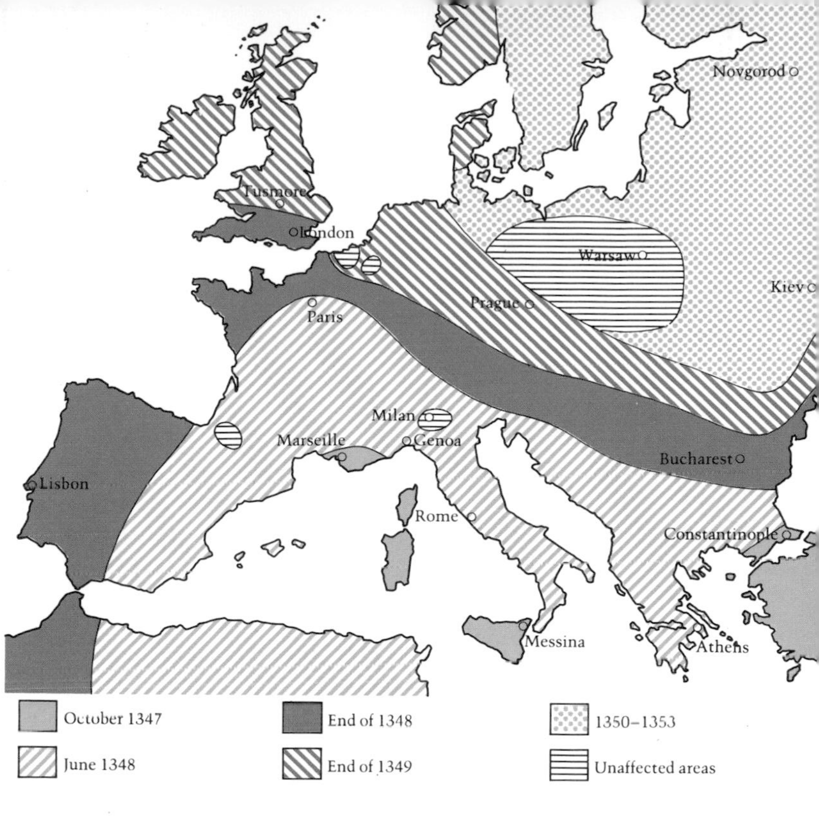

Above *Map showing the spread of the plague across Europe. It originated in the steppes of central Asia and followed the trade routes, reaching Europe in 1347.*

Below *Victims of the plague being buried in coffins. As the numbers increased, mass graves were used, one of which is now beneath London's Liverpool Street station.*

All England suffered from this sore affliction so that scarce one in ten of either sex survived. As the graveyards were not big enough, fields were chosen where the dead might be buried.

Only a few nobles died, but of the common folk, more died than could be counted, and also a multitude of monks and other clerks known only to God. The pestilence struck the young and the strong in particular, generally sparing the old and the weak. Scarcely anyone would dare touch a person who was afflicted, and the remains of the dead, which in ages before and since have been held in high honour, were then shunned by the healthy, for they were tainted with the plague.

Men who had been one day full of life, were often found dead the next. Some were afflicted with abscesses which erupted in various parts of their bodies, and which were so hard and dry, that even when they were cut with a knife, hardly any liquid flowed out. Many who suffered from these symptoms survived, either by having the boils lanced or by waiting with great endurance for them to subside. Others had small black sores which developed all over their bodies. Only a very few who suffered from these survived and recovered their health.

Such was the great plague which reached Bristol on 15 August, and London around 29 September. It raged in England for a year or more, and such were its ravages, that many country towns were almost emptied of human life.

In Germany, as Matthew of Neuenberg observes, the plague produced strange spontaneous religious outbursts.

The plague began gradually in Germany, and people started to travel across the country flagellating themselves.

Seven hundred of them came from Swabia to Strasbourg in the middle of June, together with three masters, one main one and two others, whose orders they obeyed in all respects. They crossed the Rhine at daybreak, and the people flocked to meet them.

The death of a village

THE immediate effect of the plague years on the rural population is reflected in the empty holdings recorded in manorial rent rolls, reduced revenues from tolls in market towns and tax reductions reluctantly allowed by the exchequer's collectors between 1352 and 1355. After the Statute of Labourers prevented rural workers moving to a new district, and in part as a result of the statute, villages were rarely abandoned even where the plague had been most severe. Records of the poll tax levied in 1379–81, some 25 years after the Black Death, show that almost every English village was populated despite a generation of successive plagues.

The tax collector's receipt for the hamlet of Bolton near Bradford in Yorkshire, which reported 'no one living there', is exceptional, as is that of Hilcot, a Cotswold hamlet near Stroud: 'nothing because it is not inhabited'. These rare examples are from upland hamlets where it would have been difficult to induce peasants to remain, or to come as settlers, while there were attractive empty holdings elsewhere. Tusmore in north Oxfordshire may have been one of these.

There were 23 households in Tusmore before the plague. After the Black Death, in 1355, it was wholly absolved from taxes, and in 1357 the king authorised the lord of the manor, Ralph de Cottisford, to take its fields for his parkland: 'the hamlet inhabited entirely by Ralph's bondmen being now void of inhabitants since their death in the pestilence'.

The ornamental grounds and lake are all that remain of de Cottisford's parkland. The rest is partly planted with timber but most is now agricultural land again, within large straight-sided fields. The site of the abandoned village straddles two of these fields.

Tusmore's houses in the mid-14th century were probably made from local timber, and neither house-walls or wall-footings or stone are visible, although in the aerial photograph some abandoned house sites are emphasised by water collected in small sunken rectangles. Carts and animals passing through the village streets over many centuries before the plague have lowered the surface and created straggling sunken hollow ways in the grassland, which can still be seen. The parish church was somewhere in this area, but its site is unknown. Beyond the earthworks of the former village, the regular ridges and furrows of medieval strip cultivation are imprinted on modern fields.

Right *An aerial view of the Tusmore site.*

They formed a wide circle and, having stripped off their clothes and shoes, they placed them in the middle. Wearing shifts instead of trousers, reaching from their thighs to their ankles, they marched round in a circle, and one by one threw themselves on their faces in the circle in the form of a crucifix.

Each one would step over the others and gently strike them with scourges as they lay prostrate.

Eventually the ones who had prostrated themselves first were the first to get up and start scourging themselves with whips which had knots with four iron spikes, marching round singing vernacular versions of many hymns to the Lord.

Three men stood in the middle of the circle, leading the singing in loud voices and flagellating themselves; the others followed their singing.

They went on doing this for a long time; then all of them with one voice fell on their knees, and then prostrated themselves again in the form of a crucifix, praying and sobbing.

The masters went around the circle telling them to pray to the Lord for mercy on the people, and on all their friends and enemies, and all sinners, and those who were in purgatory, and others besides.

Then the flagellants stood up, and stretching their hands to the sky fell on their knees again and sang; then, getting up, they scourged themselves for a long time, proceeding as before.

Finally they put on their clothes, and the rest of them, who had been guarding the clothes, undressed and did the same.

After this, one of them rose and read a letter out loud, which was similar in character to the letter which was delivered in the church of St Peter in Jerusalem by an angel.

In this one, the angel said that Christ was displeased by the depravities of the world, and named many sins: violation of the Lord's day, not fasting on Friday, blasphemy, usury, adultery.

The practice of medicine

THERE were two kinds of doctor in the 14th century: professional and popular practitioners. The former was university trained, generally at one of the leading European medical faculties of Montpellier, Paris or Bologna. After an Arts degree he studied for four or five years to obtain his licence to practise, and the same length of time to gain his Master's status. The training was mainly theoretical, based on studying the texts of the Graeco-Roman medical authorities, Hippocrates and Galen. Practical training was minimal.

The professional doctor's skill lay in his knowledge, licensed status, ethics and etiquette, which distinguished him from unlicensed practitioners and from surgeons, whose practical 'manual operations' were considered inferior. With the exception of Bologna, surgery was not taught in universities. It was a craft, and training was by apprenticeship. To raise their status, surgeons formed guilds to regulate their practice and to protect and distinguish themselves from the lower orders of their craft – the barbers – whose practice was to 'shave, cut and bleed' as well as dentistry. These skills were much in demand, but although barbers formed their own corporations their professional status was not always recognized. The public image of the professional doctor, with his long ermine-trimmed robe and academic biretta, was by contrast assured.

Doctors were expected to be well mannered, of sober character and morals, but contemporaries attributed three other far less flattering qualities to them: to lie subtly, to give the appearance of honesty and to kill with audacity. Their preoccupation with fees was also criticized. One anecdote tells of a physician whose dying words were 'thirteen pounds' and 'three years', so obsessed was he with this unpaid fee. Patients came principally from noble and knightly families and from the burgesses in the towns who could afford the fees. London in particular offered wealth, high social status and royal patronage, as the career of Pancius de Controne in King Edward III's entourage shows. His benefits included a salary, livery, favours and property.

Regulation of doctors was almost non-existent in rural areas, and no particular educational qualification was required to practise medicine or surgery. Barbers, wise women, and quacks or local priests tended the sick, and based their treatment on common sense experience, herbal remedies, folklore and superstition.

Professional medicine was based on the belief that there were four bodily humours (blood, phlegm and yellow and black bile) made of of four elements (air, water, fire and earth) and four qualities (hot, cold, dry and wet).

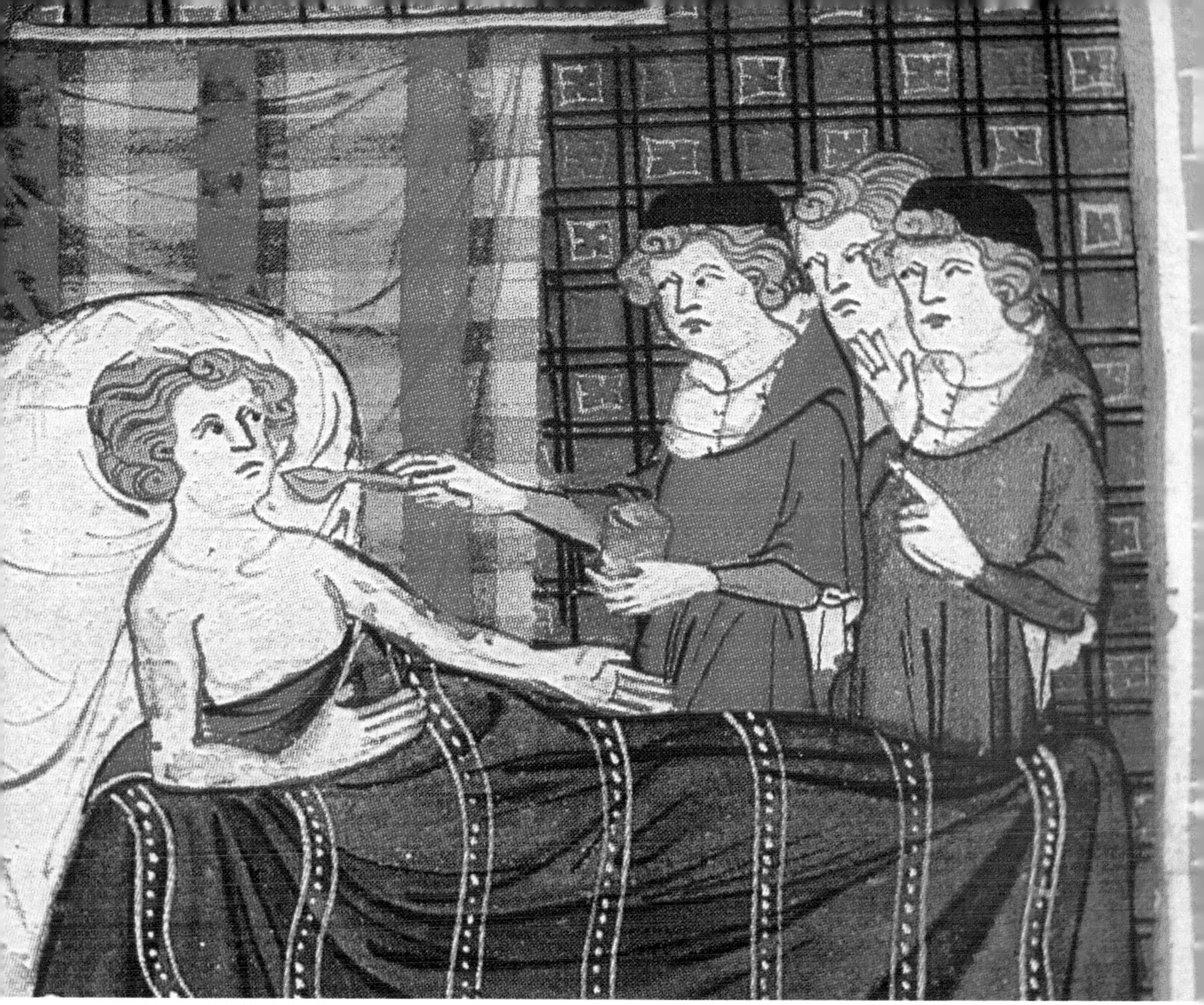

According to this theory, a combination of these determined a person's temperament: sanguine, phlegmatic, choleric or melancholic. The balance of the humours had to be perfect to ensure good health. Any imbalance caused illness, and it was the doctor's job to redress it by advice on diet, medication and, ultimately, surgery.

Uroscopy was the main diagnostic and prognostic tool, and the urine flask became the symbol of the doctor's technique. Pulse reading came next. Astrology helped calculate when an ailment would become critical or favourable days for treatment. Bird-lore was also important. If a caladrius bird, put next to the sick-bed, looked at the patient, he would recover; if it looked away, he would die. Herbal remedies in the form of pills, potions, powders or ointments were prescribed by doctors and dispensed by apothecaries. Purgatives or enemas and bloodletting by cupping or leeches were widely recommended to purge noxious humours. Stones and charms were also thought to be effective aids to recovery.

Above *Doctors prescribed special diets to redress the balance of humours.*

Below *A barber-surgeon treating a patient for haemorrhoids.*

The letter went on to say that, through the intercession of the Blessed Virgin and the angels, Christ had replied that to obtain mercy, a man should undertake voluntary exile and flagellate himself for thirty-three and a half days.

The people of Strasbourg were so greatly moved by the flagellants that they offered them all hospitality readily, so that soon everyone had somewhere to stay.

The flagellants did not accept alms, but were allowed by their masters to accept hospitality when asked; however, they did not dare change their behaviour when they were invited by the rich.

They performed their rites twice a day in the open fields, and some of them secretly once more during the night.

They did not speak to women, nor did they lie on feather beds.

All of them wore crosses in front and behind on their clothes and their hoods, and had scourges hanging from their clothing.

They did not remain in any one parish for more than one night.

About a thousand people from Strasbourg joined their brotherhood in deep humility, promising obedience to the flagellant masters for the appointed period. None was received unless he promised to observe the proper rites for the appointed number of days, brought with him at least four coins to spend each day so that he would not have to beg, and gave assurances that he had confessed and repented and forgiven all the wrongs his enemies had done him, and had the consent of his wife.

So many multitudes flocked to the flagellants, that no one could count them.

Minor skirmishes were meanwhile taking place in Brittany and Gascony, but as Geoffrey le Baker shows, Edward III was intent on chivalrous activities in England.

Left *A flagellant master leading his band of followers through a city. A multi-stranded whip is used for penance as he openly lashes his own back.*

Right *Some converts kneeling at the climax of the ceremony to hear the reading of the heavenly letter which spoke of the terrifying and apocalyptic message from God.*

Below left *Two flagellants; one has removed his cowl and wears an expression of torment and agony as a result of his self-inflicted wounds.*

The pride of humiliation

As the Black Death spread across the continent in 1348–49, it produced waves of mass hysteria that were sublimated in a new outbreak of the flagellant movement. Great throngs of people went on procession, scourging themselves in atonement for their sins and in the hope of averting divine retribution. Beginning in Hungary late in 1348, the Flagellants spread through Germany, Flanders and France during 1349, meeting with wide popular acclaim. However, although a group came to England and gave a dramatic public display outside St. Paul's cathedral, they made no converts there.

The ascetic hermit monks of 11th-century Italy had been the first people to use self-flagellation as a penance. Two hundred years later in the 13th century, the misery and insecurity caused by famine and war gave rise to organised groups of Flagellants, who survived in small numbers into the 14th century. They operated openly in Italy and France, but clandestinely in Germany, where they were regarded as dangerous and subversive heretics. Like their Italian predecessors, the Flagellants of 1348–49 wore a uniform – a white robe marked with a red cross – and were organised into groups of between 50 and 500, each under the strict control of a 'master' or 'father'. Although a layman, he assumed the power to hear confessions and grant absolution.

Flagellant leaders possessed a 'heavenly letter', which proved that, in the church of the Holy Sepulchre in Jerusalem, an angel had appeared and had read a terrifying and apocalyptic message to the multitude: God, angry with the many sins of mankind, would destroy every living creature unless people abandoned their evil ways.

To atone for the sins of the imperilled world, the Flagellants formed processions that lasted for 33½ days reflecting Christ's lifespan of 33½ years. They were not permitted to wash, shave or change their clothes, and they were forbidden all contact, including conversation, with women. When they arrived at a village or town, members of the group formed a circle, stripped to the waist, and prostrated themselves motionless on the ground in the form of a cross. They then rose to their feet and, singing hymns and praying out loud, scourged themselves with leather strips weighted with iron spikes, until blood sprayed everywhere and their flesh became bruised and swollen. The climax came with the reading of the 'heavenly letter' when the Flagellants and their audeince sobbed and groaned aloud together.

The support and admiration for the Flagellants among the general populace, and the marked hostility that many of them showed towards the Church alarmed lay and ecclesiastical leaders. In 1349 Philip VI of France forbade public self-flagellation on pain of death, so preventing the movement from spreading beyond Picardy, and Pope Clement VI issued an order to suppress the 'sect'. As a result of these measures, and with the gradual disappearance of the Black Death, self-flagellation once more became the preserve of small groups of enthusiasts.

That same year, John, earl of Lancaster, and many others crossed the Channel to Gascony in early November. Their intention was to offer some resistance to the incursions of John de Valois, son of Philip VI, the tyrant of France, who was causing trouble in that duchy.

1350

On St George's day, 23 April, King Edward III caused a great feast to be held at Windsor Castle, where he established a chantry of twelve priests and set up a hostel for impoverished knights who could not afford to support themselves. There, their daily needs taken care of, they would live in the service of the Lord, supported by the perpetual charity of the founders of the college.

Others besides the king promised their support for this foundation. Among them were the king's eldest son, Prince Edward, the earl of Northampton, the earl of Warwick, the earl of Suffolk, the earl of Salisbury, and other barons. Some knights too were of their number including Walter Manny. All were true gentlemen blessed with great riches.

All these men, together with the king, were dressed in robes of russet and wore garters of dark blue on their right legs. The robes of the order were completed by a blue mantle, embroidered with the arms of St George.

So attired, their heads bare, with great devotion they heard Mass celebrated by Simon Islip, archbishop of Canterbury, and the bishops of Winchester and Exeter.

Afterwards, they attended a feast where they ate together at a common table in honour of the blessed martyr to whom this most noble brotherhood was particularly dedicated, for it was called the order of St George of the Garter.

That year, Philip de Valois, the so-called king of France, spurred on by a sickness heralding death and calling him to appear before Him who judges the consciences of all mankind, publicly confessed that he was holding the crown of France unjustly. He ordered his son, John, to arrange a peace

The gartered few

By the mid-1400s, two centuries of essayists and romance writers had brought the code of chivalry to its fullest refinement. The code gave society an ideal of what true nobility should be, and defined its characteristics as modesty, generosity and gentleness to the defenceless, particularly women. The pursuit of honour was an essential element too, whether on the battlefield or in its substitute, the tournament. By this code, the aristocracy defined itself as the elite in medieval society. A man or a class that did not pursue chivalry was not 'noble'.

Orders of chivalry were an elaboration of this ideal. Their ultimate inspiration was in the imagination of a 12th-century Norman churchman, Wace, who added the story of the Round Table to Geoffrey of Monmouth's fictional history of King Arthur. Other writers embroidered on the idea, and during the 13th century knights in tournaments adopted the roles and fictional coats of arms of Arthur and his knights. 'Round Tables' were set up at many English tournaments, like that held by Edward I at Nefyn in 1284 to celebrate his conquest of Wales. The Plantagenet kings were the true heirs of the Celtic Arthur, he was saying, not the native Welsh princes. 'Round Tables' led to knights forming more regular tourneying brotherhoods: the golf clubs of their age.

The first European sovereign to take this development a step further was Alfonso XI of Castile, who instituted the Order of the Band around 1330. It had a written constitution, and was intended to enhance Alfonso's reputation as a patron of chivalry. When Edward III

Left ***A knight wearing the original robes of the Order of the Garter.***

Above ***St George's Chapel, Windsor Castle, home of the order.***

founded the Order of the Garter he was embarking on a more grandiose version of the same scheme. In 1344 he had held a 'Round Table' tournament at Windsor, where he had taken an oath to 're-establish' Arthur's 'order' of knights. Building works on the keep and chapel of Windsor Castle were commissioned to house his project, but it was four years before the order was finally established.

There were 26 founder knights, including the king, and the order took the military saint, George, as its patron. It borrowed much else from the Church, and was constituted as a 'college of knights' (a minster had a college of priests); its meetings, like those of monks, were 'chapters'; and its members sat like cathedral canons in opposing stalls in Henry III's rededicated and enlarged chapel in the lower bailey of Windsor Castle. The knights wore blue robes, and adopted a blue garter as their badge. According to legend the king's mistress, the countess of Salisbury, lost her garter while dancing at festivities held at Calais in 1348. To save her embarassment, the king refastened the loose article to his own knee, rebuking amused onlookers with the French words 'honi soit qui mal y pense', or 'evil to him who thinks evil of it' (the subsequent motto of the order). The story may be no more than a legend, but it is almost as old as the order itself.

The prestige of Edward III's England is reflected in the order's powerful impact. Within two years John of France had founded a rival order, the Star, and by the end of the century no great prince lacked an order of chivalry.

treaty between the kingdoms of England and of France which would bring an end to the war, warning him too, that if ever he should gain control of the land of France, he should on no account ride to arms against the king of England and make war on him.

At last, Philip VI went the way of all flesh and John, his eldest son, was made king of France. However, John had no right to the title of king and henceforth I shall refer to him merely as the pretender of the French.

In England, there was growing anxiety about the scarcity of labour to till the land, a legacy of the Black Death. The Statute of Labourers was enacted in 1351 to keep wages at their pre-plague level, and to restrict the movement of peasants from their native manors.

1353

In January, parliament met at Westminster, and it was ordained at the insistence of the people of London that no woman who was known to be a prostitute should wear a hood unless it were striped, nor should she wear furs, nor lined garments, on pain of forfeit of the same.

At the same time, the high price of wheat was brought down, much to the relief of the people, by the importation of wheat from Holland and Ireland to English ports, where it was sold.

In September, it was ordained in parliament at Westminster that the wool staples, that is to say, the places where wool merchants meet and sell their wares, which had previously been at Bruges in Flanders, should now rather be set up in various places in England, Wales and Ireland.

These wool staples were to be regulated by ordinances, with punishments prescribed for any who disobeyed, and privileges were to be granted to merchants, but especially foreign merchants, as appears in the regulations then enacted.

In October 1355, Edward III staged an inconclusive and short-lived invasion of Normandy. His eldest

Wages of scarcity

THE Statute of Labourers, enacted by the king in parliament in 1351, was the earliest systematic attempt by England's ruling élite to regulate and limit the wages of the rural workforce. In 1348 and 1349 the Black Death had wiped out about one-third of England's population, leaving land untilled and labourers in great demand. Wages had consequently risen rapidly and alarmingly. Holders of great estates who derived most of their income from rents were comparatively unaffected, but those landlords – many of them little more than prosperous peasants – who made their profits by using hired labour to cultivate the land, were badly hit. Their alarm is reflected in the wording of the statute, which castigates the labourers who, 'to their ease and singular covetousness, do withdraw themselves from serving great men and others, unless they receive wages double or treble what they took in 1347 or before, to the damage of the great men and the impoverishment of all the commonalty.'

The statute laid down precise wages for various occupations and trades, fixed at pre-plague levels. Ploughmen should be paid 10d. per bushel of wheat harvested, as in 1347, and should be hired by the year rather than the day. Master carpenters and master masons were to receive 4d. per day, other masons 3d. and their assistants 1½d. All landless men under 60 had to accept employment under such terms and their own lords had the first claim on their services. To implement the legislation, royal commissioners were to tour England holding sessions in each county four times a year; and fugitives were to be chased and brought to justice. The statute was vigorously enforced during the 1350s, with the co-operation of the minor gentry, who controlled justice in their localities and had a vested interest in wage regulation.

Potential peasant resistance was, at first, lessened by the opportunities given to many previously landless labourers to acquire smallholdings: because food prices remained high, they could make good profits.

In the longer term, however, the statute was defeated by the laws of supply and demand. Great landlords found that it restricted their ability to compete for good labour, and peasants increasingly ignored its provisions, seeking the jobs which offered them the highest wages.

Right *Masons at work erecting the walls to a palace. A master mason made 4d. per day under the statute, equivalent to the price of two chickens.*

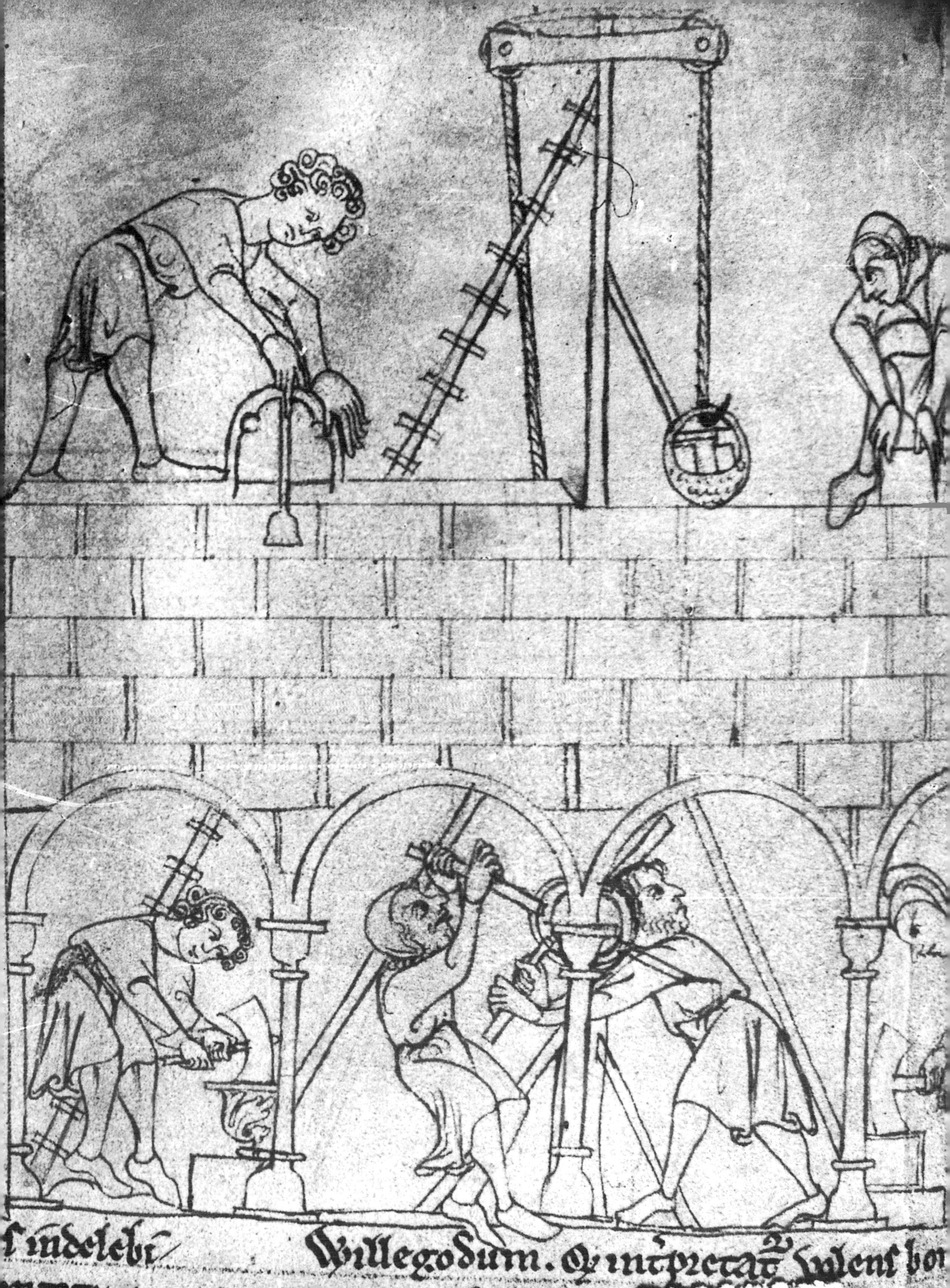
indelebi
Willegodum.

son Edward, the Black Prince, had been appointed lieutenant of Gascony in July, and he too set off on campaign.

1355

Edward of Woodstock, the prince of Wales, accompanied by the earls of Warwick, Suffolk, Salisbury and Oxford, set forth from the port of Plymouth in Devon on 9 September, and on 1 October they landed at Bordeaux. There, the prince was honourably received by the bishop, the clergy and the monks, all wearing their robes, together with the townsfolk who all came out to meet him. The lords and barons of Gascony too attended the long-hoped for arrival of Prince Edward with devotion and joy.

The prince called together a council of these men and those he had brought with him from England, and learnt that the count of Armagnac had been made leader of the opposing forces and commander of the enemy's troops.

Bearing the authority of the pretender of the French [John II], and by stirring up a rebellion throughout Languedoc, the count was causing more harm than anyone else in France to the area and to the people who were faithful to the king of England.

Prince Edward, when he heard this, was filled with rage at the actions of this man who was stirring up trouble in Languedoc. Consequently, following the advice of his noble counsellors, he determined to wage a campaign against the count of Armagnac.

And so they set forth speedily, first accepting the surrender of the fortresses in Guyenne, before laying waste the county of Armagnac, thus bringing much needed succour to the loyal people of Gascony, who, before the arrival of the noble prince, had suffered much from the fierce depredations of their Armagnac neighbours.

On Tuesday 3 November, the prince of Wales and his forces came to Carcassonne, a town of fine aspect and great wealth, well built and larger than

Women in medieval society

TWO main factors determined a woman's position in society and her prospects: her rank – whether she was noble, bourgeois or peasant – and her marital status – whether she was a maiden, a married woman or a widow. Certainly, by her sex alone she was inferior to a man; and even when an individual woman was seen to have a skill or accomplishment this did not increase society's regard for women in general.

Aristocratic women had two choices: wedlock – most women could expect to be married by the age of 14 – or the nunnery. Both required dowries and involved land and wealth transactions. The noble's wife and the nun were both important within their milieu.

The noble lady ran domestic household affairs, staff and provisioning and was also expected to manage estates, and even defend them if her husband was abroad or dead. Black Agnes, countess of March, for example, successfully defended Dunbar Castle against King Edward III in 1338. In a nunnery, an area little dominated by men, women were responsible for administration as well as spiritual growth.

The difficulty of acquiring a good education was a major handicap. Noble women might receive private tuition while nunneries provided a few schools and a rudimentary education. By contrast, most peasants' wives were illiterate. They looked after all domestic matters, plus agricultural and allied tasks such as dairying and brewing, weaving and spinning.

The economic importance of working women is most clearly seen in thriving urban commercial centres where women's occupations could place them alongside men of the same rank.

Although they were rarely given municipal or governmental roles, they could acquire the status of skilled workers, often as a result of their husbands' or fathers' occupations (most craft guilds in England debarred women unless they were the wives or daughters of members and able to carry on the craft even when widowed). In these circumstances a wide spectrum of medieval industry was open to women – from shoemakers and chandlers to gilders, painters, spicers and embroiderers. Women provided labour and technical skill in the textile industries and some, like Rose of Burford, the wool merchant, even acted as independent traders.

Women could be apprenticed to men or women traders, and so receive a vocational education. In 1364 sureties were given for Agnes, wife of a London cutler, that she would teach Jusema her apprentice and feed and

Above *Detail from an illuminated manuscript depicting a woman surgeon, with attendants, performing a Caesarean section at a difficult birth. This was one of the few professional roles available to women during the Middle Ages, though it did not lead to a wider role in medicine for them.*

Right *When a castle was besieged every available person was needed to repel the attackers; this often included women, as shown in this illustration. The awesome fate that awaited women when a castle fell made them fight all the more vigorously.*

clothe her, and not beat her with a stick or knife.

Women were also accorded a certain status in the one area in which only they could be experts: gynaecology and obstetrics. Midwives carried out surgical procedures and Caesarian sections, and all women were expected to know something of family medicine.

Nevertheless, if they wanted to be professional physicians they found that, with a few continental exceptions, university medical faculties were closed to them. Some women might reach the rank of barber, but any who tried to put their knowledge of medicine into practice were called ignorant amateurs and 'presumptuous women' by physicians.

that part of London which lies within the city walls. In between the town or burg and the city, which was surrounded by a double wall, ran a river called the Aude flowing beneath a fine stone bridge, and at the foot of the upper part of the city lay a charming hostelry.

In the town, there were four religious houses of poor friars, who did not abandon the town when the citizens and humbler folk who lived there fled into the citadel.

The whole army was lodged handsomely in the town and took up scarcely three-quarters of the houses. The troops were given plentiful Muscat wine and other victuals, both plain and luxurious.

On that day, the troops were drawn up in their proper order before the town, while many were promoted to the rank of knight.

On Wednesday and Thursday, there was a truce and the army rested in the town, while those who had been so instructed negotiated a peace treaty with the representatives of those who were in the citadel.

The citizens of Carcassonne were willing to pay two hundred and fifty thousand gold écus, if the soldiers would agree not to set fire to their town. But when they offered their money, the prince replied that he and his men had come not for gold but in the cause of justice, not to sell cities but to take them.

When they heard this, the citizens were terrified but stood by John II, the pretender of France, either being unwilling to show their obedience to their true lord, or else fearing to do so lest John II should later punish them for it.

And so, the following day, the prince ordered that the town should be burnt, with the exception of the religious houses.

On Friday, after setting light to the town, the army withdrew, later hearing through the friars and others that the town had been completely destroyed.

The Black Prince and his army next went to Narbonne, which they set alight.

1356

The prince of Wales advanced into French lands, making for the plains of the Limousin and Berry. As a good leader should, he instructed his men not to approach the enemy tentatively, but, their flesh protected with worldly armour and their souls with the sacraments of penitence, to be prepared to defeat those who had rebelled against the king of England's peace.

After a profitable raid into the king of France's lands, the Black Prince returned towards Gascony. He skirmished with a French reconnaissance party near Poitiers and, two days later, on 19 September, he led his forces into the field against the army of John II of France.

All told, the prince's army was composed of exactly four thousand men-at-arms, one thousand armed sergeants, and two thousand archers.

The French nobles drew near with great pride, thinking little of the English whose numbers were inferior to their own. The French host consisted of eight thousand men-at-arms under eighty-seven standards, and an uncounted throng of sergeants.

Many of our men complained because a large portion of our army had been sent off earlier to protect Gascony.

Prince Edward saw that the hill near to his forces was entirely surrounded by fences and ditches, its slopes being covered in one part by pastureland, thick with bushes, and in another by vineyards and elsewhere by sown crops.

It was in the cultivated area that the prince planned to stand against the French army. In between our troops and this hill was a deep, marshy valley through which ran a river.

The prince's section found a narrow ford and crossed the river with carts. They then moved on out of the valley, crossing the fences and ditches,

The young Edward

THE Black Prince has enjoyed such a high reputation since the 14th century that it is almost impossible to separate the man from the legend. His life was spent in the pursuit of chivalric ideals, whether fighting in battles and jousting at tournaments, or courting the affections of his beloved and beautiful wife Joan, the 'fair maid of Kent'.

Born at Woodstock in June 1330, the prince was christened Edward after his father. He became earl of Chester in 1333, duke of Cornwall in 1337, and prince of Wales in 1343. By his early teens he had a large household of 120 servants, and assumed the ostentatious and extravagant lifestyle expected of a Plantagenet prince. He had a taste for fine clothes, and was addicted to gambling. Like his father, the prince had few intellectual pretensions, and what little education he received was mostly in the arts of war. It was not long before these skills were put to use in the service of the Crown.

In the summer of 1346 Edward III and his son set sail for Normandy. The 16-year-old prince was knighted at Saint-Vaast-la-Hogue, and then proceeded to Caen where he first witnessed the systematic destruction and pillaging which was to be such a feature of his own later raids through France. When battle was eventually joined with Philip VI's army at Crécy, the prince was given nominal command of one of the English divisions, and acquitted himself with honour. After helping his father raise the siege of Calais in the following year, he returned home to take part in the round of tournaments organized to commemorate these English victories. He had established an enviable reputation as a military leader while still a teenager, and was duly rewarded in 1348 when he became a founder member of the Order of the Garter.

The Black Prince found it difficult to adjust to civilian life in the early 1350s. He dutifully attended parliaments and led diplomatic missions, but made no personal impression on their proceedings. He showed some interest in the administration of his estates and in 1354 went to Cornwall, where Restormel Castle was specially fitted out for his use; but he never bothered to visit his principality of Wales.

War provided him with his *raison d'être*; he was delighted when peace talks failed in 1355 and he was offered the opportunity to lead an English expedition to Gascony. This was the start of a series of campaigns in southern France which was to culminate in 1356 in the battle of Poitiers, the finest achievement of the Black Prince – by then prince of Aquitaine – and one of the greatest English victories of the Hundred Years War.

Below ***Edward III granting the Black Prince the principality of Aquitaine.***

and seized the hill; because of the undergrowth, they managed to keep themselves concealed in a strong position, higher than that of the enemy.

The enemy, realizing that the prince's standard, which had recently been visible, had become hidden from view behind the hill, assumed that the prince had taken to flight, and thus deceived, set off in pursuit of the supposedly retreating prince. Pikemen were met on the slope by knights from Uour first division stationed there, who were specially equipped to parry the attacks of pikemen.

The men came together in a fearful conflict of lances, swords and axes. Nor did the archers fail in their duty but, from a safe position protected by the mound, they attacked those above the ditch and beyond the hedge, aiming arrows which defeated armed knights, while our crossbowmen let fly bolts fast and furiously.

At the same time, the archers stood their ground in the marsh against the incursions of the French cavalry.

However, in this they were only moderately successful, for the French knights had been instructed to trample the archers beneath their horses' hooves and thus protect their own men from the arrows.

And so continued the furious carnage. The fanfare sounded, the trumpet, horns and pipes answering one another, and echoed from the stony sides of the valley through the woods of Poitou. You would have thought the mountains themselves were moaning to the valleys and resounding into the clouds.

And these mighty thunderclaps were not without their fearful lightning flashes, for the shining armour glittered golden in the light and the spears shone with their polished steel, their points like lightning bolts, shattering anything in their path. Then, the threatening mass of crossbowmen plunged the battlefield into thick night with an impenetrable cloud of their bolts, and the field was shaken by a fatal shower of arrows, sent forth by the English archers.

The battle of Poitiers

IN 1355 Edward III planned a three-pronged attack on France. The Black Prince was sent to Aquitaine, the duke of Lancaster was to lead an expedition to Brittany, and Edward's cousin Charles the Bad, king of Navarre, proposed to attack the French in Normandy. In the event, Lancaster's mission was delayed and the Normandy expedition never took place. But the Black Prince persisted with his campaign, and in August 1356 he marched northwards from Gascony to meet up with Lancaster's forces. When he reached the Loire all the bridgeheads were blocked. His army of 6000 men stood alone against the superior numbers of John II of France when battle was joined at Nouaille, near Poitiers, on 19 September 1356.

Contemporary accounts of the battle of Poitiers differ, but the main course of events is reasonably clear. The English prince occupied a defensive position on high ground, where hedges, trees and vineyards obscured the view and hindered the French attack. He adopted the tactics of Crécy, countering a French cavalry charge with a hail of arrows, then leading his dismounted knights into hand-to-hand fighting.

The battle was long and fierce, with heavy casualties on both sides. But when news broke that the king of France had been taken prisoner, the remaining French forces fled the field, and a great English victory was proclaimed. John II was escorted back to Bordeaux. In May 1357 he arrived in London, where he was paraded through the streets and greeted as an honoured guest by a delighted Edward III.

The English now enjoyed the strongest possible bargaining position. France was economically exhausted by the Black Death and the ravages of enemy armies, and politically paralyzed by the absence of her king. In May and June 1358 the Dauphin Charles had to contend with a serious revolt in the Paris region – the *Jacquerie*, from *Jacques Bonhomme*, the symbolic name for a French peasant. Under these circumstances the English king could ask what he wished.

The 'first treaty of London' of May 1358 obliged the French to recognize English sovereignty over Aquitaine and certain lands in northern France, and to pay a ransom of nearly £700,000 for John's release. When the money was not forthcoming, Edward pushed ahead with a series of outrageous and provocative demands. In the 'second treaty of London' of March 1359 he requested not only the lands and the ransom agreed in the previous year, but also the cessation of a huge block of territory in western France including Normandy, Brittany, Maine, Touraine and Anjou. The idea was anathema to the Dauphin, and the proposals were dismissed out of hand. Edward

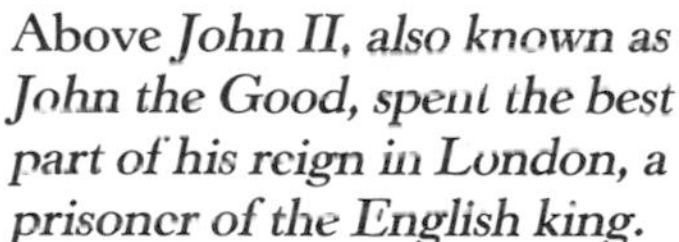

Above *John II, also known as John the Good, spent the best part of his reign in London, a prisoner of the English king.*

announced a campaign to conquer France itself.

Late in 1359 Edward and his sons landed at Calais with a large army. They headed for Reims, the traditional coronation place of the kings of France, where Edward apparently hoped to assume the title to which he had now laid claim for some 20 years. However, faced with the prospect of a long siege, he lost interest and moved south to Burgundy where he and the Black Prince contented themselves with ravaging the countryside. The English army then advanced on Paris, but a siege did not seem viable; and Edward resumed negotiations at Brétigny in May 1360.

The resulting treaty of Brétigny was a compromise. Edward III got the lands he had originally demanded in 1358, but John's ransom was reduced to £500,000. In return for France renouncing all rights in Aquitaine, Edward would abandon his claim to the French throne. The settlement brought Edward everything for which his predecessors had fought since the 13th century; but it also put an end to his pretensions to rule in Paris as well as London, a considerable blow to English pride.

Nine years of peace followed, during which Edward lived sumptuously off the profits of the French ransom. But it was not long before this valorous king and his ambitious sons looked to the prospect of further glory, and further gains, in the kingdom of France.

Top *John II is captured at the battle of Poitiers outside the city walls.*

Above *Hand to hand fighting between dismounted knights proved both bloody and fierce.*

'Madly the prince's forces hurtled on
Against the dense-packed shields, to seek a
way
To pierce their enemies' armour and to strike
The hearts beneath the breastplates' firm
protection.'

Thus Edward, prince of Wales, came to the encounter, hacking a path with steel through the midst of the enemy lines. Leaving devastation in his wake, he hurled himself into their midst:

'Savagely circling
His sword on all sides
Strikes his foes
Crushes them down.
Thus drops each man
On whom its blow falls.'

Weaving his way between the now-ragged lines of the French army, and leaving the thinly spread ranks to be defeated by his subordinates, the prince turned his fearsome advance with haste upon the pretender and his band, for they stood yet firm and close. Then the standards wavered, and the standard bearers fell. Some were trampled, their innards torn open; others spat out their own teeth; many were stuck fast to the ground, impaled; not a few lost whole arms as they stood there. Some died, wallowing in the blood of others; some groaned, crushed beneath the heavy weight of the fallen; mighty souls gave forth fearful lamentations as they departed from wretched bodies.

The blood of peasants and the blood of royalty flowed in a single flood, providing a luxurious repast for the now scarlet fish in the nearby streams.

Thus the Black Prince, the wild boar of Cornwall, he who 'loves only paths that flow with blood' raged on towards the position held by John the pretender.

Here the prince was met by a stubborn force of the bravest men. The English were repulsed by the French, whose leader, though of few years, was yet filled with youthful fury, and returned all blows with interest, crushing the heads of some, piercing the bodies of others.

Everywhere John the pretender went, he gave proof that the royal house of France was not altogether degenerate.

But at last, the wheel of Fortune swung round. The prince of Wales broke through into the French force and, with the savage nobility of the lion, crushed the proud, spared the humble and compelled John the pretender to surrender.

In the meantime, the French had scattered over the countryside of Poitou, for they had seen the lowering of the standard of the fleur-de-lis and hoped a speedy flight would bring them to safety in a nearby town.

However, the English, despite the dreadful wounds they had sustained, pursued the French fugitives to the gates of Poitiers.

The day following the battle, there was a reckoning of the prisoners. Among them were John II, the pretender, called by his own people the king of France, and Philip, his son.

The capture of John II of France was a major triumph for the English.

The chivalrous chronicler Jean le Bel relates that this was enhanced by the submission of David II, king of Scots, to Edward III.

1357

King David II of Scotland had been captured [at the battle of Neville's Cross] in 1346, shortly after the battle of Crécy, while King Edward III was besieging Calais. He remained a prisoner in England until 1357, when a peace treaty was made between him and King Edward III in the following terms:

First, he did homage to the king of England for the whole realm of Scotland, certain islands which he and his predecessors had conquered being excepted; the Scots never gave their consent to this.

Next, he bound himself to defend the kingdom of England against all men of vassal or subject rank, and to attend the four parliaments which

The game of war

EDWARD'S victories earned him a Europe-wide reputation, but after the capture of Calais in 1347 the war with France settled down again to a more normal tempo of skirmishes and sieges. In Gascony, Brittany, Normandy and around Calais a desultory war continued, with little advantage to either side. Edward had returned to England in 1347 to complaints of misgovernment. Because of his new prestige these caused little trouble, but it was clear he could not raise taxes for another great effort like that of 1346–7. In addition, he felt it was time to turn his military advantage over France into a political one.

The strength of Edward's position is shown by the demands he made in peace negotiations. A treaty drafted by the demands at Guines in 1353 proposed that he renounce his claim to the French throne in return for full sovereignty in Calais and most of western France – he would be 'king in France, if not of France'. At the last minute, however, John II of France, with the backing of Pope Innocent VI (a Frenchman) decided that these terms were too humiliating and he withdrew his offer of sovereignty. The outcome was a return to war.

Major campaigning resumed in 1355, when Edward laid grandiose plans on the pattern of 1346. Little came of this great effort, however. Later that year news that the Scots had taken the town of Berwick caused the English king to make haste for the North. In 1356, after the New Year, he burned and ravaged as far as Edinburgh but could not bring the Scots to battle.

The Black Prince's 1355 expedition from Bordeaux to the Mediterranean and back was similarly destructive. He took great plunder and burned the towns of Narbonne and Carcassonne, but these results were hardly worth the effort put into them. His victory over the French at Poitiers in 1356, in which he captured John II, was to break this pattern of indecisive English expeditions.

A peculiar feature of warfare at this time is the contrast between chivalrous conduct and brutal raiding, between professing a lofty ideal and visiting indiscriminate destruction on French and Scottish non-combatants. The reason is that chivalry was for knights – who often viewed the lower reaches of the social hierarchy with contempt. They sometimes regarded war as a game, but it was a game played in deadly earnest.

Below ***The final stage of a siege.***

were normally held each year in London. If it was not convenient for him to be present, he was to send four of his greatest barons, two prelates of the Church and two knights banneret.

He was also to renounce in perpetuity his claim to the city of Berwick upon Tweed, and to guarantee this each year by good hostages. In this manner peace was made between the two kings.

On 22 February 1358, Etienne Marcel, the provost of Paris, at the head of a rampaging mob of Parisians, rose against the French dauphin Charles (son of the captive John II), broke into the royal palace in Paris and murdered two of the leading French nobles.

1358

It was soon known in France that Edward III of England and John II of France had reached an agreement and were now in alliance against all comers.

Etienne Marcel, the provost of the merchants [of Paris], was then exceedingly alarmed, for he knew very well how bitterly Charles, duke of Normandy, son of the king of France, hated him. Charles had been loud in his complaints against the provost everywhere, because of the injury the latter had done him in the palace of Paris.

The provost therefore looked urgently for support, with the result that Charles [the Bad], king of Navarre, was sent for. When Charles II arrived, the provost and citizens of Paris persuaded him to give them his sworn word that he would stand by them against all men without exception, against even the king of France himself, which many people found almost incredible.

In that year, near the end of May, a terrible affliction the revolt of the French peasants, [known as the Jacquerie], struck many parts of the kingdom of France.

In the districts of Beauvais and Amiens, Brie, the Ile-de-France and Valois as far as Soissons, certain inhabitants of the country towns – fewer than a hundred of them to begin with – began to gather in the villages, without anyone to lead them.

They declared that the nobles, knights and squires were bringing the kingdom to shame and destruction, and that it would be a good deed to destroy them all. Each man said, 'He is right, he is right. Shame on any who hinder us!'

And so they went off at once, with no other discussion, with no weapons but knives and iron-shod sticks, to the house of a certain knight. They broke into it and killed him, his wife and children, and then set the place on fire.

Next they went to a strong castle where they did much worse, for there they took the knight and bound him to a strong stake, raped his wife and his daughter before his eyes, and then killed his wife, who was pregnant, and the girl. After that they killed the knight and all the children and burned the castle.

They did the same in several castles and good houses, and the number of these brigands grew until there were at least six thousand of them.

Wherever they went, their numbers increased, for everyone who shared their opinion joined them. Knights and squires, noble women and girls fled wherever they could, often carrying their little children in their arms distances of ten or twenty leagues, and abandoning their manors and castles.

Thus these gangs of leaderless men looted and burned, murdered men and women of good birth and their children, and raped ladies and gently born girls without the least mercy.

Never have Christians and Saracens behaved to each other with such unbounded frenzy, such diabolic cruelty.

Whoever could do the worst and vilest deeds, deeds that no human being should think of without shame, he was their greatest master.

I would not dare to write or relate the dreadful cruelties they practised against noblewomen; but,

Right Knights and squires, armed to the teeth, attacking the defenceless peasantry as they attempted to wrestle control of the countryside back from them. These outbreaks were a direct result of the intolerable strains placed upon the common people by catastrophes such as the Black Death or the terrible harvest of 1369; and by the failure of knights to perform their social function of defending the land.

William Langland in Piers Plowman *details the obligations that each section of society had towards the others; but although he lamented the plight of the destitute, he had no sympathy with attempts of the lower orders to ape their superiors. Indeed gentlemen should force the idle to perform their tasks.*

A tract for the times

WILLIAM Langland, an obscure but educated London Mass-priest, produced the first version of his great alliterative poem, *The Vision of Piers Plowman*, in about 1362. The complex allegory has been interpreted in many different ways. However, at the start of the poem Langland analyses the evils which afflicted all social classes in contemporary England. The emphasis is on sins originating from economic motives, characterised by Lady Mede, who personifies desire for unearned reward. The welfare of the community is equally prejudiced by the avarice and irresponsibility of the ruling classes and by the idleness of labourers.

Langland perceived the social and economic crisis which resulted from the continued onslaughts of the Black Death. A mortality rate of at least 30 per cent caused a catastrophic shortage of labour. In the next decade incomes for surviving peasants rose dramatically and labour services traditionally due to lords were increasingly resented as a degrading badge of servility, incompatible with rising economic status.

Great landlords, faced by falling rent-rolls and deserted holdings, automatically pressed their tenants harder. The aspirations of the peasantry and the concerted rearguard action of landlords were irreconcilable, and the clash of economic interests soon led to insurrection.

Langland, however, was no social revolutionary. Men might be equal in the eyes of God, and even before the law, but they differed in function and degree. The knight of the poem is exhorted by Piers never maliciously to ill-treat or exploit his serfs; but he should not labour at the plough himself. His function is to protect the community. In France, the nobility's failure to do this had been the primary cause of the *Jacquerie*, the peasant rising of 1358. In England refusal of landlords to channel legitimate profits into socially beneficial causes led to simmering discontent. The theme of Piers Plowman is that unless all classes dutifully discharge their divinely ordained function in accordance with natural law, nemesis will descend in the form of hunger and social disharmony.

among other wicked deeds, they killed a knight and put him on a spit and roasted him in front of his wife and children; after ten or a dozen of them had raped the lady, they tried to force her to eat some of her dead husband; then they put her to a vile death.

In the Beauvaisis they burned and threw down more than sixty good houses and strong castles.

It was just the same in Normandy, in the district between Paris and Noyon, and also between Paris and Soissons.

Wherever they went, they killed and laid waste, but God in His mercy provided such redress that all good men must thank Him for it.

You must know that when the lords of the Beauvaisis saw their homes destroyed and their loved ones so wickedly killed, they sent for help to their friends in Flanders, Poitou and elsewhere.

Then they attacked these evil creatures on every side, killing them and hanging them on the first trees they could find.

As soon as help from outside arrived in the Beauvaisis and these wicked men suffered their first defeat, they were at such a loss and so helpless that they had no idea what to do.

These wicked men had a captain called Jacques Bonhomme, who was utterly worthless; he tried to claim that the bishop of Laon had incited him to this action.

The rebellion was crushed by Charles the Bad, king of Navarre, at the battle of Mello.

The French nobles then took violent reprisals against the peasants, whom they massacred in large numbers.

1360

You must know first of all that King Edward III had crossed the sea to France on 28 October 1359 [seeking battle with the French], and stayed there until the end of May of this year.

While in France, the king of England and his men found no one to oppose them or to stop them getting supplies or going wherever they liked, except in the fortified towns. No shortages or difficulties lasted longer than three days, other than rain and winter weather while they were outside Reims.

And you must know that the noble king and his men had with them some ten or twelve thousand baggage carts, each drawn by three good horses brought from England, and on these the lords had tents and pavilions as well as forges and ovens to make whatever might be needed, for fear they would find everything in the countryside spoiled and laid waste.

They also had a number of skiffs and small boats made of boiled leather, so well constructed that each would easily hold three men who wanted to go fishing on a river or lake. In this way the nobles and gentlemen had plenty of fish during Lent, but the common people managed with what they could find.

Besides these, King Edward III had at least thirty falconers each carrying his birds and sixty or more couples of tall hounds and as many greyhounds, with which he went hunting every day.

Riding in this manner, they went on as far as Paris, seeking battle; then they moved towards Chartres, always looking for the richest country, and then directed their march towards Bonneval and the district of Vendôme.

At the request of the abbot of Cluny, the king journeyed back towards Chartres, and at Brétigny he stayed for twenty-one days, discussing the peace treaty, which was agreed on 8 May in the following terms:

That noble King Edward III and his heirs should have, hold and possess in perpetuity, in peace and freely, with no appeal lying elsewhere, the lands not being held in fief of the king of France or of any other, all the lands and countries here set out, [amongst which:] the Bigorre, the Agenais, the Périgord, Rouergue, Poitou, La Rochelle, the

War, English style

Above *English archers training; constant practice was an important reason for their effectiveness in battle.*

BETWEEN the accession of Edward I in 1272 and the mid-14th century, there was a revolution in the way English armies were raised and fought. The tactics adopted at Crécy in 1346 had been developed through long experience, brought to perfection in the long wars against the Scots. This combination of dismounted men-at-arms and archers was to remain the English way of fighting, with some variations, until at least the end of the 15th century.

Heavy cavalry had been recruited by feudal summons since 1066, although this was always supplemented by the paid services of hired knights. By 1300 there were only about 1000 active knights in the realm, and they were supported by men with lands worth about £40 a year: squires and sergeants. These were the men-at-arms. The infantry (spearmen and archers) was raised by commissions of array who toured local communities on the king's behalf. By the 1330s it consisted exclusively of archers.

During the Hundred Years War it also became increasingly common for the king to use another method of raising troops. Barons and other captains – knights, squires and even clerks – undertook by contracts called indentures to supply agreed numbers of men-at-arms and archers for a fixed payment. Henry of Lancaster took one such retinue to Gascony in 1345: it comprised 500 men-at-arms, 500 mounted archers and 1000 footmen. These 'contract armies' were effective both militarily and financially. Once in France the English lived off the land and enriched themselves: plunder, and the ransoms of captured lords or territory, were powerful incentives to supply men.

The armour of the men-at-arms developed rapidly until, by the mid-14th century, the 'suit of plates' was common. It gave more protection and mobility than the old mail – an important consideration when fighting on foot. The men often fought in pairs: each couple held a lance to meet the first shock of the enemy charge, then stood back-to-back in the mêlée, armed with sword and shield or other weapons.

A knight received wages of 2 shillings per day while his superior, the banneret, was paid double. The latter led a retinue of 15–20 men and was distinguished by an oblong banner bearing his arms; the knight carried a triangular pennon. Wealthy men – barons and peers like Henry of Lancaster – were able to raise much greater retinues. Archers were also well-equipped and disciplined. The best had breastplate and iron cap, mail gloves, longbow and arrows, sword and dagger. They were vulnerable in close combat, but their main task in battle was to shoot a hail of arrows at the advancing enemy. Trained men could shoot ten yard-long arrows a minute, with accuracy, to 200 yards. Their employers often provided them with uniforms – the Earl of Arundel's archers wore suits of red and white.

The normal English practice of fighting on foot did not reduce the horse's importance. Edward III's armies gained their mobility from being mounted, and at 4d. to 6d. a day, archers with horses received twice as much as those on foot. Men-at-arms also possessed expensive war-horses, carefully bred and trained, and reserved for battle or the tournament. The king's stud farms supplied these noble beasts for his use; and he undertook to pay compensation for horses lost on campaign. Soldiers required more than one mount, ideally four horses for a knight, three for a squire and two for a mounted archer, adding to the problem of transporting armies to France.

Limousin, Saintonge, the county of Angoulême, the whole duchy of Guyenne right up to its former boundaries, the town and castle of Calais with all its dependencies, and the whole county of Guines, towns and castles included, to its full extent.

Edward III was also to have, if he wished, the whole county of Ponthieu which had been given to his mother the queen of England [Isabella] as a marriage portion: but this he was to hold in fief of the king of France if he wished to have it back, as his father had held it.

Furthermore, for his losses and expenses he was to receive three million florins, which comes to thirty times one hundred thousand florins, to be paid in six instalments; the first was to be paid within the three weeks following 24 June 1360, and the rest within the next three years, one-third each year. All ransoms of lands, towns, houses and prisoners would remain the property of King Edward III.

In order to guarantee all this, the French were to send good and sufficient hostages, some of the greatest in the kingdom, who would remain in the town of Calais until all the terms of the treaty were fulfilled.

King Edward III, for his part, agreed and promised to bring King John II of France to Calais by 21 June, and to maintain him there at English expense for three weeks, within which period the French were to fulfil the agreed terms and to put King Edward's men in peaceful possession of all the castles, towns, places and lands which they were to have and hold without appeal.

And if this was not exactly done, King John II of France and all his hostages would have to stay quietly in Calais for three months, paying thirty thousand florins for their costs and expenses, and the English would remain in possession of the fortresses they had won in the kingdom of France, but they were not to pillage or make war.

As well as all this, the king of England was to renounce the right and name [of king] to which he laid claim in France.

Heraldry

HERALDRY – the systematic use of hereditary devices – attained its maturity under the later Plantagenet kings. Symbols like the Roman eagle, the dragon of Wessex and the Viking raven had been known for centuries, but these belonged to peoples, not particular people. The devices depicted on the shields of Norman knights in the Bayeux tapestry seem to have been personal rather than inherited. When hereditary devices began to appear in the 12th century, the famous golden lions of the Plantagenets themselves were among the earliest. In 1127 Count Geoffrey Plantagenet of Anjou displayed several of these creatures on his shield, and his son King Henry II bore two such lions. By 1198, however, the number had settled down to three which still form part of the British royal arms.

During the 12th century, developments in armour turned heraldry into a necessity. Protected by an enveloping helm instead of the old open-faced Norman helmet, knights were unrecognizable in battle or tournament except by the devices emblazoned on shield, surcoat (or 'coat-of-arms') and horse trappings. For immediate identification, these devices needed to be relatively simple; the earliest coats-of-arms are unfussy combinations of stripes, blocks, chevrons and heraldic beasts.

Increasingly the hallmark of noble birth, heraldry had become so widespread by the late 13th century that specialist 'heralds' – originally similar to wandering minstrels, but later important officials employed as messengers and ambassadors – were needed to supervise tournaments and identify opponents in war. Their technical jargon, couched in the medieval French which was then the language of polite society, is still used to describe (or 'blazon') coats-of-arms.

Heraldic arms were a man's unique property and, as such, assumed great symbolic importance; to insult the shield was to insult its owner. Edward II's fallen favourites, the Despensers, were mockingly decked in their heraldic surcoats before meeting their traitors' deaths; and the London mob who rioted against John of Gaunt in 1377 hung his arms upside-down in the streets – an affront equivalent to modern flag-burning. Heraldry was also used as effective propaganda. The most striking instance was Edward III's quartering of the French fleur-de-lis with his Plantagenet lions in 1340, thereby asserting his claim to the crown of France.

By the mid-14th century heraldry had spread from shield and surcoat to adorn tombs, castles, and manuscripts. In an age when literacy was far from general, it proclaimed more graphically than words the pride and splendour of the English nobility.

Above *An illustration from the Luttrell psalter showing the Luttrell family in full heraldic costume. The main purpose of heraldry was identification in battle and at court. This lead to elaborate and complex devices. Horses and squires were not exempt from wearing their master's livery; ladies often used blazon designs.*

Right *Inlaid heraldic tiles from the abbey church at Hailes in Gloucester. The centre top tile bears the three lions of the Plantagenet blazon.*

In order to accomplish all this, a general truce was agreed, to last until 29 September of the following year. And the French were to escort King Edward peacefully to Calais, which they did.

When all these points had been agreed, Charles, duke of Normandy, as the eldest heir of France, promised on oath to maintain and fulfil them, in the presence of Edward, prince of Wales, Henry, earl of Leicester and duke of Lancaster, and a number of English barons acting as proxies for King Edward III. Several French lords who were present took the same oath, and so, on the other side, did the English proxies.

Next King Edward III of England sent four knights to swear publicly to the treaty in the royal palace in Paris [the Louvre], at which everyone was delighted. Clergy and laity came to meet them outside the gates in a most noble procession, church bells rang and all the streets of Paris were decorated. Everyone followed the knights to the palace, where they took the oath.

The English knights were entertained splendidly by the duke of Normandy and all the nobles. They were taken into the glorious Sainte-Chapelle, where they were shown the most beautiful relics in the world and the loveliest jewels, and above all the sacred crown with which God was crowned in his most blessed passion; and Charles of Normandy gave each of the knights one of its largest thorns, gifts which they greatly valued.

Next, the duke had each of them presented with the finest courser any man could hope to see, as well as quantities of wonderfully rich jewels, and then they were nobly conducted to their own people who were waiting for them at Palaiseau. From here, two marshals of France rode with them until they reached King Edward, who was waiting for them to join him before beginning his escorted journey through France.

As soon as the English knights reached Edward III, they told him what honour and courtesy the French had shown them, and he was very pleased and gave both them and the French lords a hearty welcome.

Next morning the king of England and all his men set off in an orderly and peaceful way towards Normandy and Pont-de-l'Arche, where they intended to cross the Seine. Wherever they went, they found the towns open and plenty of goods for sale at reasonable prices, for you must know that as soon as the peace treaty was made, it was proclaimed throughout the kingdom; and indeed, the king of England had men riding in the rear to make sure that his people did no harm or violence to anyone. They stayed overnight at Pont-de-l'Arche and next morning the king went with a small retinue to the port of Harfleur, where he embarked for England.

As soon as King Edward III and the few men with him arrived in London and Queen Philippa had greeted him, he hastened to bring John II of France to London. John was welcomed by the queen and by the prince of Wales, who by no means hated him, by the duke of Lancaster and the other lords with all possible splendour. Feasting and open court continued for a fortnight.

When this was all done, and John II of France had been dressed in the fine clothing proper for a king, King Edward III and his children and all the other lords accompanied him to Dover, where Edward sent his son and a great number of lords with John to Calais, as he had promised. The English lords waited a considerable time at Calais for the French lords to bring six times one hundred thousand florins, and to surrender themselves as hostages.

When they had waited a very long time and realized that the hostages were certainly not ready nor the money collected, the English lords took leave of King John and returned to England. They left King John and his young son Philip under the guard of four knights and other very able men, who gave them all the comfort they could properly give. They allowed the French knights to talk with King John at dinner and supper whenever he liked, and they frequently took him out to enjoy himself hunting or in other ways, while they waited for the promised sum to be brought to Saint-Omer. But the French did not want to deliver it until all the hostages had arrived, as had been promised.

Bankers of Florence

'THE world', said Pope Boniface VIII in 1300, 'is made up of five elements; earth, air, fire, water – and Florentines'. With this compliment, he acknowledged the tremendous importance of Florence in contemporary Europe, and the all-pervading influence of her citizens. Along with the other great cities of northern Italy, Florence stood at the hub of European trade, and at the axis of the commerce between north-western Europe, the Mediterranean, and the Muslim East.

The basis of this economic influence was a network of agents in every major city from London to Alexandria. Members of one or other of the great Florentine merchant-banking firms, they were in constant touch with each other, and with the shifting currents of international trade. They acted as collectors and transmitters of papal taxes and – most crucially – as bankers. They also offered loans of sometimes staggering magnitude – albeit at highly profitable interest rates, disguised in various ways to circumvent the Church's ban on moneylending.

The Florentines had first been attracted to England by her wool, much the finest in Europe. They exported it to their home city, where an army of weavers and dyers – more than 30,000 according to the Florentine chronicler Villani, almost equivalent to the contemporary population of London – converted it into high-grade cloth. By the time Edward III came to the throne Italians effectively controlled English wool exports through their position as royal bankers and their stranglehold on royal finances.

This ramshackle credit system continued to work while Edward's borrowing was kept within bounds. But in 1336, when he began preparations for invading France (beginning the conflict later known as the Hundred Years War) it rapidly broke down. To buy European allies, Edward demanded loans equalling three times his annual income. He was unable even to pay the interest on these, but the Florentines, locked into the system, could not refuse. As Villani put it: 'Their great folly, undertaken through greed for profit or else to recover that which they had foolishly lent already, was to put all their wealth into the hands of one lord'.

When Edward went bankrupt in 1340, he ruined the English branches of his principal Florentine creditors, the Bardi and the Peruzzi. In Florence, there was panic among the firms' investors, and though the banks' funds were sufficient to ward off immediate disaster, both collapsed within a decade. Their crash had a domino effect on every other firm in the city, and the credit of Florentine bankers diminished almost to vanishing point. Florence eventually recovered, but never again was she able to exercise her former influence on the finances of Europe, or to dominate the export trade of England.

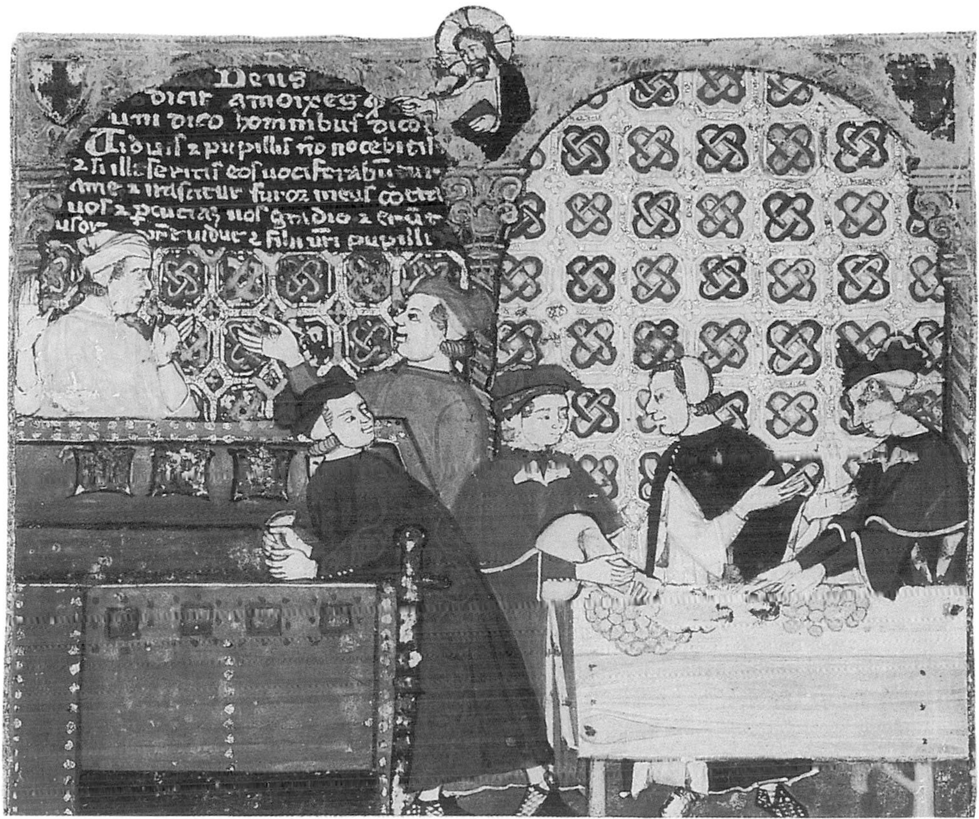

Above *A gold florin (front and back) adorned with the lily badge of Florence. It had international prestige because of its unvarying weight and quality.*

Right *Florentine bankers keep a close eye on their reserves of gold coin.*

And so matters went on until late October, when the agreed sum of six hundred thousand florins was delivered in Calais, and all the French hostages were set free with great rejoicing.

Then King John left Calais and was escorted by the prince of Wales and the duke of Lancaster to Saint-Omer, where he held high court during the feast of All Saints. On each of its three days John most lavishly entertained the prince of Wales and the duke of Lancaster and their company. Then the English lords left and returned in great joy to England.

King John II journeyed to Arras, and went from one good town to another, until just before Christmas when he reached Paris, where he and all the princes stayed throughout the winter. Wherever King John II went, people gave him a wealth of fine and lovely jewels, but he never opened his lips to say thank you.

Thomas Walsingham, a monk of St Albans Abbey, relates some miraculous and prophetic events which took place in 1361.

1361

In this year, at noon on 6 May, there was an eclipse of the sun. In the same month it rained blood on Burgundy and on 27 May, the feast of Corpus Christi, a bloody cross appeared in the sky at Boulogne from morning until six o'clock in the evening and many people saw it. Then it moved all by itself and fell into the middle of the sea. It followed that, in those parts, wolves left the woods and sought out the villages and devoured men alive.

In the summer of that year, both in France and England, in deserted and open places, many people saw two castles suddenly appear, from which two armies emerged: one army was duly equipped, and bore distinguishing knightly devices; the other, however, was clothed in black. When they joined battle, the knights vanquished the black force. Then, engaging in battle again, the black force overcame the knights. Then they returned to the castle and everything disappeared.

This year in October, the rose gardens brought forth roses of a perfect colour and odour. Deer and geese and other birds brought forth offspring.

John of Gaunt, earl of Richmond, son of King Edward III, became duke of Lancaster, in the right of his new wife Joan [the fair maid of Kent], who was the daughter and heir of the late Henry, duke of Lancaster.

Great bands of violent mercenaries terrorized the French countryside with their looting and burning.

In the same year, the famous Great Company of diverse nations was formed, whose leaders were for the most part English. They moved through France towards Avignon and took the town of Pont-Saint-Esprit, together with many towns and castles in France. The king of France was unable to expel them from his land, either by force or by skill.

At the same time, another society arose called the White Company. The leaders of this company were English, who went around living by their wits. They extorted payments from castles, towns and cities in exchange for so-called protection; nor could anyone live safely in that region unless he enjoyed their goodwill.

1362

On 29 June, King Edward III made an offering to Westminster of the vestments in which St Peter the Apostle celebrated Mass. He also gave by his charter two deer of his chase, to be taken annually from his forest of Windsor.

At Westminster on 19 July, in the presence of the nobles of the realm, Prince Edward, the eldest son of the king, received from his father the principality of Aquitaine, having performed homage and fealty. He did not give up the principality of Wales, the duchy of Cornwall, nor the earldoms of Chester or Kent. In early February [1363], Prince Edward crossed to Gascony with his wife and household.

The wool staple, despite the king's promise and that of other English lords, was moved to Calais.

Boccaccio

GIOVANNI Boccaccio (1313–1375) is the father of the European short story. The *Decameron,* his collection of tales written around 1350, was avidly received by the Tuscan merchant families who were its first readers, and continues to amuse and delight today.

Boccaccio spent his adolescence and earliest years as a writer in Naples, then one of Europe's richest cultural centres. His father, an important member of the Florentine Bardi company, was banker to Robert of Anjou, king of Naples. The works he composed there, including his long poem the *Filostrato* and the *Filocolo,* a prose romance, were inspired by the literature of courtly love and chivalry. After his return to Florence in about 1340, however, his inspiration came increasingly from the real world of bustling, down-to-earth Tuscan merchant society. In the *Decameron,* both themes – the ideals of a departed age and the reality of contemporary life – co-exist in a state of creative tension.

The imagined narrators of the tales are ten idealized young men and women of the leisured Florentine ruling class. Fleeing the danger and disorder caused in their city by the Black Death of 1348, they find an idyllic temporary refuge in the villas of the Tuscan countryside. There they create a harmonious, self-regulated society, and tell stories for entertainment.

These come from widely differing sources, including romances, moralistic *exemples,* satirical and comic *fabliaux,* folk tales and local gossip. There are characters from all walks of medieval life: powerful feudal rulers, noble ladies and their lovers; abbots, monks, nuns, friars and priests; and townspeople rich and poor, especially the adventurous, energetic merchants. While the broad geographical canvas reflects real merchants' travels in western Europe and the Mediterranean countries, their adventures are frequently elevated into human challenges to fortune. One story, set partly in England, is based on the important role played there by Italian bankers.

Boccaccio is probably best known for his swift-moving comic tales, in which quick-thinking people achieve their ends by their superior power with words. A friar improvises a sermon on false relics, other lusty clerics fool and cuckold superstitious men; and beautiful young wives, caught with their lovers, convince their dull-witted husbands they are innocent. However, alongside tales which turn on salacious word-play are stories of tragic passion, delicate young love, steadfast wifely loyalty and noble magnanimity.

A celebration of the art of story-telling, Boccaccio's ten 'days' portray humanity's weaknesses and triumphs in earthy terms that foreshadow Renaissance attitudes.

Top *A minstrel reciting a tale, very likely one from Boccaccio's* Decameron. *This was a common way for ladies of noble birth to relax.*

Above *A scene from the Death of Procris, one of the tales in the* Decameron.

Meanwhile Louis, duke of Anjou, second son of John II of France, left in England as a hostage against the payment of the French debts to Edward III, had escaped and returned to France. In 1364, his father John II honourably returned to captivity in England in his place, where he died on 8 April.

1364

The king of France was struck by a grave illness, and died in London at the Savoy Palace. On the death of King John II, the king of England solemnly celebrated Mass in various places. At his own expense, he had John's body taken to Dover by holy men, as is the custom of the realm. At length King John II was buried in the abbey church of Saint-Denis, near Paris, and his eldest son, Charles, duke of Normandy, succeeded him.

In the same year on 7 December it began to freeze, and this great frost lasted until 19 March of the following year.

1366

In this year, the king of France, Charles V, and the nobles of the kingdom requested the aid of King Edward III against the Great Company which was plundering France. Most of the leaders of the company were English, or at least from the dominions of the king of England.

At first King Edward sent letters to them ordering them to leave France and not to attempt to harass that kingdom further. The leaders ridiculed those who bore these messages, replying that they held nothing from the king of England, nor would they give up the fortresses and victuals which they had gained by such great efforts.

King Edward was enraged by their response and made ready to cross the sea. But Charles V, king of France, when he heard of the great array of King Edward was afraid, thinking that perhaps he might lose his kingdom if the king of England were victorious. On account of this he sent word to Edward, asking him to desist from his preparations and stay at home. This greatly distressed King Edward, to the extent that he swore by the Virgin

The sound of pleasure

ONLY about 30 secular English or Anglo-French songs have survived with their music from the 200 years up to 1377. They include *Angelus ad Virginem* (mentioned by Chaucer) and *Maiden in the Moor*, which is still sung as a folk song today. It occurs in the famous *Red Book of Ossory* compiled by the 14th-century Franciscan Richard de Ledrede, but this friar gave it Latin religious lyrics so that his clerical readers would not 'pollute their throats with popular, immoral or secular songs'.

The sophisticated art songs of the great French composer Guillaume de Machaut, who wrote the *Mass of Notre Dame* for Charles V's coronation in 1364 and who died in Reims in 1377, made little impact in England, though they were known to Chaucer; and at least one English manuscript of troubadour songs changes the French words to Latin religious lyrics, obscuring their origin.

Much secular music was not written down at all. For centuries musicians had improvised, or sung from memory, and minstrels, although fine performers, were often illiterate. Some were employed by town guilds to perform in saints' days processions or in mystery plays, as happened at Wakefield, Coventry and York, or were members of noble households – where harp players were *de rigueur*. Others performed near cathedrals: Edward III made several payments to minstrels playing at the north door of St Paul's, London, and in the crypt of Canterbury Cathedral.

Instrumental music and dancing played their part in court and country life. A few instrumental dances survive in a Reading Abbey manuscript which contains *Summer is icumen in*; and a volume of keyboard music (with arrangements of works by Philippe de Vitry) eventually ended up at Robertsbridge Priory. It may have been compiled for the French king, John II, who was in England after his capture at Poitiers, and who was presented with a keyboard instrument by Edward III on 4 July 1360.

In the 14th century the centre of musical patronage shifted from the monasteries to the royal court. Music flourished under Edward III, and several compositions are associated with his Chapel Royal, with St George's Chapel, Windsor and St Stephen's, Westminster. Music became more political and secular, and composers were less piously bashful about putting their names to works. *Sub Arturo Plebs* by John Alanus, canon of Windsor, celebrates the new Arthurian age and was probably performed at Windsor in 1358 at celebrations commemorating the battle of Poitiers; Alanus and 13 other musicians who performed the work are named in the text.

Top *A four-stringed gittern, dating from c. 1300, decorated and carved in wood.*

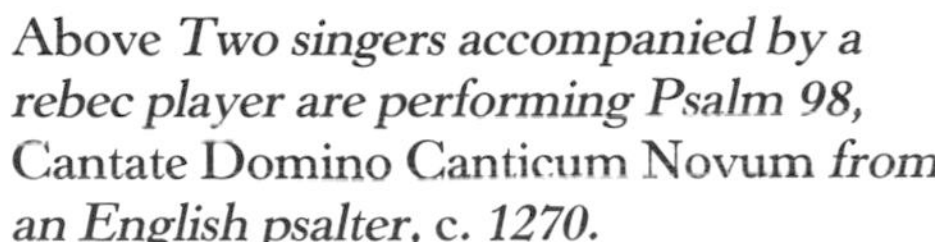

Above *Two singers accompanied by a rebec player are performing Psalm 98,* Cantate Domino Canticum Novum *from an English psalter, c. 1270.*

Right *A musical party on the Seine, complete with scores.*

> *"But here come the musicians after eating, without mishap, combed and dressed up! There they made many different harmonies. For I saw there, all in one circle, viol, rebec, gittern, lute, micanon, citole, and the psaltery, harp, tabor, trumpets (cornemuses), flutes (flajos), bagpipes (chevrettes), krumhorns, cymbals, bells, timbrel, the Bohemian flute, the big German cornet, flutes (flajos de saus), flute (fistule), pipe, bagpipe (muse d'Aussay), little trumpet, buzines, panpipes, monochord where there is only one string, and bagpipe (muse de blef) all together. And certainly it seems to me that such a melody was never seen or heard, for each of them, according to the tune of his instrument, without discord, . . . and whatever one can do with finger, and feather, and bow, I have seen and heard on this floor."*
>
> *Guillaume de Machaut 1300–77*

Mary that he would never take action to help the king of France, even though the companies tried to expel that king from his kingdom.

Then the distinguished and warlike knight, Bertrand du Guesclin [who had risen to prominence in the service of King Charles V of France], used the Great Company to march against Peter the Cruel, king of Castile, and deposed him with the help and favour of Pope Urban V. This Bertrand was always impatient of tranquillity, preferring war to peace.

It was said that King Peter of Castile lived as a vile evil-doer and a tyrant, proscribing and killing his own men. Worse was that, in contempt of the Christian religion, he consorted with a Jewish woman. When he heard of the advance of the fearsome company, Peter was soon terrified and fled into Gascony to the prince of Wales, asking him for a subsidy and help.

After Peter had fled, his half-brother Henry the Bastard was made king of Castile, with the assent of the majority of the lords of Spain and the community, and with the help of the company. There were about sixty thousand warriors in the Great Company.

Peter the Cruel of Castile appealed to the Black Prince for help against Bertrand du Guesclin and Henry of Trastamara who had ousted him from the throne of Castile. Froissart takes up the tale as Prince Edward prepares an expedition to Castile to aid its deposed monarch.

1367

Time passed while Prince Edward organized his supplies and waited for his brother the duke of Lancaster to arrive. In due course Joan, the princess, went into labour and by God's grace was delivered of her child. It was a fine son, Richard of Bordeaux, born at Epiphany, 6 January, which that year fell on a Wednesday.

The child came into the world early in the morning to the great joy of the prince and the whole household, and was baptized the following

Two cathedrals

SALISBURY and Reims cathedrals are virtually contemporary but as different as Brie from Cheddar. Reims is the archetypal, though not the earliest, French High Gothic cathedral; Salisbury is the most complete and homogeneous design to survive from early 13th-century England.

Reims, the coronation church of the kings of France, was begun in 1211, and the bulk of the building was finished by 1270. It is not only splendidly tall at 115 feet to the vault, it is the most majestic of the High Gothic cathedrals – yet it has finely cut masonry details, and its exterior is more lavishly covered with figure sculpture than any church before or since. The bar tracery window, which was to dominate later medieval architecture, was invented here.

The mysterious Villard de Honnecourt, probably a gentleman dilettante in an almost 18th-century sense, visited Reims in the 1220s, and copied into his sketch-book sections and elevations of the choir as it was being built. They are the earliest architectural drawings in existence.

Many sculptors worked at Reims, among them two of the finest artists of the Middle Ages. Both are anonymous; the Joseph master produced the saint from whom he takes his name, and also the enchanting Angel of the

Annunciation, crisp as sugar icing, with a coy giggle verging on the improper.

In contrast to the soaring height and lavish sculpture of Reims, Salisbury Cathedral is long, low and restrained, almost chaste. It was begun in 1220, and finished by about 1250. The architect's name is unknown, but the moving spirit behind its construction was undoubtedly that bishop who was later responsible for the Chapel of the Nine Altars at Durham, Richard Poore.

Bishop Poore moved the mother church of his diocese from the windswept uplands of Old Sarum, to the plain by the River Avon below. Salisbury Cathedral was the centrepiece of an entire new city, and is almost unique among its medieval counterparts in being constructed on virgin soil, with no need to accommodate or incorporate earlier remains.

Built in one more or less continuous campaign, its consistency and homogeneity are remarkable. In the English Gothic tradition of Canterbury and Lincoln, it has double transepts. Inside, there is English emphasis on horizontal lines, with a slightly cramped gallery, rather than the verticality of French Gothic. Capitals are plainly moulded and the windows simple lancets, with none of the tracery found in contemporary French churches. The west front is a patterned screen. Modelled on that at Wells, it is the antithesis of the classic French façade of Reims which resolves itself into twin towers, three splendid portals, and a great rose window.

Above left *Salisbury Cathedral.*

Above *The Angel of the Annunciation on Reims Cathedral.*

Below *Carving above the west door of Reims Cathedral.*

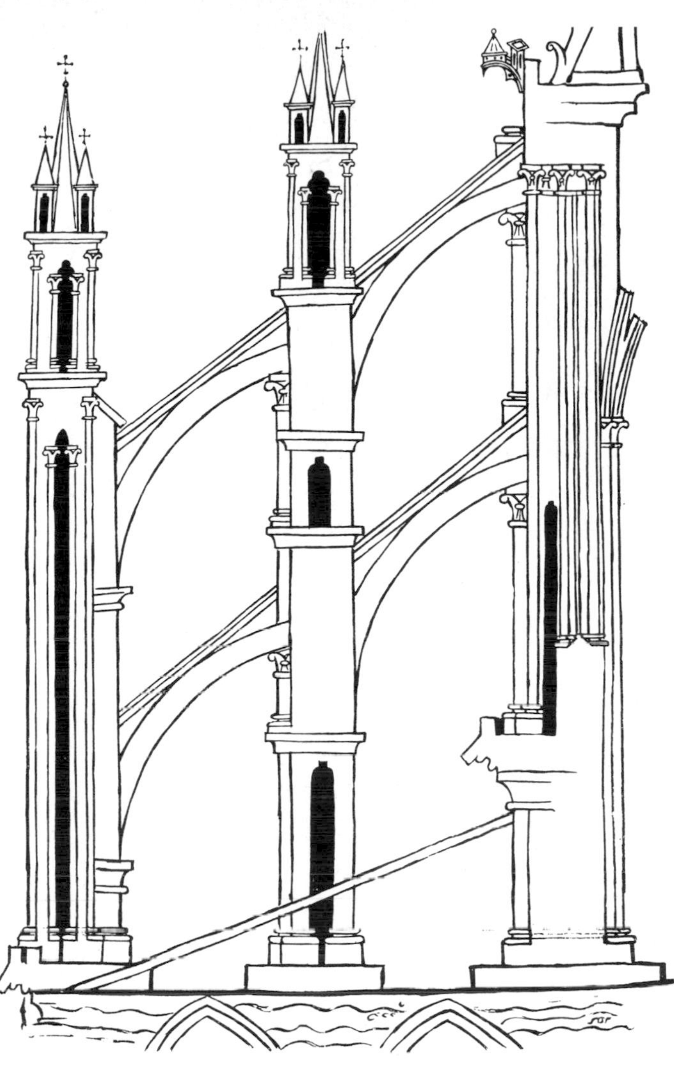

Opposite *The flying buttresses supporting Reims Cathedral.*

Left *A sketch made by Villard de Honnecourt, during construction, of the buttresses at Reims. The flying buttress, attached to the wall of the nave, took the weight or thrust from the vaulting, so allowing walls to reach a greater and more impressive height: in Reims Cathedral the vault is at 115 feet. At first these gigantic arches were concealed beneath the roofing, but later they were exposed. By using flying buttresses, more light could be let into the nave through rows of arched windows.*

Below *The nave of Salisbury Cathedral, showing both the rows of windows and the vaulting overhead. In the English Gothic tradition, Salisbury has double transepts, and a square east end with retrochoir.*

Friday in the early afternoon on the holy font of St Andrew's Church in the city of Bordeaux. The child was named Richard, and he afterwards became king of England.

Next Sunday, very early in the morning, Prince Edward rode out of Bordeaux in great array, together with all the troops who were then in the city. He joined up with his brother, John of Gaunt, duke of Lancaster, at Dax.

Between Saint-Jean-Pied-de-Port and the city of Pamplona [in Spain] are the mountain gorges and the hard crossing of Navarre. It is a difficult and dangerous pass, for there are a hundred places where thirty men could halt an army. And it was bitterly cold up there in the pass, for the prince and his troops made the crossing in mid-February. They could see well enough and were told by men who knew the pass that they could not all go over it at once, so they decided to cross in three contingents on three days, on the Monday, Tuesday and Wednesday.

Henry, king of Castile, was well informed of Prince Edward's crossing, for he had his spies and his messengers coming and going all the time. He had therefore gathered, and was still gathering, large numbers of men-at-arms and common soldiers from Castile in order to resist the prince, and he daily expected the arrival of Bertrand du Guesclin with strong support from France [which soon happened].

Moreover, he had sent special orders to all his vassals and subjects throughout his realm, that on pain of death each man must come to him, on foot or on horseback according to his rank, to help him guard and defend his inheritance.

This King Henry was much loved, and the whole of Castile had struggled to win him the crown, so that they were quick to obey his orders. Many had come and others were still coming in crowds every day to join him at his headquarters. He was encamped at Santo Domingo de Silos, where he had more than sixty thousand men, both on foot and mounted, each of them ready to do his will, whether for life or, if need be, for death.

Sons and brothers

IN 1362 Edward III appointed his eldest son prince of Aquitaine, and in the following year sent him to Bordeaux to take up his duties as resident lord. Any English governor would have found it difficult to run Aquitaine; but the prince totally failed to understand the political sensibilities of his new subjects. Disenchanted with his job, he once more yearned for a military adventure, and found the perfect opportunity in Spain.

The English king had made a treaty with King Peter I of Castile in 1362. Known as 'the Cruel', Peter was popularly suspected of having poisoned his wife. His illegitimate brother Henry of Trastamara was his rival, and just as unscrupulous. With the assistance of France, Aragon and a number of mercenary forces, Henry the Bastard overthrew Peter in 1365. The latter then invoked his alliance with England in the hope of recovering the throne. The Black Prince and his brother John of Gaunt, duke of Lancaster, eagerly prepared for war.

In the winter of 1366–67 an army of English, Gascon and mercenary soldiers crossed the Pyrenees and advanced into Castile. They met the forces of Henry of Trastamara in pitched battle at Nájera on 3 April 1367, and won a great victory. Peter was restored to power, and the Black Prince wrote to his wife: 'Be assured, dearest companion, that we, our brother of Lancaster and all the great men of our army are, thank God, in good form.'

The optimism did not last. Peter, who had agreed to pay the expenses of the English army, now informed the Black Prince that he could not meet his obligations. Furious, the prince considered partitioning the kingdom of Castile between the other Spanish rulers. However the poor health and morale of his army persuaded him to retreat to Aquitaine in the summer of 1367. Within two years Henry the Bastard had murdered his brother and re-established himself on the throne.

In Aquitaine, the prince set about raising the money needed to pay off his troops. In 1368 he imposed a *fouage*, or hearth tax, which was to last for an unprecedented five years. Encouraged by the new French king Charles V, some of the prince's subjects then chose to appeal against this levy, and registered their complaints not at Westminster but at Paris. Edward III could not ignore this challenge to his authority and in 1369 he re-assumed the title of king of France. War was once more inevitable.

In January 1371 the Black Prince returned to England from France, incapacitated by the dysentery he had contracted in Spain. He remained a virtual invalid for the rest of his life. In 1372 he was forced to abdicate his titles and responsibilities in Aquitaine, and lived long enough to witness the loss of almost all the Plantagenet lands in southern France.

The hero of Crécy, Poitiers and Nájera died, a broken and deeply frustrated man, in the summer of 1376, and was buried at Canterbury Cathedral. On his tomb are the mottoes *Houmout* ('high courage') and *Ich diene* ('I serve'), words which summarize the career and character of this knight of chivalry.

Opposite ***Peter I the Cruel, king of Castile.***

Below ***The Black Prince leading the charge at the battle of Nájera.***

You must know that the prince of Wales and his men were very short of food and supplies for themselves and for their horses, because they were in a very bad and poor district, whereas Henry, king of Castile, and his troops were in a good rich one. In Prince Edward's army, men paid a florin for a loaf of bread and were lucky to get it. The weather, moreover, was bitterly cold, with wind, rain and snow.

Edward, prince of Wales, and his army then moved to Logroño, while his opponents took up their position near Nájera.

On Friday 2 April, Prince Edward and all his forces left their camp before Logroño. They rode fully armed and arrayed in divisions, ready to fight at once, for they knew that King Henry of Castile was not far off. That day they covered two leagues and reached Navarreux early in the morning, where they halted. Scouts left Prince Edward's army and rode on until they could see the entire Castilian force, which was encamped on the heathlands outside Nájera.

The two armies joined battle on 3 April 1367.

Many were the lance thrusts, many the sword blows as they met in this battle of which I speak, and so it stood for some time, for neither side could break the other's ranks. What valiant deeds of arms were done, what men overthrown and flung to the ground, never to rise again!

Prince Edward and King Peter and their men turned their attack upon King Henry's ranks, where there were more than forty thousand, both on horse and foot.

It was a fierce encounter, hard fighting on all sides, for the Castilians and the Catalans had slings with which they flung stones and smashed helmets and headpieces, wounding and killing many. Both sides struck hard with lance and sword, many falling dead or injured to the ground. English archers, well practised, kept up a rapid fire, doing great harm to the Castilians. On one side rose the cry, 'Castile for King Henry!', on the other, 'St George! Guyenne!'

Many great feats of arms were done; on both sides men struck and cut at their opponents with great strength. Most gripped their lances with both hands and thrust them as they rode; some fought with short swords and daggers.

Prince Edward and King Peter the Cruel were the victors at the battle of Nájera, which only lasted for the length of the afternoon.

The victorious prince of Wales had his banner displayed on a bush high up on a hillock to rally his men, and there all those returning from the pursuit gathered and assembled.

And then King Peter arrived, hot and sweating from chasing the vanquished on his black warhorse, his banner with the arms of Castile borne ahead of him. As soon as he saw the prince's banner, he dismounted and went towards it.

Prince Edward, seeing him coming, went to meet him, to do him honour. Then King Peter tried to kneel as he thanked the prince, but the prince in great haste took him by the hand and would not let him do so.

'Dear lord and fair cousin,' said King Peter, 'I owe you great thanks and praise for the glorious day you have given me.' To which the prince very wisely answered, 'Give thanks and all praise to God, for the victory comes from Him, not from me.'

And so that evening they supped and rejoiced, as you can well imagine.

On Sunday 4 April, immediately after Mass and a cup to drink, King Peter mounted his horse, and rode from Nájera towards Burgos. He arrived there on the Monday morning. The inhabitants of Burgos had had news of the engagement and King Henry's defeat and had no wish or intention to close their town against King Peter; on the contrary, several of their rich men and notables came to meet him outside the town, offering him the keys. They received him as lord and brought him and his men into Burgos with much joy and solemnity.

The news spread throughout France, England, Germany and every land that Prince Edward and his forces had defeated King Henry of Castile in battle and had killed, captured, dispersed or drowned on that day, in the battle near Nájera, over a hundred thousand men.

And so the prince was honoured and renowned for true chivalry and high enterprise in every place and district where the news was known, especially in the German empire and the kingdom of England. And the Germans, Flemish and English declared that the prince of Wales was the flower of all the chivalry in the world and that such a prince was fit and worthy to rule the whole world.

In England the citizens of London marked the victory with a solemn triumph, such as was given in ancient times for kings who had won the field and vanquished their enemies.

And in France there was sorrow and lamentation for the good knights of that realm who had been killed or captured in the battle, especially for Bertrand du Guesclin [who had been captured in the fray]. They later made arrangements very easily and some were ransomed, except for Bertrand du Guesclin, who was not freed nearly so soon.

Despite the help he had received from the Black Prince, King Peter of Castile failed to pay his expenses as he had promised. He blamed the Great Company which was, he suggested, so devastating his kingdom that the people were unable to find any money; moreover, several of Peter's treasurers had been robbed.

When Prince Edward heard King Peter's excuses, he became still more anxious and requested advice on the matter. His people, who all wanted to go home, as they found the heat and air of Spain unendurable – indeed, it was making the prince himself ill and unwell – advised him to leave.

They said that if King Peter had broken his agreement, his was the blame and his the dishonour. It was then decided and generally announced that they were to go home, so the prince and his whole force set out on their return journey.

They travelled through the kingdom of Navarre, and the king of Navarre escorted him as far as the pass of Roncevaux. The prince rode on and came to the city of Bayonne, where he was welcomed with great joy. He stayed there and rested for four days and then went on to Bordeaux where he was received with great celebrations. Princess Joan came to meet him and had Edward, her eldest son, carried with her; he was then about three years old.

And so these men-of-arms separated, and the lords, barons and knights of Gascony went back to their homes.

After the prince of Wales had returned to Aquitaine, and his brother John, duke of Lancaster, to England, and all the barons to their own homes, Bertrand du Guesclin still remained the prisoner of Prince Edward, and was unable to come to any ransom agreement, much to the regret of Henry, Peter's rival, who would willingly have freed him if he could.

Now it happened, as I was informed both at the time and later, that one day the prince of Wales, in a joking mood, saw Bertrand du Guesclin standing in front of him and called and asked him how things were with him. 'Never better, my lord, I thank God,' answered Bertrand, 'and rightly so, for I am the most honoured knight in all the world, even though I am still your prisoner, and you shall know how and why: they are saying in the kingdom of France and elsewhere too that you are so afraid of me you dare not let me go.'

The prince of Wales heard this answer and thought Bertrand was quite right. So he answered, 'Really, my lord Bertrand, do you think we are keeping you here for the sake of your knighthood? No, by St George, not at all! My dear sir, pay us one hundred thousand francs and you shall go.'

Bertrand du Guesclin, who was longing for his release and to know upon what terms he could get it, seized on this remark and said, 'My lord, I swear to God I will pay no less.' As soon as the prince heard that, they say, he was sorry, for his counsellors went to him and said, 'My lord, it was very wrong of you to arrange his ransom so easily.'

The prince's people were then anxious that he should change his mind and break his agreement. But the prince, always a wise and loyal knight, gave them an apt reply: 'As we have granted him these terms, we shall hold to them and never go back on them. It would be a shame and disgrace to us if it were said that we refused to ransom him, when he is willing to undertake such a heavy burden as the payment of a hundred thousand francs.'

After this was decided, Bertrand worked hard to raise the money and pay the sum; he applied to his friends, and managed so well that with the help of the king of France and of Louis, duke of Anjou [brother of King Charles V of France], who loved him dearly, he paid the hundred thousand francs within a month. [Bertrand du Guesclin was freed on 27 December.] Then he went to serve the duke of Anjou with a good two thousand fighting men in Provence.

To pay his army for the Spanish campaign, the Black Prince raised heavy taxes from his Gascon subjects, provoking discontent. Two nobles, the lords of Albret and Armagnac, refused to pay, and took their case to the parlement at Paris. This gave Charles V of France the opportunity to find in their favour and declare Gascony confiscated once again. Walsingham describes the subsequent resumption of hostilities.

1368

In that year the French broke the peace, riding into the English lands in the county of Ponthieu and capturing by surprise castles, vills, towns and fortresses, partly by treachery and partly by force. They murdered some of the men of the king of England and captured others, but Edward III was unaware of all this.

1369

During this year, the king of France, Charles V, to deceive the king of England more fully, sent him wine from Bohemia and other gifts, as indications of his good faith and favour. And it so happened that while the French messengers were with the

The glass of fashion

WHEN Edward III ascended the throne in 1327, fashionable men and women on the continent as well as in England wore fairly voluminous long gowns with wide, loose sleeves which tapered only at the wrist. This form of dress was dignified and, unusually, attracted little criticism from moralists.

The English throne was impoverished, and in the early years of Edward's reign even clothes worn at court were not particularly lavish. Only a small proportion were made from silk – wool was far more common – while embroidery and expensive furs were rarely used.

Three years later European dress had changed. The new fashion was characterised by a tight fit – made possible by advances in tailoring techniques – particularly sleeves set into a small round armhole at the shoulder. The neckline of women's gowns became wider and men's tunics were shortened to just above the knee level. The sleeves of supertunics worn over gowns and tunics were also short, with thin strips which fluttered like streamers behind the wearer.

The new close fit necessitated long openings down the front or back of the garments and from wrist to elbow of the sleeves, which were often fastened with rows of buttons set very close together. These were unknown in Europe until the late 13th century, and were important status symbols for much of the 14th. Made of silver gilt, precious stones or enamel, they were both functional and decorative. Motley or parti-coloured garments were also decorative, as were the jagged edges and leaf-shaped patterns cut into the edges of hoods, tunics and sleeve streamers.

Moralists unanimously condemned the new tight fit and shortness of men's tunics, but by the 1350s criticism was directed at the extravagance of dress in general.

After the victories at Crécy and Calais, English exuberance was reflected in elaborate and richly decorated court clothes. More and more silks and expensive furs were imported in the late 1340s. Embroidery, with coloured silks, gold and silver thread, precious stones and besants (small ornaments cut or stamped out of thin plate gold), became increasingly popular.

For the vigil of her churching after the birth of a son, William, in 1348, Queen Philippa wore a suit of blue velvet embroidered with 400 large pearls and 38 ounces of small pearls, 13 pounds of plate gold and 11 pounds of gold thread, to which were added nearly 2000 bellies of miniver for the lining and 60 ermine skins for trimming.

By the mid-1350s pearls had become so scarce that, in France, statutes had to be drawn up governing the use of false jewels.

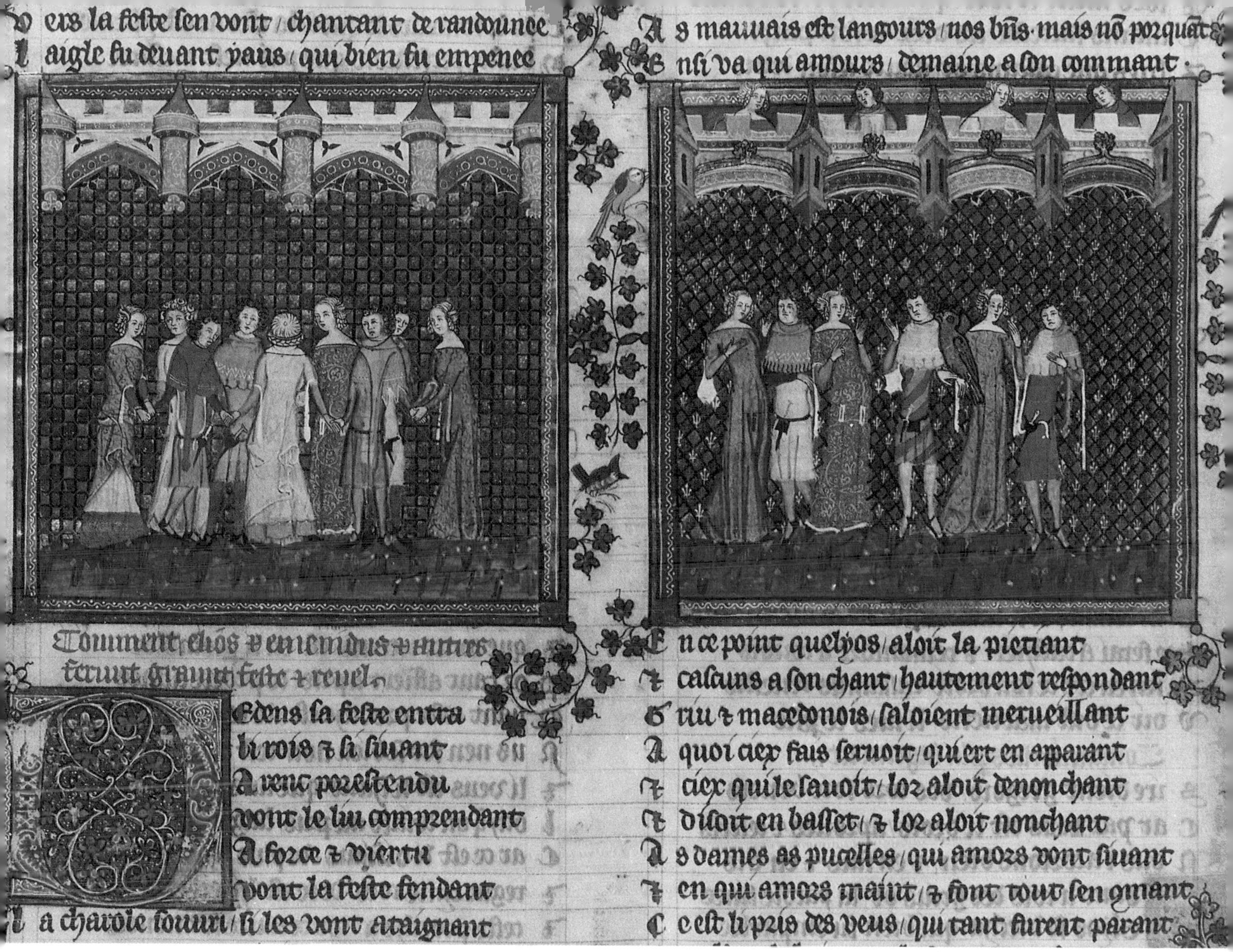

Vers la feste sen vont / chantant de randounee
L aigle fu devant paus / qui bien fu empenee

As mauvais est langours / nos biēs mais nō porquant
Ensi va qui amours / demaine a son commant

Comment clios & emenidus & autres
firent grant feste & revel.

Dedens la feste entra
li rois & si siuant
Aveuc por estendu
vont le liu comprendant
A force & viertu
vont la feste fendant
La charole souvri / si les vont ataignant

En ce point quel pos / aloit la pietiant
Et cascuns a son chant / hautement respondant
Griu & macedonois / saloient merveillant
A quoi ciex fais servoit / qui ert en apparant
Et ciex qui le savoit / loz aloit denonchant
Et disoit en basset / & loz aloit nonchant
As dames as pucelles / qui amors vont siuant
Et en qui amors maint / & sont tout sen gmant
Cest li pris des veus / qui tant furent parant

Above *A group of courtiers and their ladies wearing the fashionable clothes of the day. Since much time was spent at war, wearing armour, opportunities were readily seized to dress in soft linen and brighter colours.*

Right *The great hall at the Black Prince's castle in Gascony. This was where Edward and his guests feasted and told tales of knightly prowess. It also served as sleeping quarters for the host of servants who waited at table.*

king, news was brought to him that the king of France had attacked the county of Ponthieu as an enemy, had laid waste vills and had captured men. Besides this, he had taken the great town of Abbeville and had captured much booty there.

When King Edward III heard about the capture of Abbeville, he was thoroughly distraught, and he ordered the envoys to return with their gifts, being unwilling to injure them personally. He commanded them to report to their king, Charles V, how greatly the king of England loathed this disloyalty, which the king of France would certainly have cause to regret in the future.

As the envoys were going home, the men of Calais met them and seized the wines [which Edward had rejected as presents], which they took to Calais. The French, who are always full of falsehood and deceit, cunningly and guilefully blamed the English for breaking the peace.

On account of this, King Edward III again claimed the kingdom of France, as formerly. In pursuit of this claim, in September, he sent his son, John of Gaunt, duke of Lancaster, and Humphrey de Bohun, earl of Hereford, with a mighty force to France to fight for his right.

1370

In this year, the city of Limoges rebelled against Prince Edward, as did many other vills and castles in Gascony, because of the heavy exactions, impositions, and insupportable burdens allegedly placed on them by the prince and his men. On account of which, defecting from the prince of Wales, the citizens went over to the king of France.

The prince was disturbed at this and at first opted to crush the rebellion at Limoges cruelly, unless the citizens quickly repented and sought his grace with sufficiently humble prayers. But the citizens, protected by strong walls, with an abundance of victuals and a supply of warriors, were not intimidated by the envoys of the prince ordering them to return to his peace.

When the prince learned of their obstinacy, he sent messengers to them saying that he would raze the whole city to its foundations, and would destroy everyone he found there by fire and sword, unless they submitted to him quickly and handed over the city.

But the undisciplined mob did not wish to hear any of this and scorned the envoys arrogantly, fortifying the city more strongly on all sides. Soon the prince besieged the city and battered it with deadly assaults and attacks, giving no respite to those within its walls. Then the walls were undermined; they collapsed, and the city was taken. The conquered city of Limoges was destroyed almost down to the ground. Those found there were killed, very few being taken prisoner and spared their lives.

When he had done this, Prince Edward hurried to return to England, as much because of the infirmities which troubled him, as because of lack of money. Therefore, at the beginning of January [1371], with his wife and small son Richard, and with his household following behind, he reached Plymouth. He left behind him in Gascony his two brothers John of Gaunt, duke of Lancaster, and Edmund, earl of Cambridge, with other worthy and war-like knights. As soon as he reached his father, Edward III, he placed the whole lordship of Gascony in his hands.

John of Gaunt returned to England in 1371 with his new wife Constance, daughter of Peter the Cruel of Castile. This marriage gave John a claim to the Castilian throne, which he hoped to realise once he had firmly secured Gascony.

1373

In this year John of Gaunt, duke of Lancaster, the son of the king and the brother of Prince Edward, crossed to France with a huge army to try his fortune once again. After he had crossed, he rode through Paris into Burgundy and thus through the whole of France, and no one was willing or dared to resist him. On this expedition he did little or no damage to the French, however, except for the payments he imposed on diverse vills and places; nor did he do any harm to the enemy.

A national language

ALTHOUGH in 14th-century England everyone spoke some form of English, French was still the language of polite society, and used for less formal governmental business which was not transacted in Latin. The country gentry and middle class continued to use French for normal correspondence: there are almost no extant English letters before 1400. Proclamations in London were still made in French, which was also the language of the law, and had not yet degenerated into technical jargon. Anglo-Norman, Chaucer's 'French of Stratford-atte-Bowe', was increasingly used as an alternative to Latin in the drafting of wills and title-deeds. It was commonly spoken among all classes who could read and write, and its written usage increased as the century progressed.

The coexistence of French and English retarded the development of the native tongue as a national language. In addition, it was more difficult to translate written Latin into English than into the more closely related French. Yet, during the period when French was making inroads on the monopoly of Latin in formal business, it was gradually supplemented by English.

The transformation was almost certainly a result of the surge of patriotism and nationalism associated with the Hundred Years War: the French language came to be associated with the enemy.

In the 1320s, schoolmasters taught Latin through the medium of French; by the 1350s they used English in the classroom, and before the end of the century a statute of Oxford University enjoined the teaching of French 'lest the Gallic tongue be utterly forgotten'. In 1353 it was ordered that all cases in the London sheriff's courts should be conducted in English, and in 1363 the chancellor opened parliament for the first time with a speech in that language.

French, however, remained the courtly language and continued to be used by the military aristocracy. Libraries of the great contained hardly any books in English. In the 1360s Sir Thomas Gray wrote his comprehensive chronicle, the *Scalachronica,* in perfect Norman-French; and Henry duke of Lancaster's devotional treatise, *Le Livre de Saintes Medicines* (*c.* 1354), was also written in French.

Yet the need of religious writers to reach the widest audience foreshadowed the renaissance of English literature after three centuries of eclipse. The mystical writings of Richard Rolle (*d.* 1349) are classics of English prose and spirituality.

Geoffrey Chaucer, whose *Canterbury Tales* was written in the 1380s, recreated English as a literary language, but his full influence was felt only in the next century.

Above *English was increasingly used in schools and universities as the language of learning.*

Below *Scenes from college life, detailing the daily tasks that pupils would have to undertake, in addition to their lessons and periods of study.*

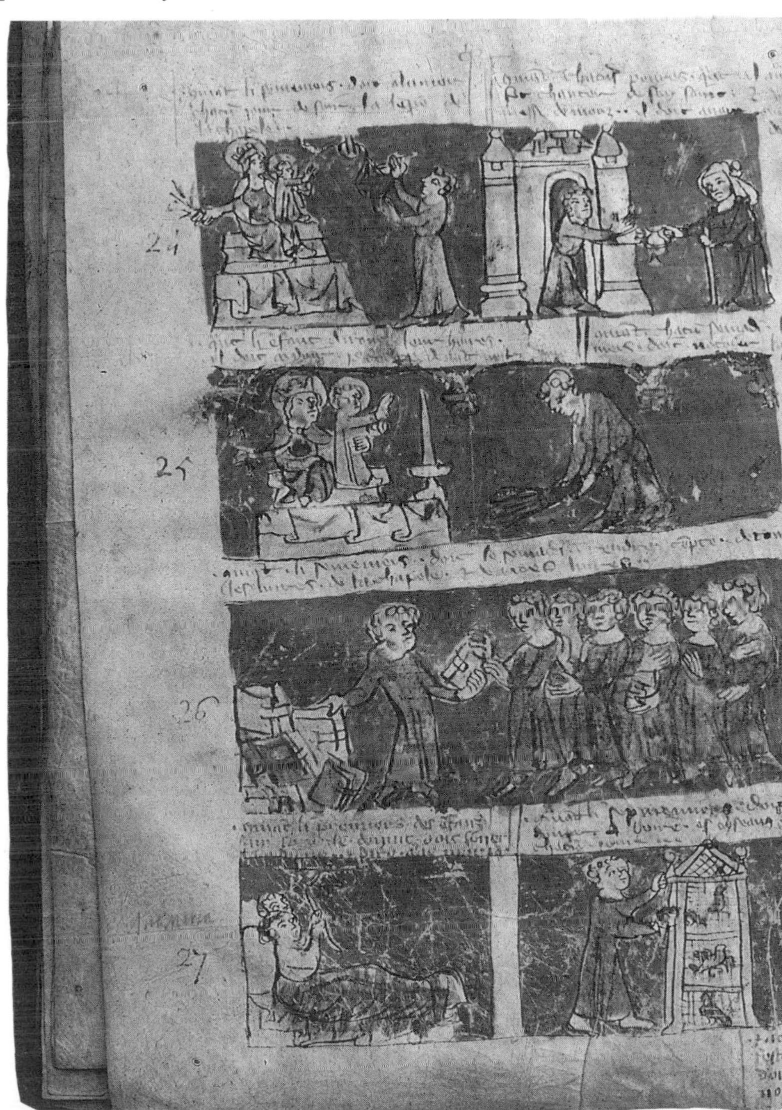

Despite such English expeditions, the king of France gradually regained ground. In 1375, when a truce was agreed, his English opponents were secure only in Calais and on the coastal strip south of Bordeaux.

1376

At the beginning of May, King Edward III held a great parliament at Westminster, in which, in the usual way, he asked that a subsidy be granted to him for the defence of the realm.

Replying, the commons said that they were weary of these continual impositions, and declared truthfully that they could not bear such burdens any longer without suffering great damage. For it was plain to them that the king had adequate resources for the defence of his realm, if that realm were governed wisely and faithfully, but for as long as wicked officials continued to conduct the business of the realm, it would never abound in prosperity or wealth.

They offered to produce convincing proof of this, and if after that the king was found still to be in need, they would help him according to their ability. Subsequently, many accusations were made concerning members of the king's household and various royal officials: many great royal office-holders were removed, and others appointed in their place.

It was decreed also, at the petition of the commons, that certain bishops, earls and other lords of good reputation should henceforth guide the king and the kingdom, because the king was growing old and required such direction. This provision, however, lasted barely three months, thanks to the interference of those who had been removed from the king's side.

Further, the parliamentary knights complained bitterly about one Alice Perrers, a wanton woman who was all too familiar with King Edward III. They accused her of numerous misdeeds, performed by her and her friends in the realm. She far overstepped the bounds of feminine conduct: forgetful of her sex and her weakness, now

The Good Parliament

THE re-opening of the war with France in 1369 marked the beginning of the final, inglorious phase of Edward III's reign. Queen Philippa was dead, the Black Prince stricken with illness and the king himself was declining into a premature old age. Effective leadership of the kingdom passed to Edward's third son John of Gaunt, duke of Lancaster, who lacked the stature and popularity of his heroic older brother.

The war went badly from the outset. The English found themselves on the defensive, fighting to hold on to the continental possessions they had won in 1360. The French king, Charles V, and his wily general, du Guesclin, pursued a policy of attrition, avoiding pitched battles and gradually wearing down the resistance of the English forces.

Within a few years, despite a crippling series of war taxes, the English had lost virtually all their French lands apart from a few strips of coastal territory.

While the French advanced, the once mighty Edward III lapsed into his dotage. His physical and mental decline was symbolised by a senile infatuation for his mistress, Alice Perrers. The daughter of a Hertfordshire knight, she had caught his eye in 1364, but after Philippa's death in 1369 her power over the king became complete. Edward could deny her nothing, and she controlled access to him. He showered gifts and grants of royal estates upon her, including jewels that had belonged to Philippa. There were rumours that she was in league with a friar versed in black magic, who made wax models of Alice and Edward, portraying the king as a puppet in her hands. England had seen royal mistresses in the past, but never one who had influenced the course of justice and the government of the kingdom. She was allowed to sit on the bench in court and bully the judges, who feared her more than they did the king.

Widespread discontent with the failures and corruption of the king's government came to a head in the 'Good Parliament' of 1376. As soon as it opened it became clear that there were members of both houses determined to attack those who controlled the king. For the first time, the House of Commons rather than the Lords took the initiative. Members refused to make any tax grants until their grievances had been redressed, and elected Peter de la Mare to act as their spokesman: the first man to serve as Speaker of the Commons.

Their main grievances were financial. They objected to demands for more taxes for the war when, in their view, previous taxes had been wasted and misappropriated by royal officials. Peter de la Mare soon began to name names, and levelled accusations of corruption and fraud

Above *The Houses of Parliament.*

against Alice Perrers, Lord Latimer, the king's chamberlain, Richard Lyons, a London merchant banker, as well as several others. When asked who was bringing the charges, de la Mare replied that they were brought by the Commons collectively, and so formulated the procedure which was to become known as impeachment. The accused were tried by the House of Lords and found guilty. Latimer and Lyons were fined and imprisoned and Alice Perrers was ordered to withdraw from court, much to the old king's distress.

The effects of the Good Parliament were short-lived: John of Gaunt was able to reverse most of its acts in the following year. Nonetheless it was of great historic importance because of the development of impeachment, which rested upon the basic assumption that the king's ministers, as public officials, were accountable not just to the king but to parliament which represented the whole community of the realm.

Impeachment was to be used frequently in future centuries at times of high political crisis, and, together with other British institutions, the process was adopted in the United States of America.

The Black Prince had died in June 1374, while the Good Parliament was sitting, and Edward III died exactly a year later at the age of 64. His personal career had always mirrored the fortunes of the nation he ruled, and his sad deterioration in old age poignantly embodied the decline of English prosperity and success.

besieging the king's justices, now stationing herself among the doctors in the ecclesiastical courts, she did not fear to plead in defence of her cause and even to make illegal demands. As a result of the scandal and great shame which this brought on King Edward, not only in this kingdom but also in foreign lands, the knights sought her banishment from his side.

On 8 June, during the parliament at Westminster, Edward, prince of Wales, King Edward's eldest son, died. That day was the feast of the Holy Trinity, which the prince had always been accustomed to celebrate every year, wherever he was, with the greatest solemnity.

For as long as he lived and flourished, his good fortune in battle, like that of a second Hector, was feared by all races, Christian and pagan alike.

When Prince Edward died, all the hope of his people died too: for while he lived, the English dreaded no enemy who might invade. It is certain too that with his death the force of that parliament died also, for the commons, with whom he had allied himself, did not obtain a result commensurate with their hopes.

Now it was said that the king no longer wished to be guided through his lords assembled in parliament, and so he had recourse to his son, John of Gaunt, duke of Lancaster, to guide himself and the realm.

Until the death of the king, the duke acted as the governor and ruler of the kingdom. He, indeed, permitted the king, against the parliamentary statutes, to receive back into grace many who had been perpetually banished from his presence by judicial sentence in parliament.

The king also recalled his mistress Alice Perrers to his company; she had been legally banished from his presence, on account of the scandal and shame which came from her wantonness. This was against the oath by which Alice had bound herself and which the king himself had ratified; namely that she would not come near the king in any way. She stayed with him until his death.

John of Gaunt, duke of Lancaster

JOHN, the third surviving son of Edward III and Queen Philippa, was born in Ghent, hence his nickname. His father provided for him financially by marrying him to Blanche, daughter and heiress of Henry, duke of Lancaster, and on his father-in-law's death in 1362 John was granted the title. This vast inheritance meant his possessions and household were second only to the king's: he held more than 30 castles and his London home, the Savoy, rivalled Westminster Palace.

John accompanied his elder brother the Black Prince to Spain in 1367, and as the prince's health deteriorated, he succeeded him as lieutenant of Gascony. He was not an outstanding general, but his lack of success was certainly not due solely to lack of ability; it also owed much to the unrealistic expectations and imprecise plans of his father.

From the mid-1370s, as Edward III declined into senility and the Black Prince's long illness ended in his death in 1376, Gaunt became the effective head of government in England. His rule was deeply unpopular. Financial difficulties caused by war led to new and burdensome taxes, and some of his strongest supporters were accused of embezzlement. Attempts by the House of Commons to curb their abuses during the Good Parliament were only temporarily successful. Gaunt's subsequent support of the reformer Wycliffe alienated powerful churchmen, and his attempts to curb the liberties of the Londoners led to rioting.

Despite the powers he exercised in 1376–7, John of Gaunt never sought the English throne and he served his young nephew, Richard II, as loyally as he had served his father. The throne he desired was that of Castile. Blanche of Lancaster had died of the plague in 1368, leaving a son,

Henry of Bolingbroke, and two daughters and Gaunt had married as his second wife, Constance, daughter of the exiled Peter I the Cruel, of Castile. For many years Gaunt's ambitions centred on regaining the throne in his wife's right. He never succeeded, but their daughter, Catherine, married Henry III of Castile, uniting the two claims.

Throughout his marriage to Constance, Gaunt maintained a loving liaison with Katherine Swynford, governess to the daughters of his first marriage. The four children she had by him were given the surname Beaufort, after one of their father's French estates. Gaunt made Katherine his third wife after Duchess Constance's death, and the children were legitimated, though on the condition that they were to have no rights to the throne. Despite this proviso Henry VII, the first Tudor, owed what hereditary right to the throne he had to his descent from John, earl of Somerset, the eldest of the Beauforts.

Opposite *The great seal of John of Gaunt in his role as king of Castile and León, duke of Aquitaine and Lancaster, earl of Derby, Lincoln and Leicester, and Seneschal of England.*

Right *A portrait of John of Gaunt. He had a warrior's build but was not an outstanding soldier or general, although no captain served harder in the protracted French wars. At home, he generally proved unpopular with the people as they laboured under the financial burdens of war.*

Below *The Savoy Palace set on the banks of the Thames. This was one of the most impressive properties owned by John of Gaunt, and rivalled the king's palace at Westminster.*

1377

In January, a parliament was held in London, at the instance of the duke of Lancaster, then vicegerent of the king, who was mortally ill.

In parliament, a subsidy was sought from the clergy and the laity on behalf of the king. An unprecedented tax [the poll tax] was granted, namely, from each lay person of either sex over the age of fourteen one groat or four pence, except from notorious paupers who begged in public.

From the religious of both sexes and from every cleric holding a benefice was levied twelve pence, and from other clergy without benefices, a groat, except the friars of the four mendicant orders, who, because they did not work like other men, were not scourged in this way.

In this parliament, the statutes of the previous parliament, deservedly known as the Good Parliament, were abrogated. And at the king's wish, the people sentenced previously were restored to their former state.

At the same time there arose in the university of Oxford a northerner called John Wycliffe, a doctor in theology, who maintained publicly in the schools and elsewhere, erroneous, absurd and heretical conclusions against the teachings of the whole Church, resounding poisonously against monks and other religious possessioners.

In order to cover his heresy craftily, and to spread it widely under a carefully chosen cover, John Wycliffe collected the iniquitors to him, namely friends and colleagues of a particular persuasion, dwelling at Oxford and elsewhere, wearing ankle-length russet robes as a sign of greater perfection, and walking barefoot, who would proclaim his errors to the populace and preach them openly and publicly in their sermons.

Amongst other beliefs, one they adhered to scrupulously was that the Eucharist on the altar, after the sacrament, was not the true body of Christ, but a symbol. Further, that the Roman Church was not the head of all churches more than any other Church, nor was greater power given by Christ to Peter than to any other Apostle.

Also that the pope of Rome does not have greater power in the keys of the Church than any ordained to the priesthood.

The lords and magnates of the realm and many of the people favoured John Wycliffe and his followers in their preachings of such errors, especially since by their assertions they gave great power to the laity to take away the temporal possessions of the clergy and the religious.

When indeed those crazy conclusions were reported and examined at the papal curia, Pope Gregory XI condemned nineteen of them as heretical and false.

He sent bulls to Simon Sudbury, archbishop of Canterbury, and the bishop of London authorizing them to seize the said John Wycliffe and examine him thoroughly on the conclusions.

When this was done, the said archbishop, in the presence of the duke of Lancaster, ordered Wycliffe to remain silent on this matter. Therefore he and his followers were silent for some time.

On 19 February, because of some injurious and insolent words of John of Gaunt, duke of Lancaster, towards the bishop of London, the Londoners united, rose up together, seized arms, and proposed to kill the duke.

But the bishop absolutely forbade this, and if he had not himself opposed their troops, they would, in their fury, have burned the home of the duke, the Savoy Palace. At length they were pacified by the bishop.

Among the insults which were inflicted on the duke, his arms were publicly reversed in the Cheapside market-place [as a sign of treason].

The duke, being warned of the great disturbance, abandoned his dinner, and fled to the manor of Kennington, complaining of the horrible insults he had endured.

The Lollard heresy

HERESY – Christian teaching contrary to the doctrine of the Roman Church – was virtually unknown in England until the last decades of the 14th century. Yet resentment against the increasing financial demands of the papacy grew as Englishmen saw streams of English gold drain away to the papal court at Avignon, in the territory of England's mortal enemy the king of France.

This resentment, however, was directed at the Church's acts, not her dogma. Before anti-clericalism and anti-papalism could turn into heresy, an entirely new way of looking at Christianity had to emerge. Its unlikely champion was a middle-aged Oxford don called John Wycliffe.

Hailed by later Protestant admirers as the 'morning star of the Reformation' but vilified by orthodox contemporaries as the 'devil's instrument', the 'church's enemy', the 'heretics' idol', Wycliffe is believed to have been born in Yorkshire in about 1330. Although he had a considerable academic reputation as a philosopher, he really made his mark when he entered government service in 1371. By that time, with Edward III rapidly declining into dotage and the Black Prince ailing, the real ruler of England was John of Gaunt.

Desperate for money to prosecute the faltering war with France, Gaunt looked to the English clergy, already hard-pressed by papal taxation. He needed to stem papal demands and also to coerce the clergy into paying even higher taxes to the state. To do this he harnessed prevailing anti-clerical and anti-papal prejudices and used Wycliffe as his propagandist. The don relished the task, developing the doctrine that it was laity's right and duty to reform the erring Church.

In February 1377, however, the English clergy counter-attacked and summoned Wycliffe to answer for his propagandising. But when he appeared in St Paul's Cathedral, Gaunt stood at his shoulder, and in the slanging match which followed threatened to haul Bishop Courtenay of London from the church by his hair. The congregation of Londoners rioted in defence of their bishop. Soon afterwards the pope joined in the condemnation of Wycliffe, who was quickly retired from government service.

His greatest work was still to come. Between 1379 and 1382 he struck at the roots of Catholic doctrine by declaring the pope to be Antichrist, proclaiming the bible (whose translation into English he sponsored) as the only true source of Christian teaching. Wycliffe became the precursor of Protestantism, and the progenitor of the Lollard heresy which rocked the English Church and state during the 15th century.

Above *Wycliffe appearing before the prelates in St Paul's Cathedral, from a 19th-century engraving.*

In this year, on 21 June, King Edward III died at his manor of Sheen, after reigning for almost fifty-one years.

Shameful to relate, during the whole time that he was bed-ridden, King Edward had been attended by that infamous whore Alice Perrers, who always reminded him of things of the flesh. She never discussed nor permitted any discussion about the safety of his soul, but continually promised him a healthy body, until she saw a sure sign of his death with the failing of his voice.

When she realized that he had lost the power of speech and that his eyes had dulled, and that the natural warmth had left his body, quickly that shameless doxy dragged the rings from his fingers and left.

A priest alone attended the dying king, the others around being intent on taking things. Since the king could not speak and make a confession, the priest persuaded him to seek pardon for his sins, offering him a crucifix, which he put in his hands. The king, indeed, took it with great reverence, kissing it devotedly, holding out his hands as far as he was able, a sign that he wished for pardon, with tears pouring from his eyes and frequently kissing the feet of the image.

At length, when, with the encouragement of the priest, with movements and signs, King Edward had sought forgiveness first and foremost from God for his sins, and secondly from all mortals, whom he had knowingly or unknowingly injured, his spirit left him.

His body was buried at Westminster with all reverence.

Indeed this king among all other kings and princes of the world had been glorious, gracious, merciful and magnificent, and was called *par excellence* 'Most Gracious' for his pre-eminent and outstanding grace. His face was more like an angel's than a man's, for there was such a miraculous light of grace in it, that anyone who looked openly into it or dreamed of it at night, might hope that comforting delights would come to him that very day.

Tempted, however, and moved by the weakness of his flesh, even in his old age, he could not restrain himself from the shameless harlot Alice Perrers; and soon, it is thought, on account of his lack of self-control, he died.

Finally it should be remarked on that just as at first both grace and prosperity made Edward III renowned and illustrious, so in his old age and declining years, with his sins, little by little that good fortune diminished; and many misfortunes and difficulties arose which, alas, tarnished his reputation.

The legacy

LIKE his grandfather Edward I before him, Edward III lived too long for the good of his historical reputation. In spite of his great military victories, the later years of decline cast a shadow over the triumphs of Crécy and Poitiers, the capture of the kings of France and Scotland and the treaty of Brétigny. He has also been accused of making damaging concessions to parliament and the nobility in order to secure their support for the war, surrendering royal power for short-term gain and storing up trouble for his successors.

It is certainly true that Edward III made concessions to his nobles and to parliament which, during his reign, greatly expanded its powers by using its control over national taxation. In particular, members from the shires, drawn from the country gentry, exploited the king's need for money and won themselves a much greater say in the running of local government. Similarly, Edward won support from the barons by relaxing many of his traditional feudal rights over their estates. But these concessions must be seen in the context of Edward's reign as a whole. When he became king in 1327, the monarchy had been at its lowest ebb and the nobility torn by murderous feuding.

Edward saw his task, above all others, as the restoration of royal prestige and national unity. To achieve this, he waged a victorious war in partnership with parliament and the nobility. Within 20 years the bitter divisions of Edward II's reign were ancient history, and England was admired and feared throughout Europe for her military prowess.

Seen in this light, Edward's concessions look like hard-headed political realism. He recognized, better than most medieval kings, that he could not rule autocratically with the limited financial and military resources at his disposal. Instead he had to secure the co-operation of all the English people, above all the barons and gentry who dominated the localities through their estates and provided the troops for his wars. The king brought these groups into government with him as junior partners; the result was the revival of royal prestige and a generation of unprecedented political harmony.

The 14th century was crucial in the growth of national identity in England, a development seen clearly in the evolution of parliament and the first flowering of English literature. Edward III's greatest feat was to embody this emergent national feeling and create a new sense of direction and unity of purpose and an intense pride in national achievements on the field of battle. In his reign, as the chronicler Thomas Walsingham wrote, 'the people thought that a new sun was rising over England, with peace abounding, the wealth of possessions and the glory of victory'.

Below *Edward III's effigy in Westminster Abbey.*

Epilogue

Edward III's reign has come to be seen by some historians as a period of superficial glory, during which the seeds of the 15th-century breakdown of the monarchy were sown.

In the words of Thomas of Walsingham's epitaph to Edward, 'as in the beginning all things were joyful and liking to him and to all people, . . . right so, when he drew into age, drawing downward through lechery and other sins, little by little all the joyful and blessed things, good fortune and prosperity decreased and mishapped'. Yet Edward has been much admired for his conquests in France, even though by his death in 1377 these had largely melted away, and the classic traditional image remains today of a great, patriotic warrior-king.

Indeed the very scale of Edward's success created problems for later kings. His string of victories up to 1360 raised popular expectations to an intolerably high level for his successors, so that when they failed to match up, the backlash of discontent was all the more fierce. Richard II in particular found it impossible to bear the burden of expectations imposed by his grandfather: it dogged his early years, poisoned his relations with the magnates, and was to contribute in no small degree to his ultimate downfall.

Glossary

Banneret: Knightly rank often granted in the field for conspicuous valour: a knight fielding vassals under his own banner.

Bezant: Gold or silver coin or plain disk used on clothes or coats of arms.

Bragget: Drink of honey and ale fermented together.

Camlet: A costly Eastern fabric made from angora goat's fleece.

Cantref/Cantred: A Welsh administrative district of 100 townships.

Carrack: A cargo ship with military capacities.

Consistory: Either the diocesan court, or the pope and cardinals' convocation from a general term for 'council'.

Convocation: Church synod debating ecclesiastical matters.

Courser: A stallion or battle-charger.

Destrier: A knight's courser led by his squire with the right hand (from the Latin *dexter*).

Dromond: A very large ship used both in peace and war.

Ecu: A French silver coin bearing three fleurs-de-lis.

Escheat: Feudal arrangement by which the fief of a man dying without heirs or declared outlaw must by law revert to the lord.

Fealty: Feudal obligation of fidelity to the lord.

Fief: Land and/or other rights held by a vassal in return for obligations to the lord, including military service.

Fifteenth: A tax of 1⁄15 similar to a tenth. (see **Tenth**)

Gris: A kind of grey fur.

Hanseatic league: Powerful mercantile league of Baltic ports with premises in London. Established in 1241, it grew to comprise around 100 towns, dominating Baltic trade.

Hundred: An administrative unit of the county or shire having its own court (hundred court) with local civil and criminal jurisdiction.

King's Bench: Court of record, supreme in common law.

Linsey-woolsey: A fabric of mingled wool and flax.

Maletote/Maletolt: A harsh tax on wool sacks.

Murrain: A plague afflicting animals, especially cattle and sheep.

Pinnace: A small two-masted tender or scout ship.

Poll tax: A capitation or head tax.

Possessioners: Someone holding a religious endowment.

Prebend: A portion of church or cathedral revenue granted as a stipend to a canon or other clergy.

Prescriptive right: A right gained via customary use.

Proctor: A steward, or the equivalent of a solicitor in a canon or civil law court.

Progress: A state journey made by a ruler or dignitary.

Provisions and Purveyance: The right claimed by the king on a progress (and extended to his suite) to seize horses, carts, food, etc., and pay what he liked (or sometimes in effect, nothing).

Reeve: A term covering various officials: baliffs, stewards, churchwardens, parish overseers, the chief magistrate of a town or district, etc.

Schiltron: A defensive ring of Scots spearmen.

Scutage: A tax levied on knights' fees, often in lieu of military service.

Seisin: The possession of feudal property.

Suffragan: A bishop assisting another bishop in his see.

Tallage: Financial aid levied by the Crown.

Tenth: Another ecclesiastical or royal percentage tax on produce, profits or property to 1⁄10 of its value.

Translate: To transfer bishops from one see to another.

Twentieth: A tax of 1⁄20 similar to a tenth. (see **Tenth**)

Verderer: A judicial officer of the King's forest, sworn to maintain the forest assizes and prevent poaching.

Vicomte: A peer acting as a sheriff for a duke or an earl.

Vill: A parish or township, the smallest feudal unit. A villein was a labourer bound to a vill and its lord.

Bibliography

This is not intended as a comprehensive bibliography of all relevant works, but is a selection of books relating to the topics discussed in the notes and the chronicles. Articles have not been included because they are more difficult for the general reader to obtain; most of the works cited here contain bibliographies which are a good starting point for more detailed reading on individual subjects.

Baker, D. ed, *Medieval Women*, Oxford, 1978

Baker, J. H., *An Introduction to English Legal History*, London, 1979

Barber, R., *Edward, Prince of Wales and Aquitaine*, London, 1978

Barber, R., *The Life and Campaigns of the Black Prince*, Woodbridge, 1986

Barraclough, G., *The Medieval Papacy*, London, 1968

Barrow, G. W. S., *The Kingdom of the Scots: government, church and society from the 11th to the 14th century*, London, 1973

Barrow, G. W. S., *Kingship and Unity: Scotland 1000–1306*, London, 1981

Barrow, G. W. S., *Robert Bruce and the Community of the Realm of Scotland*, Edinburgh, 1976

Bellamy, J. G., *Crime and Public Order in England in the later Middle Ages*, Cambridge, 1973

Beresford, M. W., and St Joseph, J. K. S., *Medieval England, an Aerial Survey*, Cambridge, 1979

Bertrand, G., and others, *Histoire de la France rurale des origines à 1340*, Paris, 1975

Bolton, J. L., *The Medieval English Economy, 1150–1500*, London, 1980

Bony, J., *French Gothic Architecture*, Berkeley, California, 1983

Branca, V., *Boccaccio, the Man and his Works*, New York, 1976

Brown, R. A., and Colvin, H. M., and Taylor, A. J., *The History of the King's Works; vol 1: The Middle Ages*, London, 1963

Buck, M., *Politics, Finance and the Church in the Reign of Edward II; The Career of Walter Stapledon*, Cambridge, 1983

Burne, A. H., *The Crécy War*, London, 1955

Bury, S., Jewellery Gallery Summary Catalogue, Victoria and Albert Museum, London, 1982

Callus, D. A. ed., *Robert Grosseteste, Scholar and Bishop*, Oxford, 1955

Cam, H. M., *The Hundred and the Hundred Rolls*, London, 1930

Clanchy, M. T., *England and its Rulers, 1066–1272*, Glasgow, 1983

Clanchy, M. T., *From Memory to Written Record; England 1066–1307*, London, 1979

Coleman, J., *English Literature in History, 1350–1400: Medieval Readers and Writers*, London, 1981

Contamine, P., *Guerre, état et société à la fin du Moyen Age*, Paris, 1972

Crombie, A. C., *Augustine to Galileo*, Harmondsworth, 1959

Cuttino, G. P., *English Diplomatic Administration, 1259–1339*, 2nd ed., Oxford, 1971

Cuttino, G. P., *English Medieval Diplomacy*, Bloomington, Indiana, 1985

Daiches, D., and Thorlby, A., *Literature and Western Civilization, The Medieval World*, London, 1973

Davies, R. R., *Lordship and Society in the March of Wales*, Oxford, 1978

Duncan, A. A. M., *Scotland: The Making of the Kingdom*, Edinburgh, 1975

English Romanesque Art, 1066–1200 (Exhibition catalogue), London, 1984

Fowler, K., *The Age of Plantagenet and Valois*, London, 1967

Fryde, N., *The Tyranny and Fall of Edward II*, London, 1979

Gottfried, R. S., *The Black Death*, London, 1983

Gottfried, R. S., *Doctors and Medicine in Medieval England*, Princeton, 1986

Grant, A., *Independence and Nationhood: Scotland 1306–1469*, London, 1984

Griffiths, R. A., and Sherborne, J. W., *Kings and Nobles in the Later Middle Ages*, Woodbridge, 1986

Hale, J. R., Highfield, J. R. L., and Smalley, B. ed., *Europe in the Late Middle Ages*, London, 1965

Hallam, E. M. ed., *The Plantagenet Chronicles*, London, 1986

Harris, G. L., *King, Parliament and Finance in Medieval England to 1369*, Oxford, 1975

Harvey, J., *The Black Prince and his Age*, London, 1976

Hatcher, J., *Plague, Population and the English Economy*, London, 1977

Hay, D., *Europe in the 14th and 15th centuries*, London, 1966

Hewitt, H. J., *The Black Prince's Expedition*, 1355–57, Manchester, 1958

Hewitt, H. J., *The Organisation of War under Edward III*, Manchester, 1966

Holmes, G., *Dante*, Oxford, 1980

Holmes, G., *Europe: Hierarchy and Revolt, 1320–1450*, London, 1975

Holmes, G., *The Good Parliament*, Oxford, 1975

Jordan, W. C., *Louis IX and the Challenge of the Crusade*, Princeton, 1979

Keen, M., *Chivalry*, Yale, 1984

Keen, M., *England in the Later Middle Ages*, London, 1973

Kenny, A., *St. Thomas Aquinas*, Oxford, 1980

Kidson, P., Murray, P., and Honour, H., *A History of English Architecture*, London, 1967

Kightly, C. S., *Strongholds of the Realm*, London, 1979

Knowles, D., *The Religious Orders in England, vol. 1*, Cambridge, 1971

Labarge, M. W., *Gascony, England's First Colony*, London, 1980

Labarge, M. W., *Saint Louis; the Life of Louis IX of France*, London, 1968

Lambert, M. L., *Medieval Heresy*, London, 1977

Landstrom, B., *The Ship*, London, 1961

Lapsley, G. T., Cam, H. M., and Barraclough, G., *Crown, Community and Parliament in the Later Middle Ages*, Oxford, 1951

Legge, M. D., *Anglo-Norman Literature and its Background*, Oxford, 1963

Lewis, C. S., *The Allegory of Love*, Oxford, 1936

Lloyd, T. H., *The English Wool Trade in the Middle Ages*, Cambridge, 1977

Lodge, E. C., *Gascony under English Rule*, London, 1926

Lucas, H. S., *The Low Countries and the Hundred Years War*, Ann Arbor, 1929

Lucas, A., *Medieval Women*, Brighton, 1983

McFarlane, K. B., *The Nobility of Later Medieval England*, Oxford, 1973

McKisack, M., *The 14th Century*, 1307–1399, Oxford, 1959

Mackinney, L., *Medical Illustrations in Medieval Manuscripts*, London, 1965

Maddicott, J. R., *Thomas of Lancaster*, Oxford, 1970

Miller, E., and Hatcher, J., *Medieval England; Rural Society and Economic Change, 1086–1348*, London, 1978

Moorman, J. R. H., *Church Life in England in the 13th Century*, Cambridge, 1946

Morris, J. E., *The Welsh Wars of Edward I*, Oxford, 1901

Muir, L., *Literature and Society in Medieval France; The Mirror and the Image*, London, 1985

Nicholson, R., *Scotland: the Later Middle Ages*, Edinburgh, 1974

Orme, N., *From Childhood to Chivalry*, London, 1984

Packe, M., *King Edward III*, London, 1983

Pantin, W. A., *The English Church in the 14th Century*, Cambridge, 1955

Parsons, J. C., *The Court and Household of Eleanor of Castile*, Toronto, 1977

Perroy, E., *The Hundred Years War* (trans. W. B. Wells), London, 1951

Phillips. E. D., *The Mongols*, London, 1969

Platt, C., *The English Medieval Town*, London, 1976

Plucknett, T. F. T., *The Legislation of Edward I*, Oxford, 1949

Postan, M. M., *The Medieval Economy and Society*, London, 1972

Power, E., *Medieval Women*, Cambridge, 1975

Powicke, F. M., *King Henry III and the Lord Edward*, 2 vols, Oxford, 1947

Powicke, F. M., *Military Obligation in Medieval England*, Oxford, 1962

Powicke, F. M., *The 13th Century, 1216–1307*, 2nd ed., Oxford, 1962

Prestwich, M. C., *The Three Edwards*, London, 1980

Prestwich, M. C., *War, Politics and Finance under Edward I*, London, 1972

Richard, J., *St Louis*, Paris, 1983

Roth, C., *A History of the Jews in England*, Oxford, 1964

Rubin, S., *Medieval English Medicine*, Newton Abbot, 1975

Russell, P. E., *The English Intervention in Spain and Portugal at the Time of the Black Prince*, Oxford, 1955

Sauerlander, W., *Gothic Sculpture in France*, London, 1972

Sayles, G. R., *The King's Parliament of England*, London, 1975

Shakar, S., *The Fourth Estate: A History of Women in the Middle Ages*, London, 1983

Shrewsbury, J. F. D., *A History of Bubonic Plague in the British Isles*, London, 1970

Simons, W. H., and Appleton, H. A., *The Handbook of Soap Manufacture*, London, 1908

Southern, R., *Robert Grosseteste*, Oxford, 1986

Stones E. L. G., *Edward I*, Oxford, 1968

Stones, E. L. G., and Simpson, G. G., *Edward I and the Throne of Scotland, 1290–1296*, 2 vols, Oxford, 1979

Strayer, J. R., *The Reign of Philip the Fair*, Princeton, 1980

Sutherland, D. W., *Quo Warranto Proceedings in the Reign of Edward I*, Oxford, 1963

Tout, T. F., *Chapters in Medieval Administrative History*, 6 vols, Manchester, 1923–35

Tout, T. F., *The Place of Edward II in English History*, 2nd ed., Manchester, 1936

Trabut Cursac, J. P., *L'Administration anglaise en Gascogne de 1254 à 1307*, Geneva, 1972

Tuck, A., *Crown and Nobility*, 1272–1461, London, 1986

Vale, J., *Edward III and Chivalry*, Woodbridge, 1982

Williams, G. A., *Medieval London from Commune to Capital*, London, 1963

Young C. R., *The Royal Forests of Medieval England*, Leicester, 1979

Ziegler, P., *The Black Death*, London, 1969

Chronicles

Part I

The History of William the Marshal in *English Historical Documents 1189–1327*, ed. H. Rothwell, London 1965; pp 82–4, 86–7. Extracts.

The 'Barnwell' chronicle in *Memoriale Walteri de Coventria*, ed. W. Stubbs in Rolls Series 1872–3. Extracts.

Roger of Wendover, *Chronica Rogeri de Wendover. Liber qui dicitur Flores Historiarum ab anno Domini MCLIV annoque Henrici Anglorum Regis Secundi primo*, ed. H.G. Hewlett in Rolls Series 1886–9. Extracts, vols II and III.

Matthew Paris, *Matthaei Parisiensis Chronica Majora*, ed. H.R. Luard in Rolls Series 1872–84. Extracts from vols III, IV, V and VI.

Building accounts of Henry III, ed. H.M. Colvin, Oxford 1971. Extracts.

Salimbene de Adam *Cronica*, ed. F. Bernini, Scrittori d'Italia nos 187, 188, Bari 1942. Extracts from vol. I.

Joinville, *The Life of Saint Louis* in *Joinville and Villehardouin: Chronicles of the Crusades*, trans. M.R.B. Shaw, Penguin Classics, London 1963; Extracts.

Chronicles of the Mayors and Sheriffs of London in *English Historical Documents*, op. cit. Extracts.

The Waverley annals in vol. II of *Annales Monastici*, ed. H.R. Luard in Rolls Series 1864–9. Extracts.

The chronicle of Thomas Wykes, in vol. IV of *Annales Monastici*. Extracts.

William Rishanger: *Willelmi Rishanger Chronica et Annales*, in part II of *Chronica Monasterii Sancti Albani*, ed. H.T. Riley in Rolls Series 1863–76. Extracts.

Part II

The chronicle of Thomas Wykes, op. cit. Extracts.

William Rishanger, op. cit. Extracts.

The Worcester annals in vol. IV of *Annales Monastici*. Extracts.

Bartholomew Cotton, *Bartholomaei de Cotton Historia Anglicana (449–1298) necnon ejusdem Liber de Archiepiscopis et Episcopis Angliae*, ed. H.R. Luard in Rolls Series 1859. Extracts.

The Chronicle of Walter of Guisborough, ed. H. Rothwell, Royal Historical Society, London, Camden Series 3, LXXXIX, 1957. Extracts.

'The Flowers of the Histories': *Flores Historiarum, per Matthaeum Westmonasteriensem collecti*, ed. H.R. Luard in Rolls Series 1890. Extracts from vol. III.

The chronicle of Peter Langtoft, in *English Historical Documents*, op. cit.; pp 264–5. Extracts.

Part III

The Life of Edward II, *Vita Edwardi Secundi*, ed., with an English translation, N. Denholm-Young, Nelson's Medieval Texts, London, 1957; pp 1–11, 25–40, 48–56, 89–92, 108–126. Extracts, selected and adapted.

Lanercost chronicle, *Chronicon de Lanercost, 1201–1346*, ed. J. Stevenson, Edinburgh 1839. Extracts.

Adam Murimuth, *Chronica Adae Murimuth et Roberti de Avesbury*, ed. E.M. Thompson in Rolls Series 1889. Extracts.

Geoffrey le Baker, *Chronicon Galfridi le Baker de Swynebroke*, ed. E.M. Thompson, Oxford 1889. Extracts.

Part IV

Geoffrey le Baker, op. cit. Extracts.

Lanercost chronicle, op. cit. Extracts.

Froissart, Chronicles, trans. G. Brereton, Penguin Classics, London 1968, reprinted with minor revisions 1978; pp 103–110. Extracts.

Matthew of Neuenburg *Chronica Mathiae de Nuwenburg*, ed. A. Hofmeister, Monumenta Germaniae Historica, Scriptores Rerum Germanicarum, nova series, IV, Berlin 1955. Extracts.

Jean le Bel: *Chronique de Jean le Bel*, ed. J. Viard and E. Déprez, Société de l'Histoire de France 1904–5. Extracts from vol II.

Froissart, *Chroniques*, in *Oeuvres de Froissart*, ed. Kervyn de Lettenhove, Brussels 1867–77. Extracts from vol VII.

Thomas of Walsingham, *Thomae Walsingham Historia Anglicana*, in part I of *Chronica Monasterii Sancti Albani*, ed. H.T. Riley in Rolls Series 1863–4. Extracts from vol I.

Manuscripts

(b. = bottom; t. = top; c. = centre; r. = right; l. = left)

2 Edmund Crouchback and St George wearing their arms. (Bodleian Librian, Oxford, MS Douce 231, f.1r.)
10 Astronomer with two assistants. (Psalter of St Louis and Blanche of Castile, French, 13th century.)
27 William Marshall at a joust (Matthew Paris: Historia Major, English, *c.*1240. Corpus Christi College, Cambridge, vol. 2 p.85)
35 c.r. Henry III in a boat (British Library, MS Roy 14 c VII, f.116v)
40 b.l. St. Francis preaching to the birds. (Matthew Paris, Historia Major, English *c.*1240. Corpus Christi College, Cambridge, MS 16 f.66v)
43 t. Frederick II's wedding. (British Library, London, MS Roy 14 C VII F 123)
55 t. Guillaume de Lorris writing the Roman de la Rose. (Guillaume de Lorris: Roman de la Rose. Bodleian Library, Oxford, MS Douce 195 f.1r)
55 b. Mirth and Gladness leading the dance. (Guillaume de Lorris: Roman de la Rose. Bodleian Library, Oxford, MS Douce 364, f.8r)
57 t. Chastity and Poverty making a bed for Hope (Guillaume de Digullevile: le Roman des Trois Pélerinages, French, 14th century. Bibliothèque Ste. Geneviève, Paris)
57 b. Wall hangings. (Grandes Chroniques de France. Bibliothèque Nationale, Paris, MS BN1400)
61 t. Mongols eating people. (Matthew Paris: Historia Major, English *c.*1240. Corpus Christi College, Cambridge, MS 16)
61 b. Genghis Khan in his tent. (Persian, 14th century. Bibliothèque Nationale, Paris, MS Suppl. Persan 113, f.4r)
69 t. Louis IX on crusade (British Library, London, MS Roy 16 G VII f.404v)
69 b. The siege of Damietta from the sea, 1219. (Matthew Paris: Historia Major, English, *c.*1240. Corpus Christi College, Cambridge, MS 16, f.55v)
73 t. Blanche of Castile praying. (Bibliothèque de l'Arsenal, Paris, MS Fr 1186)
73 b. Crusade of the Pastoureaux. (Le Livre des Faits et Gestes de Monseigneur Saint Louis, French, 15th century. Bibliothèque Nationale, Paris)
75 t.l. The mutilation of Simon de Montfort. (British Library, London, MS Cotton Nero D Roman II, f.177)
79 t. Robert Grosseteste's annotated copy of Augustine. (English, 13th century. Bodleian Library, Oxford, MS Bodley 198, f.45v)
79 b. Robert Grosseteste seated. (British Library, London, MS Harl. 3860, f.48)
81 Matthew Paris's drawing of an elephant. (Matthew Paris: Historia Majora, English, *c.*1240. Corpus Chrisiti College, Cambridge, MS 16, f.IVr)
83 t. Plan of Malacca. (British Library, London, MS Sloane 197, f.381–382)
83 b. Trading ship at Ormuz. (Bibliothèque Nationale, Paris, MS. Fr.2810, f.14v)
85 t. Matthew Paris's portrait of himself kneeling. (British Library, London, MS Roy 14 C VII, f.6r)
85 b. Matthew Paris's drawing of Lear and his daughters. (Matthew Paris: Historia Majora, English, *c.*1240. Corpus Christi College, Cambridge, MS 26, f.6)
91 t. Grape pressing in Gascony (Public Record Office, London, MS E36/275, f.252)
91 b. Henry III landing in Aquitaine. (Bibliothèque Nationale, Paris, MS Fr.2829, f.18)
94 t. St Louis dispensing justice. (G. de Saint Pathus: Vie et Miracles de St Louis, French, *c.*1330–1350. Bibliothèque Nationale, Paris, MS Fr.5716, f.246)
94 b. St Louis arriving at Damietta. (G. de Saint Pathus: Vie et Miracles de St Louis, French, *c.*1330–1350. Bibliothèque Nationale, Paris)
95 Scenes from the life of St Louis. (Grandes Chroniques de France, French *c.*1375. Bibliothèque Nationale, Paris, MS Fr 2813, f.265)
101 t. A medieval king with his master masons. (Life of St Offa, English. MS Cotton Nero D 1, f.23v)
111 Two mounted falconers. (Frederick II: De arte venadi cum avibus. Vatican Library, Rome)
113 Edward I in profile. (Public Record Office, London, MS e68–69)
121 b. Llywelyn being decapitated. (British Library, London, MS Cotton Nero D II, f.182)
127 b. A mother and children dying in the plague. (Bodleian Library, Oxford, MS Rawl D 939, part 4)
129 Nuns' service. (British Library, London, MS Add.39843, f.6v)
130–31 Persecution of the Jews in England. (British Library, London, MS Cotton Nero D II, f.183v)
135 John Balliol (left) and Robert Bruce (right) with their wives and banners. (Seton Armorial, Scottish. National Library of Scotland, MS Acc.9309)
137 Philip IV the Fair and his family. (Bibliothèque Nationale, Paris, MS Lat.8604)
139 t. Departure for the crusade. (Statuts de l'ordre du Saint-Esprit. Bibliothèque Nationale, Paris, MS Fr.4274 f.6)
139 b. The battle of Sluys. (Chroniques de Froissart. Bibliothèque Nationale, Paris, MS Fr.2643, f.72)
144 La Foire du Lendit. (French, 14th century. Bibliothèque Nationale, Paris, MS Latin 962, f.264)
145 Battle scene. (British Library, London, MS Add.47682, f.40)
146 Boccaccio: the story of Gaia. (Boccaccio: De Claris Mulieribus, French, 15th century. Bibliothèque Nationale, Paris, MS Fr.12420, f.71)
147 Men unloading a boat. (Livre des Merveilles, French. Bibliothèque Nationale, Paris, MS fr. 2810, f.86v)
151 c.l. Rome widowed. (Bibliothèque Nationale, Paris, MS Ital. 81, f.18)
151 c.r. The Smithfield Decretals. (British Library, London, MS Roy 10 E IV, f.19)
153 Avignon in the 14th century. (Le Livre de Pierre Salmon: Les Lamentations dans l'Etat de Charles VI, French, 14th century. Bibliothèque Nationale, Paris)
159 t.l. Two fashionable women. (Gervais du Bus: Le Roman de Fauvel, French, 14th century. Bibliothèque Nationale, Paris, MS Fr. 146)
161 t. A tournament. (Bibliothèque Nationale, Paris MS Fr 2829, f.18)
161 b. Knight arming, with musicians. (Roman de Troie, French, 13th-14th century)
170 Edward of Caernarvon. (British Library, London, MS Cotton Nero D VII, f.6v) Edward I making his son Prince of Wales. (British Library, London, MS Cotton Nero D II, f.19v)

173 Isabella of France (Bodleian Library, Oxford, MS CH.CH.92, f.4v)
179 c.r. Royal coronation. (Coronation order, French, 14th century. Corpus Christi College, Cambridge, MS 20, f.68)
187 t. King Alfonso X of Castile and his court. (Libro des Juegas, Spanish, 13th century. Monastery of the Escorial, Spain)
187 b. Knight leaving for a crusade. (Cantigas of Sta Maria, Spanish, 13th century. Monastery of the Escorial, Spain)
189 Edward II takes his leave of Jean de Mandeville. (Livre des Merveilles, French. Bibliothèque Nationale, Paris)
193 t.l. A banquet. (Oeuvres de Guillaume de Machaut, French. Bibliothèque Nationale, Paris, MS fr.1584)
193 b.r. Martyre de St Denis. (Vie de St Denis, French, 1317. Bibliothèque Nationale, Paris, MS Fr.2092, f.22v)
194 t. Sisinnius montre à St Denis, St. Rustique et St Eleuthère les corps des chrétiens qu'il a fait mettre à mort. (Vie de St Denis, French, 1317. Bibliothèque Nationale, Paris, MS Fr.2092, f.37v)
194 b. Conversion des Parisiens qui brisent les idoles. (Vie de St Denis, French, 1317. Bibliothèque Nationale, Paris, MS Fr. 2090–2091, f.111)
195 t. St. Denis, St. Rustique et St Eleuthère amenés par les soldats romains devant Sisinnius. (Vie de St. Denis, French, 1317. Bibliothèque Nationale, Paris, MS 2092, f.1)
195 b. Flagellation de St Denis, St. Rustique, St Eleuthère, attachés à des pieux, devant Sisinnius. (Vie de St Denis, French, 1317. Bibliothèque Nationale, Paris, MS 2092, f.42)
201 Pirates. (British Library, London, MS Roy 10 E IV, f.19)
209 Isabella and Mortimer. (Chroniques de Froissart, French, *c.* 1450. Bibliothèque Nationale, Paris).
211 r. The tower and London Bridge. (British Library, London, MS Roy 16 F II, f.73)
215 t.l. Trial and punishment. (British Library, London, Harl 4375, f.140)
215 r. The Execution of Hugh Despenser (Chroniques de Froissart, French, 1340. Bibliothèque Nationale, Paris, MS Fr.2643, f.97v)
238 Edward III doing homage to Philip VI. (British Library, London, MS Roy 20c VII, f.72v)
239 English troops embarking for France. (British Library, London, MS Roy 18 E I, f.103v)
241 t. Massacre des Jacques. (Bibliothèque Nationale, Paris, MS Fr.2643, f.226v)
241 b. Blazons. (Herald's Roll from the College of Arms)
245 The battle of Sluys. (Chroniques de Froissart, French. Bibliothèque Nationale, Paris, MS Fr.2643, f.72)
247 The battle of Crécy. (Chroniques de Froissart, French. Bibliothèque Nationale, Paris, MS Fr.2643, f.165v)
251 The burghers of Calais before Edward III. (Bibliothèque Nationale, Paris, MS Fr.2642, f.179)
255 b. Plague victims being buried. (Bibliothèque Royale, Brussels, MS 13076, f.24v)
259 t. Doctors treating a patient. (British Library, London, Roy 16 C VI, f.310v)
259 b.l. Barber-surgeon performing an anal operation. (British Library, London, MS SLoan, f.93)
261 Flagellants. (Capedimonte Museum, Naples, MS R.V. 374, f.325)
262 Garter knight. (British Library, London, MS Cotton Nero D VII f.105v)
265 Masons. (Life of St Offa, English. MS Cotton Nero D I, f.23v)
267 t.l. Woman surgeon performing a Caesarian. (Histoire ancienne jusqu'à César. University of St Andrews, Scotland, MS v.2, f.199)
267 r. Women defending a castle. (Walter de Milemete: De Nobilitatibus. Bodleian Library, Oxford, MS CH.CH.92, f.3v)
269 Edward III confers Aquitaine on the Black Prince. (British Library, London, MS Cotton Nero D VII, f.31)
271 t.l. John II of France. (Attributed to Girart d'Orléans, French, *c.*1350. Louvre, Paris)
271 t.r. John II captured at Poitiers. (Chroniques de Froissart, French, 1472. Musée Condé, Chantilly, MS 873/501, f.201v)
271 b.r. The battle of Poitiers. (Chroniques de Froissart, French. Bibliothèque Nationale, Paris, MS Fr.2643, f.207)
273 A siege. (Canterbury Triple Psalter, English, early 13th century. Bibliothèque Nationale, Paris, MS Lat.8864, f.76)
275 The Jacquerie. (British Library, London, MS Roy C VII, f.133)
277 English archers training. (British Library, London, MS Add. 421.30, f.147v)
279 The Luttrell family, *c.*1340. (Luttrell Psalter, English, *c.*1340)
281 r. Florentine bankers. (British Library, London, MS Add. 27695, f.8)
283 t. Queen Blanche of Castile with her attendants listening to a minstrel. (Miniature, French, 13th century. Arsenal, Paris. MS A5B.L.)
283 b. Illustration to Boccaccio: the death of Procris. (Boccaccio: Decameron. Bibliothèque Nationale, Paris, MS Fr.12420, f.39v)
285 c.l. Singers. (Bibliotheca Marciana, Venice, MS Cat.1.77)
285 b.r. Concert on the Seine. (Vie de St Denis, French, 1317. Bibliothèque Nationale, Paris, MS Fr.2091, f.99)
289 t.l. Page from Villard de Honnecourt's sketchbook. (Facsimile of the Sketchbook of Wilars de Honecort. John Henry & James Parker, London, 1859)
291 b. The battle of Nájera. (Chroniques de Froissart, French. Bibliothèque Nationale, Paris, MS Fr.2643, f.312v)
295 Courtiers and ladies. (Bodleian Library, Oxford, MS Bodley 264, f.181)
297 t.r. Homélie du XVe siècle. (Bibliothèque Nationale, Paris, MS Lat. 1630, f.2v)
297 b.r. Scenes of student life. Ordonnances de l'Hôtel du Roy, French, 14th century. Archives Nationales, Paris).
301 t.r. John of Gaunt (British Library, London, MS Cotton Nero D VII, f.7)

Index

Acknowledgements

Our grateful thanks to the many museums, libraries and individuals, including those listed below, who provided us with illustrations.

(b. = bottom; b.l. = bottom left; b.r. = bottom right; t. = top; t.l. = top left; t.r. = top right; c. = centre; r. = right; l. = left)

Arxiu Mas, Barcelona: 33t.; 33b.; 187t.; 187b.; 290.

Barnaby's Picture Library, London: 237; 299.
Bibliothèque Nationale, Paris: 61c.r.; 73t.; 83b.; 91b.; 94t.; 95; 139t.; 139b.; 146; 151l.; 159t.; 161t.; 193t.r.; 193b.r.; 194t.; 194b.; 195t.; 195b.; 215r.; 235; 245; 247; 271b.; 273; 283b.; 285b.r.; 291.
Bodleian Library, Oxford: 2; 55b.r.; 79t.r.; 127b.l.; 127b.r.; 141; 173r.; 267r.; 295t.
Bridgeman Art Library, London: 55t.l.; 83t.; 111; 279t.
British Library, London: 35c.r.; 43t.; 69t.; 75t.; 79b.r.; 85t.; 121b.r.; 129; 130/131; 145c.r.; 151c.r.; 170; 171; 182; 201; 211t.r.; 215t.l.; 238; 239; 262; 269; 277; 281r.; 301t.r.
British Museum, London: 4; 149; 181; 253; 279b.; 281b.

Cambridge University Library: 257
College of Arms, London: 241b.r.
Conway Library, London: 61t.; 85b.; 101t.; 265; 285c.l.
Corpus Christi College, Cambridge: 40b.; 81; 179c.r.

Jean Dieuzaide, Toulouse: 65; 89b.l.; 249b.r.; 295b.r.

Edimage/Cauboue, Paris: 57b.; 73b.; 153; 175; 189t.; 209; 219; 241t.r.; 251; 275; 283t.r.
Edimage/Goldner, Paris: 255; 297t.r.
Edimedia, Paris: 10.

John Freeman & Co., London: 303

Giraudon, Paris: 57t.; 93; 137; 161b.; 193t.l.; 260t.; 271t.l.; 271t.r.; 297b.r.
Guildhall Library, London: 301b.

Sonia Halliday: 22, 31b.; 94b.l.
Hampshire County Council: 233r.

Lord Chamberlain's Office, London: 35t. (reproduced by gracious permission of Her Majesty the Queen).

Marianne Majerus: 6; 14/15; 26; 49t.; 49b.; 50/51; 59; 63; 86/87; 87r.; 89b.r.; 101b.; 102l.; 102r.; 103; 105; 106; 117; 118; 119t.r.; 119b.r.; 127t.c.; 133t.r.; 133b.; 143; 145t.c.; 162/163; 165t.; 165b.; 167; 173l.; 176/177; 183; 191; 202/203; 207c.l.; 207r; 211l.; 213t.r.; 213b.c.; 221; 222/223; 225t.; 225b.; 226; 231; 233l.; 263; 286/287; 287l.; 287r.; 287b.; 288; 289b.; 305.
Mansell Collection, London: 40t.; 45; 152c.l.

National Library of Scotland: 135l.; 135r.
National Museum of Wales: 121t.r.

Palace of Westminster Pictures, London: 99.
Public Record Office: 91t.r.; 113; 123; 189b.

Roger-Viollet, Paris: 260b.; 261.
Royal Albert Memorial Museum, Exeter: 37; 152t.r.

University of St Andrews, Scotland: 259t.; 259b.r.; 267t.l.

Scala, Florence: 31t.; 32; 39; 41; 43b.; 66/67; 71t.; 71b.; 115; 128; 155; 197; 198t.l.; 198b.l.; 199t.; 199b.; 249b.l.
Society of Antiquaries of London: 75b.r.; 88; 300.

Victoria and Albert Museum, London: 159b.r.; 218.
Visual Arts Library, London: 27; 69b.r.